POLICING THE RISK SOCIETY

CLARENDON STUDIES IN CRIMINOLOGY

Published under the auspices of the Institute of Criminology, University of Cambridge, the Mannheim Centre, London School of Economics, and the Centre for Criminological Research, University of Oxford

RECENT TITLES IN THIS SERIES:

Prisons and the Problem of Order
Sparks, Bottoms, and Hay

Law in Policing: *Legal Regulation and Police Practices*
David Dixon

The Local Governance of Crime: *Appeals to Community and Partnerships*
Crawford

Crime in Ireland 1945–95: *Here be Dragons*
Brewer, Lockhart, and Rodgers

Sexed Work: Gender, Race and Resistance in a Brooklyn Drug Market
Maher

FORTHCOMING TITLES:

Victims of White Collar Crime: *The Social and Media Construction of Business Fraud*
Levi and Pithouse

Procedural Fairness at the Police Station
Choongh

POLICING THE RISK SOCIETY

Richard V. Ericson and Kevin D. Haggerty

CLARENDON PRESS · OXFORD
1997

Oxford University Press, Great Clarendon Street, Oxford OX2 6DP
Oxford New York
Athens Auckland Bangkok Bogota Bombay
Buenos Aires Calcutta Cape Town Dar es Salaam
Delhi Florence Hong Kong Istanbul Karachi
Kuala Lumpur Madras Madrid Melbourne
Mexico City Nairobi Paris Singapore
Taipei Tokyo Toronto Warsaw
and associated companies in
Berlin Ibadan

Oxford is a trade mark of Oxford University Press

Published in the United States
by Oxford University Press Inc., New York

British Library Cataloguing in Publication Data
Data available

Library of Congress Cataloging in Publication Data
Data available

ISBN 0–19–826553–0
ISBN 0–19–826577–8 (Pbk)

Printed in Great Britain by
Biddles Ltd., Guildford and King's Lynn

In memory of Kevin D. Carriere, 1961–1995

The influence of his scholarship lives on
in this work and that of countless others

Contents

Foreword

Professor Richard Ericson has already established himself as the most prolific and distinguished criminological researcher in Canada. In this important new book, with his colleague Kevin Haggerty, he returns to a subject to which he has already made significant contributions – policing. The authors boldly challenge many of the assumptions of other researchers and argue that it is time for a fundamental reassessment of the nature and role of policing in 'late modern risk societies.' Their thesis is that as society has become more fragmented the focus of police work has shifted from traditional modes of crime control and order maintenance towards the provision of security through surveillance technologies designed to identify, predict, and manage risks. Their empirical study of the activities of police at supervisory and management levels illustrates just how much police time and how many resources are devoted to gathering and disseminating knowledge of risk to other social institutions concerned with security. Indeed, they argue that by concentrating on how the police use information for their own internal activities, other researchers have been blind to the significance of a symbiotic relationship between the police and other bodies concerned with the management of risk. From this perspective they shed new light on a variety of matters, such as community policing and residential watch programs; connections with the world of insurance (especially relating to motor vehicles), regulation, and financial institutions; the development of technologies to obtain information useful for the control and management of high-risk territories and groups, including offenders, victims, and informants; the checking of credentials; the regulation of drugs; and the recording and systematic use of information about criminal careers. They especially draw attention to the way in which the search for knowledge to increase efficiency and predictability produces not only a 'paper burden' but elaborate mechanisms to systematize knowledge through internal supervision, policy manuals, and audits, procedural rules to guard against irresponsible use of information, and sophisticated computer technology. Furthermore, they have contributed to the theoretical understanding of the nature of control mechanisms in the 'risk society.'

Ericson and Haggerty's ambitious, wide-ranging, and impressive study lays claim to having transformed the agenda for research on the police, and there is now clearly a need to replicate their work and to test their theories in other countries. Without doubt this important book breaks new ground. It will stimulate theory and research and engender a healthy debate on the role of the police in contemporary society.

ROGER HOOD
Centre for Criminological Research
University of Oxford
January 1997

Acknowledgments

This book is the result of five years' involvement with a large number of people in many institutions. It would not have come to fruition without their enormous goodwill, assistance, and support.

We are especially grateful to the police organizations and individuals who are the subjects of our research. They have been extraordinarily generous with their time and remarkably insightful about their work. It is only through them that we are able to pursue our scholarly interest in what they know and how such knowledge is used in governance. We hope that our analysis is as helpful to them in their pragmatic pursuits as it is to scholars in their academic pursuits.

Major financial support for the research was provided by the Social Sciences and Humanities Research Council of Canada. We appreciate the extent to which that organization continues to value independent scholarly inquiry. Additional funding was provided by the University of British Columbia's Office of the Vice-President Research and Faculty of Graduate Studies.

This project was originally conceived while Richard Ericson was a Visiting Research Professor in the College of Public Programs at Arizona State University. He is indebted to David Altheide for arranging that appointment and for his wonderful collegiality. He also owes a great deal to the members of his 'Communication and Social Control' seminar at Arizona State. They not only tolerated his efforts to propose new theories of communication and social control but also made it clear when he was wrong.

The data collection phase of the project occurred while we were members of the Centre of Criminology, University of Toronto. The centre is a superb intellectual environment and we thank all of our colleagues there for their wonderful support. We are grateful for the research assistance of Marnie Crouch and in particular for her patience and good humour while undertaking the tedious work of transcribing tape-recorded research interviews.

The book was completed at Green College, University of British Columbia. Green College is the ideal environment in which to reflect, analyse, and write. One is constantly challenged and stimulated by colleagues from other disciplines and warmed by their collegiality. In particular we thank Cecil Green for making it all possible, and John Grace for his enormous enthusiasm, commitment, and support.

We wish to thank eleven scholars who read the penultimate manuscript and whose extensive criticisms have helped to make this book much better. They are David Altheide, Regents Professor, Arizona State University; Pat Carlen, Professor of Sociology, University of Bath; Malcolm Feeley, Professor in the Center for the Study of Law and Society, University of California, Berkeley; Oscar Gandy Jr, Professor in the Annenberg School for Communication, University of Pennsylvania; David Garland, Professor in the Centre for Law and Society, University of Edinburgh, and in the Faculty of Law, New York University; Anthony Giddens, Professor of Sociology, University of Cambridge; Ian Hacking, Professor of Philosophy, University of Toronto; Peter Manning, Professor Michigan Malley, Professor of Law and Legal Studies, La Trobe University; Paul Rock, Professor of Sociology, London School of Economics and Political Science; and Richard Sparks, Professor of Criminology, University of Keele.

It is once again a pleasure to be associated with first-rate publishers. Virgil Duff and Richard Hart have been very enthusiastic and supportive, and Howard Baker has provided excellent copy-editing. We are also grateful to Diana Ericson for her preparation of the index.

Edward Elgar Publishers, Felix-Verlag Publishers, and the editors of the *British Journal of Sociology* and *University of British Columbia Law Review* are to be thanked for allowing material, first published with them, to be incorporated into Part I of the present book in revised form.

RICHARD V. ERICSON

KEVIN D. HAGGERTY

POLICING THE RISK SOCIETY

Introduction

The police pervade contemporary social life. They are seen daily on the streets. Their presence is felt even more strongly through hour-long television shows that feature cathected scenarios of their heroics. They are turned to for help when people experience personal troubles, accidents, and criminal victimization. They are present at community ceremonies, sporting events, parades, and demonstrations. They are featured in full-dress uniform on postcards and souvenirs, standing for what is noble about the community and nation-state. In all of these manifestations the police simultaneously reproduce and represent order. They embody central authority as peace, order, and good government.

This book offers a fundamental reassessment of how we think about police. While research literature on policing is proliferating, it is also increasingly redundant and stagnant. There is a need to reflect critically on existing research, to provide a comprehensive theory of policing, and to undertake more-thorough analyses of the purposes and consequences of policing.

We argue that policing and the society in which it takes place are best understood in terms of a model of risk communication. In this book policing is conceived of not only in terms of what the public police do but also in terms of what is done in other institutions to identify and manage risks. Our point is that policing consists of the public police coordinating their activities with policing agents in all other institutions to provide a society-wide basis for risk management (governance) and security (guarantees against loss).

Risk refers to external danger, such as a natural disaster, technological catastrophe, or threatening behaviour by human beings. The system for communicating risk – its rules, formats, and technologies – is a part of the social meaning of risk. The risk communication system is thus a key locus for our analysis. Our research focuses on the communication systems that institutions develop to identify and manage risks, and on how the police become involved in these systems. The meaning of risk varies with the communication system used by the institutions responsible for managing it, and the police are therefore in a complex, ambiguous, shifting, and contradictory field of risk management in relation to other institutions.

Communication systems are not simply conduits through which knowledge is transferred. Rather, they have their own logics and autonomous processes. They govern institutional relations and circumscribe what individuals and their organizations are able to accomplish. There is not just an event in the world and then communication about it. The event is called into being, made visible, and responded to through the rules, formats, and technologies available in the communication system. The communication system makes things real. An understanding of the ways in which police work is done thus requires analysis of the logics and processes of the communication system the police participate in. These logics and processes *direct* how the police are organized and assessed.

The core of this book is an ethnographic study that documents how the police are organized within risk communication systems. This study is based on extensive interviews with 155 police officers and administrative personnel, observations of their activities, and analysis of their documents. While the empirical research relates to Canadian police organizations, the links made to the secondary literature on police and to social theory indicate that the features identified are generalizable to other nation-state contexts.

The data are analysed within a model that includes recent advances in social theory concerning risk, governance, and communication. While the main emphasis is on the ways in which risk communication rules, formats, and technologies structure police organization in relation to other institutions, we are also concerned with how police communications exemplify features of our society more generally. As such, the book not only provides an empirical basis for understanding policing in radically new ways, but also contributes to theories of risk society, governmentality, and organizational communication.

In developing our argument we have followed an academically unconventional path. Instead of opening with the more abstract theory that informs our analysis, we begin with a critical analysis of existing research on policing. This analysis demonstrates that other researchers have almost entirely overlooked the risk communication systems of policing. However, it also identifies how existing research at least points to the fact that policing operates in terms of the rules, formats, and technologies of risk communication systems. This identification connects in turn to features of the risk society within which policing now takes place. The abstract theory of the risk society makes more sense after one is exposed to substantive issues of policing and risk communication addressed by the research literature. Theorizing the risk society at that later point not only adds cogency to the critique of the literature that precedes it but also provides the explanatory framework for the empirical analyses presented subsequently.

In Part I our analysis of existing research on policing allows us to contend that police mobilization is not only a matter of intervention in the lives of individual citizens but also a response to institutional demands for knowledge of risk. As a result, the primary locus of police activity is the risk communication systems shaped by external institutions. Through these communication systems, external institutions are able to routinely access police for knowledge useful in their own risk management. This routine access makes police work highly visible and circumscribes both the autonomy of police organizations and the discretion of individual police officers.

The criminal justice system is but one of many institutions that organize themselves through risk communication systems, and it is by no means the central or most influential institution in policing. Most of the crime-related knowledge produced by the police is disseminated to other institutions (for example, those concerned with health, insurance, public welfare, financial matters, and education) for their risk management needs, rather than used for criminal prosecution and punishment. While they have considerable coercive power to produce knowledge of risk, the police mainly distribute the knowledge so obtained through risk communication systems of other institutions that govern in terms of a compliance mode. Coercive control gives way to contingent categorization. Policing is effected not only through territorial surveillance but also at the extraterritorial level of abstract knowledge of risk concerning securities (economic-exchange instruments), careers (life-course management), and identities (personhood).

Community policing is here analysed as a discourse that rationalizes, after the fact, the policing of risk society. Community policing turns out to be risk communication policing. It accounts for the fact that our communities are based on risk communications that give little sense of place or identity outside of institutionalized risk classifications.

Part II provides a broader theoretical discussion of the risk society context in which policing takes place. Risk society operates within a negative logic that focuses on fear and the social distribution of 'bads' more than on progress and the social distribution of 'goods.' Collective fear and foreboding underpin the value system of an unsafe society, perpetuate insecurity, and feed incessant demands for more knowledge of risk. Fear ends up proving itself, as new risk communication and management systems proliferate. The surveillance mechanisms of these systems create profiles of human populations and their risks to ascertain what is probable and possible for those populations. People are fabricated around institutionally established norms: risk is always somewhere on the continuum of imprecise normality.

Risk communication systems are entwined with privacy and trust. The more that foreboding and fear lead people to withdraw from public involvement, the more they value privacy and withdraw into privatized lifestyles. The greater the privacy, the greater the need for surveillance mechanisms to produce the knowledge necessary to trust people in otherwise anonymous institutional transactions. Paradoxically, these mechanisms intrude on privacy and are a constant reminder of the uncertainties of trust. Yet it is only in a framework of trust that patterns of risk can be adequately institutionalized and form the basis of decisions. Privacy, trust, surveillance, and risk management go hand in hand in policing the probabilities and possibilities of action.

In risk society, governance is privatized and dispersed across myriad fragmented institutions. The onus is placed on organizations and individuals to be more self-sufficient, to look after their own risk management needs. This emphasis on self-governance is underpinned by the interconnected discourses of morality, rights, responsibility, and accountability.

In the utilitarian morality of risk management, the norm or standard of acceptable risk is always both factual and moral. It signifies the typical or usual standard but also ethical constraint. Risk classifications infuse moral certainty and legitimacy into the facts they produce, allowing people to accept them as normative obligations and therefore as scripts for action. The legitimacy of utilitarian morality in risk discourse is augmented by the discourse of rights. Rights discourse has burgeoned with the decentralization of politics into risk institutions and their peculiar means of distributive justice. Rights discourse provides an ethics of the possible and probable that is embedded in legal rules of right. It forms part of the politics of difference, which contests the morality of risk classifications with respect to the security they do or do not provide. In the condition of self-governance, organizations and individuals are to contribute to the whole by being accountable for their part, including the risks they create for themselves and others. They are to be self-sufficient, to manage their own biographies competently, to be their own political economy. The result is not autonomy but rather the institutional structuration of organizational and individual careers for practical risk management purposes.

Part III provides an ethnographic analysis of how the police participate in risk communication systems designed for territorial surveillance and security. The police use a variety of electronic technologies to map the geography of trouble. They function as an inspectorate that traces population movements in time and space, for example, through street-stop checks, registration of vice practitioners, special-event security, business and residential security reviews, vehicle registration systems, and driver licensing systems. They offer expertise on environmental design to institutions seeking better territorial security in the spaces for which they have responsibility. In the aggregate, what one sees concentrated in private-security settings such as shopping malls and entertainment complexes also exists to the degree possible in more dispersed settings in the urban landscape. A combination of pervasive surveillance devices, precise regulation of movement through territories, and aesthetically pleasing design makes coercion embedded, cooperative, and subtle, and therefore not experienced as coercion at all.

Part IV provides an empirical analysis of how the police participate in risk communication systems that relate to securities, careers, and identities, which are broad areas of risk management and security provision not directly associated with the policing of territories. These systems risk-profile populations for the purpose of economic exchange, life-course management, and identity management. They are based on abstract systems of trust and risk that require sophisticated surveillance mechanisms not tied to territorial boundaries. They represent institutional boundaries that traverse time and space but still keep people in their place.

Securities such as certificates, credentials, and financial instruments attest to credit, ownership, identity, and achievements. They provide security in the form of a promise to fulfil obligations and a guarantee against any loss, damage, or default that might ensue. The police are an essential component of how institutions establish trust and efficiency through their securities. In particular, the police participate in interinstitutional knowledge coordination, risk profiling, and auditing, all to verify the integrity of securities data, products, and markets.

The police also help other institutions construct the careers of the populations that concern them. In the most routine aspects of their work – for example, reporting an accident, conducting a street-stop check or an employment screening check, and recording information about criminal suspects, victims, and informants – police officers register peoples' significant accomplishments and failures, credentials and demerits, routines and accidents.

These routines of police work also help institutions to construct population identities. Even the checking off on police forms of boxes that identify, for example, age, race, gender, and ethnicity, forces people into specific institutional identities. In this book we present illustrative cases of identities policing. For example, we analyse the policing of youth. The police help to secure the social boundaries of youth by working in the interstices of institutions that deal more directly with young people. An analysis of police programs in schools reveals that police officers function simultaneously as security officers, risk educators, informant-system operators, and counsellors, and that they mobilize students and staff to play these roles as well. Police involvement in the governance of racial and ethnic groups is also examined. In response to the urgings of other institutions, the police use racial and ethnic classifications to understand problems and to risk-profile populations. Police multicultural units select those who are in the 'other' (that is, other than 'white') category for more intensive scrutiny of the problems they experience and pose. These units also engage in extensive interinstitutional networking to foster knowledge of problems specific to racial and ethnic groups.

Part V examines how the police perceive and handle risk communications internally. It provides a study of occupational change brought about by the fact that the risk society is also a knowledge society. The police are knowledge workers who join other major social institutions in believing that the world can be made more secure by ever more perfect knowledge of risk. This belief leads them to search incessantly for whatever rules, formats, and technologies will allow them to feel that they are closer to perfection. The problem is that they are constantly faced with imperfections in those rules, formats, and technologies, which gives rise to both a sense of failure and a renewed sense that more such devices will work where fewer have not. At the same time they are faced with new demands from other institutions because those institutions are in precisely the same position with respect to knowledge risk management.

Risk society is characterized by the perpetual refinement of rules governing how knowledge is communicated. Thus the police are increasingly subject to external institutional pressures to produce and distribute knowledge in new rule-governed frameworks. For example, the criminal law dictates conditions and criteria for disclosure, as do various areas of information law regarding privacy and access to information. The need to be publicly accountable also leads the police to elaborate internal rule systems for risk communication. Rules develop to centralize the access of other institutions to police knowledge, to commodify police knowledge that is bartered or sold to external institutions, and to regulate internal systems of knowledge production and distribution. These rules protect police organizations from appearing irresponsible in the management of their knowledge assets.

The knowledge conceived, recognized, and presented through a police report depends on the format used, and is therefore always secondary to the format. Formats provide the framework through which police officers take action and regulate the actions taken. Alternative meanings tend to be seen as unrealistic, or are not seen at all. As such, risk communication formats are the focal point for an institution's selection and definition of risks. To know an institution is to know how its communication formats are used to define and select risks in ways that support and stabilize the institution.

Considerable resources are devoted by the police to regulating formats. The regulation of formats is necessary because it is the only way to guarantee that the proper classifications are in place to produce the knowledge of risk required. We analyse the regulation of forms that are created by police officers for local practical uses but do not have the official sanction of central police administrations. Our analysis of changes in forms over a sixty-year period documents a shift from the blank page and the open narrative to, as is the case today, fixed-choice risk classifications that meet the needs of external institutions. In the late 1990s the policing of narratives extends to limiting written accounts of occurrences to a specified small number of characters, circumscribing the use of abstract and interpretive language, and using scanner technologies that convert written accounts into closed-ended classifications.

The introduction of computer technology has had a significant influence on communication formats. Police officers now patrol the beat with a keyboard rather than a nightstick in hand. Every keystroke 'types' the population policed for risk management purposes. Some of these purposes are internal to the police. For example, computer terminals in patrol cars accelerate the use of street-stop surveillance, which allows the police to trace more people who appear to be out of place. Some of these purposes are external to the police. For example, police computer formats are made compatible with those of external institutions in order to increase the efficiency of risk communications to such institutions.

Every keystroke on the keyboard also 'types' police officers in terms of the quality and quantity of their knowledge production, and thereby creates the discipline that makes them useful workers, without the need for direct supervisory intervention. The computer terminal in the patrol car is a time-and-motion study that never ends. It routinely measures the police officers' activities and sorts them according to finely calibrated performance ratings and career potentials.

Regardless of the steps taken to reduce what the police call the 'paper burden,' that burden continues to weigh heavily on the police because other institutions demand more and more knowledge. This knowledge is demanded not only because of the risk management needs peculiar to these external institutions but also because of the increased capacity to provide it through computer technology, which makes new classifications imaginable and eases the task of altering communication formats to meet risk classification needs. The external demand for more knowledge, and the ease of computerized knowledge production, feed into the internal police compulsion to produce knowledge in case it might come in handy. What initially appears as an interesting technological convenience quickly becomes an expectation of supervisors and of police officers themselves.

Computer technology alters hierarchical structures of command and control among supervisors, police officers, and support staff. There is a blurring and levelling of some roles, with the result that no single person is easily identifiable as the decision maker. Decision making occurs within the criteria of risk communication formats, which have their own reality and autonomy at the system level. Hence the role ambiguity and alteration of hierarchy does not enhance the discretion of field-level police officers. Rather, discretion is at once circumscribed and dispersed into the risk communication systems that provide for routine surveillance of both the population of citizens and the population of police.

Our model provides a new window on policing and the constitutive mechanisms of society. A look through this window reveals many aspects of policing that have not been brought to light previously. Our new perspective allows us to show the limitations of other theories of policing and to open up new areas for empirical exploration and theoretical debate. Risk is a central feature of modernity, and this feature must be interrogated in fine detail and to the fullest possible extent. Risk institutions and their communication systems have become an important basis of society, and our empirical research on police participation in these institutions and systems substantiates this claim.

It is curious that researchers have been unaware of or insensitive to what is documented here. Our view is that researchers have been locked into particular frameworks for understanding what the police do, and that these frameworks are largely coterminous with popular perceptions of policing. Researchers have accepted the common view that the police are still organized along military lines to protect persons and property within definite territorial boundaries, and that this protection is effected through strategies and tactics of criminal law enforcement, order maintenance, and service provision. In particular, they have accepted the common view that police officers are primarily agents of criminal law enforcement, and that this agency gives them all of the institutional authority and coercive power necessary to maintain order.

Police officers have a similar view of their own work. On the one hand, they cannot deny that they are heavily invested in risk communication, because that work is omnipresent. On the other hand, they rationalize risk communication work as a means to the ends of criminal law enforcement, order maintenance, and service provision. When they cannot rationalize risk communication work in these terms, they see it as a self-fuelling end in itself and become alienated from it.

While criminal law enforcement, order maintenance, and service provision are obviously part of policing, they do not adequately capture the ways in which the police actually contribute to regulation, governance, and security. The police are involved in many forms of legal regulation in addition to the enforcement of the criminal law. For example, the law of insurance contracts, and police brokerage of knowledge of risk to the insurance industry, are much more significant in preventing and regulating burglaries than are criminal law and punishment. The police are also extensively involved in providing knowledge of risk to other institutions, regarding dangers that have nothing to do with criminal law and order maintenance. Their contribution to regulation, governance, and security is in terms of interinstitutional risk communication systems.

Policing through risk communication systems has grown at the same time as levels of incarceration have accelerated to record highs in many jurisdictions. Some may take this increased punitiveness as a sign that the coercive and disciplinary power of the state overshadows the subtler and gentler forms of risk management, but we argue that these are not mutually exclusive or competing trends. It is wrong to pose a simplistic dualism between sovereign/disciplinary power and risk management, as if the complexities involved could be reduced to a simple binary opposition.

Policing within risk communication systems is not separate from or in contradiction to fluctuations in punitiveness. The criminal justice system is one among many institutions the police participate in, and it too organizes itself in terms of risk management. In fact, it has a long history of devising actuarial justice technologies relating to dangerousness, release on bail, early release from prison, and so on. Increased punitiveness indicates that risk thresholds have been lowered and that new risk technologies of exclusion have been introduced. On the other hand, if the criminal justice system did not primarily emphasize risk technologies that keep most people at its margins or outside of it entirely, punitiveness would be far greater. The criminal justice system works hard to divert cases from its jurisdiction and to disperse risk into other institutions. Without this effort, and the collaboration of the police in it, a very substantial proportion of the population would be in prison. Community policing would be replaced by community prisons.

Just as risk discourse pervades all social institutions, so the discourse of increased punitiveness is not confined to criminal law. The mass media and electoral politics in particular join forces in public culture to suggest that social life would be all right if only criminal punishment were swifter and harsher. Sentiments in favour of more punishment, expressed through these institutions, certainly influence the search for new risk technologies of exclusion. However, these sentiments are otherwise distant from the routine management of crime risks. This management is based on a utilitarian calculus of loss reduction and indemnification, and disperses risk to other institutions that have higher risk thresholds and are more inclusive.

As suggested above regarding the long history of using risk technologies in the criminal justice system, policing in terms of risk communication systems is not a recent development. In many instances what are presented as new risk technologies largely entail new labels for established technologies and practices. Indeed, policing within risk communication systems has its roots in forms of governance of the late seventeenth and early eighteenth centuries. Early modern governance emphasized surveillance of populations as a way to develop statistical probabilities about them that would assist in judgments concerning social utility, health, and happiness. This emphasis was especially salient in police organizations – such as the North-West Mounted Police and its successor, the Royal Canadian Mounted Police – that were geographically dispersed into large, sparsely populated areas, for they had to represent all aspects of population governance in those territories. However, even in densely populated urban areas the police were drawn into the risk management logics of other institutions seeking knowledge for their own systems of governance and security.

In spite of this lineage, there are new and radically changing dimensions of contemporary society that justify characterizing it as being driven by institutional demands for knowledge of risk. There are new emergency needs, for example, health risks such as AIDS. Populations are increasingly mobile, which places new demands on institutions to find better ways of tracing, risk-profiling, and trusting them. There has been a transformation of structural social conditions brought on by an explosion in scientific and technological knowledge. That is, science and technology have not only identified but also have created new risks. These new risks in turn are responded to with more and more scientific and technological solutions that generate new risks, in an amplifying spiral. Risk technologies and security products flood the market, turning the 'distribution of bads' into desirable goods.

A technological change of particular significance is the rise of computers. Computers allow the development of new formats of risk communication, as well as instant dispersal of knowledge of risk to interested institutions. With a scan of one's credit card, library card, health card, passport, and so on, local knowledge immediately enters institutional databases. The databases rather than the individual bureaucrat become the basis for governance through knowledge. Knowledgeability becomes systemic, operating at collective and institutional more than individual levels.

We do not contend that the risk communication system is deterministic. The rules, formats, and technologies of that system are human creations for specific risk management purposes. They are programmable.

One must know what type of organization is desirable to be able to devise and use the possibilities of risk communication systems at all. As such, risk communication systems are meant to be determinative rather than deterministic. They are used within culturally specific interpretive frameworks and visions of social organization, and their influence is always related to these frameworks and visions.

In Foucauldian terms, ours is a study of the archaeology and genealogy of policing the risk society. We eschew evaluative questions of effectiveness that form the foundation of utilitarian efficiency in this society. We remain content to analyse the infrastructures and practices of policing within risk communication systems – the rules, formats, and technologies that structure police production and distribution of knowledge of risk.

PART I

Policing

1

Policing as Risk Communications

As was discussed in the introduction, this book analyses how the police are organized in terms of risk communications to and from other institutions such as insurance companies, regulatory agencies, financial institutions, health and welfare agencies, and motor vehicle agencies. Policing is a matter of responding not only to individual demands for service but also to institutional demands for knowledge about risk. The police are part of interinstitutional networks in which claims to expertise pertaining to a given type of risk and the need for knowledge about that type of risk among the relevant institutions determine the police jurisdiction in the given field.

'Risk,' as we have seen, refers to external dangers, such as natural disasters and threatening behaviour by enemies (Douglas 1990, 1992). There are also dangerous 'manufactured risks' (Giddens 1994) that result from scientific and technological intervention in the conditions and nature of social life. That is, in the very effort to manage external dangers through scientific and technical means, humans manufacture new dangers to their environment and lives. Pollution of the environment is a case in point (Douglas and Wildavsky 1982). 'Risk' also refers to the communication rules, formats, and technologies used to manage dangers. Our particular focus is on the rules, formats, and technologies that institutions develop to deal with the dangers they identify, and on how and why the police become involved in providing the knowledge of risk required by these institutions.

It is our contention that the risk logics of external institutions, and the classification schemes and knowledge requirements they entail, fundamentally influence the police. The framework through which police officers think and act is determined not only by formal legal rules, administrative rules, and the informal rules of the occupational culture but also by the risk communication rules, formats, and technologies of external institutions. In other words, it is the structure of institutional communications more than the legal, administrative, or informal rule-structures that circumscribes the discretion of police officers. The legal and administrative rules do have a bearing on risk classifications, but it is these classifications that in turn shape and direct police officer autonomy. Moreover, the autonomy of the police institution itself is circumscribed by these external risk communication criteria, which determine the degree of autonomy experienced by the police within the network of policing agencies and risk institutions.

We contend further that the role of the police as risk communicators in the service of external institutions changes the way in which the police provide security to individuals, organizations, and institutions. In risk society the traditional police focus on deviance, control, and order is displaced in favour of a focus on risk, surveillance, and security. The concern is less with the labelling of deviants as outsiders and more on developing a risk-profile knowledge of individuals to ascertain and manage their place in institutions. The concern is not so much control of deviants in a repressive sense as surveillance that constitutes populations of individuals, organizations, and institutions in their respective risk categories. While there is still emphasis on order within a predictable spatial environment, there is also a plethora of risk mechanisms that seek to guarantee healthy and productive 'human resources' and 'organizational resources,' and thereby provide security.

This shift in orientation toward risk, surveillance, and security is fostered by a changing legal regime in risk society. As the emphasis on control diminishes, the criminal justice institution moves away from deterrence-based law enforcement and towards compliance-based law enforcement (Reiss 1984). The emphasis shifts to acquiring the knowledge necessary to set acceptable standards of risk. This emphasis not only entails a lessening of crime control in favour of surveillance as an end in itself but also means that 'due process' protections for suspects are eroded in favour of 'system rights' to the kinds of knowledge useful for surveillance. At the same time the police must provide knowledge of risk to other institutions regarding noncriminal branches of law. For example, risk is increasingly 'legalized' in contracts, licences, no-fault mechanisms, and the use of civil damage awards to enforce liability rules and statutory rights. All of these legal methods of interpreting and enforcing social practices of risk affect the volume, direction, and nature of police risk communications. They mean that policing must be analysed with respect to theories of legal pluralism.

Finally, we contend that the changes in policing outlined here are in part already articulated in the discourse of community policing. We argue that community policing is best understood as the policing of institutional communications about risk and security, and that the community policing model serves to rationalize the changing roles of police in risk society.

The Police as Knowledge Workers

The Police and Crime

It is now well established that the police spend relatively little time dealing directly with crime. This fact is immediately evident from Canadian data on police officers and crime rates (McMahon 1992). On average, a police officer in Canada records one indictable crime occurrence a week, makes one indictable crime arrest every three weeks, and secures one indictable crime conviction every nine months. Even in New York City, which has an extraordinarily high rate of serious crime, officers spend an extraordinarily small amount of time dealing with crime and capturing criminals. Walsh (1986) found that among 156 patrol officers assigned to a high-crime area in New York City, 40 per cent did not make a single felony arrest in a year and 69 per cent made no more than three felony arrests in a year.

It is extremely rare for a patrol officer to encounter a serious crime in progress. While patrol officers are proactive, it is mainly to obtain knowledge about possible suspects who appear out of place and time, or for regulatory matters such as traffic and liquor violations (Ericson 1982). Clarke and Hough (1984) estimated that a London (England) police officer might encounter a burglary in progress once every eight years.

Reactive calls for police service are also mainly about noncriminal matters. Up to 75 per cent of calls for service are screened out without being forwarded to patrol officers for further action (Bercal 1970; Jorgensen 1981; Shearing 1984; Percy and Scott 1985; Manning 1988). Even when there is a crime call, what operators define as serious crime is changed by officers to minor incidents or no crime in one-third to one-half of all instances (Comrie and Kings 1975; Ericson 1982; Manning 1988). What officers typically find at the scene is not serious crime but a kaleidoscope of trouble that requires them to provide some combination of counsel, assistance, expertise, coercion, referral, and persuasion, and to make a report (Cumming, Cumming, and Edell 1965; Ericson 1982). For patrol officers, at least, direct involvement in crime work takes up as little as 3 per cent of their working time (Comrie and Kings 1975; Ericson 1982).

There are, of course, criminal investigation specialists in police organizations – detectives – who devote all their time to crime work. However, detectives also spend relatively little time on direct criminal investigation. Draper (1978: 31) estimated that only about 10 per cent of the investigator's time was spent this way. Ericson (1993: 45) found that detectives spent about half their time in the office and that much more time was devoted to recording investigative activities than to actual investigation work.

Studies of patrol officers also indicate that a substantial amount of their time is taken up by knowledge work (Webster 1970; Ericson 1982; Policy Studies Institute 1983; Kinsey 1985; Shadgett 1990). For example, Webster (1970) found that 39 per cent of all assignments dealt with administrative matters, which consumed 50 per cent of police time. Chatterton (1989: 112) reported on his observations of patrol sergeant activity during 152 shifts, and stated that in 9 per cent of the shifts the patrol sergeants did not leave the office at all, and that in 67 per cent of the shifts they spent less than two-and-a-half hours out of the office. A single new reporting requirement can have a dramatic impact on police personnel allocation and resources. For example, in England and Wales there is a requirement that all police audiotape interviews with suspects must be summarized on a standard form. The time devoted to this one knowledge-work requirement is estimated to be equal to the full-time efforts of 1,400 police officers, the equivalent of about 1 per cent of the entire constabulary of England and Wales (Royal Commission on Criminal Justice 1993)!

The view that the police are first and foremost crime fighters belongs to the public sphere. For the mass media the dramatization of crime is *the* staple cultural product of their industry, and the police inevitably have a leading part in crime dramatizations (Ericson, Baranek, and Chan 1987, 1989, 1991; Katz 1987; Reiner 1992: chap. 5; Sparks 1992; Schlesinger and Tumber 1994). The mass-mediated image of police as crime fighters penetrates everyone's lives on a daily basis, convincing people that the police must be as they are represented. Indeed, police officers themselves become convinced of the truthfulness of their media representation. Studies show repeatedly that within 'cop culture,' 'real police work' is defined as crime work, and everything else is seen at best as supporting that work, and at worst as peripheral or a nuisance (Manning 1977; Ericson 1982, 1993; Reiner 1992: chap. 3).

The police officer is subject to the logics of other communication media, namely those connected with institutional reporting requirements. The day-to-day reality of police work is constituted by the risk communication rules, formats, and technologies relevant to the institutions, populations, and events the police officer encounters. Moreover, a great deal of this work pertains to forms of risk management other than crime control. This reality is nicely articulated by Shadgett, a police officer who undertook an observational study of his fellow workers:

> [D]uring every facet of the police experience ... officers spent an inordinate amount of time either accounting for their work or preparing for the time when they would have to account for their work. Very little crime fighting in the popular sense was really going on. Indeed, one of the most common *jokes* around the police office, heard almost every day, was the statement, 'Well, I'm gonna go out and fight crime'... Reporting incidents was integral to investigations; in fact, the reporting of events, that is, accounting for them, amounted to the rationale and primary purpose behind many investigations, particularly those that could not be 'solved'... The production of paperwork was an aspect of 'real' police work that assisted the police in negotiating their way through the complexities ... a central aspect of the craft of police, not alien to it. Patrol officers worked very hard to patrol the streets and keep the peace. They also worked very hard, and for much longer durations, to 'patrol the facts.' (Shadgett 1990: 36, 42, 72)

Institutional Demands for Knowledge

The fact that the police are first and foremost knowledge workers leads us to ask who is demanding the knowledge they produce. The answer in existing police research is overwhelmingly that the police produce knowledge for their own *internal* management purposes. Wilson's (1968: 90) observation that the police organization's reporting system is 'not designed to ensure that the problem will be solved (often it cannot be), but to protect the department against a charge that it did nothing,' has been repeated by many other researchers. Researchers have focused on how line-officers do their paperwork with an eye toward 'covering ass' in their dealings with their supervisors (Manning 1980; Ericson 1982, 1993; Chatterton 1991). When studies go beyond the immediate gate-keeping aspects of street-level decision making, they still remain within the police institution and examine only the internal flow of knowledge (Manning 1988; Chatterton 1989; Southgate and Mirless-Black 1991). Knowledge is rarely seen as moving beyond the police institution, only into it, across it, and up it. For example, Manning (1992a: 352) states that 'The police gather *primary* information or "raw data" that is then processed within policing for crime-solving or closing the events to become secondary information. When processed twice, gathered, and formatted, it can move up the organization to become tertiary or "managerial" information.'

In this police-centred vision of knowledge work, the possibility of a communication environment outside the police institution is not even imagined. Among the few researchers who have considered police communications with external institutions, the focus has been almost exclusively on knowledge production for criminal prosecution. This focus indicates that researchers have accepted the common assumption that police work is largely crime work (Ericson 1982, 1993; McConville, Sanders, and Leng 1991; Manning and Hawkins 1989). The police-centrism of analysis has even led some researchers to conclude that police knowledge production and distribution are guided entirely by police criteria and done entirely for police purposes. Thus Chatterton (1991: 8) makes the extraordinary claim that the police 'have not been information driven. On the contrary they have made information police property. They have interpreted it in accordance with their own interests and within their own cultural assumptions and typifications. Information has been used to achieve rather than to set objectives.'

Some researchers have recognized that the police exist within a complex web of institutions and that all policing involves the policing of institutional life. However, their emphasis has been on how the police organize themselves to obtain knowledge from other institutions (Manning 1980: 34; Reiss 1983; Marx 1988; Hoogenboom 1991) and on how access is restricted by private property rights and by the state's mandate to protect privacy, both of which limit the police's ability to deal with crime (Stinchcombe 1963; Skolnick 1966; Reiss 1971; Reiss and Bordua 1967; Black 1980; Shearing and Stenning 1983). Some analysts have realized that the police's ability to penetrate other institutions has changed with changes in communication technologies and processes of bureaucratization. As Meyer and Scott (1983: 15) observe, 'The environments of formal organizations are, to a surprising degree, themselves formally organized' (see also Scott 1991: 171). This high degree of organization enables the police to acquire new and different forms of knowledge through inspections, surveillance, and audits (Reiss 1983; Marx 1988).

What researchers have failed to examine is the ways in which these external institutions access the police for knowledge relevant to their own policing needs. Regardless of the type of incident the police deal with, they are required to provide knowledge about it not only for their own purposes but also to help fulfil the risk management mandates of other institutions. The demands for knowledge made by these external institutions have a profound impact on how the police think and act. Consider the following illustration from Ontario offered by Shadgett (1990):

> An officer attended the scene of a serious motor vehicle accident involving personal injuries. Upon arrival he discovered that one of the drivers involved in the accident appeared to be impaired by the consumption of alcohol, and the necessary steps were taken to gather the evidence required for a conviction in criminal court. The result of the hour-long investigation was that one individual was criminally charged with impaired operation of a motor vehicle causing bodily harm, operating a motor vehicle with excess alcohol, and had his driver's licence suspended for 12 hours under the authority of the Criminal Code. After completing the investigation, the investigating officer then completed and submitted a total of 16 separate reports and forms regarding the incident. This total included a motor vehicle accident report; a general occurrence report; an arrest report; a 12-hour suspension of driver's license report; 2 itemized reports of property (including vehicles) seized for safekeeping; a certificate of analysis of a qualified breathalyser technician (prepared by the technician but processed by the investigating officer); a notice of intention to produce the certification of analysis at the accused's trial; a form to be sent to the local driving records registry to generate a certified copy of the accused's driving record; a notice of intention to produce the certification of analysis at the accused's trial; a 'crown brief' court package to be forwarded to the office of the crown attorney; a 'Promise to Appear' form which the accused was required to sign to facilitate release from custody and compel appearance in court; a 'CPIC' form to facilitate the entry of the accused, the charges, and the court date information into the national police computer; 2 'statistical tickets' to be forwarded to the headquarters of the force to give the officer 'credit' for laying the charges, and, any information regarding the charges to be sworn before a justice of the peace and then lodged in the local criminal courthouse for processing. With the exception of the general occurrence report and the arrest report, which were keyed into the police computer data base, the rest of the reports were completed by hand. Patrol officers perceived

> this to be another form of 'donkey-work' that required very little policing skill, particularly when it is considered that each of these reports contained basically the same information: the date, time and location of the incident, the particulars about the accused, and the charges laid. There was very little officers could do to reduce the amount of repetitive paperwork because each form was categorically different from the other and designed for different purposes. There was no possible way for the officer to accommodate a reduction in the workload to any lesser degree without neglecting force policy and due process ... Processing the incident, including dealing with any associated property, evidence and person, included first and foremost the routine processing of paper. In the one case above this took three times as long as it took the officer to initially investigate the incident. One hour to investigate, and three hours to write about it, to account for it, and to bureaucratically process it.

Shadgett shows that a given instance of police work is entwined with a number of institutions, risk logics, and legal regimes. Here the police officer is serving not only the patrol sergeant 'judge' and the criminal court judge, but also the regulatory agency judge, the insurance adjuster judge, the doctor judge, and so on. For example, the provincial motor vehicles registry requires knowledge concerning the place of the accident, the vehicles involved, and the persons involved. This is needed for risk profiling that can be used in accident prevention, traffic management, resource allocation, and automobile industry compliance. The automobile industry requires knowledge concerning the safety of its vehicles, for two reasons: first, so that vehicular safety can be improved, and second, to address the concerns of regulatory agencies and consumer groups. Insurance companies require knowledge that enables them to allocate responsibility in the particular case and to create statistical profiles for the determination of risks, premium levels, and compensation levels. The public health system requires knowledge concerning how the injuries in the accident occurred, as well as knowledge for statistical profiles that can be applied to the provision of emergency services in the future. The criminal courts require knowledge that will provide adequate evidence for prosecution and demonstrate proper procedure in generating the evidence. The police administration requires knowledge that can be used to account for property seized and persons processed, knowledge for the national computerized records system and its own record system, and knowledge for scientific 'human resources' management of police officer activity.

The police produce and distribute accounts of events within the established formats of the various institutions that might have an interest in the matter at hand. While police officers have a degree of creative latitude in how they tell the story, it is severely circumscribed by the knowledge requirements and classification schemes of the external institutions. Shadgett's police subjects believed that a lot of this reporting activity is 'donkey-work' because it is highly structured by the communication formats and purposes of institutional entities external to the event.

An institution consists of the relations, processes, and patterns associated with particular interests. It incorporates material elements (such as buildings and mechanical technologies), cultural elements (such as traditions, rituals, and scientific and legal technologies), political elements (such as the need for legitimation), and social elements (such as when all of the above are reproduced through social knowledge and routine activity). Institutions do 'a lot of regular thinking on behalf of individuals' (Douglas 1986: 47) by engaging in the perpetual elaboration of classifications and communication formats directed at the production and distribution of knowledge for risk management. This knowledge is used for entropy reduction, problem solving, and routine decisions.

'The centrality of risk assessment and risk management to complex organizations testifies to the institutionalization of risk in modern society' (Reiss 1989: 392). As new risk management needs arise, institutions develop new ways of categorizing, classifying, thinking, and acting that demand police participation. This process is not a recent phenomenon as some writers on risk and criminal justice have suggested (Feeley and Simon 1994; Garland 1996). Rather, it has been with the police since their foundation, as part of modern governance. As soon as modern institutions began devising new classification schemes for statistical understanding and risk profiling, the police were required to contribute what they could to the knowledge production and distribution effort.

Hacking observes that with the post-1820s development of 'moral science' and 'the avalanche of printed numbers,' the police were asked to help construct profiles of deviant populations on behalf of the state's health, welfare, and legal institutions. Hacking notes, for example, that in nineteenth-century France

> We find classifications of over 4,000 different crisscrossing motives for murder and requests that the police classify each individual suicide in 21 different ways. I do not believe that motives of these sorts or suicides of these kinds existed until the practice of counting them came into being ... Every fact about the suicide

> becomes fascinating. The statisticians compose forms to be completed by doctors and police, recording everything from the time of death to the objects found in the pockets of the corpse. The various ways of killing oneself are abruptly characterized and become symbols of national character. The French favour carbon monoxide and drowning, the English hang or shoot themselves ... Even the unmaking of people has been made up. (Hacking 1986: 223, 235)

Elsewhere Hacking describes a schedule devised by the French Ministry of Justice in 1836,

> in which constables should record, on the spot where the suicide was found: the sex, age and state of health; profession or social class; residence, birth place, marital status, number of children; finance: rich, comfortable, poor or miserable; education: literate, can read and write, illiterate; state of mind; morality (judicially condemned? adulterer? gambler? prostitute? concubine? drunkard?); religion. Then there should be a record of the place, the medical circumstances, the date and hour, and the weather. How was it done? Why was it done? Was a letter left? Previous attempts? A parental history of madness or of suicide? What objects were found on the scene, or in the victim's pockets? (Hacking 1990:79)

Society has become increasingly institutionalized through bureaucracy and technology, and the police role as risk communicators has grown accordingly. To borrow Hacking's memorable phrase, the police, in collaboration with a host of institutions in risk society, are 'tamers of chance.' As such, policing is a form of social insurance. A typical urban police force in Canada uses several hundred operational forms, the majority of which are for communicating knowledge of risk to external institutions. In 1992 the Royal Canadian Mounted Police had, because of the many federal, provincial, and municipal jurisdictions and private sector institutions it served, approximately 2,100 operational forms and a staff of 600 full-time knowledge workers in a special 'Informatics' Division. As we will show, this scale of knowledge work is largely a product of external demands for knowledge along with an internal police concern to ensure that knowledge is provided in proper form.

The requirement placed on the police to report to myriad external institutions suggests another correction to the conventional wisdom among police researchers. Because of their police-centric vision and their emphasis on knowledge production and distribution for internal management purposes, researchers have emphasized secrecy and 'low visibility' in police work. Following Goldstein's (1960) seminal formulation, researchers continue to contend that 'most police decisions are virtually invisible or of low visibility' and that 'Secrecy is emphasized ... information is rarely shared' (Manning 1992a: 357, 370; see also Geller and Morris 1992; Chatterton 1983, 1989; Reiss 1982: 146). To the contrary, we document that, in the context of demands from external institutions, the police engage in numerous kinds of institutionalized *publicity* that in sum make their work an exercise in high visibility. As risk communicators to various institutional audiences, the police not only distribute knowledge widely but also make their own actions highly visible in producing that knowledge. As in other knowledge-based occupations, the police worker, in the very act of producing and distributing the knowledge needed to get the job done, also produces and distributes knowledge about his or her work (Ericson and Shearing 1986; Poster 1990, 1995; Stehr 1994).

The Division of Expert Knowledge

The interinstitutional environment of policing risk means that the police intersect with, and are constituted by, a wide range of risk professions and their forms of expert knowledge (Ericson 1994a). The police profession exists within a system of professions defined by abstract knowledge of risk (Abbott 1988). The success of each profession, including the police, depends as much on the structure of the system itself as it does on the specialized knowledge and efforts of the particular profession.

In the interinstitutional environment there is constant negotiation about and adjustment to criteria of risk assessment and security provision. This state of affairs originates in the competing knowledge claims of the participants in the system and makes the police perpetually open to new, externally driven forms of risk communication and security provision. As we will show, it is therefore wrong to contend that 'criminal justice organizations are seeking to become more self-contained, more "autopoietic" (Teubner 1993) and less connected to externally driven social purposes' (Garland 1996: 16–17).

There is also a division of expert knowledge within the police institution itself. A police bureaucracy does not consist of a single professional group but is a collection of experts from many professions. For example, there are civilian professionals in information technology, law, social work, psychology, education, business administration, medicine, and engineering. There are also police officers who hold university degrees and are members of various nonpolice professions. These civilian and police professionals in the police institution work with other professionals to process abstract knowledge of risk and to turn that abstract knowledge into practical knowledge and risk technologies. But because of the research bias in favour of street-level decision making, there has been no substantial research on what these staffs do within the division of policing labour.

Although the public perhaps still believes that professionals are people who work for the most part as sole practitioners, most professionals in fact work within institutional bureaucracies. This is the case even for 'traditional' professionals such as doctors and lawyers. In bureaucracies the mix of professionals is usually very broad, and both 'turf' conflicts and assimilation into some aspects of a common organizational culture are inevitable. According to Abbott (1988: 155), 'The preponderance of multiprofessional bureaucracies among professional workplaces makes the workplace contest for jurisdiction an increasingly important part of the overall competition for control of work.'

There is no research on policing that allows us to describe the internal division of expert knowledge. The empirical analyses that will be presented in this book, especially in Part V, remedy this gap in the literature. At this juncture we can only draw on some insights of organizational theorists to suggest why there has been a proliferation of specialized experts and units in policing (Scott 1991; Powell 1991; Scott and Meyer 1991).

Organizations 'map' elements of their environment onto their own structures. When the organization has as wide a remit as the police – who deal with the full range of the risk society's institutions in complex and conflicting ways – there is an inevitable tendency toward greater administrative complexity, the creation of multiple boundary units, and less organizational coherence. Specialized units proliferate to respond to demands from external constituencies as well as to give more coherence to relations with those constituencies. Administrative complexity is further magnified when, as in the case of the police, an organization is both centralized and fragmented. As Reiner (1992: 768) observes in the English context, 'The notion of the bobby on the beat as the essential bedrock of the force, to which all other specialisms are ancillary, remains a philosophy to which most Chief Constables pay homage. But in practice, specialist departments have proliferated and foot patrol has been downgraded.'

There is also a complex division of expert knowledge within other institutions as they seek to provide for their internal risk assessment and security needs. For example, the 'taming of chance,' especially with regard to 'loss prevention,' has been a preoccupation of modern business enterprises (Shearing and Stenning 1981, 1983; Shearing 1992). As Hacking (1982: 287) observes, the 'avalanche of printed numbers' for risk management was not at all exclusive to the state apparatus of liberal governance. It was (and is) also central to business enterprises, and 'even businessmen look more at theft than trade.'

There is a complex division of expert knowledge within private security operations. Even with its narrow focus on loss prevention, private security entails risk logics, multiple boundary units, and fragmentation (Shearing and Stenning 1984: 341). There is a hierarchy of private security firms with respect to levels of expertise and specialization, with some refusing to do the 'dirty work' of low-level 'rent-a-cop' operations (South 1988: 98). Recognizing the importance of communication technology in providing both risk assessment and the feeling of security, the major private security firms also invest in communication technology industries. The English-based multinational Securicor, for example, has a cellular telephone partnership with British Telecom, as well as interests in alarm, courier, office cleaning, and insurance businesses. The cleaning business brings with it expertise in security and alarm systems (ibid.: 26–7).

The divisions of expert knowledge within the public police and private security institutions are in turn shaped and altered by relations between them. The police serve private security institutions and arrangements in many ways. As we document in Parts III and IV, the most fundamental support is via routine knowledge work within the communication formats of external institutions. As we have seen in the case discussed by Shadgett (pp. 23–4), when the police become involved in an event it is largely to account for that event according to the criteria established by external institutions for the latter's risk management purposes. However, the police also offer external institutions a range of expertise in matters of security provision. This expertise is officially recognized and indeed mandated in community policing models (Garland 1996: 9), and in at least some American jurisdictions, it has led to a fundamental shift in the division of expert knowledge between public and private policing. Thus M. Davis (1990: 250–1) observes 'an evolving social division of labour between public- and private-sector police services, in which the former act as the necessary supports of the latter ... The private sector, exploiting an army of non-union, low-wage employees, has increasingly captured the labour-intensive roles (guard duty, residential patrol, apprehension of retail crime, maintenance of security passages and checkpoints, monitoring of electronic surveillance, and so on), while public law enforcement has retrenched behind supervision of security macro-systems' (see also T. Becker 1974; South 1988: 7; Spitzer and Scull 1977; Shearing 1992).

The public police also provide a range of expert advice on nonterritorial aspects of risk. For example, they offer advice on improved information technology links that will enhance risk profiling; on security systems; on compliance standards that relate to motor vehicle, commercial, and environmental risks; and on health, education, and welfare services. These forms of expertise are recognized within the community policing model, as we demonstrate in chapters 3 and 9. For example, Leighton (1991: 492), echoing Goldstein's (1990) 'problem-solving approach' to community policing, states that

> The corporate culture becomes that of a service agency to the public, borrowing values from the private sector such as partnerships, search for excellence, continuous quality assurance, etc. The subculture becomes one of a white-collar profession that is responsible, responsive to community needs, and driven by a code of professional ethics ... Inter-agency cooperation is a key strategy involving a branching out to other service delivery agencies to form strategic partnerships and a more cooperative and productive division of labour ... within a service network of agencies addressing urban safety and, more generally, the 'healthy cities' approach.

The public police undertake routine tasks on behalf of private risk institutions, such as licensing and certifying security technologies and operatives (South 1988: 121, 135) and endorsing particular insurance products (O'Malley 1991).

It has been observed that the public police are losing ground in their relations with private security institutions and are becoming the latter's 'junior partners' (Shearing and Stenning 1983; Shearing 1992). While the public police obviously receive a great deal of knowledge as a result of relationships of reciprocity and trust with colleagues in private security institutions, the knowledge flow is clearly more from the police to outside institutions, especially via routine reporting requirements. Moreover, much of this knowledge provision has become commodified, with the external institutions paying directly for reports (such as occurrence reports for insurance companies), for officers' time (such as time spent in an interview with an insurance adjuster), and for services (such as territorial security provision).

Communication Formats, Technology, and Police Discretion

The division of expert knowledge in policing, and the associated formats by which police knowledge of risk is communicated among other institutions, has profound implications for police discretion.

Format refers to the way in which communication is organized. For example, a police occurrence report has dozens of fixed-choice categories to check off in accounting for an incident, as well as restricted space for a narrative. In some jurisdictions these reports are prepared on a computer screen, a medium that further shapes the format and becomes part of the communication process:

> Formats are metacommunication statements, or rules for the recognition, organization and presentation of information and experience ... Theoretically, formats can be regarded as central and structural properties to 'knowledgeable activities of situated actors who draw upon rules and resources in the diversity of action contexts, [which] are produced and reproduced in interaction' (Giddens 1984: 25) ... As the logic of the format pervades the everyday routines and conversations of the workplace, the terminology, metaphors and imagery of format permeate language and human and idle time; the time, place and manner of the workplace can itself be sucked into the vortex of format. (Altheide 1995: 38, 43)

Discretion is autonomy in decision making (Black 1968: 25; K. Davis 1969: 4; Ericson 1982: 11–13). All sociological research on policing addresses the question of discretion in terms of the degree of the officer's autonomy, power, or agency in relation to the various rule-structures in policing. The conventional sociological wisdom is that the most influential rule-structure is the one provided by the occupational culture of fellow officers. It is the common sense 'recipe rules' of the occupational culture – more than the laws, administrative rules, or other rules of the community being served – that most determine how the police think and act. Manning (1982: 130) says that the occupational culture is 'the lens through which the organization is seen and by which the shapes and contours of the external world are fixed and established as reality ... [It] acts as a grid or screen by which events are defined and also makes relevant internal rules. It mediates and is something of a transducer, acting to filter information and meaning moving across the posited organizational boundaries.'

While it has recently been argued that reasoning in police occupational culture is not simply rule-based – that it is also, for example, based on metaphors, tropes, and other forms of figurative language (Shearing and Ericson 1991) – this refinement still essentializes the occupational culture as the determinant of police action. Researchers have posited a sharp break or disjuncture between police administrative logic and police occupational culture logic, even to the point of depicting the police organization as a 'mock bureaucracy' (Gouldner 1954). According to van Maanen (1983: 277), 'Because police tasks at the lower levels are ill defined, episodic, nonroutine, accomplished in regions of low visibility, and are dispatched in ways that most often bypass the formal chain of command in the organization, control over the work itself remains largely in the hands of those who perform the work ... In this sense police agencies resemble symbolic or mock bureaucracies where only the appearance of control, not the reality, is maintained' (see also Manning 1983: 191–2).

This approach has led researchers to see police work as unfocused. It is said to be based on a kind of situational ad hocery. The framework through which the police think and act is their own, one for the most part unavailable to outsiders and therefore rather free-floating and arbitrary. 'All valued police knowledge is thought to be contextual knowledge, surrounded by unexplicated, tacit assumptions and meanings' (Manning and Hawkins 1989: 146). When data are captured, it is not the tightly formatted forms that are important but 'unexplicated, commonsense assumptions about the nature of police work' against a background of 'an inability to specify in advance what is needed' (Manning 1992a: 372).

While one might assume that such ad hocery would make police officers highly reflexive, it is said to have the opposite effect: policing is a 'non-reflective, action-oriented job,' a 'non-reflexive task in which intuition is valued and encouraged' (Manning and Hawkins 1989: 152). The risk communication system of policing, and the ways in which it is embedded in specific communication formats, is therefore not seen as a basis for controlling and enabling police action. Manning states that 'Information is gathered in an ad hoc manner and stored without much concern for retrieval. In other words, absent close supervision and guidance and organizational controls on the allocation of resources to cases, individual officers will determine the modes of working cases. Left to their own devices, without training or rewards to do so, officers will rarely use expert systems, network analyses or modelling' (Manning 1992a: 367–8).

The result of this view of occupational culture, which Manning himself subscribes to, is that risk communication formats are deemed marginal. They are said to be discredited within the occupational culture: 'The craftlike and clinical definition of police work, as well as its exciting immediacy and the previously described features of police knowledge, are the basis for discrediting paperwork, files, and all forms of bureaucratically ordered information' (ibid.: 370–1). Paperwork is not prospectively taken into account as a basis for thought and action, but becomes a retrospective construction for administrative purposes: 'In action, there is no thought; thought and reflection follow the act. In this sense, the environment is created and *enacted* and then naturalized and cast into organizational rhetorics' (Manning 1982: 124). Paperwork is a way of retrospectively justifying what has been done for administrative purposes, a form of account ability for accountability (Manning and Hawkins 1989: 151–2; Ericson 1993, 1995a). The huge bureaucracy of knowledge workers is said to focus on administrative 'housekeeping' rather than operational concerns. The bureaucracy's data are depicted as being for the most part merely stored rather than as moving in myriad directions internally and externally (Manning 1988: 239–40; Manning 1992a: 370–1).

Similar observations are made about information technology and its impact on police communications. The police culture is obdurate; it resists and deflects technological incursions, which is the same way it deals with the incursions of law and administrative policies. Chatterton (1991: 17) echoes Manning and Hawkins (1989: 150) in asserting that 'unless the traditional culture and structure of policing are addressed, they will condition the information technology much more than the information technology will condition police work.' The existing culture maintains the status quo and imprints its traditions on any new element: 'The technology is used to produce and reproduce traditional ways of doing things or practices, and is slowly modifying them' (Manning and Hawkins 1989: 150).

We dispute these claims about police reasoning and knowledge work. Police work is not ad hoc and situational but prospectively structured by the categories and classifications of risk communication and by the technologies for communicating knowledge internally and externally. The communication formats provide the means through which the police think, act, and justify their actions. These formats are in turn structured by the expert knowledge of risk required by police managers and by external institutions. The data thus captured are tightly formatted so that they can be entered into computers for rapid movement to a range of specialized units within the police organization, to other police organizations, and to external institutions.

In the perpetual quest for certainty the police join forces with all other major institutions in risk society. While institutions once relied on ordeals to provide conclusive answers when they could no longer tolerate uncertainty (Beattie 1986) – and still do to some extent (Nock 1993) – they now rely on risk communication formats and technologies to reduce uncertainty (Gandy 1993). They buy into the latest classification scheme, technology, or system that promises efficient risk management and 'uncluttered justice.' This reflects what Geertz describes as 'technological restlessness, a sort of rage to invent ... the general revolution of rising expectations as to the possibilities of fact determination and its power to settle intractable issues that the general culture of scientism has induced in all of us' (Geertz 1983: 171–2; see also Nelken 1990). Technology drives uses. Where there is a way there is a will (Ericson and Shearing 1986; G. Marx 1988).

The rush for technological solutions to problems of uncertainty often has the ironic consequence of increasing uncertainty. In his study of a police communications centre, Manning (1988) found that when the positions of call operator and dispatcher were combined, the worker had a greater range of sources to draw on in verifying and validating knowledge, including personal experience, radio feedback, and fellow workers who had previously served in the field as patrol officers. But when the positions of call operator and dispatcher were again separated and a single-channel technology introduced, the result was an increase rather than a decrease in uncertainty of meaning.

The introduction of more-efficient technology also produces more data, which fuel demands for more experts, communication formats, and technologies to manage such data. As Weick (1979: 168) observes, 'Technology generates a great deal of raw data, a process that places even greater demands on the organization to bracket those raw data so that they can be made manageable.'

The reduction of uncertainty is always a matter of relative power. Police officers equipped with sophisticated surveillance technology and having access to knowledge about a suspect may reduce their own uncertainty and thereby become empowered, but when they reduce the suspect's uncertainty the suspect becomes constrained. Similarly, a police supervisor can use communication technology to reduce uncertainty about his own course of action and thereby become empowered, but the resultant reduction of the subordinate police officer's uncertainty will be experienced by the latter as disempowerment or loss of discretion.

The incessant search for efficient risk management and uncluttered justice recoils on the police themselves. The very communication formats and technologies police officers use to conduct surveillance of others are also used for surveillance of their own work (Ericson and Shearing 1986). In the police call-response and dispatch room one finds the

> epitome of the assembly line worker with little or no control over the quality, pacing, content, aims or evaluation of their work. They are timed to the second on every break by the computers, they are supplied work by an automatic computer that shifts calls their way as soon as they are 'free'; the order of their work is technologically determined and demand driven. They are servants of the public in name only, for although the public pays them, they work for the machines that lurk behind them, glow in front of them, click and buzz in their ears and fill the air with dull electronic sounds. (Manning 1988: 155)

Police cars equipped with computer terminals monitor officers' movements in and out of their cars, their responses to calls for service, their checks of persons and vehicles, and so on. Some police organizations have adopted cellular telephones or laptop computers, which allow officers to immediately report on occurrences. These systems have built-in checks on every detail of the report and its completeness. Some police cars are also equipped with video cameras, which record the officer's behaviour in dealings with the public.

Police buildings are also equipped to conduct surveillance of police officer activity. Devices such as access cards, surveillance cameras, and computers programmed to check on the keeping of custody records have proliferated (Royal Commission on Criminal Justice 1993; Ericson 1994a: 168–9; Ericson 1994b: 134–6). There have also been efforts to implement surveillance of police officers who themselves are conducting surveillance of suspects. For example, in 1993 the Royal Commission on Criminal Justice in England recommended a procedural correctness overseer for major investigations and a 'helpline' or whistleblower scheme for police officers who are reluctant to report wrongdoing by fellow officers (Maguire and Norris 1993: 112; Royal Commission on Criminal Justice 1993: 22). G. Marx (1988: 57) notes a case in which a U.S. attorney who was monitoring a conversation between a police officer and a suspect telephoned the officer to tell him to redirect the conversation because his words were bordering on entrapment. The above examples again suggest that policing is at once thoroughly formatted yet reflexive.

Policing, like the knowledge-based occupations it intersects with in other risk institutions, is subject to intensive 'informating' (translating events and objectives into visible information via formats) and 'automating' or 'fordization' (machine appropriation of human skills and labour) (Zuboff 1988). Again, the goal is a simplification of choices in the face of a kaleidoscope of possible interpretations and courses of action – 'taylorization.'

The management of police officers is increasingly seen as a communications and technological problem. Inspired by progressive corporations, police managers adopt 'human resources' risk profiling techniques – the constitution of their 'population' of workers – that are parallel in logic and format to the risk profiling techniques their officers apply to members of other populations as part of their routine surveillance work. Working for 'Police Inc.,' police officers are left to perform a mental labour based on the manipulation of symbols (Poster 1990) that in turn reflexively symbolizes them as automatons.

Police officers such as those studied by Shadgett (1990) (see pp. 21, 23–4) are especially likely to feel alienated from their mental labour of symbols because they know little about its products and consequences. They are likely to feel a loss of agency because they produce knowledge within established communication formats but often have no clear idea of who this knowledge is for, where it goes, and how it is used in actual risk management. For them the experience is a 'one-way mirror.' They are in the same position as someone who uses credit cards and access cards without knowing that he or she is being risk-profiled for a variety of strategic and analytical purposes (Gandy 1993: 54). On the other hand, it might be argued that it would make little difference for police officers to have such knowledge, because in the face of a large bureaucratic machine there is little that can be done with it to enhance one's interests. As Archer (1988: 68) observes in another context, 'to be aware of the causes of inflation does not prevent it from reducing our standard of living.'

Although the police officer's discretion is severely circumscribed, it is not subject to foreclosure. It is possible to be deskilled and yet also be the broker of expert knowledge. In handling a person's troubles, for example, a police officer can take that person's definition of his or her needs and translate it into institutional, expert-knowledge renderings that establish the route for satisfying those needs. As a router of needs, it is not the police officer qua *person* but his or her *function* of mediation and interpretation within expert-knowledge systems that is important to 'clients' with 'needs' (Bauman 1992a). Thus we find that the 'taylorized' police officer is described as being like the 'taylorized' physician, a 'highly trained, relatively well-paid, white-collar professional' who examines 'underlying causes of problems using a broader range of longer-term responses, particularly crime prevention activities [that] address poverty, unemployment, poor education and work skills, inadequate housing, poor health, and underlying causes of crime' (Leighton 1991: 494–5).

This portrait of police work is of course close to Weber's depiction of bureaucratic 'dehumanized' labour. A complex division of institutional labour for risk management and security provision requires a formally detached and strictly objective expert as knowledge broker, counsellor, and advisor (Stehr 1992, 1994). The expert does nothing but transmit and apply knowledge, so that the execution of his or her work is identical with the consumption of its result, namely knowledge (ibid.): 'Automated production, mediated communication, and mediated economic exchange are offering a world wherein no one becomes implicated with another. More and more coordinated action is action that is subordinated to machines. All are becoming machine-like. Rationality is equated with subordination of human activity to machines' (Couch 1984: 369).

In the 'informated' and automated police organization, there is also a shift in discretion from the level of the individual officer on the ground to those who design the expert-knowledge system. Police managers join the risk management 'technical elites with expertise in classifying, sorting and excluding' populations (Reichman 1986: 166). This expertise also extends to moving, ordering, and coercing data (Hacking 1992: 140).

One can no more understand the expert-knowledge system of policing and its impact on police discretion if one's inquiry is limited to what police officers do 'on the street' than one can understand retailing by reducing it to what the clerk does while serving customers. The thought of a McDonald's restaurant employee dispensing 'the ever-perfect, indeed the same hamburger, designed in the laboratory and cooked by computers' (Lovekin 1991: 143; see also Boas and Chain 1976) is enough to make one realize that people with 'McJobs' are constituted by expert systems. Even in medicine the doctor on the ground is a subordinate of expert systems and those who manage them. He or she is one of many contributors to the expert system of risk management that creates the patient's dossier, and therefore loses control over particular outcomes as well as over the progress of cases. Moreover, the dossier not only constitutes the patient's medical biography but also provides data for operating various hospital, insurance, educational, and strategic planning systems: 'The operative on the ground now becomes a simple auxiliary to a manager whom he or she supplies with information derived from the activity of diagnosis expertise. These items of information are then stockpiled and distributed along channels completely disconnected from those of professional practice' (Castel 1991: 281). In turn, the hospital, insurance, educational and strategic planning schemes shape how doctors think, act, and organize.

The more the abstract system of specialized knowledge becomes embedded in communication formats and technologies, the more it takes on a life of its own. As it deskills, it also produces alienating and fragmenting effects on the occupational culture and the self. That is, local control – individual discretion, organizational authority, and the autonomy of occupational culture – is undermined with each expropriation of skill and knowledge to the level of the abstract system (Giddens 1991). Trust is also displaced to the abstract system, so that new situations and problems are dealt with by a system response. These changes in turn have a profound impact on the practices, legal regimes, and discourse of policing.

2

Policing, Risk, and Law

Risk, Surveillance, and Security

From Deviance to Risk

Sociology has been centrally concerned with the problem of order. This concern entails a focus on whether behaviour is deviant and how deviance is controlled. Deviance is defined as a straying from the normal, which encompasses not only serious forms of abnormal behaviour such as criminal acts but also violations of organizational procedures and common sense knowledge. There traditionally has been a strong moral element in designations of deviance: deviance is wicked, bad, sinful, a violation of moral order.

With regard to deviance risk has a dual aspect of identifying both problem and procedure. It designates deviance as danger. Such designations are often deeply moral (Douglas 1990, 1992). Risk also offers procedures or technologies – classification schemes, probability calculations, and communication formats – for dealing with various dangers. Risk is an invention based on imagined fears and on imaginative technologies for dealing with them. Indeed, the concept of risk is a construct of insurance technology. It turns people, their organizations, and their environments into myriad categories and identities that will make them more manageable. It makes up people and their organizations according to its own internally referential systems of rationality, rather than in terms of extrinsic moral questions and issues.

Risk does not eschew morality; rather, it fundamentally alters the basis of morality. It bears a utilitarian morality. People, organizations, and environments are sorted into whatever categories will fit the practical purpose of the institution that wishes to make them predictable. The possibilities of categorization are endless and the process of 'panoptic sorting' (Gandy 1993) is perpetual. People, organizations, and other things are distinguished from one another in terms of whether they are more or less efficient, more or less useful, more or less strong, and so on, rather than in terms of moral blamelessness or blameworthiness.

As such, the risk society is also a 'transmission society' (Castel (1991) refers to a two-speed society). It regulates the pace of contributions to society by rating credentials, personal handicaps, creditworthiness, productivity, and so on (Gandy 1993; Nock 1993). Some people are destined for the autobahn, others relegated to highways with speed limits, and still others to local roads with speed bumps. As we argue in the following section on law, justice becomes a matter of the just distribution of risks.

The police help various risk institutions regulate traffic in the transmission society. They undertake this work within the framework of official paper formatted for the needs of other institutions. They also assist these institutions by referring people to them and providing services, including the giving of expert advice on social development and the interinstitutional provision of risk management. At the same time, the police rely on these institutions for knowledge useful for their own panoptic sorting.

This cognitive mentality of risk affects moral sensibility with respect to deviance. Gutted of moral wrongdoing, deviance is treated as a 'normal accident' (Perrow 1984). Deviance is thus merely a contingency for which there are risk technologies to help spread the loss and prevent recurrence. It becomes a technical problem that requires an administrative solution, rather than an occasion for expressing collective sentiments and moral solidarity (Durkheim 1973; Reichman 1986; Garland 1990). As Garland (1996: 2) observes about criminal deviance, 'The threat of crime has become a routine part of modern consciousness, an everyday risk to be assessed and managed in much the same way that we deal with road traffic – another modern danger which has been routinized and "normalized" over time ... the normality of high crime rates in late modern society has prompted a series of transformations in official perceptions of crime, in criminological discourse, in modes of governmental action, and in the structure of criminal justice organizations.'

The moral order of wrongdoing, and of collective sentiment toward it, is played out according to the very different logic of the mass media in public culture. As in the past, public culture provides dramatizations of serious crime, morality plays through which people remember values that are increasingly at odds with those of other institutions that govern people's lives (Ericson, Baranek, and Chan 1987, 1989, 1991; Katz 1987; Schlesinger and Tumber 1994; Sparks 1992).

From Control to Surveillance

In risk society, policing is not just a matter of repressive, punitive, deterrent measures to control those who are morally wrong. It is also a matter of surveillance, of producing knowledge of populations that is useful for administering them (Dandeker 1990). The focus is on knowledge that allows selection of thresholds that define acceptable risks and on forms of inclusion and exclusion based on this knowledge.

The emphasis on surveillance redirects the law, the police, and risk institutions to continually invent new ways of accessing and distributing knowledge. The main task of the police is to 'front load' (Reichman 1986: 155) the system with relevant knowledge that can later be sorted and distrubuted to interested institutional audiences. Coercive control gives way to contingent categorization: 'The State's traditional monopoly over the means of violence is supplemented by new means of gathering and analysing information that may even make the former obsolete. Control is better symbolized by manipulation than coercion, by computer chips than prison bars, and by remote and invisible filters than by handcuffs and straitjacket' (G. Marx 1988: 220; see also Poster 1990, 1995).

No population of individuals or organizations escapes surveillance in this form. The surveillance systems people are subject to are a matter of the institutions they participate in. Those populations whose risk histories have constituted them as weak and dependent are subjected to the state's criminal, welfare, and mental health surveillance systems, among other forms of surveillance (O'Malley 1992; Simon 1993; Nock 1993). Those populations that have survived panoptic sorting, and are constituted as stronger and more independent than the populations just mentioned are subjected to the state's taxation, education, licensing, social security, and health surveillance systems, as well as a plethora of private corporate systems concerned with credit, financial securities, frequent-flyer points, and so on. Indeed, it is by no means clear that marginal populations are the ones most subject to surveillance. Those populations in the high-speed lanes of the transmission society are more mobile socially and spatially and have a much broader range of institutional commitments and entanglements. The greater a person's reputation, the greater the surveillance by a greater number of institutions. The more a person is trusted, the more he or she is subjected to surveillance mechanisms that contingently grant continuation of that trust.

The focus on surveillance for risk management means that knowledge of the person, organization, or other thing as a risk is emphasized more than the subject's moral culpability or responsibility for a particular act of wrongdoing. Everyone and everything is to be made knowable through surveillance mechanisms. Everyone is presumed guilty until the risk profile proves otherwise (Ericson 1994c):

> The focus ... on risk control diminishes the importance of moral standards in the evaluation of harm-causing activities. It is no longer useful in such a regime to distinguish between the guilty and the innocent or the culpable and the blameless. Almost every human action will increase the probability of some loss by some amount; empirically, it would be extremely rare for an action to contribute zero towards the probability of all losses in all contexts. It follows, thus, that under the modern concept of risk, no action is every truly innocent. (Priest 1990: 227)

'Guilty' becomes just another item in a person's risk profile, another mark that says he or she does not have full status or membership or citizenship in particular institutions for particular purposes. One has lost one's credit rating. One has lost some reputational credits as a result of being criminally convicted. One does not have enough credits to be admitted to university. One does not have enough credits for landed immigrant status. Each transaction in everyday life simply registers one as more or less guilty and more or less worthy to take part in instrumental exchanges governed by institutions.

From Order to Security

Existing research has focused on the police as reproducers of order. Order is conceptualized in terms of morality, procedure, hierarchy, and territorial protection.

The moral order that the police uphold is enunciated in criminal law. By ferreting out evil and subjecting it to criminal process, the police articulate local standards and provide a barometer of moral order. This is the basis on which researchers, the public, and the police themselves have essentialized the police role as criminal law enforcers.

The police are also scrutinized for their adherence to orderly procedure. A great deal of research has focused on whether the police operate within procedural requirements, for example with respect to due process norms in criminal procedure (Skolnick 1966; Shearing 1981; McBarnet 1981; Ericson 1982, 1993; Ericson and Baranek 1982; McConville, Sanders, and Leng 1991; Royal Commission on Criminal Justice 1993). As 'symbols of order' (Walden 1982) and as a model by which other exercises of authority are judged, the police cannot escape the cacophony of discourse on procedural propriety and its relation to legitimacy and authority (Habermas 1975).

The police have also been studied as reproducers of hierarchical order. They are agents of structural inequality and the status quo with respect to class, age, gender, race, ethnicity, interests, status, character, and distinctions as to quality (Reiss 1971; Ericson 1982; Brogden, Jefferson, and Walklate 1988: chap. 6). As such they have a political role and make evident the fact that order is not a neutral concept (Reiner 1992).

All of these dimensions of order are reproduced through the police's maintenance of territorial order and security of public space. Research has focused on the ways in which the police's military-style bureaucracy, discipline, deployment, and coercion fight criminal sources of insecurity. For example, research on patrol policing examines how police deployment influences crime rates and public perceptions of security (Kelling et al., 1974; Ericson 1982; Sherman, Gartin, and Buerger 1989; Sherman 1992). Research on private policing displays the same concern with securing a territory, the only difference being a focus on 'mass private property' sites (Shearing and Stenning 1981, 1983). Research that examines how environmental designs affect crime and public perceptions of security is concerned with how spatial arrangements, surveillance technologies, and security hardware secure a territory (Newman 1972; Wilson and Kelling 1982; Shearing and Stenning 1984; Skogan 1990a).

This mainstream of research on police and public order follows the consensus model of functionalist sociology. It expresses the modern dream of government, and of the police themselves, that there is a unitary order that everyone recognizes and accepts and can use to judge deviance. But in risk society, institutions are not organized around a single, cohesive notion of order. There are many institutional orders, each with unique definitions of risk and different logics for dealing with the risks so defined.

Among other things, there are risks to *securities*, which include financial instruments such as money, credit cards, stock certificates, and cheques; credentials such as passports, drivers' permits, and university transcripts; and licences such as those that allow commercial trade. These security instruments are symbolic goods that know no territorial limits and provide forms of security that cannot be assessed within the conventional framework of territorial order.

Secondly, there are risks to *careers* or the life-course of individuals (such as the viability of one's earnings and capacity as a human resource) and of organizations (such as insuring the viability of organizational resources). A wide range of insurance products are available from both private companies and the state to protect against loss caused by unforeseen hazards or by health problems, unemployment, underemployment, retirement, and so on. The police spend a great deal of time working within the knowledge formats established by insurers and helping insurers address career risks (Reichman 1986; Simon 1987, 1988; O'Malley 1991; Ewald 1991a). Career-related fields of security provision are not based on particular territorial orders and the conceptions of morality, procedure, and hierarchy that arise from territorial conceptions of order. Rather, they are moulded by institutional contexts and their dispersed and fragmented logics of risk.

Thirdly, there are risks to cultural and personal *identities*, defined, for example, racially, ethnically, regionally, and according to gender and age. As noted above, researchers have addressed how police discrimination against people with specific identity characteristics reproduces hierarchical order. However, existing research only examines how identity characteristics are 'variables' in police decision making. It does not consider how the police contribute to the constitution of cultural identities and subjectivities through forms of risk classification and security provision.

The police contribute to the security efforts of various institutions by communicating knowledge of risk relevant to each of them. These institutions, including the police, are not bound by consensual order but by communication rules, formats, and technologies that connect them to each other in time and space and provide them with the immediate knowledge of risk that becomes the basis for action. Risk institutions are characterized by 'the concentrated reflexive monitoring they both permit and entail. Who says modernity says not just organizations, but organization – the regularized control of social relations across indefinite time-space distances' (Giddens 1991: 16).

The police officer produces and distributes technologically mediated and bureaucratically formatted communications for other risk institutions, and at the same time taps into the already-processed knowledge of these other institutions to help fulfil the risk mandates of his or her own institution. A lot of this work involves appropriating knowledge already constituted in other bureaucratic settings and presupposes 'a society that is bureaucratically conditioned and prepared for data processing' (Böhme 1984: 9). Most of this work does not involve face-to-face communication with the person subject to police activity. The police officer serves as a 'faceless bureaucrat' or 'iconocrat.' Thus a substantial proportion of calls for service do not result in the dispatch of a police officer to meet the complainant, for an increasing proportion of occurrences are simply recorded over the telephone. Informants are recruited through the mass media, with anonymity guaranteed by avoiding face-to-face contact (Carriere and Ericson 1989). Investigations are conducted via computer matching that involves various institutions but no direct dealings with suspects (G. Marx 1988). Checks are run on vehicle licence plates and then on the vehicle owner, without the subject knowing that he is being scrutinized in this way. This is policing by human absence, where the 'sights' prescribed by communication technologies are more significant than the 'sites' of face-to-face communications.

Institutions are not things. They do not occupy a particular place nor are they frozen in time. They consist of expert-systems of risk that are connected to each other in time and space by communication rules, formats, and technologies. Institutional activity transpires in space, that is, in relations between absent others in different places. At the same time any given place is penetrated by knowledge from elsewhere, so that 'what structures the locale is not simply that which is present on the scene; the "invisible form" of the locale conceals the distanciated relations [that is, relations at a distance] which determine its nature' (Giddens 1990: 18–19). In a great deal of institutional activity a local interaction is also part of a transaction across distance involving expert-systems of risk communication.

What makes institutions 'social' and allows them to provide security is precisely the ways in which communications circuitry can be plugged into at any point in time and space. Police social interaction for the purpose of security provision transpires within the communications circuitry of other institutions. The communications media and circuitry become part of the system of interaction, establishing patterns of knowledge flow and therefore patterns of interaction itself (Meyrowitz 1985; Ericson, Baranek, and Chan 1989; Poster 1990, 1995; Altheide 1995).

Moreover, the communications media and circuitry have special social significance as a shared arena of security beyond their specific knowledge capacities or content. Their formats are held in common by all those who engage them, and it is media formats along with knowledge and trust that provide security.

In summary, the phenomenal world of the police is not only unified by a correspondence of territorial settings but also by the ability of the police to move through any place as members of expert-systems of risk and security:

> [T]he individual enters the social realm as a connection, a terminal or code, that is, by means of a key, which gives him access to the social networks. Although this does not mean that someone who does not have the necessary connections ... does not exist at all, it does mean that he does not exist socially ... In order for society to be controllable through knowledge, it must itself be organized in terms of knowledge. Social processes must be differentiated according to function and arranged according to models, and social actors must be disciplined in a way that makes their behaviour amenable to data collection or makes their social role and activities relevant only insofar as they produce data. (Böhme 1992 41–2)

There are signs of a shift to a broader conception of security in various pronouncements on the police role. As we argue in chapters 3 and 9, the community policing agenda can be read as an articulation of what we are discussing here. Gluzol (1981: 362) observes that the French police 'are being transformed. Their aim is no longer solely the maintenance of law and order ... but also now to assure citizens' security.' Leighton (1991: 489), a Canadian government official, declares that 'the central objective or mission of the police in Canadian society is ... to *facilitate* a sense of security among the public ... and the *promotion* of public order and individual safety' (emphasis added). Security, public order, and individual safety are not provided directly but instead facilitated and promoted in collaboration with other institutions of risk and security.

There are traces of this conception of policing in early modern formulations of police. In the eighteenth century there was a conception of 'police science' – held by Beccaria, Bentham, Colquhoun, and Adam Smith, among many others – that constituted it as a branch of political economy. Known also as the 'science of government' and the 'science of happiness,' police science aimed to develop precise knowledge of every conceivable risk, and to convert risk assessments into the management of 'everything ... unregulated, everything which can be said ... to lack order or form' (Pasquino 1991: 111). Among the 3,215 seventeenth- and eighteenth-century German works on police science was Frank's six-volume *System for a Complete Medical Policing*, which included detailed regulations designed to 'prevent evils through wise ordinances,' and covered every then-imaginable aspect of health care, such as the regulation of time for resting after a dance in order to avoid catching a cold on the way home (Bok 1979: 215–16).

As Garland (1996: 22) remarks, Colquhoun's *Treatise on the Police in the Metropolis*, published in 1795, advocated a new system of policing that involved regulation, inspection, guardianship, and environmental design, in collaboration with other governing institutions. These activities were to be based on a model of prevention and opportunity reduction and funded through the philanthropy of business enterprises, churches, and other institutions of civil society (Andrew 1989). The police were to be a superintending agency, brokering and monitoring the policing efforts of all the agencies involved.

Van Justi, in his 1768 treatise entitled *Eléments generaux de police*, said that 'the science of policing consists ... in regulating everything that relates to the present condition of society, in strengthening and improving it, in seeing that all things ... contributed to the welfare of members that compose it.' Karl Marx, writing in 1843, restated the eighteenth-century view that 'Security is the supreme social concept of civil society, the concept of *police*, the concept that the whole society exists only to guarantee to each of its members the preservation of his person, his rights, and his property' (K. Marx 1967: 236; Spitzer 1987: 43). With such a lofty conception, there were no limits to what could be policed through the application of scientific knowledge of risk. Thus Duchesne's statement in the 1757 *Code of Police* that 'The objects which it embraces are in some sense indefinite' (Pasquino 1991: 109), was echoed two hundred years later by a senior police administrator in France who declared that his task was nothing less than an omniscient 'police journalism on behalf of the state' (Brodeur 1983).

Viewed in these terms, 'police' has an obvious common root with 'policy' as something to be explained through knowledge. Policing is 'intellectual labour involving not only the invention of new forms of thought, but also the invention of novel procedures of documentation, computation and evaluation ... diversity of powers and knowledges entailed in rendering fields practicable and amenable to intervention' (Miller and Rose 1990: 3). Policing as policy transforms people and their organizations into discourse, a discourse not of deviance, control, and order but of risk, surveillance, and security.

Regulatory Law

While policing as risk, surveillance, and security has early modern roots, it takes different routes in late modern society. The risks identified change continually, as do the communication rules, formats, and technologies for dealing with them. In risk society the police are situated within a complex circuitry of public institutions on the one hand and private corporate and philanthropic institutions on the other, a situation that entails legal transformations.

Risk society is a regulatory society. There has been an expansion of regulatory systems within a compliance mode of law enforcement. This expansion is in accordance with the insurance logic of risk (Lowi 1990). The insurance logic of risk management and security provision, and the reflexivity about risk it fosters, provides the basis for endless invention of new rules, formats, and technologies.

Invention is vested in professionals who work for administrative agencies concerned with insurance and indemnification. A given professional knowledge of risk deals with each new calibration of risk management within an isolated, segmented, piecemeal, single-problem, single-solution logic rather than in terms of systemic links between its knowledge and other knowledges (Bauman 1992a). The legislation and administrative rules that result from professional knowledge are likewise piecemeal and fragmented, perpetuating the need for further refinements and more regulation to secure compliance.

Compliance-based law enforcement is 'a series of instructions to administrators, rather than a series of commands to citizens' (Lowi 1979: 106). The job of these administrators is in turn to instruct their constituencies on what risks are worth taking. In the process there is an ongoing construction and deconstruction of risks and uncertainty that fuels the enterprise (Reiss 1989).

The model of compliance-based law enforcement is markedly different from the model of deterrent law enforcement under criminal law (Reiss 1984a; Hawkins 1984; Manning 1987), for it addresses undesirable organizational activity that takes the form of conditions or states of affairs (such as pollution of the environment) rather than individual acts. The supply of the undesirable activity is endless and is tolerated to a considerable degree. Tolerance is in part a result of moral uncertainty about the harms caused, balanced against the need for organizations to operate efficiently. Enforcement, based on a scientific knowledge of risk entwined with regulations and shifting standards, is continuous. Compliance is not merely the decision to refrain from an act but the doing of something positive to ameliorate the condition or state of affairs and to reach a negotiated standard. Attitudes are as important as actions in giving signs of compliance. Formal prosecution is a sign of failure to secure compliance and is extremely rare. In its place are microrituals of negotiation between compliance officers and the regulated, and the relentless reworking of knowledge for risk management systems. All of these features of compliance-based law enforcement mean that the undesirable activity is an administrative creation, the constant administrative articulation of what risks must be taken.

In this context of compliance-based law enforcement based on regulation and the scientific knowledge of risk, the police are transformed. They become part of compliance-based law enforcement systems because they are driven by the knowledge requirements of other institutions that engage in compliance policing. Research on police has not addressed this shift. For example, Reiss (1984a: 85–6) argues that the compliance function of the public police is exhibited whenever they informally exercise their discretionary power not to make an arrest. However, he ignores how the public police serve the compliance functions of other institutions when they produce *formal* incident reports that are formatted to meet the risk knowledge requirements of those institutions. He thus fails to consider the crucial but neglected question of how rationalities of risk taken from other compliance-seeking institutions become part of police work.

In reacting to the risk knowledge requirements of compliance-based law enforcement, the police are becoming more proactive in producing the required knowledge. As Reiss (1984b: 23–4) predicts, 'The prototypical enforcement strategy for both individuals and organizations will become more like that of the Internal Revenue Service than like that of a local police agency ... deterrent law enforcement may be expected to shift more towards proactive rather than reactive forms of mobilization, especially towards the techniques of proactive law enforcement that are instrumental strategies of social control.'

Policing within compliance-based law enforcement systems is not only a matter of serving the knowledge needs of state regulatory agencies. Processes of compliance-based law enforcement are also moulded by private sector conceptions of risk and regulation and by regimes of private policing. In private policing, which is quintessentially oriented toward compliance enforcement and loss prevention, there is a 'change in the nature of surveillance as attention shifts from the morally culpable individual to *categories* of people who create opportunities for disorder' (Shearing and Stenning 1984: 340). As is the case with the public police, private policing is constituted by 'paper systems that provide for ongoing surveillance, as well as retrospective surveillance, through the paper trails that they create' (ibid.). The paper systems of the public police and the private police intersect, but the nature of this intersection has been neglected in research on policing.

The paper systems of the police and of private sector insurance institutions are closely integrated. This integration in turn incorporates *legal* integration. In all sites of police knowledge work for insurance purposes, such as traffic investigations and property crime investigations, there is legal pluralism (O'Malley 1991). For example, given a typical clearance-by-arrest rate of around 3 per cent for burglaries, the main concern in the recording of burglaries is good risk management data for insurance purposes, and the operative law is not the criminal law but the law relating to insurance contracts. Insurance law steps in where criminal law is unable to meet the needs of the parties concerned. The police accordingly become agents of insurance regulation. As O'Malley (1991: 172) remarks, 'To protect its profits, especially against forms of moral hazard that are not prohibited under criminal law (and thus potentially subject to state policing), the insurance company must establish its own legal order within the framework of the insurance contract. The insurance contract (and more recently, the law of insurance contracts) establishes the coercive conditions for the operation of an enforcement network aimed at disciplining householders, in order to minimize the assumed moral hazard.'

The legal order constituted by the insurance contract compels the insured to engage in their own forms of risk management. For example, insured householders are compelled to refrain from conducting a business or trade in their homes; to adhere to an adequate standard of security technology for the protection of their assets; to report to the police any attempted or completed act that gives rise to loss; to turn over all relevant information to the insurance company and appear as a witness in court on its behalf; and to be subject to community policing 'watch' programs as well as to instruction in better risk management. O'Malley (1991) shows how the police *are part of* this compliance-law enforcement order. The police not only broker risk knowledge to insurance companies but also function as co-promoters of insurance coverage schemes. They are an integral component of crime risk management strategies.

Various branches of law other than the criminal law have become instruments for interpreting social practices of risk. In these branches, law depends first and foremost on scientific knowledge of risk. As Foucault and his associates argued (Burchell, Gordon, and Miller 1991), science, like law, is replete with normative prescriptions not only for its own methodological practices but also for regulating populations. In particular, social science, which is entwined with actuarial science (Hacking 1990), participates in regulatory regimes by joining the law in imposing arbitrary closure on a case or problem so that it can move on to the next one. Law certifies the truth-certifying procedures of sciences that help law to get the job done. Moreover, it allocates the burdens of risk to various regulatory institutions.

Civil law in particular has expanded in the name of controlling risk. 'The principal function of modern civil law is to control risk' (Priest 1990: 209), and it is arguably far more effective than agency regulation in doing so. In all areas of civil law, risk distribution and indemnification are matters of right, and risk is further legalized (Lowi 1990). The civil courts process every conceivable risk by way of damage awards that uphold liability rules and statutory rights. Questions of motive, intention, and punishment are largely irrelevant, as the court focuses on how to allocate the risks of changes that have caused problems for the parties. Judges are the engineers of actuarial justice, fitting the parties into generic categories of actors and deciding which party is in a better position to maintain loss prevention and bear the cost of any losses or harms suffered. The final determination in litigation is which insurer will foot the bill.

In civil law the binary opposition between normal and abnormal actions breaks down. All actions are judged in terms of their probable contribution to loss. The moral quality of the actions that contribute to loss is set aside in favour of assessing quantity of contribution to risk. A utilitarian morality becomes paramount. 'The objective of controlling risk as effectively as possible prevails over all else' (Priest 1990: 209). Paradoxically, we are all guilty to a degree, that degree being calibrated according to our probable contribution to loss: 'Each of us must recognize that all of our actions are likely to harm others in the society in some way. As a consequence, every citizen stands in a position of continuous potential interaction with the law since every action is potentially subject to liability' (ibid.: 215).

The 'decline of innocence' (Ericson 1994c) is accompanied by a rise in individual responsibility. Each individual must be reflexive with respect to his or her actions to ensure that he or she does not increase the risk of loss. Reflexivity is readily available in the technologies of risk classification, and in the law, both of which provide for perpetual monitoring. The risk of failing to monitor oneself is legal action, because legal liability attaches more easily under the civil law regime of risk control:

> Our modern civil law encourages litigation as an instrument for internalizing costs to control risks ... [O]ur modern legal regime, focused on every contribution to risk, is a regime of dramatically greater dimension. Such a regime aspires to impose legal controls on all activities in the society that contribute to risk in any way. Thus, virtually every action by every citizen becomes subject to potential legal review because every action will increase the risk of loss in some way. (Priest 1990: 214)

System Surveillance and Actuarial Justice

The criminal law is also compelled to 'obey' the 'social' laws of risk that affect all institutions in risk society. As we have argued, it must therefore 'obey' the risk communication rules, formats, and technologies of other institutions. The result is a shift in the goals, principles, and procedures of criminal law in the direction of compliance-based law enforcement and actuarial justice (Ericson 1994a, 1994b; Feeley and Simon 1994).

The criminal law joins the thrust in risk society towards better risk management systems and away from sovereignty defined as the sovereign state's 'claimed capacity to rule a territory in the face of competition and resistance from external and internal enemies' [Garland 1996: 4]):

> The perceived normality of high crime rates, together with the widely-acknowledged limitations of criminal justice agencies, have begun to erode one of the fundamental myths of modern societies: namely, the myth that the sovereign state is capable of providing security, law and order, and crime control within its territorial boundaries. This challenge to the state's law and order mythology is all the more effective, and all the more undeniable, because it occurs at a time when the wider notion of 'state sovereignty' is already under attack on a number of fronts (See Hirst 1994, Lash and Urry 1987). (Garland 1996: 4)

State sovereignty gives way to fragmentation in risk management across myriad public and private sector institutions. Certainty resides less in the imagined will of strong central authority and more in the certainties that each risk institution promises. Risk society promises a world in which fail-safe risk technologies rather than fallible people rule. It promotes any technology of governmentality that might reduce uncertainty, foster self-regulation, and prevent loss.

Criminal law theory, practice, and reform are understood as existing within a binary opposition between crime control and due process (Packer 1968). On the one hand there is a need for crime control to protect citizens from capricious and arbitrary actions of criminals by ensuring that offenders are efficiently rooted out. The value of protecting the citizen from the loss of liberty suffered as a result of criminal victimization outweighs the rights of criminal suspects, accused, and offenders. There is a faith in the ability of the criminal law system, and especially the police, to detect offenders and release innocent suspects.

In opposition to this vision of the criminal process as a conveyer belt is the view that it should be an obstacle course, with the laws of criminal procedure providing the main hurdles (McConville, Sanders, and Leng 1991). There is a need to protect citizens from capricious and arbitrary actions of criminal justice agents by ensuring that suspects, accused, and offenders have rights within the law, for example to be told the reasons for their arrest, that they can remain silent, and that they can retain third-party assistance. The value of protecting the citizen from unjustified punishment and from a decline in civil liberties outweighs the community interest in effectively apprehending and punishing criminals. There is a recognition that human beings and their institutions are fallible, and a corresponding need for legal accountability on the part of the police and other criminal justice officials.

One can see this binary opposition played out daily in news stories about crime, law, and justice (Ericson 1991, 1995a, 1995b; Ericson, Baranek, and Chan 1991). However, within the legal culture of the criminal process things appear in rather different form. The binary opposition between crime control and due process blurs, breaks down, and is transformed.

It is undeniable that the police are sometimes efficient in capturing people who are subsequently subject to severe terms of imprisonment. In many jurisdictions, in particular the United States, incarceration rates have increased dramatically (Zimring and Hawkins 1991). Indeed it is the drama of cathected scenarios of the police capturing criminals, and of judges pronouncing sentences, that the media focus on in creating a spectacle out of crime control. But the media do not have it wrong: there *is* plenty of drama to be found in capturing criminals and pronouncing sentences. The media are part of the legal institution in this regard, helping it to dramatize myths about general deterrence and to espouse notions of what constitutes decent coercion (Ericson, Baranek and Chan 1989, 1991; Ericson 1996).

In the day-to-day realities of policing, however, it is sometimes difficult to discover what all the public culture's talk about crime control actually refers to. One characteristic of public policing is how rarely it deals with crime directly (pp. 19–21). Public policing has an organized incapacity to do much about crime, and it systematically displaces responsibility for crime control to other institutions in the name of community policing. This incapacity is related to the institution of privacy (Stinchcombe 1963), which makes detection difficult, and it helps to explain why, for example, the typical clearance-by-arrest rate for burglary is around 3 per cent. If you ask how many people in your city were in possession of marijuana or driving while impaired last night, you are asking a question of the same logical order as 'How long is a piece of string?' or 'How many grains of wheat are there in a heap?' (Ditton 1979).

One might argue that while the police face major limitations in detecting crime, they can be efficient in taking cases to prosecution when they do manage to apprehend a suspect. However, even when suspects are apprehended and can be prosecuted, very often they are not. For example, in England and Wales 'the number and range of cases in which people are cautioned by the police has increased steadily over the years' (Royal Commission on Criminal Justice 1993: 82). In a study of how adult suspects were dealt with in one English jurisdiction it was found that 'Case mortality is, in fact, the daily experience of routine police and prosecutorial decision making ... in all cases in which disposition was known (n = 1068), no fewer than 49.4 per cent (n = 528) were disposed of without any court action by means of no further action, caution or informal warning' (McConville 1993: 86).

The vast majority of juveniles arrested in Anglo-American jurisdictions are cautioned by the police and diverted rather than prosecuted in court. In England and Wales in 1990, 72 per cent of males and 85 per cent of females arrested were cautioned by police rather than charged and prosecuted in court (Evans 1993: 2–3). In an American jurisdiction studied by Meehan (1993) there was little community or police administrative demand for formal processing of juvenile suspects, which resulted in 'a shift to surveillance and the development of internal recordkeeping as the primary form of control.' Routinely, juveniles are not scathed by formal prosecution and punishment, but only marked on police records. These records are kept for possible police uses in the future and for distribution to other agencies and institutions.

On the statistically rare occasions when the criminally accused are convicted, sentences are often relatively mild (McMahon 1992). For example, in Ontario from 1951 to 1984 the rate of admission to prison declined by 30 per cent, and the standing-count rate decreased by 20 per cent. The most common disposition was the fine. Approximately 90 per cent of criminal cases in Ontario were disposed of with fines. Even when traffic offences are excluded from consideration, fines were still used far more than all other types of sentence combined. Moreover, fine defaults accounted for a significant proportion of all admissions to prison in Ontario (approximately one-third), creating in effect a modern form of debtors' prison. As Garland (1996: 15) observes, without these criminal justice system efforts to 'define deviance down' (Moynihan 1992), 'we would have a prison in every neighbourhood, rather than just a Neighbourhood Watch.'

The criminal statutes, of course, speak to crime control, and sometimes in very draconian terms. In Canada, recent revisions to the Criminal Code have reduced maximum sentences substantially, but these still remain high and are almost never given out. High maximum penalties are maintained because the law as written is a public text, part of public culture, sometimes having more affinity with news discourse than with what happens in legal culture (Gusfield 1981; Ericson 1996). Law reform as the end-point to political narratives must inevitably make strong dramatic statements about crime control, even if laws are typically ignored and unenforced, enforced unevenly, or subject to amelioration.

The above considerations suggest that in the operation of the criminal law institution, crime control is displaced by surveillance. We define surveillance as the bureaucratic production of knowledge about, and risk management of, suspect populations (Giddens 1985; Dandeker 1990), rather than in the popular sense of sinister police undercover intrusion meant to suppress undesirable people and organizations (G. Marx 1988). Like all other institutions in risk society, the criminal justice institution prefers knowledge to coercion where practical (Stehr 1994), although coercion is sometimes necessary to obtain knowledge.

As a system whose principal coordinating mechanism is knowledge, criminal justice seeks suspects to make into objects of knowledge for risk profiling purposes. The profiling is often an end in itself, as the hard edge of crime control, of maximal prosecution and severe punishment, gives way to a need for access to and records of knowledge about dubious members of the population. As in compliance-based law systems, prosecution is often taken as a sign of failure to secure compliance by other means, including the means available within other risk institutions. The law is still enforced, but only rarely by prosecution. The narrow focus on efficiency in crime control gives way to the efficient production and distribution of knowledge useful in the management of suspect populations. Criminal justice surveillance is designed to efficiently format, and make available, detailed knowledge about people in the hope that it will come in handy in the system's future dealings with them, or, more often, in the dealings other institutions (credit, welfare, insurance, health, education, and so on) might have with them.

Coincident with the surveillance of suspect citizens is the surveillance of the police as a suspect population. There is probably no occupation as thoroughly scrutinized as the police. This surveillance arises out of distrust, which is endemic in risk society (Giddens 1990). There is a belief within the criminal justice system itself that, given the opportunity, police officers will routinely avoid duty, make grave errors, fabricate evidence, and generally operate according to the informal rules of their occupational culture rather than adhering to formal administrative or criminal law rules. These problems are all threats to the capacity of the system to obtain knowledge useful for the risk management of suspect populations. The system's solution is to turn surveillance back on itself, to develop new communication rules, formats, and technologies that will police the police. This surveillance is intended to maintain trust in the police institution, even if individual police officers remain suspect.

Reports prepared for the Royal Commission on Criminal Justice (1993) in England and Wales reflect this culture of distrust. There is in England and Wales a law that all police interviews of suspects be tape-recorded (itself a strong indicator of distrust). To expedite review of the recorded interview, certain police officers are assigned to summarize the contents on a standardized form. Baldwin (1993: 23), the author of a Commission research report, recommended that lawyers for both the prosecution and the defence should actually listen to the tape-recorded interviews, this being, he argued, 'the only way of avoiding the high risk strategy of taking the [transcribed] records of interview on trust ... the odds at present [of the transcriptions being accurate] are greatly inferior to those that apply in Russian Roulette.' Maguire and Norris (1993: 115), authors of another Commission research report, advocated independent random checks on detectives' investigations, noting that the trust that exists between detectives and their supervisors is the key impediment to honest dealings with other criminal justice agents: 'Trust ... is a weak guarantee of compliance and, given that trust is largely a private contract, is open to abuse. To overcome this problem, we suggest that a system of "quality control" is required, whereby integrity can be demonstrated rather than assumed.'

In risk society all occupations are subject to surveillance out of a fear that their unique, informal cultures will violate procedural propriety. While craft knowledge in occupational cultures is crucial for fair and efficient social organization (Manning 1992a), it is subject to increasing administrative scrutiny and intervention in all social institutions because it is seen as too arbitrary (unsystematic) and as allowing craft practitioners to escape accountability. Thus the Royal Commission on Criminal Justice (1993: 7) asserted that the remedy for police malpractice lay 'in a better-trained, better-equipped and better-supervised police force, not in the tacit acceptance of procedural rule-bending' that they saw as the essence of the police's craft knowledge and its 'Ways and Means Act.' Maguire and Norris (1993: 109), under the heading 'Attacking the "culture"' advocated training young detectives in a way that would prevent their being 'sucked into' the 'traditional "detective culture" ("macho" and "elitist" attitudes, the belief that "rules are made to be bent," excessive secrecy and suspicion of outsiders, and so on).'

The police officer becomes acutely aware of the reality that the more one is in a position of trust, the more one is subject to surveillance mechanisms that remind one that trust is always contingent and that routinely require one to prove one's innocence. The mentality and sensibility of policing the police through the use of surveillance mechanisms was embodied in the Peel Region (Ontario) police headquarters building when it opened in 1981. A reporter for the Toronto *Globe and Mail* wrote,

> The basic idea is to control the movement of everyone who approaches and enters the building. The movement of policemen is controlled by computer access cards. There are 18 security doors, and only some cards are programmed for all of them. All entries are recorded – with card number, date and time – and entries that are unauthorized trigger an alarm.
>
> If an intruder still gains entry despite cameras outside that can pan, zoom and tilt by remote control, he will find himself in a square corridor looking into full-length security mirrors and more steel-encased tamper-proof cameras.

Controlling and monitoring all these cameras and other items, such as electronic door hinges that signal when a door has failed to shut automatically, are specially trained civilians working 24 hours a day. They sit in front of a large console with a graphic of the entire building, lights signalling exits and entries, and TV monitors for the 18 security cameras. Certain top-security areas also have sonic intrusion alarms, and the entire outside of the building is lit by high-intensity sodium lights.

The windows are all strip, ribbon windows, their double glass tilted to a 45-degree angle to deflect bullets and stones and placed seven feet above ground so they need not be draped. Besides, they are reflective, to make viewing impossible even if apartment buildings are erected around the structure. (Kashmeri 1981)

This police station is an icon of surveillance in risk society, treating both citizens and police officers as cunning, corrupted, untrustworthy, risky, guilty. As such it epitomizes risk profiling initiatives in risk society, being based on a perception that there exists an imbalance between trust and acceptable risk, which must be corrected. The station's security measures reflect a belief that the latest technologies will buy security: obtaining these technologies is seen as the 'obvious,' 'natural,' and 'progressive' thing to do. These technologies promise efficiency in determining who is to be deemed innocent and thus allowed to participate in a particular instrumental transaction, and who is to be found guilty and excluded from access, membership, and participation.

The adoption of new technologies of surveillance suggests that the nature of police supervision is changing. Traditionally police supervision has been personal and retrospective, with an emphasis on the *appearance* of complete investigations (Punch 1983). 'The focus of supervisory attention has largely been concentrated upon the *product* of police work rather than the activity itself: in a nutshell, the first priority has been to ensure that "the paperwork is right"' (Maguire and Norris 1993: 14). However, technologies of surveillance now mean that supervision is increasingly *prospective* because it is built into information systems and technologies. The computerized reporting formats for presentation of police knowledge provide classifications that fundamentally influence how the police think and act. Supervision is prospectively embedded in the formats as well as retrospectively in supervisors' checks of filed reports, and there is an increased technological capacity to monitor reporting *as it is being done*.

The police institution's organized incapacity to do much about crime control, combined with the demand for risk-relevant knowledge from other institutions, mean that it is difficult to find due process in the everyday activities of the police. Of course, due process is still played out in full criminal trials. Indeed, major criminal cases that go to trial and provide a full narrative of crime, due process, and punishment are precisely what the media focus on in their coverage of the courts. (Ericson, Baranek, and Chan 1989: chap. 2). As with dramatizations of crime control (pp. 53–4), there is plenty of drama to be found in the major trial, where the full majesty, justice, and mercy of the law *is* displayed. The media are an agency of law in this respect, helping it to sustain its myths in ways that enhance public consensus and cultural coherence as well as a sense of order. The public illusions of law are also realities (Gusfield 1981).

In the day-to-day realities of police work, however, it is rather difficult to discover what all the public talk about due process actually refers to. As was noted above, most police dealings with suspects take the form of surveillance and the giving of warnings or cautions, not formal prosecution. This 'increased reliance on surveillance bypasses not only the stigma of the formal process, but also its guarantees, and ironically increases police control' (Meehan 1993: 504; see also McConville, Sanders, and Leng 1991). Even when cases are prosecuted, the vast majority are dealt with by way of guilty plea settlements without trial. All participants know that the system would fall apart if even an additional 1 or 2 per cent of cases went to trial (Ericson 1982, 1993; Ericson and Baranek 1982; McConville, Sanders, and Leng 1991; Miyazawa 1992).

Various organizational logics merge in the production of guilty plea settlements. The police presume that the suspect is guilty and produce case material in accordance with that presumption. While there is ample academic research to support this fact (Ericson 1982, 1993; Ericson and Baranek 1982; McConville, Sanders, and Leng 1991; Miyazawa 1992), it is also evident in standard police manuals on interrogation and confession. For example, Inbau and Reid's manual (1967) includes a sixty-eight-page section entitled 'Tactics and Techniques for the Interrogation of Suspects Whose Guilt is Definite or Reasonably Certain.' Police charge suspects in ways that encourage guilty plea settlements, including 'charging up' to the highest category possible and charging the greatest number of counts possible, thus creating a situation in which charge reductions and charge withdrawals can be offered in exchange for guilty pleas.

Typically, the defence lawyer is constrained to the point where he or she begins with the presumption of guilt that has informed the police decision to charge in the first place. The lawyer is rarely present when the case is effectively foreclosed (for example by statements of confession or seizure of property) in the original transaction between the police and the suspect. Even if the lawyer is present at the original transaction, he or she is bound by the need to sustain cooperative relations with the police; by the police's selective presentation of knowledge about the case; and, more often than not, by his or her own attitudes about law and order and system efficiency that are the same as those of the police. In a general law practice criminal law work is relatively low in status and poorly paid, the main source of a criminal lawyer's income being legal aid certificates. Hence, from a business point of view, the usual provincial court case, with its presumption of guilt and its open-and-shut nature, is not worth the extra effort needed to overcome police-created barriers. The defence lawyer is a regular member of the court who must maintain relations of trust and reciprocity with the police and crown attorney to obtain the best 'deal' for his or her client. Indeed, in many jurisdictions defence lawyers also serve as part-time crown attorneys to supplement their income. In the face of all of these constraints the most the lawyer can do in routine cases is use his or her 'recipe knowledge' of the local court to make the best of a bad case. The lawyer can develop a sense of the tariff for cases of the type, what charges can be withdrawn or reduced, and the usual sentence (Sudnow 1965). He or she can also judge-shop and make favourable presentations at the sentencing hearing that might ameliorate the sentence to a modest degree.

The crown attorney is also at a disadvantage relative to the police. Typically the police and the defence lawyer speak to each other before the court date to arrive at a guilty plea settlement, and only then seek the crown attorney's ratification, in many cases during the hour before the first court session begins. The crown attorney is made dependent because the police have made the case and embodied it in the 'crown package' (case dossier), and he or she must work from their accounts. The crown attorney faces a large number of cases that day; has not read many of the files in detail (often because he or she presumes there will be a guilty plea settlement); and is a regular member of the court who must maintain trust and reciprocity with police and defence lawyers.

Based on their presumption of the accused's guilt, the police take for granted that they have done all that is necessary to secure a conviction and obtain a sentence of the kind usually meted out in similar cases, and they expect the crown attorney to share their view and simply to ratify what they have done. The following case makes this routine evident by showing what happens when it is upset (Ericson 1993: 189–90).

A detective charged two people with multiple counts of break and enter and theft as well as with other property offences. He obtained signed confessions from each accused, on each of several counts, and recovered some of the property. The potential work involved in subpoenaing all of the witnesses, bringing the seized property into court, and preparing detailed trial briefs for the crown attorney was enormous. When the crown attorney indicated that this work might be necessary the detective balked, stating that there was no call for extraordinary effort where a guilty plea settlement was the obvious solution. The following is a tape-recorded conversation from the crown attorney's office in which one crown attorney is speaking to a second:

> Look at this one, these guys have done about 900 b and e's and you get 'expected plea of guilty' [written on the file by the detective] and you know what that means, there are not going to be any witnesses here, so ah ... the old pressure is on to play Monty Hall.

Later, the first crown attorney (the one just quoted) spoke to a third:

> I've got 6 b and e's, 3 mischiefs, and a theft under and a possession. There's no brief on the possession and a big scrawl on the front of the dope sheet, 'an expected plea of guilty,' and you know, 'once upon a time there was a break and enter.'

After this, the first crown attorney asked the detective to go through each charge against each accused and supply more details. The detective became upset and started to complain that 'the system' was ridiculous because the two accused still had not indicated a plea even though there was evidence in the form of seized property and signed confessions:

> *Detective*: We got voir dires, we got statements, all kinds of stuff, property galore, it's just ridiculous.
> *Crown Attorney*: We'll just go through one at a time then.
> *Detective*: It's an injustice as far as dragging people into court and lawyers don't let us know what they're doing, or if they've retained a lawyer or what they're doing.

After going over some charges, the detective added the following:

> The thing is you know, it's ridiculous, how can you take ten statements from these guys and then they turn around and walk into court without lawyers or anything else and say they're not pleading guilty. Exhibits, just tons, boxes of exhibits, cigarettes and stuff that were stolen, you know, what do we do, bring twenty people into court and sit around on things like this all day, and carry all these exhibits in and get everything lined up, and then not knowing even what these fellows are doing.

The crown attorney then attempted to establish the order of charges for the trial but the detective balked and again protested that cooperation was needed among all parties to expedite an 'obvious' case for guilty pleas:

> 'I don't care what you say ... no way am I going to get all that fucking work and these guys, assholes, walk into court [with] no lawyers, anything. It's just ridiculous.

Eventually the detective, defence lawyer, and crown attorney arranged a guilty plea settlement that saved the detective from the extra work.

One reaction to this story is to say so what, these people are guilty. Why waste the time of costly professionals – judges, lawyers, police – and of witnesses and accused? Why make the process the punishment (Feeley 1979) for everyone? After all, the accused is the only one who should be punished. Of course, this is precisely the sensibility created by the decline of innocence. In the name of certainty and efficiency, let us not worry about process, especially costly, cumbersome process subject to human fallibility. In order to create certainty, routinism, and efficiency let us assume that people are not innocent, that they are experienced, cunning, corrupted, untrustworthy, risky, and guilty.

Discount justice has reached its most institutionalized form in the United States. In most American jurisdictions a system of open-court bargaining replaces trials in criminal cases. Cases are typically disposed of 'without a police file, witness statements, forensic evidence or courtroom officials who evidence any familiarity with the allegations or the accused' (McConville and Mirsky 1993: 1373; see also McConville and Mirsky 1995). The burden of proof – that the state must prove each and every element of the offence beyond a reasonable doubt – is negated and the adversarial model is inverted. The system is inquisitorial and depends on the defendant's public admission of guilt for its legitimacy and indeed its survival:

> Because plea bargaining turns the adversarial model on its head to one in which the individual is required to choose between a series of options which are more or less onerous rather than assuring that the state is in possession of legally sufficient evidence in the first place, little if any check exists on the case for the prosecution. By contrast, every incentive exists for the police and prosecution to rely upon a system of open discounts and penalties to pursue confessions as the principal evidence of guilt in lieu of an independent and thorough investigation. (McConville and Mirsky 1993: 1381)

The judge, plea bargaining directly with defendants and their lawyers, is no longer neutral. He or she becomes identified with the outcome of the proceedings – a guilty plea settlement and punishment within the usual limits – rather than with adversarial process. If the judge's offer is rejected and the accused is convicted at trial, the sentence 'invariably exceeds the original plea offer by substantial and arbitrary amounts' (ibid.: 1374; see also McConville and Mirsky 1995).

One view of these facts is that the system is indeed running according to the organizational logics of the occupational cultures involved in the criminal process. The informal rules of the occupational cultures are the 'real' operative rules, not those of criminal law and procedure. This has been the perspective of researchers who have immersed themselves in these cultures to read the 'real rules' (Manning 1977; Ericson 1982, 1993; McConville, Sanders, and Leng 1991). However, there are two major flaws in this approach. First is the tautology that leads to rules being inferred from observed 'informal' practices and then used in turn to explain those practices. Second, the researchers have assumed that the police and other criminal justice agents are running around ducking, circumventing or simply ignoring the law, which the researchers presume to be infused with due process provisions. However, the law itself often does not embody or even speak to due process.

For instance, plea bargaining is incorporated into the structure of the law itself. Thus a guilty plea is normally taken as a mitigating factor in sentencing. The Crown Court in England and Wales offers a standard 25–30 per cent reduction in sentence for those who plead guilty. The Royal Commission on Criminal Justice (1993) recommended that this discount be offered on a sliding scale: 30 per cent for a guilty plea on committal, 20 per cent between committal and the first Crown Court listing, and 10 per cent from the time after the first Crown listing until arraignment. We must keep in mind that the Crown Court is the highest level of 'trial' court in England and Wales, and a key symbol of English justice and its major principles, including the presumption of innocence. The court is not Harrod's on Boxing Day, nor is it the fish market at Portobello.

In all Anglo-American legal jurisdictions there is interpretive latitude for multiple charging and 'charging up', which in turn are the basis for offers of reduced or dropped charges in exchange for guilty pleas. High maximum penalties in statutes encourage guilty pleas in exchange for 'mild' sentences – in the accused's eyes, a 'deal' (Ericson 1982, 1993).

Other rights are chipped away by the courts and law reformers. The famous *Miranda* ruling in the United States has retained its 1968 status in popular culture but been fundamentally eroded in legal culture. The new *Criminal Justice Act* in Britain removes the right to silence. The Royal Commission on Criminal Justice (1993) proposed that defendants in major fraud cases who refuse to cooperate in disclosing their evidence to the prosecution should be charged with contempt of court, which 'will allow the court to deal summarily with defendants by imposing a short term of imprisonment from which we would expect them to be released once the requisite cooperation was forthcoming' (Royal Commission on Criminal Justice 1993: 115). Referring to their proposal to remove the defendant's right to choose the Crown Court as the venue for his or her trial in place of the lower magistrate's court, the Royal Commission on Criminal Justice reasoned that 'Defendants would no longer have the right to insist, as they do now in over 35,000 cases a year, contrary to the views of magistrates, that their cases should be heard in the Crown Court. We do not think that defendants should be able to choose their court of trial solely on the basis that they think they will get a fairer hearing at one level than the other. Nor in our view should defendants be entitled to choose the mode of trial which they think will offer them a better chance of acquittal' (ibid.: 88).

Various areas of criminal investigatory procedure are also without much trace of due process. For example, the recently enacted proceeds-of-crime sections of the Canadian Criminal Code offer not even the pretence of due process when it comes to seizing evidence and assets before proper adjudication has taken place. In Canada the law of search and seizure strongly favours the police, to the point where it is only the incompetent police officer who cannot prove the legality of a search. Even if a search is deemed illegal the evidence may still be admissible in court at the judge's discretion (Ericson 1981, 1982, 1993; Law Reform Commission of Canada 1983; see generally Hutchinson 1995).

In England and Wales the Royal Commission on Criminal Justice

(1993) recommended forcible search and seizure to obtain knowledge about suspects that might serve the ends not only of crime detection but also of police science. The commissioners believed, in light of developments in forensic science, that the police should be able to forcibly remove samples of plucked hair, saliva, and so on from the suspect's body. Here justice was equated with the system's surveillance needs: 'Given that plucked hair samples may increasingly be capable of providing DNA evidence, we recommend that *in the interests of justice* power to take a sample of hair should extend to hair that is plucked as much as to hair that is cut' (ibid.: 14; emphasis added). To enhance police power to pluck scientifically useful knowledge from the suspect, the commissioners recommended the reclassification of assault, burglary, and other arrestable offences to provide for sample-taking without consent.

These considerations suggest that the binary opposition between due process and crime control breaks down *within the law itself*. 'Due process is *for* crime control' (McBarnet 1979, 1981; Ericson 1981, 1982, 1993; Ericson and Baranek 1982) in the sense that procedural rules enable the police to invade personal privacy and obtain knowledge for surveillance purposes as they see fit. The strongest statement in this regard belongs to McBarnet (1979: 39):

> Legality requires equality; the law discriminates against the homeless and jobless. Legality requires that officials be governed by law; the law is based on post hoc decisions. Legality requires each case be judged on its own facts; the law makes previous convictions grounds for defining behaviour as an offence. Legality requires incriminating evidence as the basis for arrest and search; the law allows arrest and search in order to establish it. Legality embodies individual civil rights against police or state interests; the law makes state and the public interest a justification for ignoring civil rights ... Deviation from legality is institutionalized in the law itself. The law does not need to change to remove the hamstrings on the police: they exist only in the unrealized rhetoric.

In this view the law does not incorporate its own rhetoric. Alternatively, the rhetoric is external to the law, a matter of public culture and mass-media logic. Law is decidedly on the side of crime control, but also, and fundamentally, on the side of surveillance. While due process provisions still restrict some forms of police investigative behaviour, especially in the big case where a full trial with high-status participants is anticipated (Cooney 1994), the law in general broadens the legal foundations of surveillance practices (G. Marx 1988: esp. 46–54). Increasingly, '"due process" has little relevance to contemporary police actions' (ibid.: 189–90). As advances in science and technology enhance police surveillance, the law as an agency of surveillance and legitimation changes in tandem. The traditional police monopoly on the legitimate use of force is entwined with methods for the monopolization of knowledge acquisition (Ericson and Shearing 1986).

Just as crime control has given way to surveillance, so due process is giving way to system rights. That is, suspects' rights are being eroded in favour of surveillance system-rights to obtain knowledge of suspects. Rights are not only shifted away from the suspect, they are disconnected from the centralized, unitary entity of the state. Rights are increasingly bestowed on and embedded in the system itself, enabling it to produce, distribute, and use whatever knowledge is deemed necessary to conduct efficient surveillance of suspects on behalf of criminal justice and other risk institutions.

A jurisprudence of actuarial justice thus arises (Feeley and Simon 1994). The goals of public due process are displaced by the goals of private, segmented risk management. The system acts not according to consensual norms but according to security needs within specialized and functionally defined areas. The main orientation is loss prevention rather than reaction to criminal events. Deterrence and punishment through public shaming continue in the dramatizations provided by police reality programming and televised trials, but are overshadowed by, first, surveillance, and second, by exclusion through the private registration of guilt.

These legal changes derive from a number of sources, but in particular the templates of risk employed by institutions that demand knowledge from the police, and the scientific and legal knowledge requirements that flow from institutional needs in risk society. Criminology contributes to the extent that it has become a victim-focused and system-focused science of risk management (Ericson and Carriere 1994, Garland 1996). The law and economics movement participates in these changes with its focus on systems, collective goods, quantitative analyses, and utilitarian thinking (Feeley and Simon 1994). Tort law, with its emphasis on social utility and risk management, has a pervasive influence (Priest 1990). And ironically, due process rulings have amplified risk profiling of various populations, including the police and other criminal justice agents (Feeley and Simon 1994). In chapter 3 we analyse the ways in which all of these developments have been captured by community policing.

3

Community Policing and Risk Communications

Community Policing

The community policing model provides a rationale and a justification for the policing of risk society. Community policing rejects previous models of policing, including militarism (order maintenance), legalism (law enforcement), and professionalism (public service). In community policing the police are expected to work with local institutions and organizations to help them look after their own risk management.

Social scientists often read the models of social institutions as ideologies and forms of rhetoric that are separate from reality. As ideologies and rhetoric, models conceal what is really going on and thereby help to legitimate practices that are unpalatable or offensive to the population concerned. Community policing is typically read in these terms. A recent book of essays on the subject is entitled *Community Policing: Rhetoric or Reality* (Greene and Mastrofski 1988), as if rhetoric and reality are mutually exclusive or in binary opposition. Some contributors to this collection claim that community policing is more rhetoric than reality (Bayley 1988), that it is yet another example of 'police strategies aimed at shaping and manipulating public opinion' (Manning 1988: 40), and that it is 'an important new source of institutional legitimation' (Murphy 1988a: 179).

Many analysts believe that the community policing model mystifies or covers up police use of coercive force, which they regard as the essence of policing. For example, Waddington (1984: 95) remarks that '"Community policing" is a romantic delusion, not for the "world we have lost," but for one we never had. It harks back to a harmonious idyll, where the police were everyone's friend. It was never thus, and it is unlikely that it ever will be' (see also Klockars 1988; Mastrofski 1988). Waddington asserts that the police exist to contain violence and the potential for violence in society. In emergencies the police therefore need the authority to intervene with force, and models such as community policing help to give them the authority. Similarly Klockars (1988) regards community policing as an ideology of 'concealment and circumlocution.' Following Bittner (1970), Klockars sees policing as essentially a state monopoly on the legitimate use of force within a political territory. Thus Klockars explains the fall of previous models – militarism, legalism, and professionalism – as the consequence of their inability to make more palatable the fact that, in the final analysis, the police are there to be violent when necessary. Since Klockars sees models only as efforts to cover the 'when necessary' legitimation of police violence, 'community policing' is best understood as the latest in a fairly long tradition of circumlocutions whose purpose is to conceal, mystify, and legitimate police distribution of nonnegotiable coercive force (Klockars 1988: 240).

Such analyses do not address the ways in which truths are mobilized rhetorically to constitute the political realities of community, crime, and control. Instead of analyzing community policing as rhetoric or reality, rhetoric and reality should be seen as mutually constitutive components in processes of political representation (Gusfield 1981, 1989). That is, community policing is a discourse, the institutional communication of meaning via speech, writing, significant objects, and signifying practices (Macdonnel 1986; Valverde 1990, 1991). Community policing discourse does not merely represent pre-linguistic realities, nor does it serve the prediscursive interests of any institution in a simple way. As a mediating practice, community policing constitutes realities and interests. It is entwined with the social, cultural, and spatial relations that provide the context for how the police think, feel, speak, write, dress, design their stations, mobilize, and so on. Thus community police actions and the things they react to are simultaneously real, interested, and linguistic 'elements of a discourse that ... transcends and makes redundant the usual distinction between language and reality' (Valverde 1990: 71) and between knowledge and ideology (Foucault 1980: esp. 118).

As a discourse, community policing organizes and channels thought and action at every level, from official statements of police policy to everyday practices on the street. Community policing is not only an expression of preferred values but a way of embedding them in practice. As Giddens (1991: 150) observes, 'appeals to traditional symbols or practices can themselves be reflexively organized and are then part of an internally referential set of social relations rather than standing opposed to it.'

Returning to Klockars (1988), it is evident that his separation of ideology and practice means that he fails to appreciate that police efforts to monopolize force are enmeshed in the various models of policing and the mechanisms they promote. The monopolization of force is an achievement of bureaucracy and of bureaucratic mechanisms of militarism, legalism, professionalism, and accountability to the community (Dandeker 1990: 66; Giddens 1990: 59). The police, like the state itself, have no essence. They are coercive, militaristic, legalistic, professional, community oriented, and much more. These various models not only inform but also form police practices.

Writing on community policing reveals that it is a discourse, as that term is defined above. Consider the views of Trojanowicz and Carter (1988). On the one hand, they emphasize that community policing is a philosophy or sensibility rather than a tactic or practice. On the other hand, as they proceed to articulate the philosophy of community policing they do so in the language of strategic practices and tactical manoeuvres:

> A philosophy and not a specific tactic, community policing is a proactive, decentralized approach, designed to reduce crime, disorder, and, by extension, fear of crime, by intensely involving the same officer in the same community on a long-term basis, so that residents will develop trust to cooperate with police by providing information and assistance to achieve these crucial goals. Community policing employs a variety of tactics ranging from park and walk to foot patrol, to immerse the officer in the community, to encourage a two-way information flow so that the residents become the officer's eyes and ears on the street helping to set departmental priorities and policies. In addition, the officer then carries this information back to the rest of the department so that problems can be solved and the quality of life improved ... The community policing officer acts as a uniformed armed presence to deter crime, but equally as important, he or she also takes action with citizens' assistance to resolve problems before they erupt as crime. (ibid.: 17)

The 'community' solution is not peculiar to the police, but it is also evident in other areas of criminal justice, for example community corrections (McMahon 1992), and in other fields of governance through risk management, for example community health. The 'community solution ... is ... a specialized regime of environmental intervention designed to contain high levels of concentration of risk' (Gordon 1991: 46). Risk management is left to members of the 'community' institutions concerned, while governmental agencies avoid confrontations by posing as 'advisors, resource persons and friends' (Lasch 1980: 182). The role of state operatives is to decide how to justly delegate matters in dispute and distribute risks. The approach is one of

> making use of conflicts instead of trying to eliminate them, applying a new realistic awareness of conflicting needs and interests by disseminating among social partners and individual citizens new procedures for the acceptance and sharing of responsibilities (permanent retraining, self-management, decentralization) ... [D]ecentralization ... operates as a pluralization of the centre, enabling the problems of the state to rebound back on to society, so that society is implicated in the task of resolving them, where previously the state was expected to hand down an answer for society's needs. (Donzelot 1991: 178)

Communications Policing

Community policing discourse articulates developments in risk society that are already institutionalized. Community policing is an effort to mediate and appropriate what has occurred and to adjust police organization accordingly. Community policing is best understood as the policing of communications about risk in late modern society. In early modern and modern societies, community was characterized by communications that included sharing, tradition, quality face-to-face relationships, and local organization, combined with a sense of immediacy and the opportunity for direct results. Late modern society is characterized by institutions organized around fear, risk assessment, and the provision of security. As was argued earlier, these institutions – insurance companies, social security agencies, and regulatory agencies, among others – reconfigure the community into communications about risk in every conceivable aspect of life. Risk communications have qualities opposite to those of communications in earlier societies. The former involve relationships that are not face to face, but between absent others who are connected by electronic media that impersonally transmit and record their transactions. These transactions offer no sense of immediacy or direct action, nor are they tied to a given place. Community becomes institutional methodology for communicating risk management (Stenson 1993).

The literature on community policing (e.g. Greene and Mastrofski

1988; Goldstein 1990; Leighton 1991; Moore 1992) incorporates a traditional conception of the term 'community,' which emphasizes communications that involve sharing (communion) among people who hold things in common and have a sense of common identities and traditions (*communitas*). Community implies communications that foster empathy rather than fear and thus make people feel they are a part of things. Community implies communications that support 'boosterism.' Community expresses positive sentiments about collective outcomes. It is a 'hurrah word' (Bay 1981) that is used to celebrate certain forms of organization. 'Unlike all other terms of social organization (state, nation, society, etc.) it seems never to be used unfavourably, and never to be given any positive or opposing distinguishing term' (Williams 1983: 76).

Operating within these conceptions, the community policing literature treats community interests as natural, objective, and prediscursive, not as the historical manifestation of institutional intervention. The traditional community is visualized as being distinct from relationships within society and its institutions. As such, the community policing literature forms an essential part of community policing discourse. It too makes an appeal to old-fashioned values and interests as a way of easing social change in risk society. The literature fails to problematize risk communications, except in terms of giving voice to consumers of security products so that their perceptions of risk can be made part of the calculations of how the police will approach their task environment (see e.g. Winkel 1991).

Contemporary risk institutions constitute, absorb, and even extinguish traditional communities. Indeed, the greater the number of risk institutions, including the police, the less community we find (Black 1976). Community as sharing and tradition recedes 'the more thoroughly reflexivity, coupled to expert systems, penetrates the core of everyday life' (Giddens 1991: 206–7). Community as a locality where things take place with immediacy and a possibility of direct action gives way to a community of institutions that cease to offer a sense of place. Transactions mediated by institutional technologies undercut immediacy and the possibility of direct action, and replace them with the routine production of knowledge for instrumental transactions and risk assessment. Engaged in transactions based on interests, and having 'no sense of place' (Meyrowitz 1985), community members have less to celebrate and community boosterism rings hollow. That is, the term community is recognized by everyone as sheer boosterism, as a term of effusive praise for a sharing, traditional, committed, local governance that does not fit well within the everyday experience of a community of bureaucratic risk institutions that lack reciprocity, tradition, and commitment to local governance.

Community policing is a discourse for finding ways to improve connections with the communications circuitry of other risk institutions, that is, to respond to their knowledge needs in a routine manner, to provide them with expert advice, and to help them manage their risks. A 'responsibilization' (Garland 1996: 8) strategy develops, in which responsibility for crime is shifted to other institutions, while police responsibility to help these other institutions broadens to include many risk management responses in addition to crime and its regulation. Constituted as problem-solvers, the police become professional diagnosticians of every risk problem imaginable, and provide treatment directly or through referral to specialists in other risk institutions. They also develop ongoing managerial relationships with other institutions to help them assess and distribute their risks more ably.

Police supporters of community policing admit that the police alone cannot shoulder the burdens of crime control and maintenance of social order; such an expectation presents an 'impossible mandate' (Manning 1977). Other government bureaucracies, business corporations, and individual citizens all become more responsible for risk management: 'crime and disorder problems are the JOINT PROPERTY of the community as 'client' as well as the police as the local agency delivering public security services. Underlying this ownership principle is the core assumption that the level of crime, disorder and fearfulness in a community is closely related to the level of public participation in policing' (Leighton 1991: 487).

Crime is to be diverted, after initial processing, into other institutional mechanisms of resolution and management, or, better still, handled in the first instance by other institutions, so that the police become 'no more than a catalyst, involving people in efforts to police themselves' (Trojanowicz and Bucqueroux 1990: 16). This process is documented in O'Malley's (1991) analysis of how the Australian police work with the insurance industry in neighbourhood watch schemes. Mainly funded by the insurance industry, neighbourhood watch schemes become distribution points for the provision of risk lessons and technologies and for selling insurance. They promote the insurance industry and the police as partners in 'the management of normality' (Swaan 1990).

Community policing is also designed to expand the reach of the police by involving them with other institutions in a wider range of risk management activities. In 'problem-solving policing' (Goldstein 1990) there is no limit to police participation in the construction and management of social problems. While the police give up some of their direct responsibilities for crime control and the policing of risks to territories, they take on new responsibilities for the policing of risks to organizations and individuals. As Garland observes in the British context, this reconstitution yields

> A new form of governance at-a-distance ... [The state] retains all of its traditional functions – the state agencies have actually increased their size and output during the same period – and, in addition, takes on a new set of co-ordinating and activating roles, which, in time, develops into new structures of support, funding, information exchange, or co-operation. Where it works – and one should not underestimate the difficulties in making it work – the responsibilization strategy leaves the centralized state machine more powerful than before, with an extended capacity for action and influence. At the same time, however, this strategy serves to erode the notion of the state as the public's representative and primary protector ... [This strategy represents] the extension of a new form of governance, already well developed in other spheres, to the problem of crime and its control. (Garland 1996: 11)

Community policing constitutes the police as professional experts because they possess abstract knowledge about risk that is valuable to others. Professions are somewhat 'elusive occupational groups applying somewhat abstract knowledge to particular cases' (Abbott 1988: 8). Professions define themselves and their legitimate jurisdiction in terms of control of abstract knowledge and of the practical technologies and techniques abstract knowledge generates. Abstraction allows continual redefinition and defence of problems and tasks, and the securing of new tasks: 'The organizational formalities of professions are meaningless unless we understand their context. The context always relates back to the power of the professions' knowledge systems, their abstracting ability to define old problems in new ways. Abstraction enables survival' (ibid.: 30).

Community policing constitutes the broad scope of the police to engage in the professional work of diagnosis, treatment, and inference drawing (ibid.: chap. 2). This is exemplified in 'problem-solving policing,' which has the police focus on the underlying causes of problems in their diagnosis and treatment, and stresses cooperation with other professions and institutions as sources of expertise and as collaborators in finding solutions (Eck and Spelman 1987; Trojanowicz and Carter 1988; Goldstein 1990; Toch and Grant 1991; Leighton 1991).

Clearly the community police officer as expert, counsellor, and advisor (Stehr 1994) is more professional than ever. Analogies to the medical profession abound. 'The police officer is to government as the general practitioner is to the entire medical establishment' (Goldstein 1990: 106; see also Trojanowicz and Bucqueroux 1990: esp. 35–8; Sherman 1992). The medical profession analogy is especially apt because the medical general practitioner is like the police officer in being constituted by the expert-systems of external institutions. While these systems deskill many aspects of the professional's work, they also rely on his or her ability to diagnose, treat, and abstract (Castel 1991). Moreover, if the police, like the doctor, emphasize what they do for their clients, their professionalism is taken for granted and the 'professional' model is not required as ideology.

Community policing also enhances police professionalism by fostering communications and alliances among professions. 'Civilianization' (Skolnick and Bayley 1986; Leighton 1991) – hiring professionals to fill specialist positions without requiring them to have prior police training or experience – is encouraged. As discussed in chapter 1 (pp. 27–8), civilian professionals – lawyers, computer experts, behavioural consultants, public relations specialists, and so forth – not only heighten the professional ethos within police organizations but also foster professional alliances with other institutions. As well, police forces recruit officer candidates who hold graduate and professional degrees, and serving officers are encouraged to qualify as professionals in various fields, which again promotes outside professional affinities and alliances.

The police work continally with outside professionals to manage efficient risk communications. A lot of this effort is directed at finding rules, formats, and technologies that will routinize and systematize risk communications. Thus another component of community policing is to devise technological responses to the external demand for knowledge of risk. Community policing embraces communication technologies that are designed to prevent the occupation of knowledge broking from becoming a preoccupation (see especially Sparrow 1991). 'Community policing is not anti-technology ... the community policing officer is like the base of a funnel, using information filtered down from various 'hi-tech' sources and providing information upward generated from his/her neighbourhood beat' (Trojanowicz and Carter 1988: 20).

Community policing reconstitutes proactive police work as 'promoting security' (Sparrow 1988; Ericson 1995c) wherever and whenever possible, often through the development of specialized crime prevention and intelligence units (Manning 1992a: 367). Thus an Ontario government document stresses that community policing entails 'a fundamental reorientation from a narrow focus on crime-fighting through rapid response (after-the-fact reactive), to a broad focus on community security and protection through joint-problem solving and collaboration (before-the-fact-proactive policing)' (Solicitor General of Ontario 1991: 13). Reactive policing is reconstituted at the institutional level, with the police responding to and in turn shaping the knowledge requirements of other institutions in order to assist those institutions in the risk management of the special populations for whom they are responsible.

As such, community policing articulates the previously discussed move in the direction of compliance-based law enforcement (pp. 48–50). Community police officers are involved in three interrelated aspects of compliance. First, they are complaint managers who respond to grievances about the operations of other risk institutions. Each officer is an 'ombudsman, the person who receives complaints and has the knowledge, contacts, and ability to pressure other public and private agencies to provide needed services' (Goldstein 1987: 19; see also Trojanowicz and Bucqueroux 1990: 16). Second, they are inspectors of activities that take place in other organizations. Survey research and other systematic data collection methods are employed for this purpose (Toch and Grant 1991). Special units are created to inspect, for example, schools, public transit, halfway houses, and hospitals (Skolnick and Bayley 1986). Detroit police officers, like private security operatives who drop 'snowflakes' (notices about unsecured property) on the desks of offending employees responsible for insecure conditions (Shearing and Stenning 1982), 'go door to door, block by block, offering to make security inspections and enroling people in various watches. If people aren't home, officers leave Courtesy Security Awareness "tickets" that list points of vulnerability ... Residents are invited to make appointments for personal security surveys' (Skolnick and Bayley 1986: 59). Third, community police officers serve as advocates for others who need better legal or technological resources to meet their security needs. They pressure government agencies 'to carry out existing responsibilities or to invest new resources in an area. They may push for changes in the policies of other government agencies or advocate legislation that would enable police to deal more effectively with a problem that clearly warrants arrest and prosecution' (Goldstein 1987: 17; see also Trojanowicz and Bucqueroux

1990; Toch and Grant 1991). In turn, community organizations become advocates for the police, supporting their requests for increased budgets and changes in law and policy (Fleissner et al. 1991: 61–2).

The change in focus represented by community policing has been gradual. In many respects the police have always been knowledge workers, expert advisers on risk, and compliance-based law enforcers. These roles are especially apparent when the police are the only agents of government in remote areas, as is the case with some Royal Canadian Mounted Police, Sûreté de Québec, and Ontario Provincial Police detachments (Murphy 1986; Landau 1994a). However, they are also apparent in urban policing because of the organized incapacity of the police to detect and risk-manage crime and other troubles on their own. Thirty years ago Cumming, Cumming, and Edell (1965) found that half of all calls to the police concerned personal problems and another third concerned problems of property risk such as automobile accidents. The typical police response was some combination of referral to other agencies, giving of advice, and 'cooling out' of complainants (see also Punch 1979, Ericson 1982). In an analysis of British Crime Survey data, Skogan (1990b: 9) reported that the activity occupying most police time with citizen was the exchange of information, either citizens giving police non-crime-related information (16 per cent of contacts) or asking police for information (23 per cent of contacts). Reporting of crime accounted for only 18 per cent of contacts. Murphy's (1988b) study of a community policing initiative in Toronto discovered that what was accomplished was continuous with what the police had been doing previously. His conclusion was that 'Evidence that the Toronto police force already allocates police resources on the basis of citizen demand and that police officers are aware of significant neighbourhood policing problems and concerns indicates that even conventional policing is, to some extent, citizen and community based' (ibid.: 407).

Citizen calls for service have always been about many things in addition to crime reporting and control. Indeed, it is arguable that the reactive calls-for-service model offers a great deal in the way of personal service through face-to-face interaction. As Cumming, Cumming, and Edell (1965) put it, when people call for police help about a wide range of troubles, the officer is there in person as a 'counsellor, guide and friend.' This approach is in keeping with community as interpersonal communications that respect tradition, quality face-to-face transactions, and local space, and provide a sense of immediacy. The increased use in community policing of alternatives to dispatching an officer to the scene

– telephone referral to other agencies, recording complaints over the telephone or by mail, and so on – means that the police are not available in person when that is most needed. The use of alternatives to on-the-scene policing is a sign that police communications are becoming increasingly extrasituational and impersonal, and that the police are now policing a 'virtual' community.

The face of reactive policing is changing. Change occurs at the institutional level, according to institutional dictates. Other institutions – state, national, and international governments, multinational insurance companies, the mass media, and so on – operate according to knowledge requirements and interest criteria that have little respect for local community boundaries, sense of place, or feelings of immediacy. Community policing is a story of changing social institutions and social relations, in which communications with particular types of institutions – for example churches, local political machines, and local ethnic organizations – are giving way to communications with risk institutions driven by the need for knowledge that will help them construct problems, assess risks, and manage the special populations they are responsible for. As Trojanowicz and Carter (1988: 20) recognize, 'the foot patrol officer of the past had a different environmental context and different informal resources like the extended family, churches and ethnic organizations. Present community policing officers must rely on formal private and public agencies. Thus the need to be a neighbourhood diagnostician and link to community agencies.'

Community policing constitutes the police in the traditional governance role of 'making up' (Hacking 1990) people, their organizations, and their institutions. Communities are so made through a number of interconnected efforts.

Police make communities by addressing risks metaphorically, for example by using the metaphors of the 'war on crime' and 'the war on drugs.' As Nietzsche (1914) remarked, danger is the mother of morality. Communities define themselves by finding 'suitable enemies' (Christie 1986) and by busying themselves with efforts to eradicate or rehabilitate those they despise. Thus community policing makes communities by promoting reflexivity about risk: 'we begin reviving community through the prism of issues, which, in essence, constitute the most urgent kind of community interest. Within any given geographical area, the issues that provide the police with the unifying principle necessary to allow them access to the community so that they can most efficiently do their job are crime, disorder and fear of crime' (Trojanowicz and Moore 1988: 13).

The creation of communal identity through declarations of war on enemies is nothing new. That was, for example, the essence of the American Declaration of Independence (White 1984: 231–40), and has been at the centre of American public culture ever since (in the case of the war on drugs see Scheingold 1990; McGaw 1991). Community policing is designed to create a positive community self-concept in an environment of fear, apathy, alienation, and crumbling infrastructures. In some circumstances the police may be the only sign of community, of something in common, that is left to hold things together: 'In our often anomic urban society the transcendent identity of many city dwellers is that of crime victim. Their neighbours may be the very people they fear. In such circumstances police departments can facilitate, even create, a sense of community where one either did not previously exist or was faintly imprinted' (Skolnick and Bayley 1986: 214).

Thus the police are a powerful proactive force in making community organizations better. Late modern community chemistry requires 'patrol officers providing catalytic assistance and expert advice to [aid in] the formation of neighbourhood associations.' (Trojanowicz et al. 1982: 10) This entails a 'we know best' approach to selling the police as the foremost institution in the community: 'The bulk of communications is from the police to the citizen, explaining and selling prepackaged strategies devised without the particular neighbourhood and its residents' preferences in mind ... Co-production in practice means citizens doing what the police think is best' (Mastrofski 1988: 52, 56; see also Murphy 1988a: 184; Carriere and Ericson 1989).

The institutions that mediate community policing do not represent grass roots interests. Bohm (1984: 451) remarks that 'These mediating institutions are not microcosms of the neighbourhoods they are alleged to represent.' Mastrofski (1988: 51) concurs with this view, stating that 'They, like all social institutions, are heavily influenced by the distribution of power, status and wealth within their domain. Even in these voluntary associations, where membership rules are not restrictive, participation is skewed to those of higher socioeconomic status, married, and homeowners with children (Rosenbaum 1987: 108).'

Community policing is also associated with more-explicit socioeconomic inequality. Community boosterism based on threats, fear, and the urge for security is used as a vehicle for defending property values. Two solitudes are created, one for better-off symbolic workers wired into the global economy, who can pay for better security provision, the other for poor service workers and the unemployed (Reich 1991: 42–4).

'"Security" becomes a positional good defined by income access to private "protective services" and membership in some hardened residential enclave or restricted suburb' (M. Davis 1990: 224; see also Spitzer 1987).

The security of identities is also not assured by community policing. Mastrofski (1988: 50) describes an area in New York in which Italian and Jewish groups joined forces to fend off incursions from Blacks. This effort at excluding a threatening group arguably enhanced the shared sense of togetherness already felt by the Italians and Jews, but police contributions to this effort would have 'made [the police] party to bigotry' (ibid.). In other words, when the police are faced with a problem in a neighbourhood made up of a plurality of ethnic or other groups, any move by the police to support one group will inevitably exclude and create inequality for others.

There is also inequality in the institutional system for distributing risks that community policing participates in. Community policing is part of a wider trend in the risk society toward the just distribution of risk. The just distribution of risk (shared risk) becomes more important than prevention (less risk), elimination (no risk), or punishing the morally culpable. As part of this shift in the risk society, many institutions, including the police, adopt the template of insurance. Thus in community policing discourse we find statements such as the following: 'If a police department's management were strongly committed to reducing the problems it must handle, it might operate like an insurance company that, for monetary reasons, is constantly working to reduce its losses. It would have the equivalent of the researchers who study the conditions that contribute to insurance claims and the underwriters who constantly review clients' (Goldstein 1990: 73). The problem with the insurance institution is that it cannot manage the just distribution of risks and therefore also contributes to inequality in some areas. Some people are more able than others to afford insurance, whether offered by the state as social security or unemployment insurance, or offered by the private sector as property or life-course insurance. Inequality forms around insured and uninsured populations, those the underwriters favour and those they exclude. As Reichman (1986: 152) observes, 'the communities across which risks are spread do not appear to express a collective conscience or a particular form of moral solidarity. They simply form instrumental networks or relays through which control can be exercised, over dispersed populations (Donzelot 1979; Smart 1983)'.

In the communications circuits of risk management there is no single institution or person that stands above the system as *the* manager. Accountability becomes embedded in institutional networks and is diffused. The agency of institutional agents, and therefore the ability to attribute individual responsibility to such agents, recedes, while the personal responsibility of each individual who has dealings with an institution advances. The community as interpersonal communications with a defined locus and immediate reaction from responsible agents dissipates. The community as institutional communications without direct reaction from accountable agents, or a sense of place, emerges. That community is the risk society.

PART II

The Risk Society

4

Risk Discourse

In Part I of this book our critical review of research on policing pointed to many features of risk society. What is required now, in Part II, is a more thorough, abstract, and systematic examination of risk society. We first consider the characteristics of risk as a discourse of governance and examine how risk is materialized in forms of bureaucracy and surveillance. Then we investigate how major institutions organize and govern within the framework of risk discourse, in which the example of insurance is used to illustrate the institutional logics and practices of risk management. Consideration is also given to ways in which communication technologies and the processes influencing the reorganization of professions articulate with the institutional production and management of risk. Social changes occurring in the context of risk discourse, institutions, technologies, and professions are outlined. Finally, we relate our analysis of the risk society, and our earlier explorations of policing within it, to the research questions that will guide our empirical inquiry in Parts III, IV, and V.

Discourse

Discourse is the institutional construction of knowledge, which takes place within a social organization of territories, material objects, people, rules, formats, and technologies. What are constructed are representational frameworks: classifications and categories that stand for objects, events, processes, and states of affairs in the world. These frameworks provide the basis for shared understanding, including an understanding of what knowledge is required to enhance, modify, or deny the representation. Knowledge is that which is objectified in institutional representations, a property and resource that provides a capacity for action.

We make no distinction between information and knowledge. Information *is* knowledge, for to make sense of a thing there must be institutional frameworks of representation for defining and establishing its logic and what it means. While knowledge takes different forms in accordance with variations in its common sense and abstract features (Geertz 1983), even esoteric knowledge can be 'reduced to keystrokes' (Abbott 1988: 146).

This view differs sharply from the conventional wisdom expressed, for example, by Daniel Bell (1985: 17), who writes that 'Information is news, facts, statistics, reports, legislation, tax-codes, judicial decisions, resolutions, and the like, and it is quite obvious that we have an explosion of these ... But that is not necessarily (or even usually) knowledge. Knowledge is interpretation in context, exegesis, relatedness, and conceptualization, the forms of argument.' Things designated as 'information' by Bell *are* knowledge, in his own sense that they have been interpreted in context and given particular meanings. They may be given new meanings as they are transformed in the context of different representational frameworks in different institutions, but that does not make them 'knowledge' in the additional contexts as distinct from 'information' in the original context. They are knowledge in all contexts, in the sense of being given an objectified, real meaning that is used in action and has social consequences (Ericson, Baranek, and Chan 1987: 11).

The representational frameworks of institutional categories and classifications are in turn based on various forms of inscription such as writing, computation, and statistical analysis. The technical apparatus of inscription renders objects into discourse, providing conceptual forms that make them subject to regulation (Miller and Rose 1990: 5). In all forms of governance (those found in both state and private sector institutions), people, organizations, events, processes, and states of affairs 'must be rendered into information – written reports, drawings, pictures, numbers, charts, graphs, statistics. This information must be of a particular form – stable, mobile, combinable and comparable. This form enables the pertinent features of the domain – types of goods, investments, ages of persons, health, criminality, etc. – to be literally re-presented in the place where decisions are made' (ibid.: 7).

As such, discourse constitutes practice and is, in the very same process, constituted by practice. However, it is important to maintain *analytical* separation between discourse and practice. Discourse is socially organized. Social organization is conditioned by discourse (Archer 1988).

In the analysis that follows we examine the ways in which risk discourse is socially organized through the institutional defining of dangers and devising of technologies of inscription to deal with those dangers. At the same time we also consider how the representational frameworks and techniques of risk discourse provide the institutional foundations of contemporary society.

Logics

In risk society, governance is directed at the provision of security. Security is a 'situation in which a specific set of dangers is counteracted or minimized. The experience of security usually rests on a balance of trust and acceptable risk' (Giddens 1990: 35–6). Institutions that provide security offer trust and acceptable risk in the form of guarantees (commitments and warranties to take some risk out of risk), assurances (of routine, certainty, confidence, and stability), and predictability (routinization that allows one to proceed reliably and in a taken-for-granted manner).

Institutions try to make trust tangible, for example by offering written money-back 'guarantees,' by having employees represented as respectable members of the community, and, in the case of financial institutions, even by referring to themselves as 'trust' companies. However, trust is always based on a degree of faith and intangibility. Risks are also somewhat ephemeral, always subject to political-cultural revision (Douglas 1992). Furthermore, technologies of risk management provide no more than probability statements that indicate that some partially unknown level of risk must be accepted. Security is thus always more within us as a yearning than without us as a fact.

The yearning for security drives the insatiable quest for more and better knowledge of risk. However, in the search for inexhaustibly detailed and continuous risk management knowledge, each new form of knowledge and the measure of protection it makes visible gives rise to new knowledge about insecurities. This paradox was captured eloquently by Heidegger (1974: 216):

> The work for the securing of life ... must constantly secure itself anew. The guiding word for this fundamental attitude of contemporary existence speaks: Information ... In the first place, information means the reporting that instructs

modern men, as quickly and as comprehensively as possible, as clearly and as completely as possible, about the securing of his needs, their requirement and their provision ... However, while information in-forms, that is, reports, at the same time it forms, that is, it organizes and directs.

The focus on danger, and the perpetual doubt that danger is being counteracted, means that risk society is characterized by a negative logic. For Beck (1992a), risk society is driven by the distribution of 'bads' or dangers, in contradistinction to industrial society, which was principally concerned with the distribution of material 'goods.' In risk society the risk management and distribution of 'bads' itself becomes commodified as a 'good' and commands a great deal of society's resources.

As a negative logic about dangers, risk discourse produces relentless reflexivity with respect to irregularities, the dark side of life, the unknowable, and chaos. Risks become 'objectified negative images of utopias' (ibid.: 49). Reflexive foreboding operates in tandem with probabilistic thinking and risk technologies. It sometimes takes extreme forms, as in Nietzsche, with conceptions of pure irregularity and the darkest forms of humanity (Hacking 1990: 10). More routinely, it operates within institutional frameworks to interpret problems as being errors, deficiencies, cracks, and faults in what exists. Risk discourse constantly reminds us that 'knowledge is always embedded in ignorance, safety is surrounded by unsafety and natural planning inevitably frays out to incalculable evolution' (van den Daele 1992: 330). Risk discourse cultivates insecurities, focuses them on scapegoats, and forces people to accept expert knowledge of risk – a knowledge that creates new insecurities – as the only viable solution (Christie 1986; Edelman 1988; Scheingold 1990; Douglas 1992; Bauman 1992a).

The result of this negative logic is that the value system of the unsafe society gains prominence. The prevailing sensibility is that of 'the least worst.' '[R]isk society remains particularly negative and defensive. Basically, one is no longer concerned with obtaining something 'good,' but rather with preventing the worst; self-limitation is the goal which emerges' (Beck 1992a: 49). Driven by the solidarity of fear, and buoyed by the commonality of anxiety, the 'normative counterplan' (ibid.: 240) is limited to developing new, and one hopes better, technologies of risk management that will also help manage fear and anxiety.

These considerations point to another characteristic of risk logic, the control of the irrational by rational means. Fear is the basis of rational action. Irrationality is that which is unknown: lurking threats and dangers, and the unanticipated consequences of decisions. It is also the leaving of things to chance when risk technologies might be invented to tame chance. Rationality entails probability calculations that will tame chance if not eliminate it altogether. A given rationality of risk serves as 'a component in a landscape of fear because it exists to contain chaos ... [Risk rationalities provide] shelters built by the mind in which human beings can rest, at least temporarily, from the surge of inchoate experience and doubt' (Tuan 1979, quoted in Sparks 1992: 1).

Rationalities of risk are designed to reduce uncertainty to the point where the actor feels confident in taking action. Grounded in probabilistic thinking and predictions, they allow deselection of specific factors and thereby point to preferable courses of action. They are hyperrational and deeply pragmatic, always scanning for technical solutions to problems that incapacitate action. They eschew causality in favour of laws of regularity that establish standards of objective fact and the basis of objective knowledge (Hacking 1992). They turn life into the thing Max Weber believed it to be: 'deliberate, systematic, calculable, impersonal, instrumental, exact, quantitative, rule-governed, predictable, methodical, purposeful, sober, scrupulous, efficacious, intelligible and consistent' (Brubaker 1984: 2; see also Gandy 1993: 240).

Risk rationalities also make life real. As Hobbes asked in *Elements of Philosophy*, 'How can any now imagine that the names of things were imposed by their natures?' Things in nature are infused with risk rationalities that seek first to call them into being – what Foucault (1973: 131) described as 'the nomination of the visible' – and then to give them the lawlike regularity that will tame them. The process of calling them into being involves classifications of difference, classifications that not only provide a focus on what is present but also a sense of what is absent and might be.

Risk discourse is future oriented. Risk rationalities and the technologies in which they are embedded bring imagined futures to the present. People, made reflexive by risk technologies, act with reference to the future more than the past or present:

> The center of risk consciousness lies not in the present, but *in the future*. In risk society, the past loses the power to determine the present. Its place is taken by the future, [that is,] something non-existent, invented, fictive, as the 'cause' of the current experience and action. We become active today in order to prevent, alleviate or take precautions against the crisis and problems of tomorrow and the day after tomorrow – or not to do so. Bottlenecks in the labor market pro-

jected in mathematical models have a direct effect on educational behavior. (Beck 1992a: 34; see also Giddens 1990: 36ff.)

What precisely is tamed? No one can be certain. Risks always include uncertainty about the actual outcome. The best one can do is seek security through calibrations of danger that will, one hopes, reduce the imagined losses or harms. Calibrations of danger involve the development and refinement of calculable laws about threats to security. The sciences of risk join the law in providing orderly accounts of such threats.

Risk technologies presume danger, yet their goal is to ameliorate danger, to a degree. They pursue this goal by creating abstract classifications of difference that make the actual occurrence of danger contingent. The calibration of danger expresses the harm potential of an imagined event, process, or state of affairs. It is the best estimate of the probability of an event, process, or state of affairs occurring and of the harm that would result if it did occur.

Although risk logic is based on fears of threats and dangers, it results in positive effects. It provides knowledge and technologies that allow people to allay their fears and take action. It provides the bare-minimum truths that reality is certain and consistent enough for one to proceed. While outcomes are always uncertain and things are ultimately stochastic, those very facts can be used to help one appreciate the fact that risk logic offers the power to help one achieve more regularity and control in one's affairs. As William Farr recognized in 1860, people 'have the power to change the current of human actions within definite limits, which statistics can determine' (quoted by Hacking 1990: 115). This is the power *to take risks*, to take enough chance out of chance that a course of action seems worthwhile.

At the same time there are a number of complexities in the taming of chance. Knowledge of risk is not only a means of risk management but also a producer of new risks. The risk society is a knowledge society because scientific knowledge and technologies are sources of major risks and the primary basis of security efforts aimed at controlling such risks. That is, science is now called on not only to scientize nature, people, and their institutions, but also its own effects (Stehr and Ericson 1992). As Beck (1992a: 183) observes,

Society today is confronted by itself through its dealings with risks. Risks are the reflections of human actions and omissions, the expression of highly developed productive forces. This means that the sources of danger are no longer ignorance but *knowledge*; not a deficient but a perfected mastery over nature; not that which eludes the human grasp but the system of norms and objective constraints established with the industrial epoch. Modernity ... has become the threat *and* the promise of emancipation of the threat that it creates itself.

Unanticipated outcomes of previous actions occur continually. The response is to monitor actions and outcomes more precisely in the expectation that more-easily managed outcomes will be achieved. However, diagnosis always outruns remedy, and people are perpetually discharged into risk.

Risks are a matter of standards set by science and law as orderly accounts of dangers. Ironically, the higher the standard the greater the danger. For example, scientific tests are able to detect ever-smaller quantities of impurities, and the setting of increasingly demanding legal standards leads to greater levels of officially recognized pollution of the environment. This is one example of the more general point that because risks are brought into existence by scientific knowledge and law, they can also be magnified, minimized, or muzzled by scientific knowledge and law (Hawkins 1984).

Those who dispute how standards are magnified, minimized, or muzzled by scientific knowledge and law are always required to answer with greater scientific knowledge. This is because risks only exist through 'the sensory organs of science' (Beck 1992a: 162). Knowledge of risk begets more knowledge of risk via reclassification, new technologies, and new instrumentalities.

Unanticipated outcomes, negotiable standards, and the dominance of scientific risk discourse all suggest that knowledge is, and is not, power. Knowledge of risk is at once a way of proceeding and a procedure for not knowing. It is a means of deciding what to do but results in a risk of having done the wrong thing. It is at once a means of overt action but also is subversive of actions taken. As Poster (1990: 4) observes in the case of financial markets, 'the communications network that ties the world's financial hubs together for better access to information also threatens them with instant financial collapse.' 'Reflexive modernization' (Beck, Giddens, and Lasch 1994) means that power is as elusive as knowledge of risk:

Modernization is becoming reflexive; it is becoming its own theme. Questions of the development and employment of technologies (in the realms of nature, society and the personality) are being eclipsed by questions of the political and eco-

> nomic 'management' of the risks of actually or potentially utilized technologies – observing, administering, acknowledging, avoiding or concealing such hazards with respect to specially defined horizons of relevance. The promise of security grows with the risks and destruction and must be reaffirmed over and over again to an alert and critical public through cosmetic or real interventions in the techno-economic development. (Beck 1992a: 19–20)

Risk is not assessed exclusively in terms of scientific knowledge. The fact that standards are negotiable and outcomes merely probable means that they are always subject to moral, political, and aesthetic knowledges (Douglas 1992). Myriad evaluative questions arise concerning the type and extent of the danger, the populations concerned, the effects over time, who is responsible, remedial measures, and forms of compensation and indemnification. These determinations are made within the prevailing criteria of rational acceptability among knowers in a particular culture (Putnam 1981: 130) and are always a matter of ethics. One cannot enter into risk discourse without an ethical stance. In risk discourse, probability statements combine with social, moral, and political interests to constitute a kind of quantitative morality (Beck 1992a: 176).

The *social* rationalities of risk perpetually force scientific rationalities to refute their own claims of being able to investigate risks objectively. Social rationalities ensure that there is no scientific monopoly on rationality (ibid.: 29). This fact is evident in every use of risk assessment to convert uncertainty about what to do into action, because the actor is simultaneously reflecting on the risk of having done the wrong thing. As Machiavelli remarked, 'We never try to escape one difficulty without running into another, but prudence consists in knowing how to recognize the nature of the difficulties and how to choose the least bad as good.'

Nevertheless, the social rationalities depend on science. When risks are evaluated they still depend on calibrations of danger. Moreover, whatever else might be on the agenda for change, scientific rationality itself is not included. Science retains its cognitive and social superiority in managing risks, and people are forced to rely on what they are in part arguing against (Beck 1992a, 1992b; Stehr and Ericson 1992; Stehr 1994).

Unknowns linger. The social rationalities of risk never settle the question of when it is reasonable to be worried or fearful. Fear persists in exceeding the knowledge available. When 'normal accidents' (Perrow 1984) occur, the ensuing risks are not only unexpected, they are incomprehensible. We are continually reminded that 'Our ability to organize does not match the inherent hazards of some of our organized activities' (ibid.: 10). Efforts to refine or change risk technologies create new opportunities for the exercise of power, which in turn foster more unknowns. Not just accidents but also emergencies become normal. 'The exceptional condition threatens to become the norm' (Beck 1992a: 24). In consequence, new forms of surveillance arise that might have been unthinkable previously but now seem almost normal.

Biopower and Governmentality

Michel Foucault (1978: 143) developed the concept of biopower 'to designate what brought life and its mechanisms into the realm of explicit calculation and made knowledge-power an agent of transformation of human life.' Biopower is the power of biography, of constructing biographical profiles of human populations for risk management and security provision. It is distinguished from two other aspects of governmental power addressed by Foucault: *discipline,* the techniques and practices by which the human body is made subject to regular and predictable routines, and *sovereignty,* the command of central authority over territory.

Biopower, discipline, and sovereignty are not exclusive to the state and its institutions of government, although Foucault himself largely focused on the development of knowledge/power mechanisms within the state. These types of power are also part of nonstate institutions and forms of governance. In practice, biopower, discipline, and sovereignty exist in multiple spaces within and among both state and nonstate institutions. This notion is found in Donzelot's (1979) conception of the 'social,' the space between state and civil society in which numerous state, philanthropic, and private corporate institutions negotiate governance. The social is the space of biopower, as institutions negotiate classifications of populations, formats for communicating those classifications among each other, and how those classifications are to be acted on in responsible government. As such, the social is 'the field of governmental security in its widest sense; the register of government forms, in return, the surface of inscription of the security problems of society ... the rationality of security ... deals not just in closed circuits of control, but in calculations of the possible and the probable ... it structures government as a practice of problematization, a zone of (partially) open interplay between the exercise of power and everything that escapes its grasp.' (Gordon 1991: 35–6).

Biopower makes up people, literally. The risk classification and management of populations is aimed at literally fabricating people into the social body. Fabrication occurs according to the logic of the norm, the standard against which people and their institutional practices are assessed. The logic of the norm is made possible by statistics and the laws of probability, and for this reason became conspicuous in social thought and practice in the later part of the nineteenth century and dominant in the twentieth century. 'Normal people' replaced 'human nature' as the touchstone for assessing human actions (Hacking 1990). The concept of 'normal people' also allowed for social distinctions, hierarchies, and exclusions equal in power to the concept of 'human nature,' because it created ways to be both factually objective and evaluative about human actions: 'It uses a power as old as Aristotle to bridge the fact/value distinction, whispering in your ear that what is normal is also all right' (ibid.: 170).

Of course, no human being or population is ever actually normal except for the actuarial purposes of a particular institution and its risk management needs. Moreover, as Hacking stresses, measurement is inexact, statistical probabilities are imprecise, and indeterminism is therefore everpresent. Deviation from the mean is in fact the norm. Every member of a population that is risk-profiled stands along a continuum of imprecise abnormality or, simply, risk. This point addresses our observation in chapter 2 (pp. 39–41) that conceptions of risk are now displacing conceptions of normality and deviance as the dominant mentality about people and populations.

Making up people in terms of biopower also affects dominant sensibilities. Fabrication around the logic of the norm is successful to the extent that the classifications and mental assumptions behind it not only constitute populations actuarially but also become accepted by those populations objectively. If people accept the ways in which they are described in various risk population categories they will in turn act in accordance with those descriptions. If they accept that the categories *are* their identity, then indeed biography becomes power and new possibilities for action exist.

The effect of biopower on identities has been addressed by a number of theorists in addition to Foucault, all of whom stress the potency of institutional risk classifications in making people what they are. Bourdieu (1984) describes how institutional classifications impress on people who they should be and what they should do, to the point where they see themselves only through the institutional hall of mirrors. The distinctions made in institutional classification schemes mean that the social order is progressively inscribed in peoples' minds. Social divisions become principles of division organizing the image of the social world. Objective limits become a sense of limits, a practical anticipation of objective limits acquired by experience of objective limits, a 'sense of one's place' that leads one to exclude oneself from the goods, persons, places and so forth from which one is excluded ... What individuals and groups invest in the particular meaning they give to common classificatory systems by the use they make of them is infinitely more than their 'interest' in the usual sense of the term: it is their whole social being, everything which defines their own idea of themselves, the primordial tacit contrast whereby they define 'us' as opposed to 'them,' 'other people,' and which is the basis of exclusions ('not for the likes of us') and inclusions they perform among the characteristics produced by the common classification system. (ibid.: 470–1, 478)

The process described by Bourdieu is not one of passive acceptance of identities made evident in risk classification schemes. There is room to manoeuvre as people are made reflexively aware of 'different possibilities for personhood' – 'not only what we did, do, and will do but also what we might have done and may do' (Hacking 1986: 229). In other words, risk classification schemes provide scripts for actors to construct their selves and their actions, scripts that vary across institutional space and activity. There is room for improvisation, as people perpetually prove themselves to institutions by pursuing better credentials and more reputational credits that will allow them to be seen in a better light. The ability to do so of course varies enormously. For example, some institutions, such as those associated with criminal justice, health, and welfare, are in part designed to do unto others what they cannot do for themselves. The taming of chance through biopower also tames dependent populations through identity acquiescence. As Douglas (1986: 100) remarks, 'as fast as new medical categories (hitherto unimagined) were invented, or new criminal or sexual or moral categories, new kinds of people spontaneously came forward to accept the labels and to live accordingly. The responsiveness to new labels suggests extraordinary readiness to fall into new slots and to let selfhood be redefined' (see also Hacking 1986, 1995).

The redefinition of self is a means to the end of self-governance, which is achieved when people accept the models and categories for action constructed by risk institutions and use them to facilitate their activities. Models of risk, and risk profiles of populations in general, are consistent with liberal forms of governance because they construct active, autonomous, and self-regulating individuals (Burchell 1991; Miller and Rose 1990; Nock 1993).

Governmentality refers to the risk technologies and practices of ensuring liberal self-governance. Foucault (1991c: 102) defines governmentality as 'the ensemble formed by the institutions, procedures, analyses and reflections, the calculations and tactics that allow the exercise of this very specific, albeit complex form of power, which has as its target population, as its principal form of knowledge political economy [the science of policing], and as its essential technical means apparatuses of security.' Risk models and technologies fabricate people into the circuits of social life by giving them population identities, for example as members of minority groups, as holders of prestigious credit cards, as welfare recipients, as highly educated people, as people with disabilities, and so on. Risk management is a form of political arithmetic aimed at managing the destinies of various populations at a distance (Miller and Rose 1990). As Moroney (1951: 1) observes, 'Historically, statistics is no more than State Arithmetic, a system of computation by which differences between individuals are eliminated by the taking of an average. It has been used – indeed, still is used – to enable rulers to know just how far they may safely go in picking the pockets of their subjects.'

The use of political arithmetic for risk management is not a one-way process. Various state and nonstate institutions risk-profile each other for competitive and regulatory purposes. Indeed, it is a defining characteristic of liberal governance that it provides for reflexive surveillance of its own activities in ways that allow people to make claims on government. As such, liberalism and risk society go hand in hand. They provide an institutionalized critical reflection on government via surveillance. There is a suspicious vigilance *vis-à-vis* risk and rights that checks any tendency of government to exceed its brief (Foucault 1991a; Burchell 1991; Barry et al. 1996).

Bureaucracy and Surveillance

Biopower and governmentality are achieved through bureaucracy and surveillance. Bureaucracy itself is a kind of grand scheme of surveillance. Bureaucracy is a form of authority based on both the command of abstract knowledge and on risk communication rules, formats, and technologies for the production and distribution of knowledge useful for administration. As Weber wrote in 1922 (Weber 1964: 196), 'Bureaucratic administration means fundamentally the exercise of control on the basis of knowledge.'

Bureaucratic surveillance – the production and distribution of knowledge useful for risk management and administration – constitutes populations in every conceivable area of social life. Gandy (1993: 63) lists eleven broad areas in which the liberal subject's self is constituted in machine-readable, network-linked data files. His list (with examples of the sorts of data items produced) is as follows: personal credentials (birth certificates, driver's licences); financial activity (ATM cards, credit cards, tax returns); insurance (health, home, and vehicular policies); social service (files relating to social benefits, health care, and pensions); utility service (files relating to telephone, cable television, and heating service); real estate (purchase, sale, and lease agreements); entertainment (travel documents, theatre tickets, Nielsen ratings); consumer activity (purchase records, credit accounts, surveys of consumer preferences); employment (applications, examinations, performance assessments); education (applications, records, references); and legal (court records, legal aid files).

The production of knowledge in each of these areas is facilitated by a number of surveillance mechanisms (Dandeker 1990: 37). These include the collection and storage of knowledge about people and objects; monitoring of people under supervision; encouragement of people under supervision to use knowledge obtained from surveillance to construct their own self-regulated courses of action; offering of instructions to subject populations; imposing direction on subject populations via the design of physical environments; and negotiating and monitoring compliance with risk standards.

The ability to establish and sustain surveillance mechanisms varies according to surveillance capacity. Surveillance capacity is a matter of available resources; of having multiple points of contact between the bureaucratic system and its subject populations; of the ability to store and access knowledge efficiently; of the centralization of knowledge; of networking with other bureaucracies; of inventiveness; of meeting legal requirements; and of the ability to secure agreement from subject populations that the surveillance mechanisms are to their benefit, because they enable the subject populations to govern themselves.

Surveillance operates through three continuous processes (Gandy 1993: 15ff.). First there is identification of the danger, as defined by administrative criteria of relevance. Claims to danger are authenticated and authorized. Next there is the risk classification process, in which people, events, processes, and states of affairs are assigned to conceptual groupings according to identification information. Finally, risk assessment articulates standards of acceptable risk and distributes risks.

The goals of surveillance are similar to the characteristics of bureaucracy enumerated by Weber (1978: 350) in the early twentieth century, namely 'Precision, dispatch, clarity, familiarity with the documents, continuity, discretion, uniformity, rigid subordination, savings in friction and in material and personal costs.' Weber went on to say that 'all these things are raised much more effectively to the optimal level by a strong bureaucratic, especially a monocratic, administration with trained individual officials than by any form of collegiate, honorific or avocational administration.' On the eve of the twenty-first century, however, communication technologies are allowing greater perfection of surveillance without direct human agency. Through 'dataveillance' (Clarke 1988) – 'the systematic use of personal data systems in the investigation or monitoring of the actions or communications of one or more persons' – the bureaucratic database rather than the bureaucrat is the basis for domination through knowledge (see also Weber 1978; Dandeker 1990; Poster 1990, 1995; Gandy 1993). Knowledgeability is collective and institutional rather than individual.

It is in these terms that bureaucratic surveillance enables 'government at a distance' (Miller and Rose 1990). Government at a distance is made possible by communication technologies, such as computers and video cameras, which broaden, deepen, and routinize surveillance. It is also made possible by probability statistics that are produced by 'remote sensing' (Gandy 1993: 59), in other words without direct contact with those to whom they apply, and with reference to population membership categories that make no sense outside of the risk analysis system. Gandy's (1993) metaphor of the 'panoptic sort' is apt because information technology and probability statistics relating to risk allow for a new system of surveillance removed from the bricks and mortar of Bentham's panopticon. 'On the basis of the "information revolution" not just the prison or factory, but the social totality, comes to function as the hierarchical and disciplinary Panoptic machine' (ibid.: 10) or 'difference machine' for deselecting people according to institutional values and access to knowledge environments.

Reflexivity

A defining feature of risk society is ongoing and in many cases instantaneous reflexivity with respect to risk assessments made and actions taken. 'Reflexive modernization' (Beck, Giddens, and Lasch 1994) is integral to bureaucratic surveillance, science, and everyday life.

As a technology of surveillance, bureaucracy exists to reflexively monitor activities deemed to be within its jurisdiction. Surveillance 'is the condition of institutional reflexivity and at the same time also in some part its product' (Giddens 1991: 149–50). Given the sophistication of electronic surveillance technologies, almost anything can be monitored, including of course the monitoring mechanisms themselves. This is illustrated by the case of TRW, a major American defence contractor and developer of sophisticated knowledge systems directed at consumers (Gandy 1993: 92ff.). TRW maintains credit data on 138 million consumers, which it sells to retail and financial institutions. At the same time, through its TRW Credentials operation, it sells to consumers their own credit-risk profile as constituted by the very same credit institutions. And, in registering consumers for this service, TRW is able to gather even more credit data to sell to the institutions. In reaction to public criticism and legal action, TRW has even developed a privacy-risk assessment scoring system to help data subjects assess the harm that might result from the collection and distribution of risk data on them.

Social science is integral to reflexivity. Indeed, as Giddens (1990: 14, 16) stresses, the influence of social science is found not only at the level of particular policies or ways of thinking about our worlds, but more significantly in how it helps constitute institutional classification schemes and practices. Similarly, Poster (1990: 36), echoing Foucault's observations about 'the objectifying social sciences,' observes that 'the "truth" of the discourses of bureaucracy and sociology are identical.' The coincidence of sociology and bureaucratic surveillance is perhaps best exemplified by the infamous 'Sociology Department' of the early Ford Motor Company. This unit was assigned the task of keeping the company's employees under surveillance during working hours and during leisure time. Its duties included the moral regulation of liquor and tobacco consumption and other vices. Using sociology to discipline the worker as a consumer came later (Ettema and Whitney 1994).

As was mentioned earlier (pp. 88–91), another feature of reflexive modernization is that science treats itself as a risk. That is, science increasingly recognizes that risks result from its own discoveries and their embodiment in technologies, and that risk assessments and preventive measures must be built into each step of scientific production.

Hence scientific production is as much 'reflexive' as 'primary': 'Scientific civilization has entered a stage in which it no longer merely scientizes nature, people and society, but increasingly itself, its own products, effects and mistakes. Science is no longer concerned with 'liberation' from pre-existing dependencies, but with the definition and distribution of errors and risks which are produced by itself' (Beck 1992a: 158).

Reflexive scientization has the ironic effect of creating radical doubt about science because it undercuts the belief that science offers certain knowledge. Doubt becomes institutionalized because knowledge is always under revision in the reflexive practice of science, the reflexive use of expertise, and the reflexive monitoring of everyday life.

Because risks exist only as imagined constructs of science, people live with a scientific consciousness of risks in everyday life. 'The intrusion of abstract systems into day-to-day life, coupled with the dynamic nature of knowledge, means that awareness of risk seeps into the actions of almost everyone' (Giddens 1991: 111). Everyday life is experienced as situated calculations about the possibilities for action and as a dialectic of counterfactuals. People always feel compelled to know, with reference to some description of risk, what they are doing and why they are doing it. Risk discourse tells them what to do and who to be. The self itself becomes 'reflexively understood by the person in terms of her or his biography' (ibid.: 53), a biography constituted by risk discourse.

Rationalities of risk are everywhere: as we cook our meals and wonder how to minimize the harmful effects of what we eat; as we eat in front of a televised baseball game whose main feature is the creation of risk profile statistics on every movement of every player; as we buy a new television set with a credit card that immediately transmits our consumer preferences to other institutions for their consumption; as we read in the newspaper that our risk of crime victimization may be higher than we thought. Common sense is constantly altered and reconstituted by rationalities of risk. Hacking (1990: 15) records how folklore about connections between suicide on the one hand and nationality and climate on the other was refuted by the production of suicide statistics. At one time Europeans viewed the English as the most suicidal of all Europeans, and attributed this characteristic to the effects of English winters, but this common-sense view was reversed when statistics showed that the English were the least suicidal Europeans, and that suicides everywhere occurred more frequently in summer.

Reflexivity is not limited to the realm of scientific cognition. As Lash (1993; see also Beck, Giddens, and Lash 1994) argues, it also exists in the realms of aesthetics and emotional sensibility. Reflexivity with respect to risk means that fear proves itself. That is, in the very process of acting in response to risk consciousness and putting in place security mechanisms to manage risk, the perception of threat and the resultant fear are renewed. Hacking (1982: 286–7) observes that in nineteenth-century France the 'avalanche of printed numbers' on crime and deviance meant that 'every salon spoke in fear ... the illiterate were, by gossip, made fairly numerate thirty years before general education made them literate ... les misèrables created a morbid and fearful fascination for numbers upon which the bureaucracies fed.' In our own era, according to Hacking (1990: 4–5),

> There are more explicit statements of probabilities on American prime-time television than explicit acts of violence (I'm counting the ads). Our public fears are endlessly debated in terms of probabilities: chances of meltdowns, cancers, muggings, earthquakes, nuclear winters, AIDS, global greenhouses, what next? There is nothing to fear (it may seem) but the probabilities themselves. This obsession with the chances of danger, and with treatments for changing the odds, descends directly from the forgotten annals of nineteenth century information and control.

5

Risk Institutions

Risk discourse is a product of institutions. Risks exist only in institutional knowledge about them. Each institution strives to freeze risks in time in the hope of creating a sense of structure and coherence about them and of making them more understandable and certain. To know a risk is to know how an institution classifies and establishes what the risk means and how it is to be responded to. To know an institution is to know how it selects and defines risks in ways that support and stabilize the institution.

Institutionalization is a process of selection and definition of risks. Something becomes institutionalized when the risk classifications are taken for granted and when the resultant mentalities and sensibilities of institutional actors allow routine recognition of what has meaning and what actions are possible. Indeed, when institutionalized, the classifications establish the very criteria through which people discover their preferences; alternative meanings are either seen as unrealistic or not seen at all (Douglas 1986; DiMaggio and Powell 1991).

Institutionalization of risk discourse is made possible by a system of communication rules, formats, and technologies. A risk communication system provides scripts for action (what to do) and for identity (who to be). It also provides the narrative structure for reporting about the institution's risk activities in a truthful manner. Police officers, for example, could not tell the truth about events they are required to report without the relevant criteria of truth already being embedded in the classification schemes of the forms they must use to make their reports.

Institutionalization moves authorship away from the individual. Rather than improvising, people do what the institutional script provides. Institutionalization is a process of circumscribing human agency and creating routine enactments: 'If shaking hands is an institutionalized form of greeting, one takes action only by refusing to offer one's hand ... one enacts institutions; one takes action by departing from them, not by participating in them' (Jepperson 1991: 148–9). Institutionalization provides the limits to reflexivity that are necessary to get on with the task at hand.

Highly institutionalized rules, formats, and technologies allow an institution to move across space and time and to participate in systemic relations with other institutions. At the systemic level an institution becomes impervious to manipulation by individuals (Giddens 1984). On the other hand it loses much of its own agency as it becomes embroiled with other institutions in the politics of risk classification. In producing and distributing knowledge about risk to each other, institutions inevitably struggle over the definition and classification of risks. Institutional relations are both established and altered by these conflicts. Politics in risk society is a matter of which institution's risk logic applies and what is the appropriate relationship among risk institutions.

Most of the political behaviour surrounding risk classification is itself institutionalized. This is evident in relations between government regulatory institutions and regulated private sector institutions. Private sector institutions often *invite* government involvement in the regulation of risk to help protect against loss from risk taking. Government risk regulation goes hand in hand with private sector risk taking, as was revealed most dramatically in the U.S. Savings and Loan safety net of 'risk management for the well-off' (Lowi 1990: 32–3; see also Zimring and Hawkins 1993).

Risk institutions also battle for institutional hegemony. Much of the literature on risk society is the story of how in the politics of risk classification the institution of science has given ground to other institutions. Because risks exist only within institutional knowledges of risk, they are open to infinite social constructions – to being dramatized, marginalized, or changed – based on alternative knowledges. While scientific knowledge remains pre-eminent in defining risks, it loses its eminence at the points of distribution and use because it becomes politicized by competing institutional logics. The logics of markets, professions, interest groups, and the mass media are among those that demonopolize scientific knowledge. Thus scientific knowledge is not only 'more and more necessary, but at the same time, less and less sufficient for the socially binding definition of truth' (Beck 1992a: 156). It is subject to other social institutions – especially business enterprises, law, and the mass media – dictating the truth to it, so that it is at once 'indispensable to and incapable of truth' (ibid.: 166).

Professions

A great deal of what becomes institutionalized as risk is a result of the activities of risk professions and of the division of expert knowledge in the system of professions. A risk profession is an occupational group that claims exclusive abstract knowledge concerning how to address particular risks and a unique ability to provide expert services of risk management. Abbott (1988: 30) remarks that 'It is with abstraction that law and accounting fought frantically over tax advice, the one because it writes the laws, the other because it defines what the prescribed numbers mean ... It is with abstraction that American medicine claims all of deviance, the abstraction of its all-powerful disease metaphor.'

As was emphasized in our discussion of the division of expert knowledge in policing (pp. 27–30), professional expertise is not only embodied in people (experts) but also embedded in institutional systems of communication rules, formats, and technologies. Professionals are increasingly absent, their place taken by forms, computers, and step-by-step procedures that commodify expertise and reduce it to check-boxes, keystrokes, and self-help guides.

Whether in human or technological form, the task of risk professions is to be reflexive enough to capture a problem adequately, yet resolute enough to bring reflection to an end so as to move on to enactment (Stehr 1992, 1994). Risk professions make risks visible, rationalize them through processes of assessment and validation, and then offer an interpretation in order to constitute and enforce standards (Abbott 1988: 232). As such they are central to governmentality in risk society (Miller and Rose 1990).

Risk professions are also agents of dependency (Bauman 1992a). People are compelled to depend on professional knowledge of endangerment, to give up their 'cognitive sovereignty' (Beck 1992a: 53). The compulsion derives from peoples' fears and the attendant desire to make the irrational seem rational. Dependency also derives from the fact that risks only exist in expert knowledge of risk. After being evaluated by other institutions, a risk always returns to professional, scientific evaluators because it exists only in the knowledges of those evaluators. This is nicely captured in Beck's (1992b: 212) observation about environmental risks that 'no amount of collective coughing, scratching or sighing helps. Only science does.'

A profession is constituted by its institutional relations and ability to maintain institutional jurisdiction. As Abbott (1988: 320) notes, 'the state of modern medicine has more to do with the state of modern nursing, pharmacy, law and accounting than with that of nineteenth-century medicine.'

Institutional jurisdiction is constituted and contested by several interrelated elements. First and foremost, the institutional jurisdiction of a profession depends on the ability of its abstract-knowledge system to make risks visible, to dramatize them, and to provide classifications and technologies for dealing with them:

> [p]ractical skill grows out of an abstract system of knowledge, and control of the occupation lies in control of the abstractions that generate the practical techniques. The techniques themselves may be delegated to other workers ... Only a knowledge system governed by abstractions can redefine its problems and tasks, defend them from interlopers, and seize new problems – as medicine has recently seized alcoholism, mental illness, hyperactivity in children, obesity, and numerous other things. Abstraction enables survival in the competitive system of professions. (ibid. 1988: 8–9)

Consider the medical profession and its jurisdiction over crime and criminality. Doctors do not routinely provide direct service to 'dangerous offenders' or 'juvenile delinquents,' but instead abstract models and risk classification technologies for those who do. Medical models and risk technologies become part of a different institution, criminal justice, forming part of that institution's system for regulating mental and moral aspects of life (Menzies 1989).

Second, institutional jurisdiction depends on the ability to demonstrate the superiority of one's abstract-knowledge system – its models and the risk technologies that follow from them – over those of competitors. Professions market their expertise to other institutions by dramatizing the risks of other approaches and making claims about their own ways of seeing and doing things. This strategy is accomplished by institutionalizing classifications and technologies before bringing them into the public arena of policy deliberations and markets, so that they are seen as a *fait accompli*. This strategy was evident, for example, in the development of genetic engineering and its medical applications (Royal Commission on New Reproductive Technologies 1993). As Hacking

(1992: 145) observes, professionals have the knowledge system advantage of being in a position to 'decide what classes shall be counted and how they shall be defined. Commonly they are well in advance of popular distinctions, rather literally bringing the distinctions into being.' A profession maps its institutional realities and jurisdictions by employing the classifications it develops in advance of sustained public application.

Institutional jurisdiction is also a matter of regulation. Each profession tries to sustain its cognitive hegemony by defending what counts as relevant knowledge, making its knowledge sufficiently inaccessible to nonexperts, setting standards for regulatory activities within its jurisdiction, and controlling the means by which its efficiency is assessed. To accomplish reasonable self-regulation it is necessary to seek and establish various forms of external authority. The legal institution is invariably invoked in this regard, but of equal importance are more general appeals to dominant cultural values of procedural propriety, efficiency, and professional status. '[P]urely technical legitimation of professional work is impossible' (Abbott 1988: 209).

Clearly all of the above elements involved in constituting the institutional jurisdictions of a risk profession serve to institutionalize the profession itself and to firmly embed it in interinstitutional systems. Indeed, as Cambrosio, Limoges, and Hoffman (1992) show, expert knowledge is properly seen not as a property of professionals who have it but rather as a property of the institutional communication systems through which professionals interact. While professionals obviously have 'know-how,' their know-how does not become expertise until it is plugged into an institutional communication system. It is through such systems that expert knowledge becomes standardized and robust enough to use in routine diagnosis, classification, and treatment decisions by professionals.

All professionals function within risk communication systems. Risk communication systems render obsolete any notion that individual professionals operate in isolation and offer purely personal service to their clients. The main function of professionals is to enlist the help of their clients in inputting knowledge into the risk communication system:

> The essential component of intervention no longer takes the form of the direct face-to-face relationship between the carer and the cared, the helper and the helped, the professional and the client. It comes instead to reside in the establishing of *flows of population* based on the collation of a range of abstract factors

deemed liable to produce risk in general ... [In medicine] the examination of the patient tends to become the examination of the patient's records as compiled in varying situations by diverse professionals and specialists interconnected solely through the circulation of individual dossiers ... The site of diagnostic synthesis is no longer that of the concrete relationship with a sick person, but a relationship constituted among the different expert assessments which make up the patient's dossier ... There is, in fact, no longer a relation of immediacy with a subject ... but [only] factors, statistical correlations of heterogeneous elements. They deconstruct the concrete subject of intervention, and reconstruct a combination of factors liable to produce risk ... the operative on the ground now becomes a simple auxiliary to a manager whom he or she supplies with information derived from the activity of diagnosis expertise described above. These items of information are then stockpiled, processed and distributed along channels completely disconnected from those of professional practice, using in particular the medium of computerized data handling (Castel 1991: 281–2, 288, 293)

Balkin (1992: 1974) offers a similar analysis of how lawyers function in the institutionalized context of law firms:

We already have the seventy-hour billed week, the canned brief, the 500-person law firm churning out mountains of paper to prove its value to the corporate clientele. We already have mass-produced litigation and mass-produced judicial administration to deal with it. Already most federal judicial opinions are written by twenty-five-year olds, so that the language of opinions does not really mean what it says, because it was not said by the persons whose meaning really counts.

Information managers and computer specialists become increasingly influential in risk knowledge systems (Altheide 1995: chap. 2). Their influence relates to their role in helping their clients decide what is relevant information and in filtering the classifications decided on into computer formats. Similarly, statisticians exert influence as they work across the full range of institutions and professions as experts in the interpretation of probabilities: '[s]tatisticians flood their techniques everywhere, let others use them badly, and make a living repairing bad applications' (Abbott 1988: 236).

In the web of complex systems of risk management, professional jurisdiction is permanently shifting. The very same means by which professions colonize jurisdiction – abstract knowledge, competition, regulation, bureaucratization, and participation in expert systems – are also the means by which the professions can lose jurisdiction and be assimilated and destabilized.

Media Formats

Risk media formats make risks visible and subject to assessment and management. They typically include some combination of electronic and print media that effect surveillance, distribute knowledge, and provide risk analyses. Examples are magnetic access cards, market surveys, surveillance cameras, computer terminals, social surveys, bureaucratic forms, and actuarial formats.

Risk media do not stand apart from institutions but rather participate in their formation and change. They become embedded in institutions and have powerful social effects. They are the sinews that connect institutions and allow perpetual articulation of risks as reality. They broker consciousness and social existence, defining what should be taken as objective reality. They create knowledge structures concerning who knows what, and thus institutional environments of inclusion and exclusion. They organize social relations in two ways: first, in terms of population categories, and second, in terms of who should relate to whom, on what basis, and for what purposes. They 'auditize' the world, always scanning for risk and efficient management of it with reference to their own peculiar criteria of efficient management.

Risk media have no sense of place. They give institutions the late modern qualities identified by Giddens (1990): time-space distanciation, disembedding, and reflexivity. Risk media allow knowledge of risk to be produced, distributed, and managed from anywhere. They allow remote control (Cooper 1992; see also Zuboff 1988) and the abstraction of thought from action so that they can regulate at a distance. They make institutional activity not so much fluid and coordinated as displaced and transformed across the risk knowledge networks of various institutions. They organize meanings in space and time to force complexity into the narrow grooves of instant categorization for efficient risk management. Remote control, displacement, and reduction of complexity allow institutional processes to be represented as they happen and risk management, as a result, to occur instantaneously, at a glance (Zuboff 1988):

> Remote control underlies the economy of convenience intrinsic to representation: one may not be able to move the mountain itself but it is easy to move a

model or map of it. This mobility of representation helps us to understand why paperwork of all kinds is so essential to organization: mobility is central to control. Representation displaces the inevitable and obdurate; it denies the idea of fixed location and emphasizes movement. Displacement, therefore, means mobile and non-localizable associations. It therefore becomes inappropriate to talk, for example, about the organization and its environment since this gives the impression of distinct domains separated in time and space. (Cooper 1992: 257)

The risk media of a given institution penetrate other institutions and fundamentally influence how members of those other institutions think and act. A risk medium can lend its 'basic and recognizable organizing principles and features to another authority and thereby help shape the public perception, expectation and legitimation of that activity, as well as the activity itself' (Altheide 1985: 232). Risk media provide binocular vision, creating the lenses through which institutional actors convert the three-dimensional world into the two-dimensional representation of risk on the computer screen:

the power of bureaucracy derives in good part from the linguistic form instituted by computer databases, the code which generates a form of language without ambiguity ...

The establishment of modern surveillance and control is not simply a result of technical innovation, that is, the computer. It requires the encoding of language so that symbols can be converted into electronic forms ... For the subject in electronically mediated communication, the object tends to become not the material world as represented in language but the flow of signifiers itself. In the mode of information it becomes increasingly difficult, or even pointless, for the subject to distinguish a 'real' existing 'behind' the flow of signifiers, and as a consequence social life becomes a practice of positioning subjects to receive and interpret messages. (Poster 1990: 38, 14–15)

Institutional subjects are also positioned to produce and distribute messages, and therein lies their own purchase on remote control. No matter where they are placed in institutional hierarchies, people can take advantage of the fact that risk media make knowledge of risk accessible for a variety of uses, including resistance. It is impossible to control such knowledge by using institutional border-guards because of the sheer volume of risk communications, the fact that knowledge can be taken but yet remain in its original place, and the fact that once known, knowledge can never be reclaimed. Remote control means that no one is in control.

Insurance Formats

Our analysis of risk institutions, professions, and media can be made more concrete by examining insurance. Insurance is an abstract technology of risk. Indeed, the word risk itself is a neologism for insurance technology. Insurance is also an institution. As a technology and an institution, insurance is central to other security institutions. Insurance is *the* overarching technology and institution of risk, spanning all other major public and private institutions and fundamentally influencing their knowledge systems. It has become increasingly important as a model for social policy and as an institution of governance in matters of risk and responsibility.

Insurance has eight properties that make it one of the dominant templates of governance in risk society.

First, it *objectifies* everything as an accident. The world is classified into degrees of chance of harm, which are then assigned their respective costs. This entails a literal production of objective risks that is designed to make accidents normal, and in that sense not accidents at all.

Second, insurance makes untoward eventualities *calculable*. Objectification occurs through the production of concrete facts and the use of actuarial techniques to make probability statements. At the level of immediate production, the world is categorized as simply the facts, as that which can be reduced to check-boxes that in turn enable one to make the necessary actuarial calculations:

> events are facts with distinct boundaries in space and time – they are complete in themselves and have no cause, or past, or future ... They can barely be described, and their identity is reduced to the numerical quality that allows one to tabulate them as a point or a unit ... the insurer who initially notes the fact of an accident or a death is altogether indifferent to its cause ... The important thing about events is that they occur, or rather that their occurrence is repetitive, multiple and regular. They become purely accidental, and are rendered objective by comparison with themselves. (Ewald 1991b: 143)

Third, insurance is *collective*. The insurer is a kind of demographer who objectifies and makes calculable a population that has a stake in the identified risk. The reality of the risk is distributed across this population in the form of costs; each member of the population contributes a little in insurance premiums in order to save a lot if harm ensues.

Fourth, insurance forms *capital*. It is a means of capital accumulation for insurers as well as in some cases for the insured. It is also a means of protecting against loss of capital. Indeed, what is insured is not the particular calamitous event that causes harm to a member of the population concerned but the capital against which the insurer offers indemnification.

Fifth, insurance is *managerial*. It offers an alternative to direct surveillance as a means of securing territories. Insurance surveillance is extraterritorial. It manages risks on a technical basis and at a distance, for a population dispersed in time and space but bound together by a common interest. The insurer's interest is in protecting the common interest, which amounts to loss reduction for the protection of capital.

Sixth, insurance is *legal*. It makes risk subject to contract and adjudication. At the same time, it helps the law assign liability for loss to the party most able to distribute the loss through insurance.

Seventh, insurance is *cultural*. As a template for rendering the world in objectified, calculable, collective, capital, managerial, and legal terms, insurance transforms cultural mentalities and sensibilities. For example, in providing a futures market in security, insurance alters conceptions of time and destiny. In eschewing causality and making risks collective and capitalized, insurance alters notions of providence, responsibility, and justice. In propagating the managementization of the world, insurance ensures that life is experienced as a perpetual round of calculations of economic utility. By objectifying the world, insurance forces one to look at oneself in the mirror of one's risk attributes, and to do so daily to ensure that one has not been reclassified.

Eighth, insurance is *political*. It is central to liberal governance because it combines aspects of collective welfare and individual liberty. This combination can lead actuarially constituted groups, such as welfare recipients, to become effective collective actors in the struggle to secure benefits. On the other hand, it can support more-extreme forms of libertarianism and self-governance because it disaggregates people by classifying them according to their differences from others in a population. Disaggregation strips people of their political identities as sovereign subjects and forces them to stand alone and atomized, solely responsible for their own security.

Insurance also provides a framework for political trouble because of what it cannot do. Some things defy insurance, and it is precisely that realization that heightens political anxiety over potential chaos. The success of a generalizable social insurance requires 'A relatively stable distribution of risk across society; and also that risk can be depoliticized, or dealt with by being 'contained.' In an era of reflexive modernization these issues become much more problematic. Manufactured risk is unstable in relation to both human and natural environments of action. It can no longer be confronted in an actuarial way, through the control of the "routine disorder" of environments, including the environment of capitalist production as well as nature' (Giddens 1994: 150).

Environmental problems such as global warming, technological catastrophes such as the breakdown of nuclear power plants, and the fiscal problems of the welfare state all signal that some risks are uninsurable (Beck 1992a). Dangers outrun risk technologies, thereby revealing the limits of insurance and creating a limitless dread that not every chance can be tamed.

6

Risk and Social Change

Accumulating Change

Risk society is not the result of abrupt change. Rather, chance has been subject to *taming* processes over a long period (Hacking 1990). For our purposes, however, it is not fruitful to try to pinpoint the origins of risk society with regard to time, place, and cause. Instead we will look more generally at some of the antecedents of the contemporary emphasis on bureaucratic surveillance and risk management.

Governing institutions have always wanted detailed knowledge of populations. The statistical description of populations for social and political purposes goes back to ancient times. Census taking, especially in support of taxation, is a form of government surveillance firmly rooted in Judeo-Christian cultures. As Hacking (1992: 140) observes, the Bible devotes an entire book to a census of Israel, and that book is called, simply, Numbers. Hacking adds that 'Jesus was born in a manger because his parents were en route to be counted and taxed in their home town. Statistical description is so common among civilizations that it can be called a universal of human governance, a product of those two other universals of orderly society, recruitment and taxation' (ibid.).

A detailed census was taken in Canada as early as 1666, largely for taxation purposes, but also to develop an incentive scheme that would encourage families to have more children. Article 1(2) of the American Constitution (1787) called for census taking to determine congressional districts and voter enfranchisement. As Hacking (1982: 290) wryly states, 'You could say that the second most important feature of the American dream was that people should be counted ... It was to determine the size of Congressional districts, so as to give equal representation to all free persons ... all the other people, excluding "Indians not taxed," were figured in at the rate of 3/5 of a person. What we call the Enlightenment was nothing if not exact.'

In the nineteenth century the risk-profiling of populations became an instrumental part of liberal utilitarian political reform in matters of public health and security, and it has been so ever since. The dimensions and effects of policing via risk management statistics were nicely captured in remarks made by Ernst Engel in a Prussian government statistical publication in 1862, and his observations are equally applicable to the 'panoptic sort' of our time:

> In order to obtain an accurate representation, statistical research accompanies the individual through his entire earthly existence. It takes account of his birth, his baptism, his vaccination, his schooling and the success thereof, his diligence, his leave of school, his subsequent education and development; and, once he becomes a man, his physique and his ability to bear arms. It also accompanies the subsequent steps of his walk through life; it takes note of his chosen occupation; where he sets up his household and his management of the same; if he saved from the abundance of his youth for his old age; if and when and at what age he marries and who he chooses as his wife – statistics look after him when things go well for him and when they go awry. Should he suffer a shipwreck in his life, undergo material, moral or spiritual ruin, statistics takes note of the same. Statistics leaves a man only after his death – after it has ascertained the precise age of his death and noted the causes that brought about his end. (quoted in Hacking 1990: 34)

It is liberal governance's concern for the health and security of populations that has led to the proliferation of census taking beyond questions such as taxation and electoral boundaries. While the first American census (1790) asked four questions and was directed at householders only, the tenth (1880) contained numerous schedules aimed at various kinds of institutions and individuals, and in total asked 13,010 questions (Hacking 1990: 2).

The rise of bureaucratic management of populations has also occurred in response to emergency needs. Wars – imagined, threatened, or actual – have been especially fertile grounds for the proliferation of surveillance technologies and innovative risk management techniques (Giddens 1985; Dandeker 1990). The identification of major diseases that seem to spread rapidly but are difficult to capture and regulate has also led to special political technologies of risk. AIDS is a contemporary example, while the bubonic plague is a reminder from the past. The surveillance system devised for the plague in Europe, along with Bentham's model of the panopticon, provided Foucault (1977: 195ff.) with his guiding metaphors for biopower and discipline. Foucault (1977: 197) depicted the European plague quarantine system as an

> enclosed, segmented space, observed at every point, in which individuals are inserted in a fixed place, in which the slightest movements are supervised, in which all events are recorded, in which an uninterrupted work of writing links the centre and the periphery, in which power is exercised without division, according to a continuous hierarchical figure, in which each individual is constantly located, examined and distributed among the living beings, the sick and the dead – all this constitutes a compact model of the disciplinary mechanism. The plague is met by order; its function is to sort out every possible confusion: that of the disease, which is transmitted where bodies are mixed together; that of the evil, which is increased when fear and death overcome prohibitions.

Major population movements, for example those associated with rapid urbanization or massive immigration, have also led to the honing of surveillance and risk management techniques. Governments and private insurance companies were both forced to invent new forms for population welfare and security when industrialization forced people from a rural into an urban existence. The early invention of assurance and annuity mechanisms for individual labourers was very much a product of the movement from the security of communal village life to the insecurity of urban wage labour (Hacking 1991: 191).

Risk management has also proliferated with the advance of scientific knowledge. A cornerstone of Beck's (1992a) thesis is that the risk society is the inevitable product of the harmful effects of modern science and technology. Societies have always had to manage highly dangerous risks such as the plague. What is different in contemporary risk society is science and technology's transformation of structural social conditions. Science and technology are major causes of risks, which in turn are scientized. Scientization generates risk in an amplifying spiral (Beck 1992a; Stehr 1994; Stehr and Ericson 1992).

Associated with the advance of scientific knowledge as constitutive of risk society is the proliferation of professions and their expert knowledges and institutions. Risk expertise multiplies for many reasons, not least of which is that there are real, significant problems to be managed. However, there are features internal to the professional knowledge systems themselves that compel expansion. The taming of chance has always been pragmatic and piecemeal, addressing immediate practical problems rather than abstract intellectual issues. As Hacking (1982: 289) observes, the Enlightenment was not so much a great philosophical age as a matter of throwing light on practical problems of population management. In risk society the pragmatism of professional knowledge combines with a highly specialized division of expert knowledge. The result is a narrow framework within each profession that leads professionals to look at a problem and its solution in isolation from systemic consequences. Unanticipated consequences of expert decisions multiply, and these in turn foster a proliferation of counterfactual risk discourses (Giddens 1991; Bauman 1992a). As Perrow (1984; 322) remarks, 'A working definition of an expert is a person who can solve a problem faster or better than others, but who runs a higher risk than others of posing the wrong problem. By virtue of his or her expert methods, the problem is redefined to suit the methods.'

The iatrogenic effects of the single problem/single solution approach within each profession are compounded by the ways in which risk professions create dependencies. In a society based on social distance, privacy, distrust, fear of freedom, and fragmented knowledges, risk expertise finds a profitable trade in certainty: 'There are indeed many precautions to imprison a man in what he is, as if we lived in perpetual fear that he might escape from it, that he might break away and suddenly elude his condition' (Sartre 1966: 59). Expertise is also iatrogenic because people come to depend on it rather than on each other, and there is a professional rage to invent new *its* in order to stay in business and find a niche in the security market.

As producers of risk, scientific knowledge and professional expertise are entwined with technology. Like expertise, risk technologies are self-legitimating. Their very availability justifies the need for them, as well as their claims to prestige and a greater share of resources (Ellul 1964). As they set out in search of problems, risk technologies masquerade as solutions. They also create fragmentary effects as they turn danger, formerly defined as fate, into options on behalf of others, who are thereby excluded from participating in the decisions and made dependent.

Two technological inventions in particular have made a profound contribution to the constituting of risk society. Statistical thinking has reached a point where the decisions of every organization are made on its terms: 'No public decision, no risk analysis, no environmental impact, no military strategy can be conducted without decision theory couched in terms of probabilities. By covering opinion with a veneer of objectivity, we replace judgement by computation' (Hacking 1990: 4). As Simon (1987: 87) notes, when we are driving at high speed on the freeway our being together with other drivers has a quality of nothingness about it, with one exception, namely the danger we create for each other, and how it is managed by risk technologies such as road design, vehicle design, driver's licenses, demerit points, photo-radar, aerial surveillance, and accident reports.

The second great technological construction of risk society is communication technology. Computers and their associated telecommunications infrastructures have made it easier to collect, process, store, and distribute risk knowledge, which in turn increases pressure on risk institutions and their experts to produce and use even more risk knowledge. Computers broaden, deepen, and routinize surveillance because they transcend space and time, permit invisible or barely visible forms of monitoring, involve people in self-monitoring, and open the door to actuarial analyses that allow institutions to create categories of suspicion and automatically exclude some groups from institutional benefits. As Poster (1990: 38) emphasizes, these powers of the computer are not attributable to the technical capacities of the computer alone, but to how that instrument creates a new form of language, a language of fixed-choice check-boxes that provides certainty where there was none: 'the power of bureaucracy derives in good part from the linguistic form instituted by computerized databases, the code which generates a form of language without ambiguity' (ibid.; see also Altheide 1995: chap. 2).

Statistics and probability theory, constituted in computer formats, structure truth. They present risk data as the basis of an objective standard that people *must* accept as objective reality and therefore use to form their identities and behaviour. Although the risk classifications and categories, and the resultant identities and behaviour, are socially constructed, once in place they are 'relative to nothing' and become *the* standard (Hacking 1992: 135). They become truly rational and drive social change by routinizing it in institutional procedures.

As Weber realized, the rationality of bureaucratic surveillance for risk management is not open to rational critique and change except within its own criteria of rationality. In risk society these are the criteria of statistical probabilities and computer formats. 'Let a man propose an anti-statistical idea to reflect individuality and to resist the probabilification of the universe, the next generation effortlessly coopts it so that it becomes part of the standard statistical machinery of information and control' (Hacking 1990: 141). Populations are changed to fit the formats, not vice versa: 'We obtain data about a governed class whose deportment is offensive, and then attempt to alter what we guess are relevant conditions of that class in order to change the laws of statistics that the class obeys. This is the essence of the style of government that in the United States is called "liberal" ... the intentions are benevolent. The *we* who know best change the statistical laws that affect *them*' (ibid.: 119).

The rise of risk society is also associated with cultural shifts that transcend particular institutional changes. There is a shift from a materialist 'standard of life' orientation to a postmaterialist 'quality of life' orientation that includes incessant demands for freedom from risks. The emphasis is now on risk management products, that is, on professional expertise and technologies of risk that promise a better quality of life. The genealogical interdependence of risk, enterprise, progress, and modernity – first evident in the nineteenth century – has new cultural life, and there is a thriving market in risk and security products. An inflationary logic develops with the commodification of risk. Market forces encourage novelty that will create new demand, as opposed to merely adjusting the level of supply to meet existing demand (Bauman 1992a).

With market forces at work in the distribution of risks, new forms of inequality ensue, and with them further demands for risk management. The law becomes a product for assisting in risk management. Equality of condition *vis-à-vis* risks becomes the guiding legal force, even at the expense of liberty. Liberal governance's public policy must now, more than ever, address as a matter of legal right the democratization of risk management and indemnification (Lowi 1990; Priest 1990). The law increasingly forces risk producers, who are in the best position to prevent risks and to insure against harms caused, to take responsibility for prevention and insurance. It also participates in the construction of scientific knowledge of risk, including how risk becomes embodied in professionals and embedded in technologies. As Cambrosio, Limoges, and Hoffman (1992: 354) show with respect to the release of genetically engineered organisms, regulatory categories 'participate in the construction of risk assessment facts ... [and] are themselves a result of a hybrid construction process whereby different kinds of scientific work ... interact with performative pieces of legislative discourse.'

The accumulated changes analysed here constitute a risk society that has several cumulative effects. Four such effects require further elaboration: changes in privacy and trust, fragmentation, new forms of inequality, and a new constellation of morality, responsibility, accountability, and rights.

Privacy and Trust

Privacy can be defined as 'places, spaces and matters upon or into which others may not normally intrude without the consent of the person or organization to whom they are designated as belonging' (Reiss 1987: 20). Risk society values privacy, which finds symbolic meaning in the sanctity accorded the individualized, privatized lifestyle of the home. But people also value privacy in personal affairs and the freedoms that come with anonymity in public spaces. As such, privacy is constituted by what escapes institutional risk management surveillance. Both state (Giddens 1991: 51) and nonstate (Gandy 1993: 97) institutions are involved in setting legal and other standards that define the limits of surveillance and the public/private divide.

The quest for privacy results in part from structural features of risk society. The more people fear the risks of public involvement, the more they withdraw into a privatized lifestyle. The more people are risk-profiled according to their population identities, the more they feel individualized and separated from those not so identified.

As Tocqueville (1840) observed, bureaucratic surveillance becomes ever more necessary as the privatization of the citizenry increases. Surveillance makes the relevant characteristics of people and organizations known so that their trustworthiness can be gauged for the purpose of a particular institutional transaction with them. People are known by and trusted because of their credit cards, building access cards, driver's licences, passports, psychological screening tests, and the like. Organizations are known by and trusted because of routinized auditing techniques and forms of accountability. Privacy can expand only with trust, but trust can expand only with surveillance.

In summary, accompanying privacy is a greater intrusion into privacy so that people can be known in risk management terms. The 'backstage' of private places, spaces, and matters breaks down, and personal and organizational life is experienced as porous (Meyrowitz 1985; G. Marx 1988). The more often surveillance mechanisms must be used to create trust, the greater is the realization that trust is doubtful. The greater the presumption of distrust, the greater the space for surveillance, and so on, in an amplifying spiral.

People who take part in a particular institutional relation face a paradox. They perceive that they are treated as not fully trustworthy, as a risk, yet they must put *their* trust in the institution's risk management practices. Trust resides in the institution and in the capacities of the institution's abstract system of risk management, not in the individuals within the system (Giddens 1990, 1991; Nock 1993). People become dependent on the system, and a kind of 'trust inequality' results. As Lash and Wynne note in their introduction to Beck's (1992a: 4) book on risk society,

> risks are always created and effected in social systems, for example by organizations and institutions which are supposed to manage and control the risky activity ... the magnitude of the physical risks is therefore a direct function of the quality of the social relations and processes ... the primary risk, even for the most technically intensive activities (indeed perhaps most especially for them), is therefore that of social dependency upon institutions and actors who may well be – and arguably are increasingly – alien, obscure and inaccessible to most people affected by the risks in question. Thus the issues of trust and credibility have been raised in the risk field.

Trust presupposes some awareness of circumstances of risk, yet most people are not sufficiently aware of such circumstances to take action on their own. They are forced to put their trust in the reliability of the institution and its expert systems to help them manage their risks, a trust that fills the gap between their limited knowledge and the need to take action. Indeed it is only within a framework of trust that patterns of risk can be properly institutionalized and converted into routine action. Paradoxically, privacy, trust, surveillance, and risk management go hand in hand in creating the probabilities and possibilities of action.

Fragmentation

Risk society is fragmented. Fragmentation results from the fact that risk as danger subverts institutional boundaries. Risks blur the boundaries of professional knowledges, raise complex ethical issues that require interdisciplinary approaches, force the adoption of more-stringent institutional responsibility and accountability, and forge new interinstitutional alliances.

Fragmentation also results from several features of risk management technologies and practice. Risk management is future oriented. The past – with its traditional ways of doing things – gives way to the construction of frameworks for the future. The past retains meaning only if it does not clash with present knowledge and plans for future action. One may possibly escape one's past, but never institutional futures. Risk society's orientation towards the future is blatantly obvious in, for example, insurance provision and the 'futures market' of stock and commodity exchanges. However, it is also present in all institutions through their proliferation of 'instant' risk profiling and counterfactual thought. Individuals and organizations become obsessed with accessing communication flows that will create futures that can then be colonized for personal profit and security. Discontinuity with the past and with fragmented futures is an everpresent reality.

A related aspect of risk technologies and practices is the need to sell efficient solutions to specific problems. Efficiency requires that problems be extracted from their wider social context and that their 'totalities' be dissolved. The resultant solutions are piecemeal, segmented into manageable bits. The bits make no sense beyond the domain of the temporary solution to a local problem, except to give a sense of fragmentation.

Fragmentation is also a result of how governance in risk society is pluralized and dispersed across multiple public and private institutions and spaces. As Beck (1992a) observes, 'the political' (meaning a strong state) is depoliticized, and 'the nonpolitical' (meaning institutions not formally part of the state) is politicized: 'The political institutions become the administrators of a development they neither have planned for nor are able to structure, but must nevertheless somehow justify' (ibid.: 186–7). They become organizers on behalf of politicized, nonstate institutions, helping them produce, distribute, and use risk knowledge to manage their futures. As such they are less and less the innovators in risk management, but merely agents – knowledge brokers, regulators, and legislators of things that cannot be changed – within the technical systems of nonstate institutions:

> This division of labour in the power structure of modernization discharges the state into a multiple belatedness ... the 'alternative society' is no longer expected to come from parliamentary debates or new laws, but rather from [institutions and their] ... application of microelectronics, genetic technology and information media ... Everyone else – even the most responsible and best informed people in politics and science – more or less lives off the crumbs of information that fall from the planning tables of sub-politics. (ibid.: 213, 223)

Fragmentation is experienced at the personal level in the form of population identity categories provided for one by major institutions. The self becomes a reflection of risk profile after-images, images that are as fractured as the number of institutions the self participates in (Gergen 1991; Gandy 1993). Institutions governed by risk management break down social solidarity and foster selfish individualism.

The breakdown of social solidarity does not mean that social integration evaporates, only that it changes. Integration is now based on common interests in the management of a particular risk, and on the risk logics of the institution charged with the task (Douglas 1986, 1990, 1992). It is also based on one's associated connections to the social circuitry of risk communication, connections that provide knowledge for security purposes.

Inequality

Not everyone has the same interest in and connections to a given area of risk. There is inequality with respect to risk. Class divisions exist in risk society, but they are fundamentally different from those of industrial society. However, the traditional question of class remains: how is a market economy made socially possible? Risk society answers this question by addressing a range of risks different from those addressed by industrial society, in addition to making changes in economic security provision. In risk society, the possibilities of a market economy depend on the probabilities of risk management that relate to territories, securities, careers, and identities.

The probabilities themselves make classes. In each area of risk they construct the other, the population that is to be determined, analysed, and regulated, and thereby brought into being as a social reality (Hacking 1990: 120). They constitute a 'risk position' as the class position for the particular risk. A given individual or organization is a member of many such populations and therefore has multiple risk positions. Moreover, an individual or organization has different class standings within each risk position held. Some risk positions are held only temporarily, in connection with specific threats and interests. Other risk positions are held over a longer term, for example in connection with insurance schemes that provide life-course security. There are also very long-lasting risk positions, for example those associated with age, race, ethnicity, gender, and chronic disabilities.

There is inequality with respect to risks as dangers. Some risks have a levelling and democratic quality because they affect everyone. Beck uses the term 'boomerang effect' to refer to the fact that those who, for example, own factories that pollute, may also suffer from pollution: 'Necessity is hierarchical, smog is democratic' (Beck 1992b: 204). Nevertheless, the wealthy can often buy some immunity from risks, whether by having their homes in safer neighbourhoods, escaping to second homes in more environmentally friendly areas, or purchasing healthier products. Even things that are promoted as being 'on average harmless' may, according to the law of averages, adversely affect those whose risk position is at the bottom of the hierarchy: 'A person who inquires about the average already excludes many socially unequal risk positions. But that is exactly what that person cannot know. Perhaps there are groups and living conditions for which the levels of lead and the like that are "on average harmless" constitute a *mortal danger*?' (Beck 1992a: 25).

The wealthy also benefit a great deal as risk takers. Despite talk about too much government regulation, they invite such regulation when it is to their benefit in risk taking. Those who pollute the environment are happy to receive government subsidies for new equipment or tax incentives for implementing higher safety standards (Pearce and Toombs 1990, 1991; Hawkins 1984, 1990, 1991). The U.S. Savings and Loan crisis made clear that financial institutions are happy to take risks with ordinary people's money when losses are covered by a government's deposit insurance scheme and its willingness to mortgage the future of the entire population. Furthermore, the same people and organizations that benefit from producing risks as dangers also benefit from marketing risk management technologies for dealing with the very same dangers they have produced. Risks as dangers create market opportunities for risk technologies, which are incorporated into the regulatory dance. There is structured inequality in this regard. As Perrow (1984: 311) observes, 'it is striking that those who feel we have abandoned risk in our search for security are speaking only of technological risks associated with large corporations and private profits, or aggressive military postures. The corporate and military risk-takers often turn out to be surprisingly risk averse ... when it comes to risky social experiments which might reduce poverty, dependency and crime.' Meanwhile, faced with dangers they themselves have contributed to, people in lower social risk positions perpetually reinterpret and redirect their fears by scapegoating and demonizing people in higher social risk positions (Christie 1986; Edelman 1988; Beck 1992b).

Inequalities also arise in various components of risk management. There is inequality in knowledge of risk and therefore in reflexive capacity to deal with insecurities. 'The reflexive conduct of life, the planning of one's own biography and social relations, gives rise to a new inequality, *the inequality of dealing with insecurity and reflexivity*' (Beck 1992a: 98). Risk knowledge is hierarchized in bureaucracies' abstract systems so that even those bureaucrats who front-load this knowledge do not know where it goes or how it is used in risk profiling. People depend on such expert systems, as well as on individual experts, to take the risk out of their risks, only to discover that they themselves have been 'taken' and exposed to further risks.

Risk management technologies institutionalize bias and selective discrimination. People are excluded from risk pools by statistical probabilities that often rely on poor or false indicators of offending behaviour (Reichman 1986). Unable to take into account context and circumstance, these technologies either misrepresent them or simply fill in the blind spots with local bureaucratic custom. Gandy (1993: 131) offers the example of a college graduate who responded to an advertisement inviting graduates to apply for a credit card, but was rejected because her area of study, English literature, disqualified her. For those who are accepted into the pool, risk technologies establish a standard of measurement that initially makes one equal to everyone else in the pool, but only as a stepping stone to creating distinctions and inequalities:

> This is, in fact, the only objectivity that it provides: the norm invites each one of us to imagine ourselves as different from the others, forcing the individual to turn back upon his or her own particular case, his or her individuality and incredible particularity ... the norm is most effective in its affirmation of differences, discrepancies, and disparities. The norm is not totalitarian but individualizing ... However, despite the strength of various individual claims, no one can escape the common standard. (Ewald 1991b: 154)

Risk technologies construct destinies in terms of competitive ability. People are neither expunged from risk society nor fully reintegrated into it, but only assigned to a category tied to their competitive capacity. Marginality is managed as much as centrality. Management occurs within a 'regime of downward mobility' (Gordon 1991: 44) that features vigilant recycling efforts to give marginality a function, even if it turns out to be an inferior one.

The inequalities of risk management can no more be eliminated than the inequalities of risks as dangers. That much is assured by risk discourse itself. Inequalities of risk can only be altered by new knowledge of what constitutes a risk and how it is to be managed. Indeed, such alteration is precisely what politics is about in risk society. 'Prejudiced and exclusionary behavior validates itself' (Douglas 1990: 15) in the politics of the classifying, stereotyping, and stigmatizing processes that alter the just distribution of risk. At the same time, it is the politics of 'How fair is safe enough?' (Short 1990: 186).

Morality, Responsibility, Accountability, and Rights

Some analysts argue that risk discourse expels morality. Giddens (1991: 445) asserts that there has been an 'evaporation of morality ... [in which] moral principles run counter to the concept of risk and to the mobilizing dynamics of control. Morality is *extrinsic* so far as the colonizing of the future is concerned.' While morality plays are still on offer in the mass media, even they become saturated with risk discourse (Stallings 1990; Coleman 1993). Within risk institutions, computer technology (Poster 1990), risk technology (Simon 1987), professional experts (Bauman 1992a), and legal regimes (Priest 1990) combine into complex systems of risk management that effect a decline in morality.

It is wrong to contend that morality is extrinsic to systems of risk management. Rather, moralities are built into the technologies and expert systems of risk management, and these moralities in turn foster a new range of demands for the improvement of democratic institutions and equality rights.

Morality is embedded in risk technologies and systems of risk management. When the science of probability analysis was first developed in the nineteenth century it was known as 'moral science,' and morality continues to be embedded in the classification schemes and risk assessment data used for probability calculations today. As Beck (1992a: 176) remarks, 'Statements on risk are the moral statements of a scientized society.' More precisely, what is constituted as the standard or norm by risk analysis bears both factual and moral imprints: 'The norm may be what is usual or typical, yet our most powerful ethical constraints are also called norms' (Hacking 1990: 104). People experience the facts of risk assessment as normative obligations and therefore as scripts for action.

Institutional classifications for risk management have evaluative rules embedded in them. Even in their binary fixed-choice extremes, these classifications produce moral meanings that in turn produce further classifications. Thus institutional classification schemes infuse regimes of moral truth and legitimacy into the facts they routinely produce. The body of facts surrounding a risk is a moral construction. As Gusfield (1981: 74) argues brilliantly in his analysis of public discourse on the risks of impaired driving, accidents are still seen to be caused by people who behave immorally:

> The discovery that alcohol is associated with an auto accident is turned into alcohol as *the* cause of the accident. The rapidity with which alcohol is perceived as villain exemplifies the moral character of factual construction. Without that moral direction the transformation of data into policy directives is difficult. Multicausality weakens the capacity and purposefulness which make control seem possible ... The story of the 'killer-drunk' is then a story that is deeply embedded in an individualistic world in which moral actions lead to safety and immoral actions threaten me and you and the actor himself.

In the context of practical institutional decisions about risk, morality is the rule. Gusfield (1981) shows, for example, how actual law enforcement decisions about impaired driving involve fine-grained moral evaluations of the drinking driver and the circumstances of his or her accident. Similarly, Hawkins (1984: 207) shows that decisions about pollution are not confined by the strict criteria of scientific testing and scientific standard setting: 'Pollution control is done in a moral, not a technological world.' Our point is that the moral and technological worlds constitute each other. The moral world is understood and acted on within the framework of the risk classification scheme of the technological system. This point is exemplified by the insurance industry's use of the term 'moral hazard' to describe a thing that is statistically out of line to the point where it is wrong and requires remedial and preventive attention.

The morality of risk society is thus thoroughly utilitarian. Efficiency in loss reduction is *the* moral imperative. Otherwise, absolute and fixed values and standards give way to unstable determinations of what is adequate and acceptable for practical purposes in particular circumstances. Values are not established a priori, but through endless comparisons in which a given standard 'is a form of compromise, the common denominator, a point of reference that is destined to disappear – a measurement that expresses the relation of a group to itself' (Ewald 1991b: 152).

The above-mentioned shifts in the morality of risk society are accompanied by the ascendancy of rights discourse. Economic rights (such as those relating to welfare and financial security), political rights (such as those relating to political accountability and participation in the exercise of political power), and civil rights (such as those relating to the rule of law and freedom of expression) are the key tools for articulating democratic moralities in risk society. They go hand in hand with the decentralization of politics into risk institutions, which promote a peculiar means of distributive justice. They are necessary for addressing the structure of exclusion that is built into the operations of risk institutions. At the same time, since these rights are presented politically and legally as universal moral values, they lead to contradictions when used to address specific conflicts among risk institutions. The fragmentation of risk management into strategies for the management of numerous special populations means that economic, political, and civil rights are only realized in sectorial, partial, and exclusive terms, prompting more rights discourse in a continuous feedback loop.

Rights discourse addresses the question of which institutional risk logics should apply when confronting a particular danger. It articulates the appropriate relations among risk institutions and how those relations should be regulated. Rights discourse is therefore central to the politics of difference that has arisen in risk society. The politics of difference questions, on moral grounds, whether people should be classified in particular ways and risk-profiled as members of particular populations. It also questions the relative harms that may ensue if people are or are not given particular security arrangements as members of those populations. It represents the ethics of probability in risk society, an ethics that is embedded in the legal rules of rights. The legal institution acquires a new political and ethical importance in legalizing risk, for it increasingly takes the distribution of risk out of the hands of the political institution and makes distribution a matter of right. Determinations of right within the legal institution serve to make organizations and individuals responsible for managing their own risks, and for their failure to do so.

Mary Douglas remarks that 'a culture is a system of persons holding one another mutually accountable' (Douglas 1990: 10). In Western cultures the 'system of persons,' as embodied in liberal forms of governance, is conceived in atomistic, individualistic, and libertarian terms. People are expected to contribute to the whole by being personally responsible for their part, including the risks they create for themselves and others. Individual competence is defined as self-sufficiency in this regard, and people are labelled culpable if they fail and thereby create risks. Indeed culpability is deemed essential for creating a sense of competence in self-governance. The individual as 'the reproduction unit of the social in the lifeworld' (Beck 1992a: 88; see also Giddens 1991: 5) is thereby made responsible for his or her own biography, his or her own life-course. The individual is to be socialized and educated – by family, school, and mass media – to become his or her own political economy. That is, the individual must create his or her own biography and then manage it competently in order to capitalize on life-chances.

Of course, more individual responsibility does not necessarily mean more autonomy. The individualism and individuality of social life in risk society are highly institutionalized by risk communication rules, formats, and technologies. With institutionalization comes standardization, the continual comparison of oneself to others in the hall of mirrors of institutional norms and the differences they reflect. Thus individual situations

> are no longer merely private situations, but also always institutional. They have the contradictory double face of institutionally dependent individual situations. The apparent outside of the institutions becomes the inside of the individual biography ... the liberated individual becomes dependent ... [as a result of the actions of] secondary agencies and institutions, which stamp the biography of an individual and make that person dependent upon fashions, social policy, economic cycles and markets, contrary to the image of individual control which establishes itself in consciousness ... Individualization thus means precisely institutionalization, institutional shaping and, hence the ability to structure biographies and life situations politically. (Beck 1992a: 130–2)

Beck's observations indicate that even though personal responsibility is fostered at the individual level, it is actually governed at the institutional level. At the latter level, and even more so when interinstitutional transactions are involved, personal responsibility and accountability again evaporate, and rights are given to the system to acquire the knowledge it needs for risk management. Within the system 'one can do something and continue doing it without having to take personal responsibility for it. It is as if one were acting while being personally absent. One acts physically, without acting morally or politically. The generalized other – the system – acts within and through oneself: this is the slave morality of civilization, in which people act personally and socially as if they were subject to a natural fate, the "law of gravitation" of the system' (Beck 1992a: 33).

Researching the Risk Society

Since all major institutions are organized around risk knowledge, it is possible to ground a study of risk society in any institution. The police, however, are an especially instructive vehicle for understanding risk society. The police intersect with all other major institutions, and their primary function is to communicate knowledge of risk to them. As such, the police are governed by the risk knowledge formats of those other institutions. The ways in which the police think and act illustrate how risk knowledge structures govern social life more generally.

In Foucauldian terms, ours is a study in genealogy, archaeology, and knowledge/power relations. With regard to genealogy, we wish to see how institutions visualize their activities by adopting rationalities of risk. We focus on 'how forms of rationality inscribe themselves in practices or systems of practices, and what role they play within them, because it's true that "practices" don't exist without a certain regime of rationality' (Foucault 1991b: 79). What is the 'regime of rationality' of risk institutions as understood by the police in their communications to and from those institutions? What does this regime tell us about how risk rationalities become institutionalized to the point of being the governing basis of social life?

With regard to archaeology, we examine the conditions under which risk discourse exists, the ways in which it is configured institutionally, and the practical fields in which it is deployed. As Beck (1992a: 23–4) observes, in risk society 'knowledge gains a new political significance. Accordingly the political potential of the risk society must be elaborated and analysed in a sociological theory of the origin and diffusion of knowledge about risks.' What is the knowledge of risk produced? Who is the audience? Why is it demanded? How does it move within and between institutions? Who moves it? How is it useful? What are its effects? As Foucault (1991a: 59–60) asks about discourse in general, 'What individuals, what groups or classes have access to a particular kind of discourse? How is the relationship institutionalized between the discourse, speeches and its destined audience? How is the relationship of the discourse to its author indicated and defined? How is the struggle for control of discourses conducted between classes, nations, linguistic, cultural or ethnic collectivities?'

With regard to knowledge/power, we seek an understanding of governance as the art and activity of risk management. This pursuit requires scrutiny of how governance is accomplished at the most everyday, routine, and mundane levels of risk knowledge production and communication. As Miller and Rose (1990: 8) argue,

> To understand modern forms of rule ... requires an investigation ... of apparently humble and mundane mechanisms which appear to make it possible to govern: techniques of notation, computation and calculation; procedures of examination and assessment; the invention of devices such as surveys and presentational forms such as tables; the standardization of systems for training and the inculcation of habits; the inauguration of professional specialism and vocabularies; building designs and architectural forms ... 'a microphysics of power,' an attention to the complex of relays and interdependencies which enable programmes of government to act upon and intervene upon those places, persons and populations which are their concern.

A 'microphysics of power' is necessary to build a macrosociology of risk society. It is the basis for linking the governmentality tradition of Foucault to the risk society theorizing of Beck, Giddens, Lash, and others.

So informed, we entered into the everyday, routine, and mundane world of policing the risk society by conducting field research in police jurisdictions across Canada. Our focus was the demands for risk knowledge external institutions place on the police, and how the police respond to those demands through communication rules, formats, and technologies. Both of this book's authors took part in the field research, to which ninety-two days were devoted in 1992 and 1993. Our methods included open-focus interviewing, direct observation, and document analysis.

We conducted 155 open-focus interviews with police employees selected on the basis of theoretical sampling. These employees represented a diversity of knowledge-work roles at various levels of police organization. A summary of the types of police employees interviewed is presented in table 6.1. We interviewed forty-nine operational police officers, including fourteen administrators (inspectors and higher-ranking officers), twelve supervisors (corporals, sergeants, and staff sergeants), and twenty-three constables. We also interviewed forty-eight police employees responsible for various information system and records functions, including employees whose work involved telecommunications, computer systems management, records management, forms production, forms management, and the security of all of the preceding. Another thirty-one interviews were conducted with employees

TABLE 6.1
Police employees interviewed

Employee Type	N	%
Operational		
Administrators	14	9.0
Supervisors	12	7.7
Constables	23	14.8
Subtotal	49	31.5
Information systems and records		
Systems administration	21	13.5
Records administration	13	8.4
Forms administration	9	5.8
Information security	5	3.2
Subtotal	48	30.9
Special surveillance units		
Organizational surveillance	15	9.7
Population surveillance	6	3.9
Territorial surveillance	3	1.9
Credential surveillance	3	1.9
Surveillance tactics	4	2.6
Subtotal	31	20.0
Planning, crime prevention, and crime analysis		
Planning	7	4.5
Crime prevention	4	2.6
Crime analysis	5	3.2
Subtotal	16	10.3
Rules systems		
Administrators and auditors	5	3.2
Subtotal	5	3.2
Consultants		
Consultants	6	3.9
Subtotal	6	3.9
Total	155	99.8

working in special surveillance units concerned with organizations (such as banks, insurance companies, automobile manufacturers, schools, and government regulatory agencies); populations of individuals (such as children, older youths, and racial and ethnic groups); territories (such as those relating to dangerous goods and the protection of special properties); credentials (such as security credentials for employees and for participants in special events); and surveillance tactics (such as electronic monitoring and surreptitious entry). We interviewed sixteen police employees involved in planning, crime prevention, and crime analysis. Interviews were also held with five employees who looked after the drafting of internal rule-books and audited their forces for compliance with the rules. Finally, we interviewed six people from nonpolice organizations who were employed regularly as consultants by the police, for example as police station architects and information systems specialists.

Our observations of police knowledge work occurred in various contexts. We spent 170 hours observing patrol work in the various divisions of several police organizations. Forty-six days were devoted to looking at other aspects of policework, during which we observed routines and forms of knowledge work and interviewed police employees as they worked. Our interviews also gave us additional access to police offices, which allowed us to add to our stock of observations.

During our interviews and fieldwork we were given copies of police forms and documents that have proved useful for our analysis. From some police organizations we acquired complete sets of forms. We also obtained superseded forms dating back several decades, instruction manuals for police officers on how to complete forms, administrative manuals dealing with form-related procedures and other operational procedures, internal reports on information systems and managerial activities, internal reports on the units we studied, and security advice pamphlets distributed to various institutions and publics.

We are now ready to proceed to our empirical study of policing the risk society. In Parts III and IV we examine how the police serve the knowledge needs of institutions concerned with risks to territories, securities, careers, and identities. In Part V we consider how the police perceive external institutions' demands for risk knowledge and how they respond to those demands by creating more-elaborate communication rules, formats, and technologies.

PART III

Risks to Territories

7

Tracing Territories

Tracing and Governance

A defining characteristic of the state is its claim to a monopoly on the legitimate use of force within its territory. Despite risk society's fragmented sources of institutional power, the state remains dominant in matters of internal territorial security and in the use of force required to sustain such security. Although some of the state's fiscal and knowledge-based forms of power are rivalled by globalizing institutions in the private sector, the state still claims territorial monopolies: 'All modern states have a more or less successful monopoly of control of the means of violence within their own territories. No matter how great their economic power, industrial corporations are not military organizations (as some of them were during the colonial period), and they cannot establish themselves as political/legal entities which rule a given territorial area' (Giddens 1990: 71).

The emphasis on knowledge production and distribution in risk society does not mean that the police have abandoned their traditional focus on the coercive policing of populations in legally-delineated territories. It does mean, however, that the ways in which that policing is conducted have changed. Policing today is not a matter of order maintenance, law enforcement, or social service as ends in themselves (Wilson 1968). Rather, coercive policing is underpinned by surveillance devices that facilitate the governance of territories and populations. When they are working properly – as most often they are – these surveillance devices create a situation in which the coercion is not manifest.

'The exercise of discipline presupposes a mechanism that coerces by means of observation' (Foucault 1977: 170). The built environment is constructed with opportunities for observation in mind. As Shearing and Stenning (1984) show in the case of Disney World, the categorization of populations, the precise tracking of movement through space, the pervasive use of surveillance devices, and reliance on aesthetically pleasing design combine to create coercion that is embedded, cooperative, and subtle, and thus not experienced as coercion at all. In the broader urban landscape, however, the subtlety and the aesthetic features give way to blatant efforts to demarcate policing zones. In extreme cases such as Los Angeles, 'obsession with physical security systems, and, collaterally, with the architectural policing of social boundaries, has become a zeitgeist of urban restructuring, a master narrative in the emerging built environment of the 1990s ... an unprecedented tendency to merge urban design, architecture and the police apparatus into a single, comprehensive security effort' (M. Davis 1990: 23).

Observation of the built environment rests on other forms of surveillance. The police have equipped themselves with sophisticated telecommunications systems, electronic surveillance devices, and risk profiling technologies to help regulate those who inhabit and pass through territories. These systems, devices, and technologies are evidence that monopolization of force and territorial regulation are achieved through bureaucratically organized surveillance (Giddens 1985; G. Marx 1988; Dandeker 1990).

The fact that surveillance and the coercive policing of territories are entwined is evident in the language of police officers. In the police cultures we observed, militaristic and coercive metaphors related to knowledge work were used continually. While in public culture many police-related 'metaphors are misleading because they suppress the essentially violent nature of policing' (Manning 1993: 17; see also Klockars 1988), in the occupational cultures in which the job of policing gets done coercive metaphors are part of the most routine aspects of knowledge work. Thus police officers referred to themselves as 'armed stenographers' for whom 'information is as much a weapon ... on the street as the .38 they carry on their hip.' Those working as knowledge brokers and system managers off the street commented, for instance, that 'This whole organization *marches* on information.' They also lauded new information technologies that '*disciplined*' officers 'into the flow of data,' and thereby made the officers and the data 'a little more *regimented*.' Some cases of police action against offenders were described as '*slapping* them with paper.'

In Part III we show that this coercive cultural language employed by the police in risk society connects with the knowledge work that the police perform. In the present chapter we examine how the police organize themselves to trace and map the territories and populations they govern in collaboration with other institutions. In chapter 8 we analyse the ways in which the police mobilize segmented territories and fragmented populations for governance. In chapter 9 we return to a consideration of community policing as the enactment of governance in risk society.

Policing is driven by demands for ever more perfect knowledge of the territories and populations policed. For this reason a substantial proportion of police resources is devoted to tracing territories and populations. By 'tracing' we mean 'to observe,' 'to investigate for signs and vestiges,' 'to discover.' Observation and investigation involve following, tracking, and marking the position of something as it moves from one point to another. The emphasis is on detail, looking for 'traces' or marks or vestiges that will provide a more accurate map of the territory and a more reasonable profile of the organizations and people who inhabit it. What is discovered is 'traced' – marked out, sketched, and delineated in a laborious manner – in order to represent the ground covered.

The police have developed sophisticated electronic media infrastructures, spatial arrangements, and inspection devices to maximize their tracing capacities. Although we examine each of these tracing technologies separately, it is important to keep in mind that they operate simultaneously in the actual practice of tracing.

Electronic Infrastructures

The modern police organization equips its members with electronic technologies for tracing risks that threaten territories. Police cars have become mobile offices and technological laboratories. They are 'wired' with voice radios, cellular telephones, computer-assisted dispatch terminals, laptop computers, radar, video cameras, remote microphones, breathalyser equipment, fax machines, printers, and vehicle locators.

Patrol cars are sometimes incapable of handling this technological congestion. In some cases the front passenger seat is removed and the officer is left with technological partners rather than a human partner. In other cases the shotgun or other weapon harnessed between the driver's seat and the front passenger seat is removed, an action that signifies a shift from symbols of force to symbols of knowledge as power. The wired nature of the police car is evident even when one looks at the vehicle's exterior, which, because a separate antenna is required for each electronic device, takes on the appearance of an 'antenna farm.' A somewhat exasperated police executive said, 'We are already stretching the limits of the power source for a standard car. General Motors is currently trying to figure out how to increase the power load available for police cars just to run all our equipment. We may end up towing a diesel generator around behind the car!'

In addition to what they manage to fit into their patrol cars, police officers have access to other electronically equipped vehicles for tracing purposes. We accompanied a patrol sergeant in his van to a town house complex where some people were believed to have an illegal handgun. The equipment check-list for this van included various tracing devices such as printed and computer-generated city maps, a map of the complex, binoculars, a telescope, a polaroid camera, and special tools for wire-tapping. Some of this equipment was used to monitor the suspects while a strategy for forcibly entering the premises was developed. Among other things, a powerful telescope was used to peer into the premises and a remote wire-tapping device was attached to telephone lines to monitor calls.

Larger mobile surveillance and command vehicles are also available to map territories and what happens within them. A police organization we studied received a gift of a large truck from a private company. The organization decided to equip the truck with sophisticated electronic surveillance equipment, including full telephone facilities, wire-tapping and video surveillance devices, and television monitors to keep abreast of news coverage of critical events the police were involved in.

Police managers are acutely aware that major events are subject to the gaze of the news media and that news formats often govern how those events are understood and responded to (Ericson, Baranek, and Chan 1989; Schlesinger and Tumber 1994). In consequence, they develop vehicles to trace how the news media trace events. One police organization had a large mobile home dedicated to the 'accommodation' of the news media at major events. As we toured this vehicle our police host commented that it was 'a place for them to get out of the cold. We find it better to accommodate them, to keep them informed about what is going on rather than having them cross over lines and try to find out for themselves. You find the odd one is not cooperative but generally they are OK.'

There are still other territory-mapping technologies that the police use to trace territorial populations and the risks those people pose and confront. Precinct and detachment profiles are developed to provide an overview of the territories and populations policed. One police organization had a five-page form for establishing precinct profiles, which required a description of the precinct's boundaries, roadways (length in kilometres), population characteristics (such as age structure and ethnic composition), and special problems. It also asked for information on police strategies for monitoring and dealing with problems in the precinct.

Many police organizations in Canada are buying computerized mapping systems (Gandy 1993: 88) that rely on American military technology adopted by the Canadian Department of National Defence. These systems allow territories to be broken down into ever smaller units, the smallest unit being only one square metre in size! Equipped with this technology, the patrol officer can obtain detailed knowledge of officially recorded crimes and other problems that have occurred in narrowly defined zones within a patrol area – blocks, buildings, and even parts of buildings. One system we examined identified population characteristics such as race. The police official who demonstrated this technology to us said, 'You can see where this would be a big help to the community police officer. He can come back to the station and search his specific area for crimes that have been occurring. He could get a geographic feel for the location of prostitution or sexual assault cases for a specific period if he wanted them.' When asked whether he saw difficulties arising from the fact that the system recorded only crimes officially known to the police, he replied, 'That is what is real for us. We can only deal with what is real not with crimes that we only think are occurring.'

Crime itself is defined by the police with reference to territories and the problems people create in such territories. For example, as part of a change to a new voice-entry system for reporting occurrences, a police organization revamped its entire reporting format and classification system. New classifications were developed for crime 'hot spots' (see Sherman 1992) such as residences where 'domestics' occurred and places in the public transit system where youths congregated and created trouble.

As we have noted, video surveillance devices are also used to trace risks to territories. The video production unit in one police organization was officially described as being 'equipped with a broadcast-quality camera and full editing facilities.' Such units produce public relations and police training videos, monitor major events such as demonstrations, and conduct surveillance of places and people.

Some police organizations have also placed video cameras in their patrol vehicles. During our fieldwork in one jurisdiction we witnessed the introduction of video cameras into patrol vehicles. The patrol officers we studied believed that the video cameras would serve many purposes. One interviewee remarked that these devices would be useful for 'Anything that your imagination could come up with.'

There was a firm belief in this jurisdiction that the video cameras would provide more-certain evidence. They would show a violator that the police 'had him' and thereby facilitate confessions and guilty pleas. As one officer said, 'If they have something to query, they cannot query it if it's involved with a taping. It's right there. There are no ands, ifs, or buts about it. It's cut and dried.'

Video cameras were also seen as useful for surveillance of suspects. They were used with radar to detect speeding vehicles, for the video image itself was able to display the speed of the target vehicle. They were also used to conduct surveillance outside a notorious club. People entering and leaving the club were filmed, and their licence plates and the criminal records of the vehicles' owners were checked on the police car's computer system. Video cameras were also believed to be helpful in identifying people involved in major disturbances such as riots, picket line confrontations, political demonstrations, bar fights, and noisy parties (see Doyle and Ericson 1995).

Another function of video cameras was as investigative tools for accident reconstruction. One officer imagined that in the long term videotaping might be one way to reduce the paper burden associated with major accident investigations: 'There is no amount of paper that you could shove into a court that would give you that great a view of "Here's where she died, here is where he came across." And you could still-frame those things and enlarge them up.'

Police video cameras come with an audio intrusion capacity. An officer can wear a transmitter on his or her belt and have any conversations relayed to his or her partner in the police vehicle some distance away. This capacity was seen by officers as especially useful for handling the always troublesome domestic disputes:

> One guy's got a mike and the other guys can sit out in the car and listen. If things are getting out of hand they can go in; if they are not getting out of hand they can just sort of back off. Another thing is that you've got the 'record' on in the car and if the old guy is on the couch here and he yells, 'As soon as they leave, you slut, I'm going to beat your head in' – too bad, he's history. So then

you can take him out and there's your evidence. It's all on tape. Actually, you could use it in a million different ways.

Video cameras in patrol vehicles offer opportunities for the police to produce training material that depicts actual instances of good and bad policing. Film from the same source can also provide exceptional visuals for televised police reality programs (Doyle 1996).

Like other police technologies (see chap. 16), video cameras are potentially able to trace police officer activity. However, we found that there were a number of ways in which this capacity was circumvented. For example, officers might position the camera in a way that would produce a recording fashioned to induce the viewer to empathize with the officers rather than the suspect (cf. Holloran, Elliott, and Murdock 1970; Tumber 1982; Ericson, Baranek, and Chan 1989). As one officer declared, 'I'm not a great lover of Rodney King or anything, but it will be nice to have the camera show our side of things for a change.'

The patrol officers maintain technical control over every aspect of taping. They can turn the tape recorder and microphone on and off as they choose. The tape recorder is kept in the trunk and the only key is fastened to the car's key-chain. Although tampering can be detected, officers can simply remove a troublesome tape, reinsert it, and six hours later the entire tape has been erased.

During our fieldwork a supervisor expressed a concern that the video system he was about to have installed would display the speed of the police vehicle as well as the speed of the vehicle being pursued. He worried that police vehicles would regularly be shown to be travelling at excessive speeds, even during routine patrols. For example, a police vehicle on radar patrol might be moving at 125 km/hr in a 100 km/hr zone, and the video system would register its excessive speed at the same instant that the patrol officer was 'catching' another speeding vehicle. The officer would thus be shown to be enforcing a law that he himself was breaking. The installer agreed to remove the speed display for the police vehicle, so that only the speed of the oncoming vehicle would be registered.

Still photography is also used regularly for surveillance. Polaroid cameras are employed to record suspects *in situ*. One police organization had a 'Noisy Party Reference Report' that called for each apprehended culprit to be photographed at the scene standing alongside the arresting officer. Next to the photograph were to be recorded the details of the place of arrest and the person arrested. Below the photograph was a space for a detailed description of the charges (if any) and the circumstances of arrest.

The same police organization took polaroids of all known prostitutes in order to make a record of the locations in which they worked. Notorious hotels frequented by drug dealers and fences as well as prostitutes were also sites for taking polaroids of anyone who regularly used the premises.

In visually recording risk in these ways, the police use the same technologies as the news media, and therefore can selectively supply the news media with material that the latter see as helpful (Altheide 1993). By the same token, the media sometimes produce material that helps the police find what they are after (Doyle and Ericson 1995). The 'simulations' (Baudrillard 1983) involved here are at times complex. During one of our ride-alongs a message appeared on the officer's computer screen warning that the robbery squad was filming a training video at a certain location, and that the staged robbery would include gunshots and other realistic features. This prompted the officer to recall a case in which one of his colleagues had noticed that a disqualified driver was in a television commercial driving a car. The officer proceeded to charge this person with driving while disqualified, which in turn was deemed newsworthy and resulted in further television coverage!

The police are also connected to a variety of electronic infrastructures that give them instant knowledge of people and places. Computer terminals in police vehicles provide immediate access to the Canadian Police Information Centre (CPIC) system, which maintains data on criminal records, outstanding warrants, and so forth. During their 'down time,' when they are not filling out reports, patrol officers conduct random checks on vehicles and people with the aid of the computer. We found that up to 15 per cent of shift time was spent on random checks of vehicles on the road or in parking lots. A licence plate check supplies the identity of the vehicle owner, and a check of the owner reveals whether he or she has a criminal record or is wanted on an outstanding warrant, either of which prompt further investigation. The only limits on such checks are the officer's time and keyboarding speed. The experience of using this technology was described by one of our interviewees, who had only recently received a computer terminal for his car:

> It's right there beside you, and it takes two seconds to type a name and a date of birth and you can query anybody. Plus if you query somebody and get a hit on

them you can send a message anywhere in Canada to any other CPIC terminal. You can ask if this is the person, if they want him or whatever the story is ... You can go along and query plates as you drive around. You are constantly checking anything suspicious. Vehicles. People. If you stop somebody you can query them right on site. I have a tendency to drive down the street and query anybody. Just query vehicles as they go along ... I do more haphazard queries now, because I could be driving down the road and could see a car that I just basically want to find out about them. Maybe I want to know who it is, who the car is. Maybe it's not doing anything at all, just driving down the road.

The computer terminal also provides links to data systems developed by other institutions. In many police jurisdictions there is a link to the provincial motor vehicle agency database, which provides information on driver's-licence status, vehicle registration, and vehicle safety inspections. There are also often links to municipal utility billing systems, which offer a convenient way to trace a person's address, telephone number, and credit history. These connections are facilitated in many jurisdictions by direct links between the patrol vehicle and police computers, but where such a system is not in place the telephone provides the necessary link. One officer remarked, 'We all retain certain contacts with different agencies. My pet people, my favourite one is the [provincial] power security because everyone has power. If I come across a house and want to know who lives in a certain place I call them up and talk to a guy in security. He'll go to his computer and I'll give him an address and he'll tell me who lives there.'

The police also maintain specialized databases on particular types of risks to territories. For example, the Canadian Bomb Data Centre collects reports on all bomb-related incidents in the country, which are categorized by target, official response, and the characteristics of the people who make the bomb threats. Callers are profiled according to such subtleties as accent, voice, speech patterns, diction, and manner, the goal being, in the words of one interviewee, 'tracking a serial bomber ... [and tying] these incidents all back together in a forensic pattern.'

Police electronic infrastructures are also designed to intrude on private spaces. Police organizations retain specialists in what is variously called 'technical intrusion,' 'technical services,' and 'security engineering.' These specialists enter private locations to install surveillance equipment and conduct investigations. In one police organization the mandate of the Technical Services Unit was officially described as the provision of 'specialized electronic surveillance expertise to all areas of the [organization].' The Unit was required to 'administer and control Part VI of the Criminal Code [Invasion of Privacy] as well as fulfil all reporting requirements as requested by the Attorney General and Solicitor General ... [and] through research and projective budgets, maintain a modern and technically advanced electronic surveillance capability.' Another organization had over forty employees in its unit, most of whom were technicians trained in community colleges and university-educated engineers. A member of this unit said one of its major purposes was to 'bug telephone lines, put room audio in, video surveillance, tracking, all that.'

In another unit we studied, the employees specialized in what was termed 'offensive assistance,' in other words, to invade private locations for the purpose of investigative tracing. A subgroup was dedicated to 'skilled forced entry,' such as how to 'circumvent a lock to get into a place so that the appropriate listening device could be installed.' A member of this subgroup told us how it had a research and development program for improving the technical expertise needed to ensure that entry could be effected as unobtrusively as possible, even in the face of resistance:

A: [We engage] in various types of research such as looking at skilled forced entry. Considering the times we live in, there are occasions when it is necessary to have a quick means to gain access where you might be looking at a barricaded door, that type of thing, and so they're involved in that type of research ... how to go through a barricaded door ... outside of taking a front-end loader and driving through the side of the wall, which isn't very practical, it's been difficult.

Q: Doesn't look good on television.

A: No. You're absolutely right. So one of the things that they look into is various methods without the use of explosives which obviously isn't the way to go. I mean, you risk the injury to not only your police officers but also your people inside. So they look at various engineering issues like that.

Members of this unit were required to file a report on each incident of technical intrusion. The form was designed very much like a burglary report, except that it was the police who were breaking and entering. The officer would be asked to indicate, among other things, how he or she had effected entry, whether there had been an alarm system, whether there had been any locks or safety devices, and the 'type of attack,' to be described by the following fixed-choice responses:

'punch, pry, peel, chop, grind, drill, torch, thermal lance, explosives, clandestine.'

Such units try to centralize their electronic intrusion capabilities and the expertise in forced entry needed for their work. Their existence is based on an assumption that the average officer lacks the expertise needed to effect subtle forced entries and install electronic tracing devices. Nevertheless, officers outside these units do on occasion employ their own surveillance devices. A patrol officer informed us that he had been conducting surveillance of suspects whom he believed to be hiding two separate stashes of stolen goods. Since he could only observe one stash area at a time, he borrowed a friend's electronic baby-monitor to cover the other area. This device alerted him to the suspects' presence at the second stash, and he moved in to arrest them.

The expertise developed by these units is also used for 'counter-technical intrusion,' that is, protection against the electronic intrusions of others. One of our subjects described this specialization as 'methods and means of defeating and bypassing certain [electronic] systems.' She said much of the expertise is attained by attending scenes where 'electronic security systems have been bypassed or defeated in some method to commit a criminal act.' In addition to improving the compromised security system, the knowledge derived from such investigations is used to defeat efforts by others to electronically intrude on people and spaces under police protection.

Police organizations are charged with the responsibility of protecting secret or confidential knowledge held by various clients, especially members of municipal, provincial, or federal governments of which the police are a part. Therefore, technical intrusion and security engineering knowledge is used in patrolling access to spaces where confidential discussions occur. The task of experts in this area is revealed by an interviewee who talked about maintaining 'line security': 'With line security ... we get into data encryption. Encrypt the data so that I can't break into that line, decode that signal this computer is receiving here to say everything is OK and then black-box it ... [this is similar to the way in which] ADT [a private security company] will sell you a double-A line for a bank which means it is encrypted and it does certain handshakings through the day and checks to make sure everything is OK.'

Of course not everything is so high tech. At the low tech end, police knowledge security units take an interest in rating shredders, document containers, and other devices that help to keep knowledge confidential. A security engineering specialist in one police organization described her testing of shredders for government 'in terms of the dimensions of the cut and various other physical requirements.' She also described a rating system for document containers: documents with lower risk potential if lost or stolen were placed in less secure boxes:

Probably more than occasionally there's been a tendency to err on the side of extreme caution when dealing with documents. For example, you might classify something at very high level when really all it talks about is something that wouldn't be harmful in the public interest or the national interest or wouldn't compromise anything. And so all that has an effect on your security containers because if you classify something very high then, of course, you need a container that will withstand the attacks and that kind of stuff. So now there's quite a reviewing of security requirements ... if you have a container that only requires a minute of protection, it's a lot cheaper to build than one that requires twenty minutes.

Spatial Arrangements

The police, as was mentioned earlier in this chapter, also trace territories by establishing spatial arrangements and processes for the exclusion of undesirable populations. In public territories they work with business and residential groups to discourage selected populations from using particular spaces. This 'architectural policing' is designed to constitute a more homogeneous population for a space, by constructing 'architectural and semiotic barriers to filter out undesirables' (M. Davis 1990: 257; see also Bauman 1992a). The deselected undesirables are those who have already been panoptically sorted and excluded from many other spaces. This spatial exclusion combines with the exclusionary effects of electronic risk technologies to institutionalize their personal failure (Gandy 1993: 228).

Armed with an official report that claimed 'the high visibility of the homeless and the "perceived threat" associated with them seriously affects the public perception of safety downtown,' police environmental design specialists in one of the jurisdictions studied by us transformed a downtown outdoor mall that was a gathering place for undesirable youths and homeless people. Aesthetically pleasing benches, trees, planters, and the like were removed to make the space less comfortable. As an additional deterrent, the public mall area was converted into a road for vehicular traffic from 6 p.m. to 6 a.m. According to one of the environmental design specialists we interviewed, the goal was to remove 'A lot of the desirable elements that might legitimize loitering.' The loiterers were indeed displaced to another area, but the same problems arose there. 'Improvements' were therefore made in the newly threatened area as well. For example, as a condition of obtaining renovation permits, businesses were required to provide high-intensity lighting for the public spaces outside their premises.

As M. Davis (1990: chap. 4) observes, 'bum-proofing' devices can be very inventive and elaborate. One architectural policing specialist discussed the possibility of importing American-designed telephone booths built with a slanting floor to discourage people from lingering too long on the telephone. An interviewee in another jurisdiction criticized the poor security design of commuter-train stations in the following way: '[The stations] have become the second hangout of the 7-Eleven crowd. The shitbags just take a tour of the city at will and commit crimes here and there ... [Now] you go down there at any given time and they play classical music. Drives you nuts. Of course, the kids won't hang around ... the boom boxes won't overpower it and it just drives them crazy ... it was copied from some other place.'

The police provide spatial design and protection services for a number of clients. For example, they work closely with liquor licence authorities to regulate the spatial arrangements, crowd capacity, and clientele of troublesome bars. Schools are similarly managed in cooperation with school officials. In some jurisdictions there are police officers who work full-time in schools to exclude trespassers, organize School Watch programs, and oversee video surveillance of classrooms (see chap. 12). Organizations designated by governments as 'vital facilities' are subject to a police 'vital points' risk scoring system. Those with high scores are given thorough advice on security engineering and design.

The security relationships between the police and organizations within the government sphere are especially highly institutionalized. Whether the relationship is between a municipal police force and local schools, a provincial police force and a provincial legislature, or a federal police force and federal ministries, the result is that the police operate like a private security organization. The Royal Canadian Mounted Police in particular functions as a general security agency. An example of this is the force's work at airports on behalf of Transport Canada. Almost eight hundred RCMP officers were assigned to Canadian airports in the early 1990s. Their responsibilities included mapping spatial arrangements for airport security and monitoring all private security personnel and airline workers involved in the pre-boarding screening of passengers. Daily reports on this activity, and on the passenger populations under surveillance, were forwarded to Transport Canada. If any ordinary Criminal Code matter arose, it was not dealt with by airport RCMP officers but instead turned over to the local municipal police. Certain RCMP officers were also responsible for forwarding information on territorial security risks to Transport Canada's own security officers. In its relationship with Transport Canada, the RCMP devoted a substantial proportion of its budget to providing full-time inspection of spatial security arrangements in a narrowly defined territory.

Inspection Devices

The RCMP has always acted as a government inspectorate. This role was necessary in the past because its officers were dispersed into remote territories where there were usually no other government officials. The RCMP's involvement in the federal government's regulation of such things as immigration and customs also contributed to its work as an inspectorate. Many of its early inspection functions remain in place today; the force, for instance, continues to inspect storage facilities for explosives on behalf of the Ministry of Energy, Mines, and Resources. It has also acquired new inspection functions, such as those relating to airport security, that arise out of government ownership of special properties.

Inspection functions are also at the centre of routine public policing. As we saw in chapter 2, the police have become regulators and compliance-based law enforcers far more than deterrence-based criminal law enforcers. Their primary role in this regard is tracing people in order to slot them into their proper place.

The 'contact card' is the most pervasive device for police inspection of a population. It is used to report police observations of people suspected of being out of place or associating with undesirables. Patrol officers are required to satisfy quotas for the submission of contact cards. The cards are sent to analysts who computerize the data and prepare and distribute profiles of suspect populations and their proper places. As described by one such analyst, contact cards 'are a great source of information. They tell me all about who has been hanging around. You see, the officers don't fill these things out unless they feel that someone has been up to no good. They may not have the exact proof but they know the guy is up to no good.'

Contact card reports often result from random checks. During one of our ride-alongs, an officer stopped a vehicle driven by someone he knew to have a criminal record. He charged the driver with failure to produce a valid driver's licence and issued him a demand notice requiring him to produce evidence of auto insurance. The officer also submitted a contact card indicating the association between the driver and his passenger, justifying this action to the researcher by saying that 'this [neighbourhood] is a problem area. There are a lot of banks in this area and these two are not above robbing one. They weren't doing it this time, but who knows in the future?'

Contact cards are usually produced on an even more random basis. An officer in another jurisdiction said that 'In the summertime we [routinely] check hitchhikers. You never know who or what you are going to find there. *It's always right to know.* It places people in the right place at the wrong time, somehow. You don't necessarily know that at the time but you might come back two weeks later.'

Computer terminals in police vehicles permit the electronic entry of street-check information. This technological innovation has, along with increased quota expectations, encouraged greater numbers of random checks. At least in the eyes of police officers who have computer terminals, it has created the potential for more pervasive and systematic inspection of populations that appear out of place. As one patrol officer said,

> You can program into this machine a street check ... Whereas before I wouldn't have bothered filling out a form ... because they were time consuming, a pain in the ass and nobody ever bothered to do anything with them ... What we are doing is a proactive patrol ... go out in residential areas ... and just write down anything suspicious. Vehicles, young fellow walking down the road at two o'clock in the morning. But it is relatively a lot simpler to do a street check ... It will increase our street checks something like 700 per cent ... [Previously] there was no way we could keep track of who was on the go. Now you do your street checks, stop a specific car in a neighbourhood at four o'clock in the morning and someone may find out that that night there was a specific break [burglary] or car broken into. You can go back and check this person and maybe they are responsible. The more people you know who are moving or who are on the go then the more people you are keeping track of ... We do the subdivision areas late at night and just kind of sneak around and park on the side of the road to see who is moving and do spot checks [on] who is driving or walking. Maybe we get to know who is roaming around at night-time [*sic*],

maybe looking to break into cars or break into vacant homes ... It's generated because we want to be able to identify potential criminals and what kind of patterns they might have. Because you can call up street checks for the month of February and they will give you all the street checks for February, who was checked where and when.

Another contact card system provides a means of tracing populations that reside in targeted residential areas. Inquiry forms are used to record systematic data on householders interviewed in connection with a crime or other risk in the area. In one police jurisdiction, the attending officer was required to complete a form for each person in the household aged fourteen or older, which had spaces for, among other things, name, marital status, vehicle ownership, occupation and employer, name and address of ex-spouse, and number of persons living in adjacent houses (adult males, adult females, and children). The form included an admonition to the officer to 'Be alert for spontaneous response.' In light of the typical clearance rate of 3 per cent in residential burglaries, police officers viewed this brand of police census taking as a tracking device for possible future use, rather than as a means of solving the crime that initiated the inquiry. As one interviewee remarked, 'You have to check with neighbours on the left side and on the right and across the street. To some people that seems like a pain in the ass and you are not going to find anything, but we have found very often that you may be looking for the guy who is across the street down the road. And all of a sudden you have that in your computer.'

Similar census taking is conducted even without the stimulus of a particular incident or problem. One of the police departments we studied had 'liaison contact record' forms for apartment buildings and businesses. Constituting populations of organizations as well as of those who managed them, these forms were intended to provide detailed knowledge of territorial units. The form for apartment buildings included, for example, questions on the number of suites and on the building owner, manager, and caretaker. The form for businesses included questions on the type of business, the nature of the property, and security arrangements. Both forms provided a space for comments on attitudes toward the community among the owners and senior staff listed.

Inner-city 'deviant ghettos' (Scull 1984) are also subject to inspection and census taking. The downtown division of a police organization we studied had four special-information rooms related to populations and spaces in the immediate area.

In the first room was a large wall-map of the division, with recent criminal incidents identified and colour-coded. Other items included a clipboard of reports on recent incidents; several books prepared by the division to facilitate various aspects of its work, such as one containing profiles of 'habitual' young offenders; a bulletin-board to which were affixed photographs and descriptions of the same young offenders; and an American poster listing 'the 10 most wanted Asian criminals.'

In the second room were computer terminals, which gave the officers access to personal information on suspects beyond what was available from CPIC.

The third room held additional internally produced books, including a scrapbook containing information on recent incidents and troublesome people, such as an account of an incident of the previous day in which a female known prostitute had 'rolled' a drunken British soldier and stolen $270 from him. However, because the soldier was about to be transferred to Germany, the police made no effort to charge her, despite the fact that she was known to be the thief. The account concluded by saying that this woman was obviously shrewd in choosing her victims and therefore she should be watched closely.

The fourth room was devoted exclusively to information on a notorious hotel. An entire wall contained photographs and descriptions of the hotel's regular patrons, mainly prostitutes, pimps, and drug dealers. High up on the wall were copies of orders banning people from the hotel, as well as photographs and descriptions of those banned. There were also large books containing polaroids of prostitutes working in and around the hotel.

We visited the hotel during a ride-along. On this occasion the officers noticed someone new occupying the traditional drug dealer's chair near the rear entrance of the hotel bar. After learning this person's name from the proprietor, they discovered through a CPIC check that he had an extensive criminal record. The next step was to write up a contact card noting his newly acquired position in the hotel's social ecology.

Such approaches to inspection and census taking reflect the risk management orientation that governs the policing of territories. The goal of the police is to regulate risks to territories and their populations in a compliance-based law enforcement mode, rather than by cracking down on troublesome or illegal behaviour. Benson (1993: 87–8) offers a similar ethnographic example of how the police tolerate and manage some risky populations:

> The new management in the club wanted to change the type of customer the club serviced and decided to take the club 'up-market.' In order to do so it was felt necessary to remove permanently the drug users from the club ... [but] the drug squad had talked to the club owner with a view to maintaining the status quo. The club was useful to the squad as a place where they could see what drugs were around, which persons where involved, who was spending money, who was 'new' to the area, and the like. Such information was necessary for the practical purposes of controlling local drug use and for gaining access to drug suppliers rather than drug users.

Risk management also guides the policing of prostitutes and their territories. As we saw a moment ago in connection with the notorious hotel, the police in that jurisdiction devoted much effort to learning about prostitutes and their 'strolls.' Indeed, those police had a special contact card dedicated to prostitution and related trades, which recorded whether the subject was a prostitute, exotic dancer, pimp, or escort; his or her name, social insurance number, and police polaroid number; and the telephone number of his or her next of kin or closest friend. Photographs were required because, as one officer said, the police wanted to 'know who's who and which pimp is dealing with which ... they can say no [to being photographed] [but] they never do, probably because they don't know they can say no.'

Our ride-alongs in this jurisdiction revealed that the patrol officers had a detailed knowledge of the spaces where prostitutes worked. During one evening ride-along an officer we were with drove behind an abandoned warehouse, where he correctly predicted he would find a prostitute with her customer. After questioning the two individuals, computer checks were run on both. The prostitute supplied details of her criminal record and that of her pimp, which proved very accurate when checked against the data on the computer system. She explained that she usually worked another 'track' that supplied a higher-class clientele, but that she was under a probation order banning her from working the streets in that area. She also said that the customer had only hired her for a 'blow-job,' and that she would have preferred taking him to a private room, but he refused. The officer asked her to take her business somewhere else, explaining that the seniors who lived in the area became upset during their evening constitutionals at the sight of prostitutes plying their trade.

Prostitutes working in less public settings were traced in other ways. For example, all escort services in the city were licensed. The licences were processed by the police unit responsible for all municipal licences, but the vice squad carried out additional checks on the escort services and their clientele.

These forms of tracing prostitutes represent the technological advancement of a long-standing desire for regulation through knowledge. Moral science has always been interested in 'The prostitute and the statesman ... the *them* that is watched and the *we* who engage in the necessary surveillance' (Hacking 1990: 120). As one delegate said at an international congress on statistics held in 1867, 'It is evident that the statistics of this class [prostitutes], if followed and made precise according to age, family condition, and movement, will be found very useful to the statesman in determining the first motives for bad morals, the lifestyle, the probability of culpability, and the organization of surveillance' (ibid.).

The police must also inspect people and things that pass fleetingly through their territories. Chief among their tasks in this regard is the tracing of vehicles and their owners and operators. The police perform a great number of vehicle inspection functions. For example, they run contact card tracing systems on drivers and vehicles as a part of random stop-and-search programs. These include 'check-stop' inspections for impaired driving and safety infractions, which also allow them to run computerized checks to look for outstanding warrants and other matters. These programs are largely compliance oriented, but backed up by threats. For example, one police organization we studied issued a warning notice regarding vehicle safety deficiencies which contained the following statement: 'This notice is issued with no monetary penalty and relies on your voluntary compliance. Failure to comply with the requirements stated on this document will result in prosecution ... for the above-indicated infraction(s).'

In addition to routine patrols, the tracing of vehicles is carried out through aerial surveillance and the use of photo-radar devices. The latter are able to produce data on traffic flows and trends for use by provincial motor vehicle and transportation agencies. The police also provide traffic analysis reports based on systematic observation, as well as highly detailed traffic-accident reports (see chap. 10). A government transportation analyst we interviewed told us 'A road safety problem doesn't exist unless you have [police] data on it ... If you want to do anything from a regulatory perspective you've got to have data to back you up.'

For an example of how the police conduct vehicular tracing and regulation we can look at the operations of the 'Truck Unit' in one of the municipal police departments we studied. This unit, which comprised five officers at the time, is responsible for all aspects of tracing and regulating commercial vehicles. The concentration of expert knowledge in a separate unit was deemed necessary by the department because of the high degree of specialized knowledge required for carrying out inspections and because of the complexity of the applicable regulatory laws.

Truck unit officers must be certified by the Commercial Vehicle Safety Alliance (CVSA), an association that encompasses Canada, the United States, and Mexico. Certification follows a two-week course. Members of the Truck Unit must also be fully trained truck drivers and pass a two-week hazardous materials course offered by the local fire department. Their main task is to conduct random check-stops on commercial vehicles in accordance with a CVSA inspection form used throughout North America. The form is based on standards set by government and industry, not by police agencies. The data from these inspections are sent to the provincial government and then to the CVSA. If a vehicle passes its inspection it is given a sticker of approval. If minor repairs are required a fourteen-day notice of correction is issued; if major repairs are required the vehicle is towed.

The Truck Unit is entangled in a network of relationships with many other government and private sector institutions. It cooperates, for instance, with the provincial motor transport services agency that does CVSA inspections in areas outside the municipal boundaries policed by the Truck Unit. This cooperation includes using each other's equipment and the carrying out of joint inspections. The Truck Unit is also a member of a multi-agency committee responsible for determining truck routes for the transportation of dangerous goods. As a unit member said in an interview, 'We don't want dangerous goods going by hospitals, senior citizens' places, anywhere there's lots of people.' Another involvement of the Unit is with municipal government committees concerned with offensive industrial odours and the management of hazardous spills. Unit members work with the city's inspectors of dangerous goods and with the fire department's specialists in hazardous materials. They sit on the safety committee of the provincial truckers' association, which entails monthly meetings with safety supervisors from all of the major carriers to discuss new safety equipment, road and bridge restrictions, consistency in compliance-based law enforcement, and 'grey areas.' Unit members also judge trucking-industry driving competitions.

The mass media also have an important relationship with the Truck

Unit. The mass media are regularly used to announce changes in routes and regulations and to publicize the need for community sensitivity to traffic problems. A unit member said the mass media are turned to 'Instead of trying to sneak around and catch people and trick people,' and for communicating the message that 'This is what we want, this is what we're looking for.' He gave the example of a media blitz following repeated complaints from motorists – and from their insurance companies – about cracked windshields caused by debris falling off trucks. As part of the subsequent 'Operation Cleansweep' local television stations showed unit members handing out brooms and information stickers to truckers. The stations also carried the message that the applicable fines were being increased from $60 to $200.

The above examples indicate that the Truck Unit operates within a compliance-based mode of law enforcement. Improved cooperation and better standards are the measures of success, whereas the issuance of a summons is a sign of failure. A unit member described the work in this way:

> More often than not, there's federal and provincial and city acts that govern the same occurrence, so you sort of have to pick out. That's got to be tough on the truckers ... It's sometimes confusing for us and it's got to be terribly confusing for them ... More than anything, they want to know what we're looking for. We strongly stress cooperation. It's the easiest thing in the world to go write a summons. Anybody can do that. But if you make people comply by other means, you know, follow the rules and regulations, then that's what we're looking for ... There's no real pressure on this unit to produce X number of summonses ... More than anything, it's encouraged that we go around and talk to these groups.

While most of the work takes the form of proactive inspection, the unit also reacts to complaints that come in from individuals and institutions, as in the cracked windshield cases. In one instance the routing of trucks through a new subdivision resulted in noise complaints, which were dealt with by the unit holding meetings that brought the residents and the truckers' association together, and resulted in a new weight limit for trucks and a new routing by-law. Reactive policing also occurs when truckers inform on their employers, such as when they are given the option of either driving an unsafe vehicle or losing their job. Such drivers sometimes collaborate with the police in a ritual of capture and law enforcement that is directed at building a case against the employer. Competitors in the industry also inform on each other.

The typical enforcement response is to begin with a warning issued to the problem company. If this proves unsuccessful, a Truck Unit member visits the company and offers his expert advice on how to meet standards. Only when there is a failure in the negotiations at this stage does stricter enforcement ensue. A unit member told us that at that point '[we] sit and wait for them and we'll just hound them until they comply. And it starts costing a lot of money.' A recent violation involving an overweight truck had resulted in an $8,700 fine, and as he said, 'Something like that goes through the whole industry, and then you see more of these outfits are phoning us for permits from the city for overloads, for bridges.' He also noted that persistent failure to comply can mean the end of a business because it will lose its licence to operate. In the end 'they have no choice, they have to comply.'

The Truck Unit is an example of how the police engage in environmental regulation. In some cases, such as the regulation of environmental hazards caused by vehicles, the police are involved directly in regulation. Shadgett's (1990: 14) observational study of patrol policing in Ontario reports that officers are given a one-day course on 'the enforcement of the *Environmental Protection Act*. [An] officer stated that during the course he was required to observe plumes of black smoke emitting from a smoke stack designed to produce exhaust emissions similar to those from motor vehicles. He was then to decide if the smoke was black enough to warrant a charge under the above-mentioned act for the offence of "unreasonable smoke." The certificate he received enabled him to give evidence in court regarding the offence.'

More often, the police work with other compliance-oriented law enforcement agencies in regulating the environment. An officer we interviewed discussed a case of commercial fraud and illegal dumping of chemicals by a waste disposal company. He recalled being 'out in the dump, I don't know how long, in coveralls, supervising all of the excavation and movement of these drums and the counting of the drums and the sampling of the contents.' Police in some rural jurisdictions report to federal wildlife authorities on the status of endangered species, on animals killed by hunters, and on hunters checked. An urban police organization we studied worked closely with fish and wildlife officers in areas adjoining the city. These fish and wildlife officers were tied into the force's radio system, reported offences using the force's occurrence forms, and were assisted by the force during check-stops for fish and wildlife violations.

As we saw in the case of the Truck Unit, the police also sit on policy and planning committees that trace risks to the environment. These committees are established to cope with specific risks to local territories, for example river flooding or the transportation of hazardous materials. They draw on the expertise of many private institutions and government agencies, and also, with the police, engage in community education.

The police also undertake special territorial inspections as the need arises. For example, major events where there is presumed to be a substantial risk of disruption or terrorism, such as sporting events, political and business conventions, and international political summits, are subject to a plethora of inspections and risk analyses. In the case of government meetings, the analysis includes ensuring that the site is not owned or otherwise used by opposition parties. An alternative site is also selected to cover the risk that some natural disaster or terrorist attack might preclude the use of the original site, and the alternative site must then also be risk-profiled. Risk analysis is also employed in the issuing of credentials to people connected in any way with major events, such as hotel and restaurant employees, security guards, and journalists. Employers are asked to have all employees submit an accreditation application. An application form we saw stated that the process was voluntary, but 'should you refuse to respond accreditation will not be granted.' In Canada applicants are checked by sending computer tapes to the Department of National Defence, the Canadian Security and Intelligence Service, and CPIC and other police intelligence organizations. As one intelligence operative said in an interview in which he described a computer program that links networks of people and organizations, 'You just fill in the information ... and then when it's all done, you just push a button and bang, it's done. Just like that.'

The examples in this chapter illustrate how the tracing of territories involves a combination of electronic infrastructures, spatial arrangements, and inspection devices. It also requires the cooperation and compliance of the people and organizations traced. In the next chapter we will explore how considerable resources are expended on mobilizing people for self-policing.

8

Mobilizing Territories

Watch Programs

The police mobilize territories by setting up residential, business, and general watch programs whose purpose is to persuade people living in or travelling through specific territories to reflexively monitor their own risks and to feed relevant risk knowledge to the police.

Residential watch programs such as Block Watch, Neighbourhood Watch, and Apartment Watch mobilize the residents of local territories to become reflexive with respect to risks. Reflexivity is not only intended to prevent crime and capture criminals but also to help residents confront their emotional responses to risk and to become responsible for policing their own territories.

A residential security brochure distributed by some police forces urges people to join Neighbourhood Watch because '*Crime Preys on Apathy.* Public apathy towards crime is not easily measured, but we do know for certain that it's growing – almost as rapidly as the incidence of crime itself.' No data are provided to support these assertions. A Block Watch brochure says that the program is designed to help people deal with their fears, as well as with crime, through intensive territorial surveillance that includes self-policing: '[Block Watch is] to deter *fear* and incidence of crime ... through saturation ... increase the identification and reporting of suspicious activities ... [and] provide neighbourhood cohesiveness ... getting to know your neighbours ... works best in low transient populated communities ... [Block Watch requires] an observant eye for an unusual activity and common sense precautions ... Crime prevention is not a series of lectures but a part of daily life.'

Apartment Watch is sold to the public in similar terms, but with some special features for people in high-rises. The idea is to make communities by creating a communality of fear. An Apartment Watch brochure distributed by the police states that the program is aimed at higher-density and less stable communities. The brochure promises that stability will increase because the program helps apartment dwellers get to know their neighbours, promotes neighbourhood cohesiveness and a safer community, and provides a communication link with the police and instruction on the proper reporting of suspicious activity. As with all other watch programs, people are given a highly structured form that guides them on how to classify suspicious people, vehicles, and events. This is the citizen's version of the police contact card system. Even in the big city, Apartment Watch is advertised as being 'based on the small-town concept where people know their neighbours well and therefore care and look out for each other ... If a stranger is seen where he is not supposed to be, the police are called. Upon implementation of Apartment Watch, the apartment or complex in effect becomes a small town environment and hostile to the criminal.'

In practice these residential watch programs have proved difficult to implement beyond the symbolic gestures of putting up street signs and window stickers proclaiming that the territory is 'protected' (Bennet 1993). A police interviewee responsible for mobilizing people to participate in these programs said that it is much easier to do so when data can be produced showing high crime rates and fear of crime in the area. In risk society, negativity and fear must be kept alive in order to mobilize the population and sustain reflexivity: 'Block Watch ... [is a] difficult program to keep people motivated. It's good if something negative is happening. When things get quiet it gets hard.'

The police offer other means of residential protection that are similarly multifaceted in their symbolic functions. For example, some Canadian police organizations have adopted the 'Shield of Confidence Home Security Program.' Working in conjunction with home-builders, insurance companies, and government building code regulators, the program involves the police in certifying the security technologies and design features of new homes. The builder is required to contact the police crime prevention branch on three occasions: before construction, on completion of the frame, and on completion of construction. The police are required to inspect the frame and the completed building. If the home passes both inspections, the police provide a certificate and supporting documentation that indicate that compliance standards have been met. The standards are very detailed, as the following extract shows:

20(b) Outside lighting in 20(a) shall be controlled by switches in the
(i) Master bedroom
(ii) Front entrance area
(iii) Rear entrance area or kitchen.
(c) Outside lighting in 20(a), and within 3 meters (10 feet) of grade shall be protected against tampering.
(d) Excepting those in 20(a), all exterior lights will be at least 60 watts incandescent per unit.

Here inspection, training, and residential watch functions come together in police compliance work on behalf of developers, insurance companies, and residents.

Residential watch schemes also operate within electronic infrastructures. An example is a program known as the Personal Computer Community Organization Prevention System, or PCCOPS. This program is based on a computerized telephone dialling system that automatically sends out prerecorded messages to member residents. In a jurisdiction we studied, eight divisional police stations had acquired the system. In one division there were approximately 13,000 residences and 1,500 businesses in the contact database. A program organizer said that survey research had been used to determine residents' definitions of what constitutes a neighbourhood. The surveys established that people see neighbourhoods as spatial constructs, as areas bounded in each direction by the second or third street from the place of residence, 'and beyond that they're not concerned.' The program accordingly was 'mapped' onto neighbourhood units defined in these terms, with about 300 telephone numbers in each unit. The system operated four lines, each capable of making four calls at once, which allowed up to 320 three-minute calls to go out each hour.

PCCOPS does a number of things for its members. It makes 'alert calls' regarding urgent matters such as recent criminal acts, threats posed by rabid animals, and lost children. It also makes 'information calls' reminding people of their responsibility for managing their own risks. Other functions include informing people about upcoming Neighbourhood Watch meetings and in some cases about territorial inconveniences such as public works projects. In the words of one interviewee, the system is intended as an educational alternative to 'boring' community meetings. With PCCOPS 'You've got a better educated and much more aware community, for one thing. They don't feel like they have to go out every two weeks to this meeting and whatever and talk about things that they don't want to do.'

In the jurisdiction we studied, the impetus for the PCCOPS program came from a municipal politician, whose photograph, name, address, and telephone number were prominently featured in the promotional leaflet sent out to residents. The police officers and other people we spoke to saw his selling of the program as an integral part of the selling of his political self.

In the jurisdiction we have been discussing, PCCOPS began as an outgrowth of the local Neighbourhood Watch program. In the eyes of one of its initiators, it was a big step beyond Neighbourhood Watch, which 'just doesn't work anymore ... People have their signs up and their stickers on the door, but big deal.' The local Neighbourhood Watch committee raised enough money to provide a dialling system for the local police division. The committee also signed up an initial 10,000 telephone owners (who thereafter received messages that began, 'It's the City Police – Neighbourhood Watch Computer-Dialled Alert Calling'). An interviewee who played a key role in the development of the local system said that some Neighbourhood Watch members were concerned that they were being displaced by computerization. However, he reassured them that such a risk was 'A big fallacy ... [the system is] going to enhance the Neighbourhood Watch program. We still need Block Captains to go out and greet the new people in the neighbourhood and tell them about the dialler.'

PCCOPS was sold to the community as a highly effective way to reduce risks. One publicity brochure claimed that it had reduced 'crime' in the area by 38 per cent, but there was no specification of the time period or substantiation of the claim. Another benefit, supporters said, was that a feeling of community would be engendered by fighting 'crime.' One of the supporters we interviewed observed that 'Residents would not only be informed about happenings in their community, but would also *feel* that *somehow* they helped in resolving crime ... It takes a few phone calls, but after that you really start to feel like you are a partner in this, you know.' This feeling of partnership was said to encourage other forms of participation in the program, including participation in fund-raising activities such as bingo nights.

While PCCOPS relied on people's feelings about their community to generate participation, its supporters were concerned about the risk of people becoming too emotional. As a condition of participation, people were required to sign a form consenting to the receipt of calls that might be alarming. A police officer explained that 'Our fears were ... we get in touch with an elderly person and say there's been a rash of break-ins, we have to consider that perhaps they might really get upset. They could have a heart attack. We don't want that happening. So by asking for the written consent, people are saying, yes, we want to participate in this program.'

He went on to say that he did not see the possible creation of fear by PCCOPS calls as a significant problem. In his view, 'The public *should be* a little more concerned about crime. They can do something about it and they can be our eyes.'

In addition to liking its surveillance and community-building functions, the police viewed PCCOPS as a convenient tool for making some of their routine tasks easier. When involved in direct, face-to-face relations with the police, people can make annoying demands that are tangential or irrelevant to the task at hand. It is far better, the police think, to avoid face-to-face contact by relying on computer-assisted dialling systems such as PCCOPS:

> [When you go door to door] and you tell them that little Johnny or Mary from next door is missing, they're concerned but they're going to say, 'Are you going to my neighbour?' And you say 'Yes.' [They reply,] 'When you tell them could you also mention that their dog is awfully noisy at night?' This happens. So you go five minutes at every house. For the missing child you don't want to spend five minutes at every house because you get twelve houses on one side of the street and you've used up an hour of your time ... I can record a message on the dialler and call sixty to eighty houses in that hour because they're not expecting to tell that machine about the barking dog next door, and it cascades ... I can't be rude. I'm there as a professional so [when] it's a two-way conversation ... I have to, because it's face to face, listen to whatever you're going to say to me.

Even when safely insulated by the computer system, however, the police act to forestall possible complaints that they are not doing their job properly. During the seven years the system we are describing here had been in place, the police recorded *every* call made by it. A police interviewee described the risk logic involved in this monitoring by saying, 'If there was an inquiry down the road, and someone felt that maybe the police had not done as much as they could have done or should have done, I can go back and say, "Well, yes, we did put out a computer message and, in fact, the person that has complained, they answered their phone at 1:30 in the afternoon and we did give them the message ... and *this* is the message that they were given."'

PCCOPS exemplifies community policing as communications policing. A police officer told us that even though there were some cases in which the program had led to the capture of suspects, that function was not central to it: 'You can't evaluate its effectiveness [in crime prevention and detection] ... It's provided us a means of communicating with the community on a regular basis without having to go and knock on the door to do the town crier bit. We don't have the manpower to do the town crier.' A local government official said that the system was, despite appearances, 'still policing ... police and community policing community.' He observed that crime prevention was the best message to initially put forward in selling the program, but that in the long term the program could be used for governance much more broadly. He had become involved in developing the system, he said, in response to citizens who complained,

> 'How come I didn't know what was going on or why wasn't I informed, and how come I didn't see the police, or why was there no meeting in my neighbourhood?' So there's a sort of isolation that occurs in the inner-city communities whereby you may be two blocks away but perhaps you're not informed of an event or so forth, so I thought the best way of keeping people informed is through a computer link-up. Rather than have the police force or myself, whatever, these constant meetings, constant dropping-off of pamphlets, letters, it really is a waste of time and money and resources are limited ... So you sort of involve yourself in community building, at the same time it's crime prevention ... So I really think it's part of policing in the future.

As we noted above, there are watch programs designed specifically for businesses. Their goal is the same as that of the residential watch programs, namely to make participants responsible for their own risk management.

Responsibility begins with businesses being reflexive with respect to 'defensible space' within their own territories. As a police-distributed 'business security' brochure remarks, 'The stronger the security image, the less likely the robber is to select your business as a target.' In many jurisdictions the police undertake business security inspections, which help businesses trace their territories and ascertain their risk management needs. At the same time, these activities allow the police to construct risk profiles of business owners and managers and the security risks they pose.

While business watch programs focus primarily on providing advice and help with respect to technologies for the protection of defensible space, they sometimes enlist volunteer or paid security officers. In one jurisdiction studied, businesses in industrial parks were informed that the police could no longer conduct preventive patrols. The businesses involved then formed their own territorial security association, which hired private security officers at seven dollars an hour and then tried unsuccessfully to bill the city for this expense. They also formed a 'Fleet Watch' organization of truck drivers who made pick-ups and deliveries in the industrial parks. Equipped with citizen's band radios and their trucking companies' dispatch systems, Fleet Watch members conducted surveillance as they went about their work. A police officer involved with this organization referred to them as 'more eyes and ears out there, making it uncomfortable for the individuals that want to do crime because they never know if they're going to be seen or not.'

In some business territories the police sit on risk management committees that decide how to respond to specific problems as they arise. For example, a downtown shopping district had a management committee that included as members the constable who policed it and the inspector he reported to. A restaurant, bar, and entertainment district in another part of the city had a risk management committee of police, business owners, liquor regulators, and city officials, which oversaw the monitoring of the spaces under its authority, especially regarding liquor consumption, dance floor areas, and noise levels. The police provided full-time officers for compliance-based law enforcement in this district.

Many watch programs have an even broader remit. For example, Radio Watch, as described in its official brochure (distributed by the police), enlists 'the expertise of citizen's band radio operatives ... becoming extra eyes and ears.' Radio Watch volunteers are assigned in pairs to a police officer. They are sent to locations such as the parking lots of shopping malls and industrial areas to conduct surveillance and report any suspicious activity to their officer. In some jurisdictions people who do not have a citizen's band radio are given old police radios set to a frequency the police do not otherwise use. They use these radios to report impaired driving and other troublesome activities observed during their patrols.

The police also recruit auxiliaries and other types of volunteers to conduct specific forms of territorial policing. One police organization had a

'Police Ventures' program that enlisted Boy Scouts and Girl Guides for police-related work. Another organization had an elaborate volunteer program coordinated by a full-time employee. This program was a classic example of 'moral entrepreneurship' as defined by H. Becker (1963: chap. 8). It began with a special festival for which volunteers were recruited. After the event almost three hundred volunteers wanted to continue working with the police. A police official talked with us about this:

A: [This group of people] that now we had activated, and now what were we going to do with them?
Q: You say the spirit was there first and then they had to think, 'Oh, what are we going to do with them?'
A: Absolutely, absolutely. So not the best way to run a volunteer program ... It was a bit backward ... Unlike a lot of other volunteer agencies, we're swamped with people wanting to volunteer.
Q: Do you proactively recruit?
A: [Shakes his head]
Q: The answer is no?
A: No! Emphatically No!
Q: You proactively discourage them?
A: It's really tough when somebody comes forward and they want to give of their time and we don't always have places for everybody ... We get calls daily, people coming to the counter daily as well, wanting to find out how they can be involved.

This interviewee went on to state that the reasons for volunteering vary enormously, but include the fact that people who want to become regular police officers believe that service as a volunteer improves one's chances. More generally, the residents of this police jurisdiction simply seemed to enjoy policing. In a local crime and safety survey 37 per cent of the respondents 'indicated that they were personally involved in some crime prevention program.'

According to one of the program's annual reports, volunteers participated in 109 different policing tasks, which included serving as report takers and information providers at police station desks, delivering subpoenas, staffing Crime Stoppers and victim-assistance lines, conducting telephone surveys, hosting the police graduation ceremony, delivering crime prevention pamphlets, offering computer programming expertise, sorting risk profiles on habitual offenders, sorting other investigative data, acting in police-produced videos, organizing National Crime Prevention Week activities, participating in line-ups, working as security guards at viewing sessions where large amounts of stolen property were on display, acting in police training exercises, crowd control, marching in a parade held during a local festival, making presentations to Block Watch meetings, and fund-raising. The imaginative discovery of policing tasks for volunteers to perform, and the attendant expansion of the program, led to division of labour problems and complaints by unions. As a result, volunteer activities were made subject to review by the police personnel office, the police officers' association, and the clerical workers' union.

Another watch program with a general patrol mandate is Realty Watch. The history of this program shows how residential, business, and general watch programs are not always absolutely distinct from one another.

According to the *Realty Watch Manual* produced by the Canadian Real Estate Association, Realty Watch is a 'roving crime watch system ... an extra set of eyes and ears for the police ... a proactive instead of reactive method of policing that enhances the Neighbourhood Watch and Block Parents programs.' This publication also states that 'Traditional police methods of law enforcement are failing to curb rising crime rates in Canada. The key to curbing this increase is for the public to become more closely involved in preventive policing ... If all of Canada's 112 real estate boards opted for Realty Watch, it would add more than 72,000 pairs of eyes helping keep communities safe. Why Realty Watch? So the real estate industry can become aware, involved, and assist the crime fighters of our community to protect property, possessions and personal security.'

The police coordinator of a Realty Watch program said that its main benefit, from his perspective, was its fostering of a more extensive surveillance capacity during the peak residential burglary period of 10 a.m. to 3 p.m.: 'We have 3,800 realtors out there all of the time. And those are the hours they're always out there ... they know the communities.'

The manual is explicit about the program's surveillance function. Real estate agents are expected to be vigilant and reflexive in all situations: 'Trained real estate practitioners watch and listen for suspicious activity wherever they go.' Agents should be suspicious at all times, even during their leisure time, when they might have their guard down: 'Realty Watch is common sense, caution and cautious awareness of what is happening around you as you walk, drive, work and relax ... Some people fail to call [the police] simply because they are not aware of what seemingly innocent activities might be suspicious.' To guide their surveillance work, agents are given a seventeen-point 'Checklist of Suspicious Activity' that reads like a police guidebook on clues to suspicious behaviour (Sacks 1972; Shearing and Ericson 1991). Among the seventeen indicators of suspicious activity are the following:

- One or more juveniles walking casually through a neighbourhood looking into backyards, automobiles etc. (Particularly during school hours when they should be in a classroom.)
- A person running, particularly if she/he is carrying something valuable.
- Parked, occupied vehicles holding one or more persons at an unusual hour and an unusual place.
- Apparent business transactions being conducted from a vehicle, especially around schools or parks. If juveniles are involved, it could be a drug sale or involve stolen property.

Agents are warned not to neglect reporting *any* potential risk to the police: 'Anything a Realty Watch participant finds suspicious should be reported to the police. Don't worry about "bothering" the police – they urge all citizens to report anything out of the ordinary ... Any type of criminal activity should be reported. As should any hazardous situations such as children playing by railroad tracks or downed hydro wires.'

In some jurisdictions reflexivity with respect to risk comes back to real estate agents in the form of a subprogram that addresses their own safety. In one police organization we studied, this aspect of Realty Watch was downplayed in public relations because the police and the realtors wanted to show that the program was a selfless effort on behalf of the community. Moreover, risk as a threat to real estate agents was something that the Realty Watch organizers had not emphasized before the police increased their sensitivity to it by developing the subprogram. We questioned a police officer on this point:

A: [The] incentive was community involvement. They [realtors] wanted to *show* that the real estate board and the realtors ... are helping the police service. We had just an excellent press conference ... [but] we didn't really want the media to know that [realtors'] personal safety was an issue ... We wanted the positive feedback from Realty Watch. We didn't want any prospective ... criminal out there to say, 'Gee, now that's a good time to maybe nab a woman, when she's doing an open house on Sunday in an area that maybe she shouldn't be in.'

Q: Were the realty people concerned in the beginning about safety issues?

A: Not really. Not until we brought them up. But there certainly is concern in the States because they had a lot of problems in the States.

In addition to being the proverbial 'eyes and ears' of the police, Realty Watch members help to make local residents watchers as well as watched and 'the bearers of their own control' (Shearing and Stenning 1983: 504). In one jurisdiction the real estate board paid for security pamphlets on personal and home safety for seniors and on the street-proofing of children. The design and distribution of the streetproofing pamphlet was a collaborative effort of the real estate board, the local Block Parents organization, and the police force's school safety and crime prevention units. The seniors' home safety pamphlet included a highly structured guide for recognizing suspect people and vehicles.

The *Realty Watch Manual* instructs realtors on how to promote the program. The aforementioned security pamphlets, the general Realty Watch pamphlet, and other crime prevention pamphlets, it advises, should be distributed to clients at every opportunity in order to demonstrate a concern for the value of security. The effectiveness of the program in reducing crime should be stressed. The manual mentions, for instance, that the program originated in Philadelphia in 1981 and that there was a 27 per cent drop in 'crime' in the city during its first year of operation! Suggestions for promotional activities include the advice that 'When a Realty Watch tip to the police results in a crime being prevented, make the most of it with major announcements to the media.' Also suggested are promotional videos, awards programs, the issuance of certificates of participation, and fund-raisers for Crime Stoppers. To create a sense of security people are encouraged to place Realty Watch signs at municipal boundaries (these signs are similar to the well-known 'This is a Neighbourhood Watch Community' signs). A Realty Watch sign, the manual says, 'lets criminals know what they face, keeps Realty Watch on the minds of the public, and enhances the image of the real estate industry.' Placing the Realty Watch logo on everyday items is also advised as a way to solidify an identification of the industry with what is morally worthy in security risk management: 'Handing the Realty Watch stickers, buttons, refuse bags and key chains to clients is more than just reminding them about crime prevention. It is also a reminder of the broker's service to the community – which helps when sellers are scouting for a real estate professional to market their property ... Board members will look forward to taking part in the program if it helps to increase business.'

The corporate underpinnings of the program are obvious. By doing good for the community – or at least making a show of doing good – realtors also advance their own business interests. The *Realty Watch Manual* is replete with statements that participation creates pay-offs for the real estate industry. Indeed, the manual begins with the promise that Realty Watch 'is an excellent community service project that is bound to pay *big dividends* in enhancing the real estate industry in your board area' (emphasis added).

Our analysis of Realty Watch has shown how police mobilization of territories is intimately connected with corporate relations and sponsorship. We now turn to a more systematic examination of the corporate connection and its implications for the ways in which risks are constituted and managed.

Corporate Programs

In the mobilization of territories for risk management the police interlock with public and private corporate institutions. The police offer corporations their expertise in territorial security design and risk analysis, and test private security systems for corporate clients. They also join with corporations in the commodification of risk management devices, and in turn receive corporate sponsorship of their own activities and programs.

Police experts in territorial security design and risk analysis operate within units devoted to prevention and analysis. These units – the research and development branch of the police – work closely with corporate security designers and analysts in other institutions. In what follows we illustrate these operations by drawing on examples from one of the police organizations we studied.

In this police organization a full-time territorial design expert served as an advisor to public and private corporations. She said that much of her work was inspired by Oscar Newman's (1972) 'defensible space' arguments and aided by courses she took in the United States that taught her how to present her ideas in an attractive fashion. As she explained it, these courses taught her how to convince clients to 'buy into the proposition that it's going to work. There's a certain element of marketing ... [that] goes on in the course itself ... [and] provides a person with the vocabulary [needed] ... to put in visual terms what it is you're seeing in two dimensions.'

This expert served on municipal committees that included representatives from social service agencies, the city planning department, the city transportation department, the city parks department, retail business associations, community associations, development companies, and large private corporations. In addition to providing these committees with 'statistics and advice,' she collaborated with them in developing safety-audit systems and long-term plans for revitalizing territories suffering from urban decay. In her view revitalization meant such things as increasing the population density and improving the 'public life' of neighbourhoods so that people could keep a better eye on each other; 'natural surveillance,' for example not building tall fences or other obstructions to visibility in high-risk areas; and improving the lighting, colour schemes, and music played in areas, such as commuter train stations, where people might feel vulnerable.

The expert also worked with zone sergeants and constables to conduct security design assessments related to development permit applications. The officers provided written security assessments based on their knowledge of patrol areas, which were used by the expert in reports to the chief of police. Another of her tasks was to advise private corporations on architecture-related security issues. For example, she offered advice on the location of automatic banking machines. In one case, she recalled, 'I dealt directly with the architect, negotiated some changes – lighting level, landscaping features.' She said that this architect later realized that 'if I can deal with these [issues] up front, then submit my application saying that I've already addressed the concerns of the police department, then I have a smoother course than if he bothers to draw plans and has to change them.' She also helped a utilities company that needed a new office entrance design to protect against threats from hostile customers whose service had been cut off.

The analysis unit of the same police organization employed people with master's and doctoral degrees in sociology, environmental design, statistics, economics and finance, and other disciplines. Advice was given to large corporations on office relocation and security protection. This unit also performed a number of tasks similar to those performed by our design expert, such as 'target-hardening' of retail businesses that were especially vulnerable to victimization. During the research for this book cigarette prices were very high because of heavy taxation, which resulted in cigarette cartons being an especially attractive commodity for thieves. The unit developed a 'cigarette crime' database that profiled victimization patterns, and thus provided information for the development of preventive measures.

The unit also supplied expertise to corporate executives. For example, corporate executives coming to live in the city were advised on which residential areas were the most secure. An interviewee said that this was done as 'a favour because down the road there's probably information that may be resonant in that corporation that maybe it helps us.' Dignitaries visiting the city for special events were also given security advice by the unit's experts. There was, for example, a restaurant screening service. We were told that dignitaries 'don't want to read an advert and say, "Hey, that's really good food, we're going to take this guy for a big dinner," and then find out it's where the majority of our shitbags hang out.'

The unit also had a number of specialists working full-time on particular sorts of crimes. For example, one analyst maintained databases on street robberies and robberies of financial institutions and retail stores. His job was described by an interviewee as one in which he was incessantly 'looking through the databases we have, looking for patterns and similarities, looking for things that ... we're missing and we need to dig up to clarify either identities or proof on individual cases.'

The interviewee just quoted emphasized that the unit was committed to the widest possible mandate for its activities: 'Everything that's possible we look at.' He said that computer technology and data analysis techniques made its tasks limitless. Everything was not only looked at but also treated as potentially useful: 'Electronically we don't throw anything away. There's no tidbit that can't, or might not someday, be of use.'

Police specialists in territorial design and analysis are also willing to go to extraordinary lengths in testing on-site security and providing advice on how to correct problems. A police interviewee offered the example of a private corporation that was concerned about the security of an area in its plant where dangerous materials were kept. He assigned two plain-clothes officers the task of breaching plant security and gaining access to this critical area to prove its vulnerability. The officers, wearing white coats and carrying clipboards, entered the plant. Someone did stop them to ask them their business, but when they responded, 'You are the first person to ask who we are, that's going to go into our report,' they were able to proceed without further questioning. They then entered the critical room and placed two coins, given to them by the interviewee, inside a container. The interviewee later visited the room with the company president and retrieved the coins. The interviewee concluded the story by remarking, 'Now I tell you his face was as fucking red as this binder here. So they had to sit back and review their security provisions.'

Some police organizations have units to help with the acquisition of security devices. Corporate executives hoping to justify expenditures on new security devices sometimes seek official police endorsement. The police also help to install security devices such as surveillance cameras, alarms, and automatic door locks that can trap suspected wrongdoers until the police arrive.

Large police organizations employ full-time electronic security experts. One urban police organization we looked at had a full-time alarms officer. He described his role as giving advice to alarm companies on how to improve their products, and to large corporations such as banks and oil companies on how to enhance their electronic security. As a matter of policy he did not explicitly endorse particular products, but he was willing to advise against hiring alarm companies with poor records. This advice was not based on casual assessments, but on the expert's own sophisticated risk-profiling of alarm companies. The expert's system, which was, in effect, a risk assessment system directed at a risk management technology, was constructed around a city by-law requiring the registration of alarm systems so that keyholders could be traced and alarms monitored. The by-law provided that when the number of false alarms in one place exceeded a certain level, the police would no longer respond to the affected premises. But faced with a 91 per cent false alarm rate, the police over a four-year period lowered the no-response threshold from forty to twenty to fifteen to ten, and finally to three, false alarms in a twelve-month period.

The alarms officer said, 'We enforce that alarm by-law to the letter, and every time somebody reaches three false alarms, a computer prints out a letter saying you're going to be suspended.' But as is typical of compliance-based regulation, enforcement was 'to the letter' only in the sense that letters would be written to alarm owners. The next step, according to the alarms officer, was that he 'negotiate[d] with them on ways that the false alarm problem can be diminished ... If they do things I consider proper to stop false alarms, we'll take them out of suspension, so we're on the phone daily with people like that.' In the eleven-month period preceding our interview with the officer, about 1,500 suspensions were handed out, so there must have been many such calls every day.

The alarms officer told us that the major effects of this compliance-based law enforcement crack-down were to foster sales of upgraded and more expensive alarm systems, and to lead some of the larger corporations to entirely privatize their alarm-response systems: 'There are some of the bigger corporations that have, for instance, two hundred alarm systems and they've had to face the suspension of one or more of those alarm systems almost on a daily basis. They've actually gone to a private response to all of their alarms.'

Suspension of police service in responding to alarms does not mean that the police thereby transfer exclusive responsibility for alarms management to private security operatives, for they continue to work with the private sector in other alarm-related areas. For instance, police electronic security experts help private corporations develop new and improved alarm systems. They share information with experts employed by major corporations such as Bell Canada and ADT. A police electronic security expert told us that these relationships are sometimes complex. For example, an urban police department that provides assistance to a bank may turn for help to RCMP electronic security experts, who themselves will ask ADT or Bell Canada for advice. According to our expert, there is an 'extremely high level of industry contact ... unless we do that we're going to end up in a real nice isolated shell out there that doesn't have access to the latest things that are out there – the thinking and so on.'

Technical cooperation includes seconding police officers to private corporations and corporate experts to police organizations. An interviewee said that some of her police organization's electronic security specialists worked in a plant owned by an alarm systems company. The goal was 'to make sure we got what we needed and they know what our requirements were. So there's lots of companies out there that we've done some pretty hand-in-glove type of business [with].' This same police organization also offered temporary placements to corporate experts, who thus had the opportunity to become familiar with police technical standards and requirements, and to take this knowledge back to their corporations for use in research and development:

> So we work very closely with any companies that we've looked at. And basically we try to let the company solve the problems. We've got to be careful, from a mandate point of view ... we cannot be the R and D centre for a private company, so it's a funny balance there. We may tell them, well, this is the problem. No, we're not going to tell you how to fix it. That's your job ... [but] let's say [it] is the only system that is of the quality or the level that you want to go in and you do

see a problem. You may be forced into saying, 'Well, it's this thing *right here*, but if you only did this or did that, it would be good.' But we try not to.

Another link the police maintain is to insurance company investigators with an interest in electronic security devices. A police electronic security specialist mentioned that he worked with the Underwriters Laboratory of Canada to develop standards for intruder alarms and closed-circuit television systems. He said that this work was important because there was no value in writing 'a great UL [Underwriters Laboratory] standard for an alarm system if you forget something or leave [out] something that is so basic with regard to defeat of the system ... that it renders the system just basically useless ... So we're there to make sure that UL doesn't write a standard that forgets these types of things.'

Commodification

The police join with corporate allies in applying a business sensibility to the mobilization of territories. They engage in creative advertising and marketing strategies to convince consumers to accept their programs. They finance and market these programs by identifying themselves with corporations whose main interest is the marketing of consumer security products. They thus create opportunities for such corporations to market their products with police endorsement and collaboration. A police middle-manager had this to say:

You can use all the same techniques that the business uses to sell a product, and to move your product in the police world as you do in the business world ... We'll call a meeting, and, OK, we got them in to talk about streetproofing. That might have been a community concern, it might have been ours. *It doesn't really matter.* But while we got them on the streetproofing, we're going to sell them a residential security program called Block Watch. So you've got a captured audience to say, 'Look, seeing as you're here, I've got some other thing that I want to show you, this particular product' ... It's a sales job is what it is ... Once you've got people and sold them the product, now you've got to give them a warranty in terms of keeping them informed of the information and changes ... You say, 'OK, we have a product on the shelf that can fit your need or fit your concern' ... I think of Block Watch as a pyramid-sales organization ... It's the old multilevel marketing system ... the tendency to package this nice little program, give it a name and sell it for Christmas.

The selling job includes dramatizing crime and other risks to induce fear and make people reflexive enough that they will accept the need to buy the product. This approach is standard in the mass media and security industries (Spitzer 1987; Featherstone 1991; Sparks 1992; M. Davis 1990; Massumi 1993). As was explained to us by the manager of a police district station, 'You have to sort of seek out and raise consciousness and awareness. One of the things I use is those community newsletters, writing articles ... to raise sort of a *fear factor* so they get the interest in the community up.' One time, she discovered that a particular neighbourhood that did not have a Block Watch program had a higher official crime rate than surrounding territories with Block Watch. She then 'made a nice little graph and chart ... That's when the excrement hit the air-circulating mechanism. Everybody started phoning everybody.' Shortly thereafter, the neighbourhood signed up for Block Watch.

Victims of serious crimes or accidents are sometimes used to help sell a program. As one police interviewee remarked, the police give the victims the 'authority to say, yes, crime is alive and well in your community and to this extent.' In authorizing others to induce fear under specific conditions, the police can use the legitimacy of personalized and dramatic voices to convince consumers 'to buy into the program because it's really a community concern.'

Consumers also need to be sold on the idea that a territorial risk management program works best in partnership with corporate sponsors. A police middle-manager who worked as a sales agent for Block Watch said that his job entailed having potential consumers rethink the meaning of community. In sales meetings he told potential customers,

> Don't think of it just as a residential program. You have to go back to your sense of community because you've got local businesses that are part of your community ... What's that got to do with residential security? Well, two things. One, these people want to come in and sell you their product – bars, locks, and so on. The other is you need their money to help you produce newsletters, so we have an exchange now. I can give you advertising to sell your product if you'll help me print the brochure that I can drop in mailboxes. So again we, the police, assist in planting the idea, How about having a home security show? ... [so that you can] make contact with some of the local businesses down here in the business of selling security products.

The signs of this police–corporate quid pro quo are everywhere. Corporate-sponsored logos appear on crime prevention advertisements, pamphlets, trinkets, drinking-cups, and so on. Corporations fund the establishment of community police stations, for example by paying for signs, office equipment, and office furniture that bear their logo. They also sponsor crime prevention videos featuring their products. A police organization we studied produced residential and business security videos with a subsidy from a lock manufacturer. A police interviewee noted that although the lock was not explicitly endorsed, it was the only one depicted in the video, despite the fact that the video's narrator 'very generously talks about types, different styles of locks and stuff – we don't think that's a conflict of interest at all.'

Special police events promoting risk management strategies also feature the corporate advertising connection. In one jurisdiction the school safety patrol program benefited from having its brochures printed gratis by the local newspaper in return for the newspaper's name appearing on them. A police officer told us how a local snack manufacturer also participated in the program by providing 'little bags of snacks ... over the years ... the number of bags of snacks is humongous ... whatever the commodity is ... it's the old barter system ... Again, we, the police, are facilitators because X gets advertising out of it, kids eat their snacks, so they sell more of their product.'

Many other examples of corporate involvement can be cited. In Canada major airlines and railways offer free travel to missing children traced by Child Find, helping to reunite them with their families that cannot pay the costs themselves. A retail mall paid for a computer upgrade of the PCCOPS system described earlier. In one police organization an investigator of automobile thefts was negotiating a deal that would see the insurance and automobile industries making financial contributions to the police in exchange for the police endorsing their strategies for vehicle theft protection:

> [The two industries would like to advertise] *on behalf of* the police service ... use me in an advertisement, recognizing that I'm a ranking member of the police service and saying, 'Myself and my fellow members of this committee would like to show you what we would try to do with the long-term problem solving.' They would like to actually buy advertising for us. Do the video at their own cost and then buy the video or buy the space to actually go forward and advertise ... We would be able to use resources that we just haven't had before ... I'm seeing ... more and more how we have to use outside help.

Many of the developments described above are recent, the result of police budget stringencies. They are also fostered by a public culture that is increasingly saturated by mass-media dramatizations of crime that promote fear and reflexivity with respect to security. On the other hand, there is a long tradition of the police being associated with certain businesses. This was pointed out by a police officer who identified the security benefits to fast-food outlets of offering free or subsidized food to officers: 'Every couple of hours they get to have a marked police car parked in front of their restaurant. That's great security for the price of a hamburger. If you were to pay for that, it would cost you hundreds of dollars [each time], with a three-hour minimum. What does it cost? A couple of hundred dollars [a week] for some hamburgers.'

Police images are used by corporations to symbolize the security features of their products. A large billboard seen during our field research showed that, in a sense, the police are *virtually* everywhere. This billboard featured a very large male police officer standing on a very small stool. Under him was the caption, 'Put a police officer wherever you put your phone.' The advertisement was for a telephone receiver that displayed the caller's telephone number; the police connection obviously highlighted the security aspect of the device. Advertisements for cellular telephones also emphasize the security aspect, namely that calls for help can be made from anywhere.

Much of the security work that the police engage in with electronic security and communication companies also involves commodification and marketing. For example, the false-alarm compliance system described earlier gives alarm companies the opportunity to sell costlier products to people who have lost the privilege of police response. Police research staff who test electronic security products for police purposes also help private companies to improve and sell their products. As a police research executive observed, 'Although we don't get involved in actually testing products for home security and that, nevertheless ... we get involved in testing products for our own security which have an industry spin-off.' An individual in another branch of police product research said, 'most of our stuff that we've done has commercial application, has been exploited commercially ... a royalty spinoff ... taxes from the company ... help Canadian jobs.'

The police also help private security companies by providing them with risk profiling and research data relevant to the development, marketing, and servicing of their products. A police data analyst said that private security companies selling security products are 'probably a bigger caller than anybody from the public ... If the information's handy, they'll be given it ... They want to go to the local areas ... to sell their product.' His counterpart in another jurisdiction said that after the police made improvements in neighbourhood crime data collection, he had 'security people breaking down our doors to try to get that information ... There is big money in this type of information.'

An Imaginary Community

We can best conclude this chapter by imagining a stranger who drives into a medium-size town. She is greeted by signs showing that the community is associated with Neighbourhood Watch, Block Watch, PCCOPS, Block Parents, Realty Watch, and other name-brand watch products. Pulling into a name-brand fast-food restaurant, she immediately notices members of the local constabulary eating hamburgers. While waiting in line for her food, she reads a pamphlet with tips on personal security, which comes complete with the corporate logos of its sponsors. Because she is in town during National Crime Prevention Week, her coffee is served in a free crime prevention souvenir cup. At least until the cup breaks, it will remind her, with each and every sip, that she takes risks and needs to protect herself against them.

The restaurant alarm goes off. There is no need to worry, because the police are already there. In any event, it is a false alarm, and the only consequence will be a suspension of police response service until a better alarm system is purchased.

The driver leaves the restaurant and proceeds farther into town. Still sipping, she notices a colourful celebration taking place in a school playground. It is a school safety carnival, the town's featured event of National Crime Prevention Week. She stops for a closer look, and finds that people are being given free snacks. Those participants who have put up displays and given security demonstrations receive extra free snacks as a reward. Already full from her hamburger, she is not interested in a free snack. However, an especially cheerful police officer insists, and she is unable to resist his gesture. She munches on her snack as she enters a tent for a free video show on personal security.

Back out on the highway, the driver is warmed by the feeling that this community is somehow familiar, although she has never been here before. This feeling of familiarity leads her to conclude that she is in a secure place, a place where she is not really a stranger. This feeling has been brought to life by her consumption of the products the community has to offer. Still sipping, she sighs, then smiles and says to herself, 'This must be a real community.'

9

Territorial Communities

Making Up Communities

In chapter 3 we outlined the ways in which community policing is an official discourse that constitutes changing mentalities, sensibilities, and practices in risk society. In this chapter we show that the tracing and mobilizing of territories exists within the ambit of this discourse and in turn helps to constitute it. As community policing discourse suggests, the police *do* join with partners in other institutions to make up communities.

The police operate with a strong sense that a community is represented by a territory and by those who belong in the territory. When conceptualizing community policing they therefore emphasize 'turf.' Typical of this outlook is a statement by one of our police interviewers that community policing is 'old-style policing with turf ownership. And people want to know all about the turf.' As this person's comments suggest, the focus on turf is not new, but how the turf is focused on has changed.

In describing the changes that are occurring under community policing, our interviewees drew parallels with what was done in times past. They observed, for instance, that RCMP and provincial police officers in remote areas have always, out of necessity, been community makers. One interviewee told us that 'When I was in detachment we were actually the centre of community. We acted as everything to everybody. People would come to you with all kinds of problems because you just know what is going on so well. The police were a valuable source of information. We provided a valuable service to the community.'

Urban police officers made similar remarks about their work in the days before community policing initiatives. One example mentioned was the Community League system in Western Canadian cities, a locus of community policing in that it was used to provide risk knowledge to local people, and as a vehicle for the police to learn about risks that they might wish to address. Certain long-standing police programs were also conceived of in community police terms by our interviewees. Programs for placing police officers in schools, which had existed in one jurisdiction for more than two decades, were viewed as an expression of the quintessence of community policing. An interviewee looked on the school-based officers in his jurisdiction as 'the forerunners of this community-based policing ... you're putting a uniformed officer ... under one roof with 2000 citizens, into a school community with all that interaction going.' He went on to observe that school officers were 'basically the small town policeman ... we never had the label for it, but ... we end up solving problems in some of these schools that basically are not a police problem. If we're on the street it wouldn't be anything you'd ever call the police for.'

The label of community policing is now applied to virtually every aspect of Canadian police organization. Traditional police functions now bear its name. For example, entire patrol divisions have been reconfigured under the name 'Bureau of Community Policing.' Such changes in labelling point to changes in how the police communicate with other communities in risk society.

Community policing is part of the police's new corporatist approach to their work. A police middle-manager who started his police career 'pounding the turf' as what he called a 'night-watchman,' described for us the shift to 'business-oriented' policing:

> When I first started, we were in the old-style municipal policing where it was a platoon system. We had 30 cars, we had 22 beats ... You worked either afternoons or nights and there really wasn't a lot of integration with the community. When you started off on the job you basically were like a night-watchman. You walked the beat, you rattled doors, you found an open premises. Then you'd call the car crew [and] the car crew would stand by until the detectives came. And then you go back rattling doors ... [A new chief of police] brought in a more community-oriented concept. It would be a lot like small-detachment policing by the RCMP, where the members in a specific area would be responsive to the community, to what the community's needs were, to interact with the community more. As we developed along further, the demands on the police department became more for more services, more programs; we needed crime prevention

programs of any nature that could be seen as being proactive to reduce crime. And in those time-frames, in the late seventies and early eighties when money was abundant, we had lots of manpower. Money wasn't a problem. We could hire lots of people. We had a high level of, number of actual street personnel to citizens. And we were able to provide all these programs that the community wanted or that we perceived that the community wanted ... As we become more business oriented, paperwork is going to increase. The reports, when you look back to the original reports, they were very, very simple. I came. I saw. I did. I left. With your assessment periods for people, one a year, the sergeant would come out and he would say, 'Here are seventeen categories and, from one to seven, this is how I see how you fit on the scale. And I think that ... on a one-to-five scale, here's where you are for promotability.' And that was basically all that was done for the person for career-pathing or to determine the effectiveness that you had at doing your job. As we became more business oriented we went through the same things as any other company – goals and objectives and all that ... *Everything* seems to be done now by paper. Any complaint that comes in, there has to be a paper trail where before it was, 'Yeah. Right. I'll get to it at some particular point in time.' Whereas now there's more due dates and more pressure being put on by the public, more pressure by the politicians, more pressure by the police commission. And the accountability factor is coming down and down and down, so you're doing more nonreport writing to the point where now you're looking at, OK, how am I going to solve the problem of putting together a proposal, putting together responses to the alderman or the police commissioner, or to the chief, or to the deputy, or to whoever.

The 'business orientation' of community policing is based on new reporting requirements and the attendant proliferation of paperwork. These new forms of reporting are driven by demands for accountability from an increasingly diverse range of institutions. The police manage these demands by acquiring additional knowledge about the risk management requirements of community populations. For example, they conduct public surveys to ascertain what various groups see as the most pressing risks and how they think the police should manage them. These surveys help the police to think in terms of population categories (such as race, ethnicity, gender, age, and class) and how these relate to specific problems in the territories policed. As a police manager in charge of a community policing operation said, such surveys help to 'force police officers who may be resistant to adopt community policing.'

The same function is served by various auditing procedures directed at community policing programs. These audits are conducted to ensure that representatives of diverse populations are found on community policing boards and in community policing programs generally. The community policing audit in one police organization, for example, was designed to ensure that the community advisory body was 'made up of a cross-section of the community, i.e. youth, aged, poor, minorities, professionals.'

Community policing and communication technology evolve in tandem. In all of the police organizations we studied, communication technology was promoted to prospective buyers as a tool for managing the new reporting requirements of community policing. A computer specialist who worked for the police gave us an example of how this was done. At the time of our interview with him, he was helping his organization implement a new laptop computer system for patrol officers. He said that this initiative, and indeed all other technical initiatives in the organization, had to be justified to the senior administration and to the police commission as a brand of community making: 'So if we go around and say, "Give me a million dollars," they will laugh you out of the building. But [not] if we say, "Give me a million dollars, or half a million dollars per subdivision, and your aboriginal policing will be supported, your community policing will be supported, we'll be cutting back, we'll increase our efficiency and cutting back on administrative work in the office, we'll be able to do other things instead, all related to community policing."'

This selling of communication technology as an aid to community policing is not mere rhetoric to acquire more toys. Rather, the police recognize that communication technology is central to community making in risk society. Communication technologies are necessary tools for tracing and sorting populations and thereby defining what the community is and represents. A police interviewee spoke with delight about his computerized territorial mapping system:

> We use a great deal of data supplied to us from the city. Things like automated mapping. When you look at the dispatch system it contains a map of the city that can be overlaid with a great deal of intelligence. There is a ton of data behind that map and a variety of different systems feed that program. It also contains a complete listing of legal addresses in the city ... This can bring us down to street level much more efficiently. I think that is related to some of the community policing initiatives because you can use that program to identify addresses that produce a large number of calls. When the person is dispatched,

the officer can be told that there have been X number of calls there recently and to act accordingly.

On the other hand, those involved in devising computer systems and programs for community policing realize that things are not quite so simple. Indeed, the need to fit what a community means into computer formats proves to be perpetually troublesome. A colleague of the interviewee just quoted, who was involved with the conceptualization and design of the mapping system, observed 'that for the different computer systems there are different definitions of community. With the first system communities were based on a geographic grid system. Since then we have come up with boundaries that more accurately represent the different [population identity] communities.'

For an information technology specialist employed by a police organization to develop an expensive information system to support a new 'neighbourhood policing' approach, the expense was justified because 'Neighbourhood policing is going to greatly increase the amount of information that will be coming into the police force from the community. This information must get to the officers. They have to have information on things that are part of their community. This will allow them to do their own thing within their geographic boundaries.' However, he also said that in spite of his best efforts to collaborate with his police colleagues, it was extremely difficult to determine exactly what constituted a neighbourhood. He pointed out that neighbourhoods do not exist naturally, nor can they be made up simply through signage that gives names to parts of the city as if they are villages. With some exasperation, he said that 'Looking at the neighbourhoods ... is a difficult task because we don't know what a neighbourhood actually is! ... The problem of geography is a real big problem because we are trying to figure out an entity that does not currently exist.'

This information technology expert experienced similar difficulties in fitting the meaning of policing into his computer formats. If policing becomes defined in terms of community, it inevitably fragments into multiple communities and multiple forms of policing. It becomes simultaneously the policing of public spaces in collaboration with myriad watch programs; the policing of private spaces in collaboration with various institutions (such as schools, malls, and workplaces); and the policing of identities in collaboration with minority groups (such as gays, racial and ethnic groups, the elderly, youths, the disabled, and the poor:

What will change ... is the information exchange between the community and police under neighbourhood policing. This is the second phase of this project that will come into effect when we know what community policing consists of ... There are different people from different groups involved in this and their opinions often differ according to the groups that they are involved with ... Currently we are at the initial stage and are dealing only with police matters. Right now it is hard to know what is a policing matter and what is not a policing matter. The definition of policing is not clearly defined.

Other interviewees said that they were facing similar struggles over how to make their communities. Some said that particular populations would never 'buy into' community policing initiatives. One police officer observed, for instance, that 'southern' formats such as Neighbourhood Watch would never fit into 'northern' communities, including native communities: 'It just does not fit the native form of social organization.' Recruitment of laypeople for participation in community policing efforts was a problem in many jurisdictions. Community was often defined by local groups only as a community of interest in a particular form of risk management. A police manager remarked that in his district 'There's not a viable community per se ... Sometimes community people are just an interested bunch of victims of crime. That suddenly makes a community whereas before they had no real interaction or link to anything.'

Despite the attractive packaging of watch programs, people often remain uninvolved, and the sales campaign has to be stepped up. A police manager said that in order to recruit community policing board members, some of his officers 'have advertised in newspapers and others have had to drag people in kicking and screaming. Initially a lot of the officers just appointed the people that they knew. However, they were instructed specifically against simply appointing the town councillors and local politicians ... At this point we are trying to get people to buy in.'

Faced with such difficulties, the police devise various ways of placing themselves symbolically at the centre of a community, and are willing to form partnerships with any institution or group they deem legitimate. A key aspect of symbolization is police station architecture. In contrast to the Peel Region police station described in chapter 2 (pp. 57–8) stand new community police stations that appear more welcoming. The headquarters building of the Metropolitan Toronto Police Department, for example, includes an aesthetically pleasing police museum as part of its large entrance area. Passers-by are enticed into this museum by a large display window similar to the type used in nearby up-market department stores. Some new divisional police stations feature a 'community room' that is available for use by any legitimate organization. Whereas community groups would previously have met in churches, schools, and town halls, they are now encouraged to meet in the police station, the putative centre of the community. The role of the community room as a communications room – as a beacon that beckons all – becomes clear when we consider the interview comments of an architect who helped design one such room:

> It jutted out from the main police reception area. It is quite physically removed from the station. We used glass brick for that. One of the reasons for that was because you could leave the lights on in that room and there would be a constant glow. We knew that the room would be sitting empty a great deal of the time. If we just had traditional windows then people passing by would see this unused room. And even when it was in use the people inside would probably close the blinds. With the glass brick we can leave the lights on all the time and you don't know whether or not people are using it. This lighted room becomes a symbol for the community and the symbolism works twenty-four hours a day.

Apart from user-friendly entrances and comforting community rooms, community policing stations retain many of the environmental design and electronic technology features of the Peel Region station. For example, a promotional brochure put out by a firm of architects specializing in community policing stations points to a number of security-enhancing features, including, 'a wiretap facility; a separate medium-security corridor for young offenders; audio monitoring in cells ... [and] electronic keypad-controls on each entrance at grade.' In risk society, community policing discourse focuses on communications technology and security.

Efforts are also made to modify existing police station territories to establish links with members of the community. Police managers at a station located next to a high school decided to ask the transit authorities to move the school's bus-stop to a position directly in front of the police station. This move encouraged high school students to use the police station entrance as a bus shelter during bad weather. An interviewee said that this innovation made young people more familiar with the police – and 'they are not going to be dealing drugs in the front lobby.'

Special police facilities are also used as community makers. In one jurisdiction the police had a separate training facility for their emergency response team. In an attempt to encourage community involvement with the police, the facility's managers turned to the world of televised entertainment for inspiration, and made the facility a tourist attraction. One of the designers commented that '[this] is now a high-profile policing facility. People can go there and visit and watch the guys rappelling ... business groups and scout troops go in there for a visit. The guys in there can give you an unarmed combat demonstration at the drop of a hat ... they give a first-rate tour. It also gives a human face on a bunch of guys you normally only see in black pyjamas. There is no downside to it whatsoever.'

Community Networks

The police clearly see community policing as a construct of communication networks. For them community policing is indeed communications policing, a matter of devising new reporting classifications and formats for risk management. It involves increased communication to institutions that demand knowledge of territories and populations at risk. It also involves increased communication to various publics, whether by selling participation in watch programs or by cultivating an appreciation of the aesthetics of police buildings that place the police at the centre of their community. It entails the centrality of communication technology in police work. Communication technology helps the police efficiently classify their community – its populations and its territories – in terms of who belongs where, and to broker this knowledge to other institutions in the network that share this understanding of community.

A police organization that had changed the name of its patrol division to 'Bureau of Community Policing' also had a 'Field Support Division.' This division was responsible for a number of special services including crime prevention, multicultural liaison, school safety, youth liaison, victim assistance, and volunteer coordination. The official description stated that the division was 'Comprised of areas responsible for enhancing the professional image of the Police Service with the public, media, and members of the Service. This is done through the development of positive public relations, effective avenues of communication, and innovative community-based policing programs.'

A district manager in the organization observed that all police communication activities are sensitive to the philosophy of community policing. The idea is to set up communication links with the community that will enhance surveillance, allow knowledge brokering, and create police legitimacy in the eyes of the community. He defined community policing as 'a satellite, kind of going around the rest of society' and allowing the police to function as 'conduits of information and facilitators.'

The police define community with reference to the institutional communities they see themselves as serving. One of the designers of a new community police station told us that her design group of police officers defined their community as a collection of corporate and service institutions such as business enterprises, the YMCA, the Kiwanis club, and the provincial housing corporation. A police manager responsible for downtown Bureau of Community Policing operations said that, 'What the community consists of for me in the downtown core will be the businesses and offices that are there during the opening hours. And that becomes, in essence, my community ... car problems, office thefts ... Chinatown, there is a specific community there.'

A police manager in charge of a community policing unit said that his organization did not think in terms of a single community, but of multiple communities: 'within any one community you may have multiple communities. If you have a lot of NSF cheques your community for that issue is essentially the business community, different communities that are not clearly geographically defined.' Another police manager involved in community policing echoed his colleague's sentiments in asserting that 'My community is not kids on a bicycle or people that do traffic in uniform. My community is the business professional – the lawyer, the accountant, the business executive that's out there having problems that deal with the economic system as it occurs today and the abuses of it.'

The people we spoke to emphasized that community policing improves communications with institutional constituencies. Improved communications in turn enhance surveillance capacity and efficiency, which results in greater public satisfaction. A police specialist in automobile theft investigation said that community policing had enabled his unit to conduct joint investigations with Insurance Crime Prevention Bureau investigators and to develop improved knowledge exchanges with automobile industry officials. He enthused, 'I think that the community will realize that the police working together with the insurance [industry] is something that is workable. We've never done that before. Community policing may be a new term but we never have worked as radically close to the community as what we're getting now.'

During basic training, in-service training, and professional development days devoted to community policing, the emphasis is on outside institutions and what the police can do to improve risk management communications with them. We were told that the entire membership of one police organization was required to take a one-week training program entitled 'Enhanced Community Policing Problem Solving.' The main goal of this program 'was [for the participants] to be exposed to these different agencies with the understanding that ... when you get into a situation ... you identify that there's a need for someone with that kind of expertise.' Another person said that professional development days on community policing usually involved having a representative from a particular institution give a talk, followed by a discussion of ways that the sharing of risk knowledge could be enhanced. She gave the example of immigration officials speaking 'on what we at immigration can do for you the local police service, or what we can use your help in, in providing us with information.' The cooperation of the immigration authorities in community policing work proved useful in efforts to exclude certain people from the community:

> Police officers are aware of a couple of bad guys but we can't get evidence on them to get them to court ... However, part of that knowledge might be that they just recently came to the country or whatever, in terms of our investigation. So while we can't get them on a criminal charge, we phone immigration and say, 'Look, here's the situation. This is what we're dealing with.' They do some background checks, they do document checks and everything else and find out, hey, wait a minute, your visa has expired or they're in the country illegally or whatever it is. So while you can't get them on the criminal side of the house, you can get them on immigration ... There are greater federal powers to get your fingerprints under immigration, if you fall in there, than there are under the local police under the Criminal Code ... That's a case of what they were saying. This is how we can help you and then, too, ensuring what we would like from you, is we would like some information. If you come across situations that might be of interest to immigration, either in documentation or a credit card fraud – [for example,] somebody who is landed and ends up getting into credit card fraud – historically we, the police, in isolation, have been dealing with that, not telling anybody that we've dealt with it and now all they want over here is just a phone call to say, 'Yeah, we've picked up Mr X, he's a landed immigrant or whatever it is and we've got him charged with credit card fraud.' So he might go through the criminal courts and be convicted or not be convicted but then, through immigration, get in on the act and he's gone, out of the country ... I think we've

only hit the tip of the iceberg in terms of, back under that broad title of community policing. Historically, we've done business with other agencies that we've been most in contact with and then, too, really on a limited basis.

A police manager said that community policing was designed to enhance all forms of communication between the police and other institutions, especially with respect to systematized communication networks for risk profiling. His description of a disaster management program coordinated by the Red Cross and involving a number of other institutions was as follows: '[they have] a very nice computer program to collect all the information pertaining to disasters ... so it's a case of working together ... [where] the common denominator was the collection of information.' He also mentioned his work on a city health care advisory committee. The purpose of this committee was to provide hospitals with better 'information on things like the victim' by trying 'to work out some protocols in dealing with information as it pertains to victims.'

The use of communication networks is vigorously promoted in community policing. Data on crimes, accidents, and disasters are routinely produced for various community organizations interested in assessing their risks. A police interviewee who specialized in the production of risk data said that

> We may release information [to the public] that will tell them when they are more vulnerable to certain types of victimization in different areas. This information is supplied to the district and zone level. People can use this information to find out what sort of crimes are happening in their neighbourhood and then target-harden ... [real estate agents, for example,] use crime data as a real selling point ... We will supply information to real estate groups. We may caution them about certain interpretations, but we don't try to restrict their access.

Community policing officers sell themselves by communicating the message that they are experts in risk management. A pamphlet distributed by a police organization to business and residential 'clients' emphasized the following points:

- The officer's role is to show you how you can reduce the risks of being victimized by a wrongdoer.
- Your police officer will show you how to improve your level of security, both in your home and in your district.

- Follow his advice. He's a specialist in the field of crime prevention.
- Do not hesitate to call him whenever you need him. He is 'your' police officer and his primary concern is your protection.
- Foster relations between you and your neighbours in the fight against crime. As in other fields, there is strength in numbers.
- Promote dialogue among you, your neighbours and the Police Service.
- Advise you personally about security matters.

The emphasis here, and in all other community police initiatives, is on risk knowledge networks. Communicate with us, supply us with knowledge of risk, and we will offer you risk management expertise in return. The director of a police organization's computerized information system observed that 'As we move toward community-based policing the requests for statistics and information will increase ... There will be an increased need for intelligence sharing.'

The architectural features of police buildings and police information systems are designed to meet this need. In describing a new community policing 'satellite' station that had been set up to manage youth violence at a shopping mall, we were told by an interviewee that after the police 'kicked some ass and banned some kids' from the mall, they found the station to be such an important centre for attracting informants that they kept it operating. The police see Crime Stoppers as an electronically mediated version of an informant centre (see Carriere and Ericson 1989). A police officer who supervised a Crime Stoppers program defined it as community policing, pointing to a board of directors composed of community leaders and to the community volunteers who took informants' calls. She described Crime Stoppers as 'one of the first community-based programs that we really got into ... as far as an investigative area, that was the first that really got the community involved ... even when the [volunteer] fellows and girls answer the phones in there I've heard them say, "Crime Stoppers is not a police program. This is a community program."'

Community policing emphasizes the need for knowledge to the police as well as from the police to other institutions. Knowledge flows to the police not simply as idiosyncratic tips from individual informants who drop into the community policing satellite station or call Crime Stoppers anonymously, but also takes the form of active police structuring of communication networks that ease the flow. For example, a police interviewee stressed how various 'partners' in watch and other surveillance programs collaborate with the police in systematizing the knowledge flow. To assist people who want to report suspicious activity, security products companies print watch program brochures that include detailed forms for the description of suspects and vehicles. Insurance companies and driver education companies provide brochures that include forms that the public can use to report their own driving accidents to the police. The interviewee said animatedly that this was 'the whole idea' of community policing: 'We, the police, are not in this alone. We're part and parcel of this and so are you ... [We've] really been fortunate and really benefited from the support from behind a lot of our programs by major corporations and by making efforts to be good corporate citizens.'

The problem-solving orientation of community policing (Goldstein 1990) was also seen as necessitating routine knowledge flow directly from external institutions. If the police are to be experts, counsellors, and advisors on all manner of social problems, they require systematic data from public and private health, welfare, education, and insurance agencies. An interviewee pointed to an important internal document on the future of his police organization and said that it 'focuses on the police as problem-solvers. In this regard information gathering and sharing is central to the process. There is the emphasis on drawing upon agencies and resources in the community. This makes the information side of what we are trying to do very important.'

The discourse of problem solving was seen by the police as the primary vehicle for shifting responsibility for problems onto other institutions. For the police, the goal is to achieve the outcome they deem to be just and reasonable, but through the offices of other institutions. The following case of communications networking provides a helpful illustration:

> He was an elderly person who had one of those lifeline buttons so that when they fall out of bed and are unable to help themselves they can push the button and get some emergency response. This person had been doing that constantly and the police – those are *very* high-priority calls – have lights flashing, are driving through rush hour traffic, doing all of this, getting to the home, having to break in, doing this regularly, the paramedics as well, to find that the person was really inebriated. That was basically the problem, that, yes he did have a medical problem and was in bed, but the biggest problem is that he was drunk, passed out and fell out of bed. And so now here they were sort of lifting him back into bed, knowing that at any stage he may fall out again. And they were saying that, first of all, they found it a really appalling situation to see this one person living

in with, just sort of lying at the side of the bed with a bottle and nothing else. But also had some concerns about the amount of times they were responding ... What we were able to do is plug in immediately to Community Health who have nurses who go out and do assessments. They went out and assessed and, sure enough, felt that there was an alcohol problem. And they can access physicians better than someone else can. So they call right in to the physician and say, 'We've been into the home. We see this. Is this a problem?' And this man had a chronic problem of alcohol ... So that was pretty clear that we had an alcoholic and we guessed then, the question became do you just leave it at that with no end to this problem? What I chose to do is be in touch with the, it's a corporation for profit that runs these lifeline systems, and be in touch with them and say something must be wrong with your screening process here, because surely your intention is that this is for people with medical problems primarily, and not for people with alcohol abuse problems. They had never, it was a new system [in our jurisdiction], an American system. They had not been addressed with that. It's obviously been a problem elsewhere. They changed their corporate policy. They flew into [our jurisdiction] from wherever their offices were to meet with us and were able to recognize the fact that their whole existence was tied to the cooperation of the emergency services personnel. If emergency services personnel didn't respond or didn't respond well, there's a good chance that the public wouldn't buy their monthly program. So they rectified the problem very very quickly and what happened is when they were able to go back to their customer and say, 'We are no longer going to be able to keep you as a customer because of this kind of behaviour,' the man was then, he said, 'I'm no longer going to be able to stay in my home.' Well, that's exactly what was needed. We were then able to convince him to get into a treatment program, into a nursing home. So to me that's a classic problem-solving kind of case.

Problem-solving policing is the basis for constituting the police as knowledge brokers for institutions that are more directly responsible for governance. A police manager said his first consideration was, 'whose problem is it? And the second is don't make your problem my problem ... say, "Wait a minute, we, the police, aren't going to do this anymore because there's in place another agency that has the mandate to do this, especially in social services programs." So it's a case where we have to clean our plate a little bit ... Now you get into an accountability problem and people don't like being held accountable for something because you start to shift the problem in their direction.'

Knowledge brokering and displacement of responsibility are accomplished within the formats of communication technologies. As is stated at the beginning of a police-distributed booklet on police and other community services, 'We are dedicated philosophically and operationally to the concept of community-based policing ... our most effective tools are positive community relations, education, problem-solving and use of current technology to analyze conditions, project trends and deploy resources.'

The police officers we interviewed stressed that community policing has put an end to the foot-patrol, watchman-type policing of the past, and does not rely on face to face encounters with one's neighbours: 'I don't think that [watchman-type policing] makes sense in this type of community. I mean we are out here in the suburbs and we're supposed to walk around in –40°C temperatures and rattle door-locks? Come on! And where are we supposed to work? Everyone needs their office. Am I supposed to carry my forms and paperwork around in a knapsack? There would be no place for the forms at all.'

This officer's comments indicate that the police feel tied to their reporting requirements. The officer cannot function without the knowledge-work tools of his or her trade at hand. Because the officer must be mobile, the goal is to make the police car the office. During our ride-alongs with patrol officers, we heard frequent references to 'community policing,' meaning simply that the officer now had information technology in the car that allowed him or her to be out on the road often, rather than sitting in the police station doing paperwork. The community was said to appreciate seeing more officers in its midst, even if all the community saw was officers using their computers and doing their paperwork in their mobile 'offices.'

Making the patrol car the office often means that the officer is surrounded by technology and has little room for other people. As was mentioned in chapter 7 (pp. 135–41), police cars are now equipped with a plethora of electronic and computerized devices. In some instances this paraphernalia takes up the entire front seating area and makes friendly dealings with the public more difficult. During a ride-along a disgruntled officer complained that communications policing had run rampant, displacing his beloved shotgun and placing obstacles in the way of his attempts to create a reassuring environment when trying to obtain information from distressed people. 'They moved the shotgun rack over so you can't have someone in the front seat with you. That's an example of how our new computer system is really nice, it's a type of luxury, but a shotgun is a necessity! If you pick up a sexual assault victim, you can't put them in the back seat of your car! Go to an accident scene and you have people hurt but don't require an ambulance, the back seat of the police car is too small.'

People, and the traditional coercive symbols of policing, are likewise displaced in satellite community policing stations. A police information systems manager observed that such stations are only made possible because of the ability to wire them up with electronic technology: 'So we're *infiltrating*, if you will, communities to a greater degree. And every time we do that, we need more hardware, we need more communication lines, we need printers.'

Similarly, Neighbourhood Watch and related programs rely increasingly on computer-assisted technologies to activate surveillance and to risk-profile the information received. An example of this trend is the PCCOPS program analysed in chapter 8 (pp. 158–61). To repeat the words of a PCCOPS officer, 'It's provided us a means of communicating with the community on a regular basis without having to go out and knock on the door to do the town crier bit.' PCCOPS epitomizes community policing as communications networking, as the constituting of communities through information technology. Another interviewee excitedly remarked that PCCOPS means 'you sort of involve yourself in community building, at the same time it's crime prevention ... [so it's] police and community policing community.'

Electronic technologies are also used to reach particular communities. For example, some police organizations use videos and computer games in schools in place of the traditional visit from the local police officer. A police manager in charge of community policing spoke with delight about

> Computer programs revolving around the police that have been incorporated into the school community ... There is also a computer game called 'Know Your Cops.' It works with the alphabet and you press the screen and get a different police officer from around the world telling you about his country and culture. So if you press 'M' you get a police officer from Maui telling you about his country. I think that this kind of thing has tremendous potential because it could free us from having to speak to the kids one-on-one. That takes a tremendous amount of time that could be used for other things ... I think that there is a program dealing with the police in X that actually has the chief of police of X giving a little 'hello' to the kids before the program starts. Going to the schools used to take a lot of time for the officer and the teacher ... Now they don't have to take up a block of their time. The officer visiting the school is now a video clip.

'The officer visiting the school is now a video clip.' The enthusiastic way this fact is talked about and promoted indicates how communications policing has become *the* mentality and sensibility of community policing. The officer in the mobile patrol car who responds to calls for service and deals with people face to face is being displaced by the police officer who responds only in virtual reality. A police communication technology executive observed that 'Over the years the police moved into police cars and became more concerned with responding to individual calls in a large area. They lost their earlier contact with the community. What the new technologies are enabling them to do is to replace that lost contact. Communications technology where everyone has their own telephone number or where they can talk through satellites enables the police to remain in touch with the community.'

The policing of territories is being transformed by risk technologies. These technologies trace populations as they move through public and private spaces, and register errant moves. Under the rubric of community policing, the policing of territories becomes the responsibility of each institution *vis-à-vis* its specific territory and particular populations. The transformation of territorial policing is largely attributable to advances in risk technologies for tracing and mobilizing populations, and to the attendant advances in communication systems that allow immediate readings of who belongs where and when.

These advances also mean that the police are in touch with much more than is on the ground. The policing of territories through technologies of tracing, technologies of mobilization, and the discourse of community policing is only one aspect of risk knowledge work. The police also produce knowledge for risk management of securities (symbolic properties), careers (life-courses), and identities (collective subjectivities). These forms of risk management are not tied to territorial boundaries. They demarcate institutional boundaries that traverse space and time, yet they still manage to keep people in their place. It is now time to examine these forms of risk management more closely.

PART IV

Risks to Securities, Careers, and Identities

10

Securities

Policing the risk society involves policing forms of risk that transcend space and time. In Part IV we consider risks to securities, careers, and identities as nonterritorial dimensions of risk society that the police participate in.

In this chapter we examine how the police help to manage risks to securities. Securities are symbolic instruments – financial instruments, certificates of ownership, credentials, and so on – that attest to credit, ownership, identity, and achievements. Securities give assurance of the fulfilment of obligations and guarantee against the risk of loss. Securities contribute to the foundation of trust that is essential for the routine flow of institutional relations. The police are an important part of how institutions establish trust and efficiency through their security instruments.

In chapter 11 we study risks to careers. The focus is on two kinds of careers: those of individuals (where the risks are to the viability of people's earnings and to their lifestyle capacity as 'human resources'), and those of organizations (where the risks are to the viability of organizational resources). We also study risk technologies used to manage individuals' careers and police participation in this management. For example, for individuals insurance products are available through private companies and state social security agencies to protect against loss as a result of health problems, unemployment or underemployment, retirement, and other welfare risks. The police act as knowledge brokers and regulators with respect to these forms of insurance and thereby play a major role in providing for the security of individual life-courses.

In chapter 12 we consider risks to personal and cultural identities, defined, for example, racially, ethnically, regionally, and in terms of gender and age. In risk society, policing takes place within risk-relevant classifications of identity. The police respond to institutional demands for knowledge about people, demands framed within specific identity categories. Police thinking and acting are, in turn, shaped by those categories. In providing knowledge of identities to other institutions, the police constitute and confirm the culturally salient features of those identities. While some aspects of this classification work help the populations involved, others create their own risks of deselection, marginalization, and exclusion on the basis of cultural-identity criteria.

Securities Policing

Securities provide a pledge or formal promise made to secure one against loss, damage, or default. They are always backed by institutions, whether public or private. They provide an institutional warrant that permits the holder to claim ownership of a property or identity and to have a reasonable probability of making that claim stick. They provide a crucial sign that the person or organization making the claim can be trusted because he or she is backed by an institutional guarantee (Nock 1993). As Reiss (1984b: 33) observes, in risk society 'The inherent fragility of trust relationships leads to a parallel emergence of institutions built around mistrust and distrust as well as those of trust. There are, for example, a series of institutions that are designed to minimize the risk of harm when fiduciary responsibility is violated. There are institutions of distrust such as collateral security and the collectivization of risk to minimize losses from turns due to violation of trust.'

The trust embedded in securities facilitates freedom of action and communication. It allows transactions to occur in a routine and taken-for-granted manner even when they happen at a distance rather than face to face. It allows institutions to engage in efficient transactions with others who are strangers except for the securities they bear.

The security instrument itself lacks tangibility. It always represents or stands for something else, and transcends space and time. Although a security may only have validity within particular institutional territories and contexts, it can also transcend institutional and territorial borders. Indeed, securities are designed to transcend boundaries freely, to constitute rights of ownership, identity, and exchange across space and time.

These features of securities introduce unique nonterritorial aspects into policing. Securities policing *necessarily* entangles the police in complex interinstitutional communication networks. This entanglement not only relates to the fact that symbolic property is a product of other institutions but also to the ways in which symbolic property moves so freely across institutional boundaries. Because the policing of securities is entirely knowledge-based, the police are involved in appropriating and redistributing other institutions' security symbols, and the risk criteria relevant to such symbols.

The symbolic and interinstitutional dimensions of securities policing also mean that this form of policing often seems intangible. For example, when a commercial securities investigation involves trying to access computer trails of complex financial transactions across both nation-state and institutional borders, policing is itself transitory. It is an attempt to police information, and information is the hardest thing in the world to guard because it can be stolen without being removed from its place. As one of our police interviewees observed, tangibility depends on the type of security policed: 'So somebody breaks into a bank vault and steals $100 million. It's money, it's gone. You know it's gone. That's all there is to it ... [But with complex financial transactions conducted via information technology] we need to know that information is gone. Information can go without the actual document disappearing or the computer program being tampered with.'

The abstract quality of symbolic transactions involving many institutions also makes it difficult for the public police to convince others that the matter is clearly within their jurisdiction. The people we spoke to noted that it is much easier to justify police resources for drug enforcement or combatting street violence because those areas can be made tangible through dramatization and personalization (see Manning 1980). In contrast, securities offences represent something abstract and complex that most people do not grasp, let alone become alarmed about. As a result the police often give up some jurisdiction to other institutions in the division of labour in securities policing. They depend on other institutions and they must work hard to maintain the ties with those institutions that will facilitate their policing.

The abstract and complex dimensions of securities transactions, and the dependency on other institutions, mean that the police often face substantial barriers to effective securities policing. As one police interviewee said, even in simpler matters such as credit card or telemarketing frauds, 'Crooks have no boundaries, we do.' When it comes to more-complex financial transactions, the people involved and the symbolic property they trade in seem to be everywhere and nowhere, 'And that's the best part of it all [for culprits]. They don't have to touch it. It's an easy game for them. They can do it from Switzerland, they can do it from Germany, they can do it from anywhere. And when you try to chase money or chase shares and that, you've got to go through so many treaties it's unbelievable. But that's the new world of global policing.'

The police must develop new and varied strategies to gain some purchase on securities policing. As G. Marx (1988: 34) observes, 'concrete property rights and visible offenses seemed to call forth uniformed patrols and coercion for protection, while more abstract property rights and invisible offenses called forth invisible police and deception.' However, the main police response is to function in a compliance-based mode of law enforcement on behalf of securities institutions. The police are knowledge brokers and advisors to securities institutions and help them to establish and maintain *their* standards. This approach includes operating within the risk logics of those institutions. The focus is not on criminal law enforcement per se, but on reducing loss through the perpetual refinement of technologies and standards. As a police interviewee said, 'We define security as the protection of assets from threats ... whether it's accidental or deliberate.'

In the following sections of this chapter we analyse different fields of securities policing to illustrate its unique extraterritorial features. We initially examine how the police join with other institutions in regulating commercial activity. We then analyse the regulation of selected types of securities, including vehicle registration systems, credit cards and cheques, stock markets, and computerized financial transactions.

Commercial Regulation

In police commercial regulation units, the emphasis is on prevention and compliance rather than investigation and enforcement. Some commercial units have full-time prevention officers. When advice on commercial regulation is given to another institution, it is on the understanding that prevention, as well as investigation and enforcement, is the institution's responsibility. As is stated pithily on the back cover of an instructional pamphlet on commercial security distributed by a police organization, 'Security is *your* responsibility.' The main regulatory tasks are interinstitutional knowledge coordination, risk profiling, and auditing. Direct criminal investigation and prosecution are rare.

A look at the field of bankruptcy investigation will show what we mean. With respect to bankruptcy, the police are an investigative arm of the federal Ministry of Consumer and Corporate Affairs. The police's goal is to avoid direct investigatory involvement and to have the investigation in question constituted by the expert knowledge of other institutional players in the system. A police investigator working in this field described the process as follows:

> We have the complainant deal with the trustee who administers the bankruptcy who, in turn, deals with the official receiver ... That way we try to get each party to do their share of the work, rather than having the complainant coming to us directly. I take the position that we're on the outside looking in and the creditor, the trustee, and the official receiver have all the information. So they deal with it, they direct the complaint to the official receiver. The official receiver, in turn, makes a judgment in consultation with us as to whether or not there's an offence. At that point we agree to take on the investigation and they would issue us with an investigation order. There's a lot of people involved, but ... in this day and age, when resources are stretched to the limit, you have to task the proper people to do their fair share of the work ... [Some police organizations require the complainant to hire a forensic accountant] to do the major part of the forensic work, to substantiate the criminal offence.

The police focus in commercial regulation is on establishing risk profiles of individuals and organizations. Parties suspected of wrongdoing are subject to 'financial intelligence report' profiling according to standardized criteria. An officer working in a specialized area of securities fraud was asked what training was required to do his work. He replied that the regulators he worked with in another government institution offered a special two-week course where the police were instructed on investigatory procedure and taught how to fill out forms for the profiling of products, people, and organizations. A supervisor of a police commercial unit said that computer technology, standardized forms, and the routine nature of the work meant that supervision was minimal: 'The ideal for my people is to give them a laptop or a notebook, a car, and a set of files, and to see them once a week.'

Police commercial regulators are placed in a position of dependency on external institutions and their knowledges. They respond to this by networking with representatives of external institutions. Such networking helps to routinize the formal and informal exchange of information. We observed, for example, a 'contact' party organized by a police commercial unit that was attended by more than one hundred representatives of the government regulatory bodies and private financial institutions the unit worked with. The officer who organized this party told us that its purpose was to foster knowledge exchanges among all of the agencies involved, with the police at the hub. Those who attended were asked to drop their business cards into a basket, thus indicating their willingness to serve as contacts for the police in future transactions.

The police offer various forms of knowledge and expertise to external institutions involved in commercial regulation. As the custodians of criminal records, the police can supply criminal history profiles to financial institutions and business enterprises. A police commercial unit specialist said he regularly met requests from bank officials for criminal history and other investigative information on bank customers involved in major financial transactions. He also assisted the local Better Business Bureau in the risk profiling of businesses. For example, people who contacted the Better Business Bureau about companies being considered for contracts were sometimes referred directly to him, especially if the company had had previous dealings with the police or was otherwise rated poorly. All such exchanges were *sub rosa*. As the specialist stressed, 'We certainly tell everybody we deal with when we're giving information away that they cannot say they got it from us.'

The police also offer commercial regulators their expertise in loss prevention and in how to conduct legally acceptable investigations. One police organization seconded one commercial unit officer a year to a bank's audit department. The pay-off for the bank was that it learned how to recognize criminality by learning how to carry out risk assessments of financial transactions. A police officer in this unit said that the officer seconded to the bank was there to 'offer some insight to an auditor how somebody would steal money from them, and not from an audit point of view, but high living and stuff like that ... The policeman would be naturally suspicious.'

Commercial unit officers react to demands for their expertise as the need arises. An interviewee in another police organization said that there were many such demands from large corporations, and that they invariably were met:

> The corporate security people of those companies are coming to us for resource material ... lesson plans ... pamphlets ... The corporations are cutting back their security staff ... and they're coming to us more and more for information and resource material and direction of programs they've never been involved in before ... We're pretty much on call for anybody that needs assistance. We don't refuse anybody. Anybody that has a concern over business security and safety,

we're there. It's as simple as that. And I don't know of any cases where we've ever refused anybody.

Generally speaking, police commercial units depend more on the specialist knowledge of corporate accounting experts than vice versa. However, the police have begun to construct their own expertise for court purposes, especially when the investigation involves smaller businesses. In a large urban police organization we studied, such expertise had existed only for six years. Officers in the commercial unit were sent to university for two years to study commerce full-time. Combined with their experience as investigators, this education gave them expert status in court when financial evidence was presented. Whereas this police organization had previously hired outside experts to determine whether commercial cases should be treated as civil or criminal matters, much of the decision making was eventually transferred to the commercial unit's specialists.

Police interviewees said that they also offered commercial security operatives their expertise in communication. There were ongoing efforts to ensure that commercial regulators in private corporations learned proper legal communication formats. An interviewee said that a large part of his job was helping these commercial regulators learn to communicate via police forms used for the risk-profiling of problems and for reporting occurrences.

In some commercial fields, the police assist businesses in guaranteeing their products. For example, municipal and provincial police forces collaborate with the RCMP and Interpol in maintaining a registry of stolen artifacts and works of art. The RCMP cultural property unit includes two civilian art historians and is the fulcrum of a broad interinstitutional network of art organizations, museums, galleries, auction houses, and insurance companies. The force's records of cultural items (some in book form, others computerized) allow prospective purchasers, through their dealers, to check whether the item they desire might be stolen or fake. These police thus help the private market to authenticate and guarantee the security of its products.

In exchange for the provision of knowledge services to commercial regulators, the police receive knowledge in return. A commercial unit officer said that his contacts allowed him to obtain any financial information he desired, even if it was given in violation of legal regulations. He described this situation as 'freebie information ... a two-way flow. You scratch my back, I'll scratch yours':

There is not a financial institution in the city that you could deal with that I can't find out any information I want on your account. By a phone call I can find out where you've got the safety deposit box, I can find out where you've got term deposits, RRSPs ... balances on your account ... if you're a good credit risk, or a bad credit risk through contacts. That information is, some of it is legally obtained, some of it is not. The Bank Act is very strict in so far as customer confidentiality is concerned. Over the years, because of your contacts, you can build your credibility to the point that you can get the information that you need or want that private industry has. Now to massage that information, get it ready for court purposes, is another matter. But you can, of course, do that at later dates through search warrants and through whatever, on the process, to get it before the courts ... All the crimes we see are monetary crimes so we really try to feed into the financial institutions ... [For example, in a recent case of a car salesman who fraudulently converted cheques, there was] a quick phone call to the bank. I say, 'Who owns this account? Did this cheque go into it?' 'Yes it did.' 'What kind of balance does that account have in it?' 'Oh, it's got $80,000 sitting in it?' 'Do you think this guy is an auto-parts man?' 'How much does he make a month?' Bingo! So [contacts are] very, very important.

The police pay for credit information in some cases, though they receive special treatment from the providers. For instance, the police buy memberships in credit bureaus in order to obtain routine computerized access to employment histories, credit account details, risk ratings, and information on others who have made credit inquiries about particular individuals or businesses. Describing one such arrangement, an interviewee said that 'Every time we do an inquiry it's $7.50 and we pay for that information. We belong to the credit bureau as a member ... so they are not a free contact.' However, the credit bureau did favours for him. It notified him about any credit inquiries concerning designated individuals, and it did not record his own credit inquiries:

If I want to do, let's say a money laundering inquiry and I don't want somebody to know that the city police have been poking around, the [credit bureau] will do the inquiry and immediately scrub the screen that we've inquired ... A week later somebody else phones in, they don't know that we've inquired ... they scrub it off totally. So if the individual goes in and their rights, in so far as freedom of information, you go in and say, 'OK credit bureau, I want to see my file,' they have to show it to you. So this way, if a fellow goes in he will never know that we inquired.

Government bodies involved in financial regulation are also useful knowledge sources for the police. A municipal police organization we looked at had computerized access to the data bank of the provincial ministry responsible for consumer and corporate regulation. A police officer said that on occasion he was able to obtain confidential information on individual tax returns from contacts at Revenue Canada. Routinized relations were also established with people involved in the administration of the Goods and Services Tax: 'We call them GST police ... Many times, of course, where we have a corporation accused we find that they're collecting GST and not submitting it. We'll report it to them and they'll feed us information back and forth. It's a two-way flow. I think they are probably covered by the Tax Act as well. I'm sure they have a confidentiality clause, but for them to do their work they have to have information from us as well.'

The police also have access to the records of bodies responsible for regulating the financial and ethical conduct of professionals. A police interviewee said that he had a good working relationship with his province's law society, which gave him access to information on lawyers' trust accounts and complaint files. His ease of access was due to the fact that his law society contact was a former police officer, and to his willingness to supply the contact with information on police suspicions about particular lawyers.

Pawnshops are a reminder that collaboration between businesses and the police in the regulation of symbolic property has a long history. Many police organizations have a pawnshop squad that has access to all the records of all pawnshop transactions in the jurisdiction. Pawnshops function, in effect, as licensed informants, because they must provide information about their transactions as a condition of municipal permission to operate. In one jurisdiction pawnshops were required to submit a daily report accompanied by the following statement: 'I hereby certify that the following is a correct copy of the entries in my book of all articles received during the twenty-four hours preceding the hour of date of this certificate, in compliance with the by-law regulating the same, and that the said entries are true.' In another jurisdiction the pawnshop unit was officially described as a surveillance operation with interinstitutional connections. The description contained the following language: 'Monitors transactions of licensed pawn brokers, secondhand dealers and coin dealers; disseminates information on the transactions to service investigators or other public agencies; and seizes and/or coordinates the seizure of stolen property. Members of the unit assist the City

Licence Department in the granting of secondhand and pawn shop licences. Unit members are available to investigators to locate and/or seize stolen property.'

Private corporations offer the police expert knowledge in the area of commercial regulation. If the police are looking at contraband items that require scientific analysis – such as fuels, pesticides, or drugs – they depend on specialists to tell them what they are dealing with and what regulatory standards and issues are involved. In thefts of information from computer and telecommunication systems, the police typically turn to corporate experts hired by the victim. An interviewee reported a case in which computer hackers had accessed the long-distance network of a telephone company and were using its services without charge. The telephone company sent a computer expert to work with the police on this case for one month.

Such arrangements are also common in cases involving complex financial transactions. Take, for instance, forensic accountants, who usually work in-house for large corporations or as consultants to large corporations on a case-by-case basis, and can be found managing all aspects of financial investigations, including such crucial decisions as whether to bring a matter to civil or criminal court. Forensic accountants sometimes begin as bank auditors or accounting firm experts who are seconded to the police for an extensive period of time to provide expertise and to learn about how the police handle the legal aspects of cases. Armed with this knowledge, they then are able to specialize in forensic accounting, their job being to steer cases of corporate wrongdoing away from the police and the criminal justice system. The police end up as a minor component of a compliance-oriented regulatory system, and criminal prosecution is rare. When criminal prosecution does occur, it is within narrow limits defined by the forensic accountants. A commercial unit officer explained what happens and why:

A corporation that's getting ripped off, they [private forensic accountants] can do the work for you and you don't have to report to the police ... They're going to go into the civil courts and that's where the criminal courts want it to go. They don't want to charge anybody. It's too costly on taxpayers ... The day of the long-winded, long-trial paper crime is gone. Courts don't want to do them ... so what you do is you put together a case that's got all the best evidence rules, you pick your best case and give full disclosure ... because you've got the evidence. So you use a forensic accountant to tie up any loose ends ... to get it in there. So that's why we hire them.

What we have learned about commercial regulation supports our model of policing as the interinstitutional exchange of risk management knowledge within a context of compliance-based enforcement. Regulation works only to the extent that the police maintain contacts, whether electronically via computers and telephones or interpersonally via relations of personal trust and reciprocity. A police commercial unit officer told us that the police

> would be dead without contacts ... A policeman has a lot of general knowledge ... [but] has to seek out the information from the people, from the experts. And without the contacts to get that information to find out what he wants, a policeman is nothing ... A policeman is a gatherer of information ... so we've got fantastic contacts: Land Titles Office, Motor Vehicles Branch, Better Business Bureau, Consumer and Corporate Affairs both provincial and federal, Excise, Tax, Law Society, Agriculture Canada, telephone company, airport, Gaming Commission, Securities Commission, Social Services, Treasury Department, brokerages, co-op, Canada Customs, Immigration and Employment, Unemployment Insurance Commission, Central Registry, City Licensing, it just goes on and on.

Vehicle Registration

The policing of vehicles has both territorial and securities dimensions. Although vehicles move across territories and are traced by a variety of observational and electronic devices (see chapter 7), they are also constituted as securities that bear risks. Vehicles come with certificates and credentials that attest to ownership and identity, give assurance of the fulfilment of obligations, and guarantee against risk of loss. These certificates and credentials include, among other things, driver's licences, insurance cards, and vehicle registration document. In this section we focus on vehicle registration to understand how, in the policing of securities, the material is embedded in the symbolic.

A great deal of police work in relation to vehicles involves the authentication of registration and ownership. In this work the police serve the auto industry in much the same way that they serve the art industry (see p. 203), by assuring consumers that the goods are not stolen or fake. For example, the police work with Consumer and Corporate Affairs compliance officers to enforce the Weights and Measures Act provisions against the selling of second-hand vehicles whose odometers have been rolled back. The police also expend considerable resources on detecting the fraudulent alteration of vehicle registration numbers. We interviewed a motor vehicle unit officer who had developed an expertise in this area of the securities trade:

> It took me two years to gain my expert status ... I needed to make sure that I knew almost ... every aspect of vehicle identification from every manufacturer's point of view. Then I had to view and probably work on three or four hundred stolen renumbered cars. I had to go to every wrecking yard and virtually observe thousands upon thousands. So I had to set a standard for what I considered to be expert status and I did that ... So in my work with a prosecutor here, I set up my status to indicate long research, long analytical, long personal investigation of all the theft-related matters ... VIN identification ... heat and acid restoration ... all the courses ... [previously] there was no formalized concept ... no documentation supporting it ... Now we've got, at least, a standard, one that's been accepted by the courts, by all of my people here now ... Now you have to be more formalized and more professional about what you do ... I had to establish ... a concrete base for my status in court so that I couldn't be challenged ... [Now] there's nobody that wishes to challenge us because they just don't have the resources available to challenge us.

The registration of vehicles is also related to the risk management of vehicle, road, and driver safety. Transport Canada and provincial government motor vehicle agencies maintain very detailed records of accidents, which are then risk-profiled for the purpose of improving the safety of vehicles, roads, and drivers. An official responsible for improving the collection and use of this data described the efforts of Transport Canada to develop a system for accessing every province's records on

> what it is in certain areas that keeps causing accidents, so that they can plan on redoing roads, as an example. They want to know if one specific car keeps having the same accident and killing people. Therefore, they will turn around and insist that any cars manufactured should have this and that. So they established standards. So in order to establish that database, they are asking the municipal and provincial police force or province now to supply them with all of that information ... They want to know the alcohol count number because they want to see if the blood alcohol count is too low and even people with the 0.8 or less are having accidents all the time ... They're going to request to the province to see if they can modify their form to have this thrown in ... [At present] you need to bring them back to the detachment where he has this [breathalyser] count that you can fill the form out ... [but it is possible to] devise a mobile unit that has a

count, with possibly – assuming it has the proper interface – connecting it to the side of the laptops and it automatically puts it on the form.

The reporting of accidents is highly structured and formatted, the purpose being to serve the needs of external institutions – motor vehicle branches, insurance companies, vehicle manufacturers, health care providers, and so on – that require risk knowledge of vehicles, roads, and drivers. In figure 10.1 we reproduce the 1991 Alberta Collision Report Form. This form requires the police and the parties involved in an accident to provide fine-grained detail on the background to the accident, on the parties involved, on the vehicles and their owners, and on road and environmental conditions at the time. It comes with a forty-eight-page *Alberta Manual on Classification and Reporting of Vehicle Collisions,* which provides highly specific coding instructions for each category and classification on the form. The form and the manual together turn the investigating officer into, in effect, a social scientist fieldworker guided by fixed-choice criteria designed to facilitate systematic observation (see chapter 15). Thus formatted, the officer is bound to report the accident within the constraints imposed by the risk-relevant criteria of external institutions. Every detail of context, people, vehicles, roads, and environments is registered and subsequently risk-profiled to ascertain the norm and the anomaly. That is, the job of the police, and of all other institutions connected with the accident event, is to ensure that the event is interpreted in terms of whether it is or is not a 'normal accident,' for a 'normal accident' is no accident at all.

Police organizations also employ traffic analysts who undertake separate follow-up investigations using a different set of forms. One police organization had a very detailed five-page form that included a full page for the lamp examination and another full page for the tire examination. The data that these analysts collect are useful not only in investigating particular cases but also in helping vehicle manufacturers and regulators monitor and improve standards.

By law, accidents must be reported when certain conditions occur. A reportable accident is typically one that occurs on a public road and results in death, injury, or property damage that exceeds a specified dollar amount. Escaping the scene of a reportable accident one has caused is a criminal offence, commonly referred to as a 'hit and run.' Special police units are responsible for tracking hit-and-run suspects and their vehicles. In one municipal jurisdiction the members of the 'Hit and Run Unit' were described not in the language of investigation

FIGURE 10.1

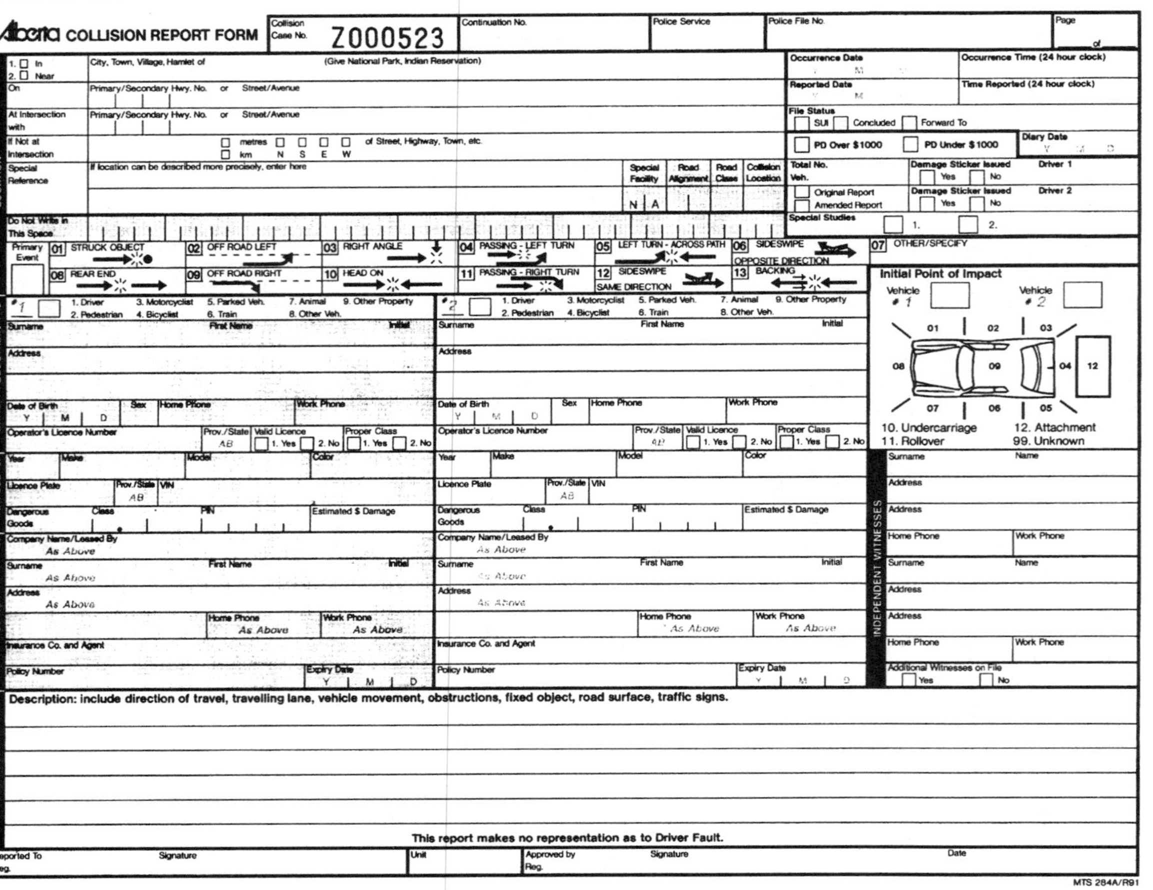

Alberta COLLISION REPORT FORM

Collision Case No. Z000523 | Continuation No. | Police Service | Police File No. | Page of

LOCATION

1. In / 2. Near — City, Town, Village, Hamlet of (Give National Park, Indian Reservation)

On — Primary/Secondary Hwy. No. or Street/Avenue

At Intersection with — Primary/Secondary Hwy. No. or Street/Avenue

If Not at Intersection — metres / km — N S E W — of Street, Highway, Town, etc.

Special Reference — If location can be described more precisely, enter here

Special Facility | Road Alignment | Road Class | Collision Location — N A

Occurrence Date Y M D | Occurrence Time (24 hour clock)

Reported Date Y M | Time Reported (24 hour clock)

File Status: SUI / Concluded / Forward To

PD Over $1000 / PD Under $1000 | Diary Date Y M D

Total No. Veh. | Damage Sticker Issued Yes No — Driver 1

Original Report / Amended Report | Damage Sticker Issued Yes No — Driver 2

Special Studies 1. 2.

Do Not Write in This Space

Primary Event: 01 STRUCK OBJECT; 02 OFF ROAD LEFT; 03 RIGHT ANGLE; 04 PASSING - LEFT TURN; 05 LEFT TURN - ACROSS PATH; 06 SIDESWIPE OPPOSITE DIRECTION; 07 OTHER/SPECIFY; 08 REAR END; 09 OFF ROAD RIGHT; 10 HEAD ON; 11 PASSING - RIGHT TURN; 12 SIDESWIPE SAME DIRECTION; 13 BACKING

A DRIVER PEDESTRIAN

#1 — 1. Driver 2. Pedestrian 3. Motorcyclist 4. Bicyclist 5. Parked Veh. 6. Train 7. Animal 8. Other Veh. 9. Other Property

Surname | First Name | Initial

Address

Date of Birth Y M D | Sex | Home Phone | Work Phone

Operator's Licence Number | Prov./State AB | Valid Licence 1. Yes 2. No | Proper Class 1. Yes 2. No

B VEHICLE

Year | Make | Model | Color

Licence Plate | Prov./State AB | VIN

Dangerous Goods | Class | PIN | Estimated $ Damage

C OWNER

Company Name/Leased By — As Above

Surname — As Above | First Name | Initial

Address — As Above

Home Phone — As Above | Work Phone — As Above

Insurance Co. and Agent

Policy Number | Expiry Date Y M D

#2 — 1. Driver 2. Pedestrian 3. Motorcyclist 4. Bicyclist 5. Parked Veh. 6. Train 7. Animal 8. Other Veh. 9. Other Property

Surname | First Name | Initial

Address

Date of Birth Y M D | Sex | Home Phone | Work Phone

Operator's Licence Number | Prov./State AB | Valid Licence 1. Yes 2. No | Proper Class 1. Yes 2. No

Year | Make | Model | Color

Licence Plate | Prov./State AB | VIN

Dangerous Goods | Class | PIN | Estimated $ Damage

Company Name/Leased By — As Above

Surname — As Above | First Name | Initial

Address — As Above

Home Phone — As Above | Work Phone — As Above

Insurance Co. and Agent

Policy Number | Expiry Date Y M D

Initial Point of Impact

Vehicle #1 | Vehicle #2

01 02 03 04 05 06 07 08 09 12

10. Undercarriage 11. Rollover 12. Attachment 99. Unknown

INDEPENDENT WITNESSES

Surname | Name

Address

Address

Home Phone | Work Phone

Surname | Name

Address

Address

Home Phone | Work Phone

Additional Witnesses on File Yes No

POLICE STATEMENT

Description: include direction of travel, travelling lane, vehicle movement, obstructions, fixed object, road surface, traffic signs.

This report makes no representation as to Driver Fault.

Reported To Reg. | Signature | Unit | Approved by Reg. | Signature | Date

MTS 284A/R91

Alberta COLLISION REPORT FORM | Collision Case No. Z000523 | Police Service | Police File No.

D

Object Identification (1 2)

- 01. Passenger Car
- 02. Pick-Up/Van <4500kg
- 03. Mini-Van/MPV
- 04. Truck >4500kg
- 05. Truck Tractor
- 06. Motorcycle/Scooter
- 07. Pedestrian
- 08. Bicycle
- 09. School Bus
- 10. Transit Bus
- 11. Intercity Bus
- 12. Other Bus
- 13. Fixed Object
- 14. Train
- 15. Animal
- 16. Motorhome
- 17. Construction Equipment
- 18. Emergency Vehicle
- 19. Farm Equipment
- 20. Off-Highway Vehicle
- 21. Motorized Snow Vehicle
- 22. Moped
- 98. Other/Specify
- 99. Unknown

Light Conditions (Choose one in A and one in B)

A (1 2)
- 01. Daylight
- 02. Sunglare
- 03. Darkness
- 99. Unknown

B (1 2)
- 01. No Artificial Light
- 02. Artificial Light
- 99. Unknown

Traffic Control Device (1 2)

- 01. None Present
- 02. Traffic Signal/Lights
- 03. Stop Sign
- 04. Yield Sign
- 05. Merge Sign
- 06. Pedestrian Cross-Walk
- 07. School Bus
- 08. Lane Control Signal
- 09. RR Crossing
- 98. Other/Specify
- 99. Unknown

Contributing Road Condition (1 2)

- 01. No Unusual Condition
- 02. Under Const./Maint.
- 03. Hole/Ruts/Bumps
- 04. Slippery When Wet
- 05. Oily Pavement
- 06. Soft/Sharp Shoulder
- 98. Other/Specify
- 99. Unknown

Environmental Condition

- 01. Clear
- 02. Raining
- 03. Hail/Sleet
- 04. Snow
- 05. Fog/Smog/Smoke/Dust
- 06. High Wind
- 98. Other/Specify
- 99. Unknown

Surface Condition

- 01. Dry
- 02. Wet
- 03. Slush/Snow/Ice
- 04. Loose Surface Mat.
- 05. Muddy
- 98. Other/Specify
- 99. Unknown

INSTRUCTIONS

This form is **NOT** to be used if there has been **A FATALITY OR INJURY, A HIT AND RUN CRASH, OR A CRASH INVOLVING A NATIONAL SAFETY CODE VEHICLE** (school bus, truck >4500 kg, truck tractor).

PLEASE HAVE YOUR DRIVER'S LICENCE, VEHICLE REGISTRATION, INSURANCE (PINK) CARD, AND THE VEHICLE WHICH WAS INVOLVED IN THE COLLISION WHEN REPORTING TO THE POLICE.

EACH DRIVER SHALL COMPLETE EITHER THE BLUE OR YELLOW SECTIONS OF THIS FORM ONLY.

A. DRIVER INFORMATION
OPERATOR LICENCE NUMBER - This number should appear on the top portion of your Alberta Driver's Licence (Example: 123456-999)

Alberta OPERATOR'S LICENCE — NO. 123456-999 — Smith, Bill

B. VEHICLE INFORMATION
Please take the following information from your vehicle registration documents:

YEAR: Enter the year of vehicle using the last two digits only. ("86" for a 1986 vehicle)
MAKE MODEL: EXAMPLE: Ford Bronco or Chev Camaro.
COLOR: Enter the color(s) of the vehicle as per registration.
LICENCE PLATE: This is the plate number on your vehicle.
VIN: This is your vehicle identification number found on your vehicle registration.
This number is a long one, please make sure you have copied it correctly.

Vehicle Make: Chevrolet — Year: 86 — Vehicle Access Code (VAC): 01078-4700 — Alberta Vehicle Registration Certificate — Tab Validation Number: 91012007517
Model or Series: Camaro — Body Color: Blue — Fuel: Gas — Licence Plate No.: DRS 123 — Class: 3 — Licenced Mass: kg
Vehicle Style: 2 door — Licenced Mass: kg — Expiry Date (Y/M/D): 1991/01/31 — Type of Operation: Passenger
Vehicle Identification (VIN): 1G3AH46R2SP241378 — Unit Number — Bus Capacity — If Leased Vehicle, Leasing Company Name and MVID

C. WHO OWNS THIS VEHICLE?
Please use your insurance pink card to assist you in completing the following:
Owner Name and Address.
Insurance Co./Agent:
Write the name of the insurance company and the agent in this area.
For example: XXX Insurance Inc., Protect Agencies Inc.
Policy Number: Write the policy number from the area on the pink card.

XXX INSURANCE INC.
BILL SMITH
77 MAIN STREET
EDMONTON, ALBERTA T5T 2J6
217408
86 CHEV 1G3AH46R2SP241378
15 | 09 | 90
15 | 03 | 91
2698 PROTECT AGENCIES INC.

D. Please select only **ONE** item from <u>each</u> of the sections listed: Check only the <u>one</u> which best describes.

Printed on Recycled Paper

POLICE COPY

and enforcement, but as advisors, compliance officers, and knowledge brokers. According to an official description, the unit 'advises other police members and victims on hit and run accidents, and monitors auto body shops in the city to ensure compliance with provincial regulations. Also, records all hit and run accidents on the computer system, which enables a search of victim and accused vehicles, and the search of partial plates.' This unit was also responsible for monitoring the use of the province's 'Damaged Motor Vehicle Clearance Sticker,' which included the statement that 'the damage indicated hereon has been reported to police as required by law. This damage may now be repaired and sticker must be left on windshield until this is done. Sticker must be removed when damage is repaired.' There was a brisk local trade in stolen stickers, which was also subject to policing by the Hit and Run Unit.

The interinstitutional nature of motor vehicle securities policing is obvious. A motor vehicle unit officer told us that he and his colleagues 'try and infiltrate, and I use that word kindly – befriend would be a better word – infiltrate the [motor vehicle] industry. Infiltrating the industry means to go out there and solicit assistance, to speak to the used [and] new car dealerships, wrecking yards, insurance companies, motor vehicle outlets, et cetera, et cetera, and try and convince them that we're fighting this war together.'

In addition to being sources of information in the investigation and verification of motor vehicle registration systems, industry contacts collaborate with the police in the refinement of prevention devices. A police motor vehicle unit officer said that he received 'a dozen, maybe two dozen calls a day from managers and salesmen with problems.' He was also a member of a committee of manufacturers' representatives that met monthly to discuss security problems. The focus of his work was to provide compliance-oriented technical advice to the industry on weaknesses in the security of their vehicles:

> We find a weak product, as we found with Toyota, weak ignitions, and they rectified it right away ... [We are] specifically telling them if they don't do something – for example, General Motors with the number one stolen car here is the Camaro – if you don't do something with your ignition system then the juveniles will continue because it's susceptible, it's a weak product, it's susceptible to the scissors, juveniles, and screwdriver. We are trying to lobby for change but this has to be federal lobbying. The manufacturers come under the direction of the federal government.

As this interviewee indicated, compliance is effected at several levels. There is direct dealing with manufacturers to correct particular problems, as well as collaboration with federal compliance officers in searching for long-term regulatory solutions. The main compliance lever available to the police is the industry fear that the police will publicize information on which cars are least secure, and that this publicity will harm sales.

The police work closely with other public and private sector agencies to regulate the securities aspects of vehicles. One police organization we studied had cooperated with local bailiffs to set up an information system to ensure that vehicles stolen had not in fact been seized under legal process. The police also have a close working relationship with the insurance industry. A motor vehicle unit officer said that investigators from the Canadian Automobile Theft Bureau of the Insurance Crime Prevention Bureau of Canada 'virtually use our office. We're very much in tune with some of the big insurance companies and we're doing a lot of work for them now ... [For example,] we're starting to see fraudulent-accident investigations here where stolen vehicles reported are actually set up for an injury accident, civil litigation ... setting up accidents for lawsuit purposes.' This officer was also responsible for a motor vehicle theft complaint information system that ascertained which cases should be selected out as 'insurance problems' to be dealt with by the insurance industry rather than by the police.

Police motor vehicle specialists and civilian experts employed by government motor vehicle registries both yearn for technical devices that will ease their work. One thing they hope for is a 'smart card' that will contain all the necessary information on the driver and the vehicle (including ownership and insurance). As imagined by a government motor vehicle registry officer we interviewed, 'All he [the police officer] will have to do is pass his wand over it and he's got basically all of the material that he needs.' A limited version of the smart card is, in fact, already available in some American jurisdictions, where title-registration schemes are in effect and provide the basis for the information on the cards. The cards record ownership, offer a way of knowing about liens when a car is sold, and prevent salvage yards from switching vehicle registration numbers (because the title itself cannot be altered).

Financial Instruments

Just as the police authenticate and guarantee tangible goods such as vehicles and works of art, they also support the financial securities industry by helping to identify fraudulent cheques. The police readily accept this role, including the substantial subsidy to the industry that their work represents. They embraced this role because they see the community as including major financial institutions and their securities systems. It thus seems natural to the police that they should serve the community of financial institutions by helping to constitute its securities knowledge and thereby bolstering trust in the financial system.

A police officer working as a financial securities analyst observed that the police support 'big outfits, loss prevention outfits that are looking for ideas or assistance or anything that comes off Translink ... Bay, Woodwards, Eatons.' He drew a moral distinction between offering help to the 'big outfits' and not to security products companies and real estate companies that profit directly from crime prevention, reasoning that the latter kinds of companies

> target people. You know, 'You've got the worst break-in rate in the city. You should buy my product.' And it's *not* what we're about. When we supply information ... [to companies] it's almost sort of a tacit approval of their solution ... bank security or Visa or Mastercard or telephone security who we work with quite a bit. Those kinds of organizations that are trying to prevent crime as opposed to somebody who's going to try and sell a service off of the crime, or in their case, sell real estate in our area because there's a low crime rate in that area, so buy a house here.

Police participation in the financial securities system is extensive. The RCMP, for example, operates a system for recording cases of fraud throughout Canada. The system is managed by the Handwriting Analysis and Data Centre, which in 1992 had twenty-six employees devoted to the operation. Police departments send in occurrence reports, fraudulent cheques, and other documents for examination and sorting. In 1992 there were 35,000 exhibits available for viewing on search-wheels and a main collection of one million exhibits. Over one million items were examined and sorted each month. Similarly, local police organizations maintain their own fraud identification and tracking systems. An organization we studied hired a computer specialist to develop a tracking system for use by the fraud squad. The officers we interviewed believed that it was necessary for them to police fraud against the financial securities industry because the industry itself deliberately fails to adequately look after its own interest. The reason, we were told, is that excessive vigilance by the industry would offend honest customers and upset the routine flow of transactions.

The police assist the financial securities industry in a number of ways beyond the panoptic sorting of securities documents. There are, for instance, committees that include representatives from the industry and the police, which focus on transjurisdictional cases and problems, especially those involving credit cards, ATM cards, and marketing scams. The police also design communication formats for financial institutions to use in reporting suspected frauds and in scrutinizing employee behaviour. Another thing the police do is organize fraud alert systems whereby information on major suspected frauds is distributed to financial institutions and police units. Police efforts also include the brokering to financial securities institutions in the private sector of credit-risk knowledge obtained from other government insitutions such as welfare agencies and utility companies. A police interviewee said that in investigations of welfare recipients suspected of passing bad cheques, he could routinely obtain and broker knowledge concerning 'their welfare. How much are they getting? What are their assistance? What is their needs?'

The police also produce and distribute information on loss prevention on behalf of financial securities institutions. One police organization supplied a brochure to retailers that included fifteen tips on detecting fraudulent cheques, such as 'Beware of strangers who are name-droppers' and 'Beware of cheques that have the company name stamped on rather than printed – means a very small company or a bad cheque passer.' Another police organization offered retailers a brochure on credit card fraud prevention that warned them that 'The universal acceptance of credit cards as a means of payment has created a new type of criminal ... the plastic criminal.' The brochure identified three kinds of plastic criminals: loners, members of loosely organized gangs, and big-time operators. The best way to detect them, the brochure said, was always to be suspicious, especially 'of newcomers, in-a-hurry shoppers ... the customer who buys clothing but doesn't want to wait for alterations ... someone who buys several sizes of one item.'

Individual consumers are also given lessons in credit card security by the police. A 'Protect Your Credit Cards' brochure issued by one police organization consisted of a long list of dos and don'ts emphasizing the need for distrust and suspicion. No place, the brochure warned, is safe: 'At home, keep your credit card out of sight to avoid unauthorized use by people such as babysitters, guests or neighbours.' This brochure came with a list of its corporate sponsors, which included Consumer and Corporate Affairs Canada, banks, oil companies, a major retailer, and American Express. For all concerned, it pays to be secure.

The enormous police investment in supporting the financial securities industry explains why it is so free with its credit information when dealing with the police (pp. 203–4). A district staff sergeant said that even at his level – let alone in special fraud units and at more senior levels – it was very easy to obtain information from the financial securities industry. He observed that the industry had the advantage over the police of up-to-date credit information and that the industry was happy to disclose such information because 'they have to minimize the losses ... A lot of times they rely on the police department basically to do their job.' For credit card inquiries from the police 'they'll put a run on and they'll draw all the receipts that have been used on that credit card during the time frames that we need. They'll do all the background work on that, provide us with all the information that we need.'

Equities

The police justify their policing of equity markets by arguing that it helps to maintain public trust in those markets. The police join with regulators of equity markets and securities markets to conduct surveillance of suspected wrongdoers. Such surveillance takes place within expert-systems of compliance-based law enforcement. Although the police orientation in these matters is largely towards compliance, in exceptional cases they take on a prosecutory role. And as is generally also true of compliance-based law enforcement (Hawkins 1984), prosecution is symbolic. It lets potential violators know that systematic and persistent violations that challenge the authority of regulators and undermine public trust will not be tolerated. An equities market police officer remarked that 'That's why we're into it ... to maintain the confidence of the general public in the stock market, equity field ... Every once in a while we'll get people in court and [they] pay fines or go to jail because they haven't been operating as the rules require ... So that's ... say the ideal reason for us being here, same as if you're out doing traffic enforcement, catching speeders to slow people down, so no more bad accidents.'

The police work hand in hand with investigators employed by securities commissions, many of whom are former police officers who share police investigative logics. They work on joint investigations out of each other's offices. Many of these investigations are very lengthy and complex.

The police depend heavily on the expert knowledge of securities specialists who work for securities commissions and accounting firms. The police are primarily responsible for developing and maintaining expert-systems of surveillance; deciding whether violations should be proceeded against and, if so, whether criminally or civilly; and for devising preventive strategies. When the need arises, the police hire private accounting consultants to work with them on a case.

The police also have in-house expertise. All the members of a police equity market unit we studied were experts in one field or another. One was a former stock broker, another a former banker, a third a lawyer, and the others had degrees in business administration. Most had taken a course offered by the provincial securities commission. Such expertise is needed by the police not only to understand the complexities of securities markets but also to share the cultural logics of the regulated.

On some occasions the police are called on to offer their expert knowledge to people in the equities and securities businesses whose knowledge is deficient. For example, an equities market police officer said he was asked by the director of security of a trust company about how to handle a case of insider trading. This trust company employee did not understand the mechanisms for using insider knowledge to sell short and make a profit when a stock price declines:

> it's difficult for him, as a director of security, to say 'I don't know anything about it.' So because of his relationship with me, he felt comfortable coming here and asking me about it ... Again, that's an important function because next time something comes up that ... I need some information from him as to ... not necessarily what's in a person's account, [but] does a person have an account with this bank or whatever, and is it worthwhile me going to the trouble of getting a search warrant.

While such contacts are important in equity market policing, most of the work is accomplished via routine surveillance that uses risk profiling technologies. An equities market police officer said that her job was not a matter of her immediately being able to supply expert knowledge with regard to the facts at hand, but rather 'knowing how to operate the systems to go and find out.' She added that 'the information systems of the stock market are very key to our investigations and to manipulations ... I don't know what we deal with that isn't dealt in information systems.'

Some of these information systems are developed and maintained by the police. For example, the RCMP has a Security Fraud Information Centre that risk-profiles securities transactions. The centre's mandate is 'to maintain a national repository of criminal intelligence information on fraudulent and illegal activities in the security field and disseminate information to securities commissions across Canada,' and 'to check against repository of fraud activity by provincial securities commissions.' Its risk data are crossreferenced with similar profiles prepared by other RCMP branches, including Criminal Operations, Policy Centre, Commercial Crime, and Commissions. The RCMP system is one mechanism through which the police act as inspectors of stock exchanges. It is used, for example, in reviewing the prospectuses of all companies seeking a new listing on an exchange. According to an RCMP officer, 'Every new prospectus that is going to be listed comes through us. I'll look ... through it, see if there's anything that has to do with any of the investigations we're doing, or some of the people named in it might be ... familiar.'

The Security Fraud Information Centre operates a surveillance system known as Simulated Market of Reconstructed Trade (SMART) to detect trading irregularities in stock markets. Among other things, SMART matches buy and sell orders. Surveillance data-tapes on trades in particular stocks are used to detect irregularities such as 'wash trading,' where the same party is on both sides of the trade and no change in beneficial ownership takes place. The tapes also help identify cases where brokerage houses conspire to buy and sell shares among themselves in order to boost the price and thereby attract unsuspecting buyers.

The police receive 'stock watch' surveillance reviews and other risk profile knowledge from a variety of agencies, including stock exchanges, securities commissions (including the U.S. Securities and Exchange Commission), and the Canadian Investor Protection Fund (an insurance protection fund for stock brokers). This information is used to identify potential targets for further risk profiling and possible investigation.

In equities policing the focus is on the manipulation of the symbolic aspects of capital in order to sustain the symbolic canopy of public trust in the financial system. This symbolic policing of trust is based on risk management systems governed by the needs and expertise of external institutions. Police work of this kind, therefore, deals in abstractions and things that often are intangible, but as we will now see, abstraction and intangibility are even more apparent in the policing of other types of computerized knowledge.

Computerized Knowledge

While all areas of securities policing involve computerized communications, the protection of computerized knowledge is a field unto itself. Computerized knowledge is treated as a security because, like registered credentials, financial instruments, and equities, it is a symbolic currency. Indeed, because of the similarities between computerized knowledge and other forms of symbolic property, police computer protection specialists sometimes work within commercial crime units.

Protecting computer hardware is becoming increasingly difficult because of the greater portability of the machinery. This fact, combined with the development of new telecommunications networks and the fact that computerized knowledge can be appropriated even though the knowledge remains in place, means that the policing of computerized knowledge is increasingly difficult to secure. A police specialist in computerized knowledge observed that

> At one time we were originally looking at most of the computing resources in one room ... There's less physical security that can be applied to it [now] ... At one time you could do almost everything with access-control mechanisms in the system and physical security of the system. And that's changed pretty dramatically and, of course, the interconnection of systems has been a big change too. Most systems were a sort of star-type network. You had the system in the middle and then a bunch of lines and users ... Now ... there's interconnections with other systems which the whole world is connected to.

As is typical in compliance-oriented policing, the protection of computerized knowledge does not entail a sharp distinction between mistakes, accidents, and criminal intent. Instead there are 'normal accidents' (Perrow 1984) and 'normal crime' (Sudnow 1965). All involve losses, and the goal is loss reduction. We can see these ideas at work in the comments of a police officer specialist in computerized knowledge: 'By far, the incompetents outnumber the crooks. There's more mistakes made. Most of them are accidental problems. Bigger threats from accidental ... We define security as the protection of assets from threats ... whether it's accidental or deliberate.' The primary police response to these concerns is to refine the systems that will avoid or correct both technical and human fallibility. According to the officer just quoted, his unit focuses on developing 'a lot of automatic controls you can put in systems to verify the integrity of data.'

Prosecution is rare in cases involving computerized knowledge. Prosecution is avoided where possible not only because of the system's focus on compliance but also because of the evidentiary difficulties presented by the ephemeral nature of computerized knowledge. A police specialist remarked that 'Most people are not going to plead guilty to this kind of thing. A lot of these kinds of cases that involve computers, there's a lot of circumstantial evidence. You haven't got a smoking gun. There's not a guy standing there over a body so you have to build up a lot of evidence to get a conviction.'

Another problem in some cases is that building a case necessitates actual seizure of computerized knowledge assets. Seizure can sometimes put a company out of business even before adjudication has taken place. The police are reluctant to prosecute in such cases unless conviction appears certain or they have other reasons for wanting to shut the company down.

These features of policing computerized knowledge lead the police to orient themselves towards prevention rather than enforcement. As a police interviewee said, 'computer crime is a serious problem but people will not report it, they just refuse to report it because of all the impacts. So the best way to approach it is to develop talent that can investigate, identify, and relate to them and have them on-side as a preventive security aspect.' One police organization we studied sought to 'develop talent' by creating an electronic data security branch staffed by twenty-five employees, who served as both investigative experts and preventive security advisors to government and private sector organizations.

The point at which electronic-data security specialists are brought in as experts is when their clients decide a violation has taken place and there is a need to seize evidence in an electronic form. For example, in a fraud investigation in which the relevant records are electronic, police specialists are called in to help execute the warrant. Execution of a warrant sometimes involves removing knowledge from a system and finding another system to process it. It also involves attention to procedural propriety and to ensuring that the seized knowledge is presented in ways that are understandable in court.

The police preventive role is multifaceted. One facet is the extensive risk-profiling of people and territories to determine who can be given permission to access computerized knowledge sites. Similarly, data systems are risk-profiled to establish how much security they require. This risk profiling for the security of securities was described by a police specialist in the field:

> [We do] risk analysis of your systems so that you know what kind of security to apply ... We give advice on how to do it and we teach courses on it. And we help people do it. We try not to do it for them ... There's a lot of subjectivity to it ... the assets that you have, whether they be human resources, financial resources, a service that you're providing, whatever it is ... Then you look at the threats against those assets from destruction, theft, corruption, disclosure, modification ... You combine the threat likelihood with the asset value and you end up with an *expected* loss, which they call a cost exposure. So you look for your biggest cost exposures and apply your security to that.

The electronic data security branch of which this officer was a member also functioned as an inspectorate for scrutinizing government. The computer systems of government departments, as well as of private companies that contracted with the government, were inspected for flaws in security. The contracts with private companies often contained security clauses, and these were used as the standard for assessment in such cases. We were told by a police interviewee involved in inspection work of this kind that the contracts had

> security clauses ... that relate to how they [the private companies] protect information that they have in their custody while they're doing that contract. And we go and do an inspection, based on those contract clauses, of their security and provide recommendations to bring it to the standard that the government uses itself to protect its information ... It's a verification of security clauses in the contract ... [to establish that] security mechanisms are in place, and [that] they're operating ... [this] is what they're looking for.

The branch also played a major educational role. It published a data protection bulletin that had a print run of 20,000 copies and was circulated internationally. It trained government department security coordinators responsible for safeguarding computerized knowledge. Many of its staff eventually exported their expertise by joining other government outfits and private companies.

The flow of expertise was never one-way. Computer companies exchanged expertise with the branch on an informal basis. They also entered into more formal arrangements to conduct joint investigations and to train police staff for expert-witness appearances in court. Naming three major computer companies he worked with, a police officer with the branch said that joint investigations were common but were conducted on the understanding that company experts would not be involved in court proceedings. The companies insisted on this arrangement because it protected them from the appearance of undertaking 'vendettas' against their customers.

Police expertise risks appropriation for private marketing by the computer industry. Although the police may be willing to offer their technological security creations to other police organizations, and perhaps other government departments, they are uneasy about sharing them with the private sector. A police specialist explained their position as follows: '[We are] reluctant at times if we have developed something to give it to a private sector company that's going to remarket it ... We have some investigative tools that, software tools that one of the members wrote here that have been very successful and they're used by police forces ... all over the place. And the company approached us recently, wanted to take that over and market it. Well, we didn't ... I probably get on average, a call a day probably, from somebody who wants to sell us something or [wants us to] help them market something.'

The policing of securities exemplifies trends in policing risk society. It involves the interinstitutional exchange of risk management knowledge within a framework of preventive loss reduction. The police selectively broker their data and expert knowledge to external institutions and receive data access and expert knowledge in return. They normally do not seek to criminalize risks, but to standardize them by applying panoptic sorting techniques and risk management practices. As we will see in chapters 11 and 12, the same techniques are evident in the policing of careers and identities.

11

Careers

People's life-course careers are managed by institutions responsible for insurance, education, employment, welfare, sport, criminal justice, health, and finance. These institutions register accomplishments and failures, credentials and demerits, routines and accidents, experienced throughout the life-course. This knowledge is used to profile careers and to etch them into the institutional class structure of risk society. Class is constructed in terms of groups of people who share a particular institutional classification: high school graduates, recipients of $5,000 lines of credit, Alzheimer's patients, people with criminal records, and so on. These classes exist as definitional sets for institutional purposes, not as communities that share a self-defined common interest.

The police help to maintain the institutional class structure of risk society by inspecting, investigating, and registering career-relevant knowledge on behalf of other institutions. Their classification work helps to construct individual career profiles as well as population classes. In this chapter we analyse four areas in which the police help to construct the careers of individuals: the provision of insurance against accidents and criminal victimization, the issuance and verification of credentials, the management of risks to health, and the management of careers within the criminal justice institution. Our examination of these areas extends the analysis in chapter 10, in which we considered how the police join with financial institutions in constituting the credit and financial security careers of individuals and organizations. The present analysis also provides a framework for chapter 12, in which we examine how police classification work with educational and welfare institutions helps to constitute life-course identities related to age, race, and ethnicity.

Insurance

Because insurance logic dominates risk society, the insurance institution is especially pervasive in police work. The influence of insurance on policing has major implications for the use of police resources and for how police officers think and act.

Insurance deterritorializes regulation into multidirectional classes of populations and their careers. With insurance, the world is mapped and plotted not as physical space, but as abstract classifications in which risk is defined as danger, as populations exposed to dangers that can be measured and made subject to premiums and indemnifications. Defert (1991: 215) remarks that 'In its form as a *generalizable technology* for rationalizing societies, insurance is like a diagram, a figure of social organization which far transcends the choice which some thinkers are putting to us between the alternatives of privatization and nationalization of security systems.' Insurance establishes insurable classes and deselects those classes that are uninsurable, thereby constituting forms of hierarchy and exclusion. Everyone is assigned careers within insurance's institutional class structure.

Working within the institution of insurance, the police also deemphasize territorial surveillance. In traffic regulation or property protection, for example, territorial surveillance is minimal, or at best highly selective. In place of territorial surveillance, the police work with insurance companies to effect regulation within a framework of insurance logics. In remarking on how burglary reports are completed for insurance rather than criminal justice purposes, a patrol officer said the following:

A: Do you have any idea what our clearance rate for break and enters was last year? Three per cent! We have almost no opportunity to catch people breaking into homes unless we just happen to stumble across them.
Q: Or unless they run into the side of your car?
A: They would have to run right into an open door and into the back seat for us to catch them.

Taking a back seat to the insurance institution, the police become reactive servants of that institution. They collaborate with insurance companies in joint investigations, routinely act for insurers as brokers of insurance-formatted knowledge of crimes and accidents, and serve insurance companies by producing and distributing information on how to reduce loss and prevent accidents. In the process they bring into existence the insurance-relevant careers of individuals as victims of crime and accidents, and thereby contribute to one important dimension of the security and identity of those individuals.

The police see themselves as deskilled servants of the insurance companies and their knowledge needs. Spending a good part of each working day checking off boxes on forms based on risk-relevant insurance criteria leads them to think of themselves in that way. An officer in charge of a regional police information centre, whose responsibilities included the brokering of knowledge to insurance companies, observed that 'a lot of people will call in the theft of an item – they know there isn't a hope in hell of finding it and they really don't have an interest in reporting it to the police, but they know they can't get their insurance claim until they do report it to the police ... It's almost a paper exercise.' A station-level officer indicated that the only community policing done out of his station was the brokering to insurance companies and Statistics Canada of knowledge concerning impossible-to-solve crimes. 'If somebody comes to the front counter here and reports something stolen and there's no suspect, there's no evidence, well what can we do? ... We take a report for the insurance company, and for the crime stats ... that this event has occurred ... So we still have *that* community involvement.' Referring to a traffic accident report form similar to the Alberta form discussed in chapter 10 (pp. 210–11), a patrol officer exclaimed, 'That's the form we're *forced* to fill out, so that's the information the insurance company can have. That's all there is to it.'

Many police organizations have specialized units to handle the brokering of knowledge to insurers. One organization we studied had ten employees in a unit that, among other things, was in charge of correspondence with outside institutions. The unit supervisor said that about 85 per cent of their work was for insurance companies.

This unit included a full-time coordinator of traffic accident insurance paperwork whose job was to review the completeness and consistency of police accident reports. She ensured that full reports were distributed to the relevant parties, including the people involved in the accident, their insurance companies, the lawyers, and the provincial motor vehicles branch. At the time of our research she was working with a university research team, to which she submitted every twenty-fifth report on accidents involving noncommerical vehicles. She said she received an average of fifty calls a day from insurance adjusters and investigators seeking clarification of or further information on accident reports. She also looked after the sale of police accident reconstruction reports to insurance companies for $1,500 each.

Property crime reports were handled in a different way by the unit. Insurance-relevant information was extracted from the reports and supplied to insurance companies for a fee. The information usually was supplied in a standard letter that bore the warning, 'Police Property. For Your Use Only. Not To Be Distributed Further.' If the insurance company wanted more detailed information, or suspected fraudulent reporting by the complainant, the unit directed the adjuster to talk to the police officer who took the report or was investigating the case. In some jurisdictions, the time a police officer spends with the adjuster is billed to the insurance company. In one police organization we studied the billing rate was seventy-five dollars an hour.

The unit received considerable assistance from other parts of the police organization, particularly a victims' assistance unit staffed by both police employees and volunteers, which helped to broker insurance-related knowledge. This brokering included assisting victims to report and pursue insurance claims by giving them necessary information (such as police occurrence numbers), helping them to complete the required forms, and giving advice on how to collect on unsatisfied judgments.

The police in Canada have been trying to improve reporting formats and communication technologies so that they can expedite the brokering of knowledge to insurance companies. In one police organization we examined, about one-quarter of all occurrence reports were taken from the complainant over the telephone by a clerk, without the involvement of a police officer. As was explained to us by a police officer, 'If somebody steals your barbecue off your balcony or off your deck, you're not going to get it back. But a lot of people like to report it, like to have a case number for insurance purposes. And so we put them right through to the four girls ... dedicated to Victim Voice Entry.' Victim Voice Entry was a system in which calls for police service that were judged by the police operator to be a low priority were directed to clerks or voicemail for report taking without the dispatch of a police officer. A supervisor in the records section of the same police organization said that the Victim Voice Entry system was used to reduce the police workload but still meet the risk knowledge needs of insurance companies. In his view:

A: [If] somebody threw a rock through your car window, well, you know, who are we taking the information for anyway, basically?

Q: Insurance companies.
A: Exactly. They've been ... so spoiled ... they've been living on a freebie for a long, long time.

Insurance companies and their investigative units are routinely given access to police records. In one jurisdiction they had unhindered access to the accident-history profiles of drivers. A police employee who was responsible for transmitting this information to the insurance companies explained, 'Maybe the guy's had twenty accidents and he's claiming injury every year. So they're looking to see how many accidents he's had and I give the case numbers. They order all those. It just means more business for me, right? And they can order them and look and see how consistent the guy is.'

Although the police can do little to solve property crimes by arrest, they do collaborate with insurance companies in investigating matters that threaten the integrity of the insurance institution itself. Most of this investigative effort is directed towards detecting fraudulent insurance claims and towards tracing people who fail to acquire mandatory insurance (such as uninsured drivers). In such instances the police grant insurance investigators routine access to data that they can then match to their own records and thereby detect fraudulent claims. For example, a police organization we studied granted investigators from the Insurance Crime Prevention Bureau (ICPB) permission to read police files. This was justified on the grounds that ICPB investigators usually are former police officers and thus can be trusted. In another police organization, the operations manual formalized the trust relationship with the ICPB by stipulating that criminal records, fingerprints, and photographs could be released to the 'Insurance Crime Prevention Bureau for use when assisting Canadian Police Forces in the investigation of arson, auto theft and related offenses, such as conspiracy, fraud, and possession of stolen property.'

There are other forms of institutional collaboration between the police and insurance companies in the construction of insurance risk careers. There are, for instance, police programs that encourage people to make full and accurate disclosure of the knowledge needed for insurance purposes. One police organization gave people involved in traffic accidents a form entitled 'Information Required by Your Insurance Agent,' which instructed its readers how to obtain the required particulars on the other vehicles and drivers involved. Many police organizations now have a system for dealing with minor traffic accidents that requires the parties to drive their damaged vehicles to the reporting centre or local police station and report the accident themselves by filling out a special form. This, however, has created problems in educating citizens about what information is relevant. A police interviewee said that his organization dealt with the issue by creating a brochure that instructed drivers on the required reporting format: 'We enlisted the support of the insurance industry to help us sell that education to the public through putting in a little brochure from the individual brokers when they send out the new pink card ... for new insurance.'

Mandatory self-reporting of accidents is a form of diversion from the police to the insurance institution that has clear parallels with police diversion of criminal cases to the social welfare institution (Law Reform Commission of Canada 1975). In both cases the goal is to reduce the police workload by shifting responsibility onto the parties involved and other institutions. However, as is the case with criminal justice diversion (Cohen 1985), the police often find that their workload has increased, and that the difficulties they face have been compounded rather than alleviated. A police employee who acted as an accident report broker said that the self-report system adopted by his organization made 'twice as much work for everyone, really, like even insurance companies because then they've got to get people to go out and look at these cars and cover them. And then ... they don't know there's no accident until I do a check on it to make sure there isn't one, which takes time up for them and me.'

The police and the insurance companies also collaborate in promoting loss prevention schemes that place the onus on citizens to reduce risk and disclose information. Many of the crime prevention pamphlets and programs analysed in chapter 8 are backed by insurance companies (see also O'Malley 1991). In some jurisdictions insurance companies sponsor a program in which drivers agree to place a 'Stop Thief' sticker on their vehicles, on the understanding that the sticker gives the police the right to stop and search such vehicles at night during certain hours. This prearranged consent to give up knowledge of oneself to institutions concerned about loss reduction casts greatest suspicion on drivers whose vehicles are not so labelled.

The police and insurers also collaborate by taking steps to improve standards. The police serve with insurers on interinstitutional committees set up to monitor standards. They also belong to insurance associations of various kinds, such as their local claims adjusters' association. A police interviewee who dealt with Underwriters Laboratory Canada

(ULC) said that he 'couldn't even begin to think of all the groups [ULC has], addressing everything from textiles to machine parts to automotive to alarm systems.' At that time he was working with ULC in developing security classifications for closed-circuit television and alarm security systems.

The police also respond to the enforcement needs of the insurance institution. An important aspect of police patrol work is checking whether drivers have the required insurance. During patrol ride-alongs we witnessed several instances in which officers pointed out vehicles that they suspected were being driven without insurance, and they were often correct in their suspicions. In one case an officer followed a very old and dirty vehicle with a fresh-looking licence plate, telling us that the vehicle was probably unlicenced and the driver uninsured. His suspicions were confirmed: the licence plate had been taken from a vehicle owned by the driver's parents, and the driver had no insurance. Another patrol officer described in an interview how he looked for people driving without insurance: 'You try to pick out offenders. And now, people with no insurance is [a] very common [situation] now because there is a lot of people not working. So, saying that you get a guy between 9 in the morning and 5 in the afternoon who is coming towards you in the check point and the vehicle is a bit of a shitbox, I always pull him over because he is probably not working, he can't afford a thousand bucks for insurance for PL [personal liability] and PD [property damage].'

When property crimes and traffic accidents are recorded by the police, investigative responsibility is shifted to the insurance institution. Insurance company adjusters do most of the work, backed up by the ICPB, and by the police in cases of serious fraud. A police administrator who coordinated joint police-ICPB investigations and ICPB's access to police information defined the police role as 'sort of watchdogs to make sure that the people don't cheat.' As in other areas of law enforcement we have discussed, the police are overseers within a compliance system that treats criminal prosecution as an exception.

An attitude of suspicion is central to the police occupational culture (Reiner 1992: chap. 3). People and situations are constantly read as if they are not what they appear to be, and complainants and victims are routinely viewed as having ulterior motives and hidden agendas (Waegel 1981; Ericson 1982; Ericson 1993). Police interviewing of complainants and victims in insurance cases typically includes questions designed to vet exaggerated and false claims. A patrol officer who had just finished speaking to a complainant told us, 'Sometimes you get people who are just looking to take their insurance company for a bath. That is why I am hesitant to give the victims the number that was on that form I had the woman fill out. If you give them the number of the Victims Assistance Unit they might call them up and add a whole list of things that they never owned in the first place. Sometimes you get a case you can just tell is fishy. Like if someone contacts the insurance company before he contacts the police.'

Another patrol officer said that he met more often with adjusters in insurance cases than with lawyers in criminal cases. On average, he said, he met once a week with an adjuster. The main purpose of these contacts was to get at 'the truth – they want to know what really went on, if the guy is bullshitting or what.' When asked whether he framed the narrative portion of occurrence reports to flag suspicious cases for the insurance companies, he replied, 'Oh, sure.' His partner added, 'Shit, we write [on] the thing, "I think this guy is lying." Even then sometimes the insurance people don't come out, it is just too much trouble for them in relation to small claims.'

The police administrative units whose job is to forward reports to insurance companies also flag suspicious cases. Knowledge brokers in these units are not permitted to offer opinions in writing or otherwise second-guess the police investigators who compiled the reports. Instead, they use a coloured marker to mark reports that they think require the adjuster to consult the investigating officer regarding suspected fraud:

A: We don't release ... officers' opinions, that type of thing ... if the insurance company needs some further information or wants to know what's happening in regards to a file, we would direct them back to an investigator. Or if, for example, they felt that their client was not being honest with them as far as reporting crime to the police, we would channel those sorts of things back to the investigator rather than provide the insurance company with the officer's opinion prior to them not having the opportunity to talk to the investigator ... If a victim is reporting to his insurance company that his home was broken into and a $10,000 diamond ring was stolen, [and] if, when we pull up the report, it says 'unfounded,' in the top left-hand corner, that means it never happened. We won't say this never happened to the insurance company, but we will take a highlighter and we'll highlight this line right here, which says [in effect] 'For further information, please contact the officer because we're not allowed to say that this was unfounded.'

Q: So your highlighter, is that sort of a cue to them that they should be looking into this?
A: It is standard. They're all aware of it, all of the insurance companies. If we have a new insurance company and it's highlighted then we'll certainly explain to them, but it's such a daily thing that everybody is aware of what we're actually saying by highlighting that you'd better contact the officer because it's something you need to know. It's just something that we can't tell you.

While insurance adjusters take the lead in investigating fraudulent claims, they depend on the police for routine disclosure of relevant knowledge. Police willingness to disclose varies depending on formal and informal exchange agreements. A key variable is whether the insurance representative is a former police colleague and therefore judged to still be a member of the police fraternity. As was said to us by a police interviewee, collaboration is routine 'if we know it's a reputable outfit, like for example this one is a retired staff sergeant ... and the head of that firm is quite well known, his brother is a retired superintendent, you know, those types of things.' Another officer, who worked regularly with insurance adjusters on arson cases, said that relationships of trust facilitated routine information exchanges 'on the QT.' Referring to a case he was investigating, he said that 'The adjuster is passing our guys information on the financial status of the client because we're on the arson-for-profit angle.' In turn, adjusters seek full disclosure of the police case, such as what the police know about the client and their opinion of the claim. A police interviewee with extensive experience in working with adjusters likened the situation to his dealings with criminal defence lawyers. Adjusters, like lawyers (Ericson and Baranek 1982), take the police file as *the* factual standard for the case and rely on it in deciding whether to negotiate a settlement: 'Let's face it, the insurance companies are in the same boat as the lawyers are. The lawyer admits freely that his client isn't always going to tell him the truth. The insurance company is in the same boat ... Eliminates a lot of their anticipation of a guy going to full disclosure.'

As was mentioned earlier (p. 227), police relations with ICPB investigators are formalized and highly institutionalized. A police officer we interviewed said that his unit had an ongoing working relationship with local ICPB investigators. This relationship was based not only on formal procedures for ICPB access to police files and data but also on the trust that came with all eight ICPB investigators in the region being former police officers. From the police perspective the ICPB was 'being used as a [clearing-house] to at least take all the information and then give it back, saying, "You've been victimized."' The officer pointed to a number of police initiatives with the ICPB that both enhanced his unit's capabilities and served the community better. Indeed, he believed that the police relationship with the ICPB was an example of community policing, and brought his force 'radically closer to the community':

> We communicate daily now. We do ... joint-force operations together ... [for example, we take] one of their investigators, I'll give them one of my detectives and we, for a three-month period, will review and analyse every [vehicle] theft report taken in the city ... with one objective: [that] by any way, shape, and any number of different avenues of investigation ... they interview these individuals to determine if the original report of the theft of the vehicle is valid or not. I want them to do a three-month evaluation interview, all the people that reported their car stolen and give them *carte blanche*, let them say to these people, 'There will be no charges. Is this an erroneous report? Did you want to get rid of your car?' I want to evaluate the number of vehicles that are specifically insurance problems and specifically not a police problem and see what that percentage is ... I think that it will really influence the insurance industry as to making more of their own in-house prevention or their own in-house tactics stop the car theft problem.

These comments reveal that even at the investigation stage, detectives are deployed to risk-profile cases with the goal of ascertaining which ones should be diverted into the compliance mechanisms of the insurance institution. The emphasis is on risk communications that broaden the responsibility of the insurance institution to deal with vehicle theft, not on criminal law enforcement against thieves.

On the rare occasion when a culprit is apprehended and prosecution is contemplated, diversion to the insurer is still sometimes used as a form of alternative justice. The police see the criminal justice institution as a set of procedural obstacles requiring extensive knowledge work, whereas the insurance institution can seek compliance or effect its own forms of summary justice such as denying claims or refusing to insure. A police administrator who worked closely with ICPB investigators described the insurance institution's alternative justice in the following way:

> We [can] have a circumstance where we may not have sufficient grounds to pro-

ceed criminally, but we have problems with a report ... We don't have enough to go and say, 'OK, well listen, he's criminally trying to pull the wool over somebody's eyes.' We can go to the [ICPB] investigators and say, 'Look, we have a problem here. Something doesn't ring right.' And they have other means by which they can proceed ... leverages to get to the root of the matter, whether it be a fraud or whether it just be a person [who] is trying to claim more ... They have abilities to say, 'No, we're not going to pay out the claim.' What can we do? Really, as the police force, we sit down and we say that we can't force the person to make a statement that would put him in jeopardy. We can't tell him that we're forcibly going to make you give us a photograph or we're going to browbeat you to death until you tell us what we want to hear. But instinctively, policemen have an idea that there's something that stinks. The damage that we're seeing isn't consistent with the story and, realistically, we don't have the availability to go out and say to him, 'Look, you're a liar. You did this damage yourself.' We don't have any evidence that would substantiate it but we have that gut feeling that the damages are inconsistent with what is going on ... [we] just phone down [to ICPB] ... 'Has this guy ever made fraudulent claims? Or has he made a lot of claims? What's some of the background on him?' ... They can go to the insurance company and get further background from them no matter where he's lived.

The vast majority of cases never reach the investigative stage. Instead there is only the routine brokering of risk knowledge to insurance companies for a fee. This commodified brokering is highly institutionalized and systematized through established communication rules, formats, and technologies. Problems with claimants are routinely dealt with through the insurance institution. The operative law is the insurance contract and the operative model is compliance (O'Malley 1991). On the rare occasions when police investigators become involved in investigating fraudulent insurance claims, the focus is on the improvement of the risk communications relating to the claimants, not on criminal law enforcement.

Credentials

A credential is an indication of society's confidence that a person is qualified for the performance of a particular task (Nock 1993). Some credentials, such as driver's licences, are widely held and relatively easy to obtain, while others, such as university degrees and qualifications for professional practice, are more limited in number and more difficult to obtain.

Credentials also provide a means of tracing and regulating populations. The regulatory capacity of a credential can go beyond the specific role or function for which it is issued. For example, driver's licences are used by the police to obtain the name and birthdate information needed for a CPIC check. They are also used by retailers to validate signatures on cheques and to trace customers whose cheques bounce.

Risk society is credentialized. Because credentials are required for routine institutional transactions in a society of strangers, we carry many of them with us in our pockets and purses. We cannot live without them, nor can the police. Just as the store clerk addresses you by name only because he or she glanced at your credit card as it was swiped through the clearance machine, so the police officer only knows you by the credentials you present.

One of the authors of this book observed a patrol officer at the scene of an accident involving three vehicles. She became flustered when she ran out of room on the patrol car dashboard after laying out nine documents supplied by the drivers. Muttering that police cars need to be equipped with filing cabinets, she enlisted the author and other police officers present to hold the remaining documents. After sorting through driver's licences, insurance certificates, vehicle registration certificates, Canadian Automobile Association membership cards (needed to arrange for towing), and other items, she proceeded to complete the vehicle collision reports, drivers' statements, and traffic ticket that would affect the future driving and insurance credentials of the people involved.

While such credentials are continually used to trace, register, and risk-profile their holders, they must also be policed for authenticity. Credentials are easy to obtain and falsify. A police interviewee recalled, 'I had five driver's licences when I was an auto theft detective, in five different names. Two I got the same day from the same lady ... I arrested ———, another long-term criminal, and he had seven of them. Three he got in one day from the same lady.' The falsification problem necessitates a special police form and computerized data input system. A report on 'Vehicle or Licence Name Variations' is inputted into criminal intelligence information systems to assist in tracing fraud.

The police issue, authenticate, inspect, and investigate an enormous range of other credentials, ranging from immigration documents and employment licences to bravery awards and good-citizenship certificates. In every case the police job is to vet, on behalf of other institutions, people's claims about their accomplishments and rights of access to roles and functions. The police thereby help the institution concerned to foster public confidence in its credentials and career-pathing. An officer who conducted bravery award investigations explained the importance of his role:

> We look to see if the person actually did what they claimed that they did. You would be surprised at the people who claim to have done something and it turns out that they were not even at the scene ... One of the advantages of using the police is that they know a lot about their communities. They can tell when people are telling lies or even if the person was in the place he said he was. Another group we have contact with is the [Andrew] Carnegie organization. They give out awards and we do investigations for them ... It's a PR sort of thing to do. It's a good-citizen thing.

Police involvement in credential systems is exemplified by the work they do for employers in various institutional contexts. In this regard we examined how the police help to construct employment careers by serving the risk profile systems of private businesses, municipally regulated trades and services, government institutions, social service agencies, welfare agencies for the unemployed, and volunteer agencies.

The police undertake security-risk checks on behalf of private business employers. In many jurisdictions such checks are routine when private security guards are hired. Elsewhere, however, checks on private security guard applicants are confined to a limited number of private employers (such as the railways) and public institutions (such as universities and colleges).

The 'Security Clearance Unit' in one police organization we examined charged a fee to large private corporations for employment screening checks. While these checks focused for the most part on the criminal history of the applicant, they sometimes embraced other sources of police information. A police officer in this unit said that he was often directly involved in the hiring decisions of corporate clients. He indicated that such decisions were not always simply a matter of excluding people with criminal records. For example, some companies were concerned only about a person's possible involvement in particular types of offences, and would therefore ask the police to report only on selected aspects of a criminal record: 'I have a lot of companies saying, "Is there any way that you could formulate it where you can make the decision, where you can just say, 'Look, he hasn't got any sexually related type convictions.' 'Because that's all we're interested in. We don't care if he's stealing or whatever, it's just *that* that bugs us."'

This officer said that he often intervened on behalf of people with criminal records who he did not feel should be excluded because of their past unlawful behaviour. He recalled the case of a person with an old conviction for imparied driving whose employment application had been rejected for that reason. The officer called the company and argued that the person was otherwise 'first class.' This led the company to reverse its decision. The officer also told us he was careful about the accuracy of records. In one case a company rejected an applicant because of a supposed criminal record, but there was some question about whether the applicant and the criminal were the same person: 'I said, "It could be the wrong John Doe." "Well, it doesn't matter to us. It's close enough." "No," I said, "You're out. We won't be doing security screening for you anymore" ... I don't know if I should be doing it, but I'm telling them they won't be getting them through us. You can try another police service, or whatever you wish.'

In some circumstances deals are struck with private businesses to offer selected information in a systematic fashion. One police organization had an arrangement with a private courier company in which the police would run criminal pardon checks. As a condition of employment the courier company required each new employee to submit a form requesting a criminal pardon. This form was then processed by police in accordance with standard procedures. Pending completion of the check, the employee was on probation. If it was found that the employee had never been convicted, or had received a pardon, he could be hired permanently. But if there was a criminal record with no eligibility for a pardon, employment would be terminated. This system was obviously designed as a roundabout way of investigating a person's possible criminal past in the face of laws prohibiting the police from conducting criminal background checks for private businesses.

As was mentioned above, the police also screen potential employees in various municipally regulated occupations. Checks are run on, among others, strippers, 'escorts,' movers, home renovators, janitors, realtors, taxi-drivers, and street vendors. A police administrator in a large urban jurisdiction said that his organization processed roughly a thousand licence applications a week. He said that each application required an average of one-and-a-half hours to process, and that the service was provided without charge. This was the equivalent of fifteen hundred person-hours a week, the same as forty-three full-time employees each working thirty-five hours a week.

With some municipally regulated occupations the police play a more active role in the regulatory process. For example, licences for strippers and escorts are also checked by vice squad detectives and are subject to continual monitoring. Whenever an occupation is the focus of continual monitoring, the process always includes tracing criminal and other activities that might lead to denial or revocation of a licence. A specialist in a municipal force's licensing unit explained that 'We check them on CPIC ... [but also on] our local files ... Of course, if a person has a history of a particular type of offence, even though they've never been convicted, we can make a determination that they would not be the most suitable candidate for a specific licence. Like, if they've been investigated four or five times for fraud, for example, but we've never been able to lay a charge, we can, in fact, not recommend the licence.'

Government employees at all levels are the targets of intensive police screening. One jurisdiction maintained an elaborate system for the risk-profiling of government documents, which were given the designations 'unclassified,' 'sensitive,' or 'classified.' The intensity of the screening depended on the security classification of the documents to which the employee was going to be given access. The screening formats were incredibly detailed, being directed at every aspect of the employee's life. An employee would be risk-profiled, for example, in regard to his or her attitudes towards democratic institutions, including law and law enforcement; organizational memberships; credit history; possible drug use; family and social connections, including friends living outside Canada or who were recent arrivals in Canada; sexual activity; possible mental illnesses; possible associations with representatives of foreign countries; and possible criminal record. Each item was scored to establish risk thresholds and criteria for rejection. A police interviewee working in this area said that '[we] come up with a score at the end of it and that will determine whether you go [further] in the process or not. And that's all done with greater minds than mine. A bunch of PhD guys over there that are helping them develop those things.'

The police also collaborate with government and private sector social service agencies in employment screening. Screening of employees who work with children, for example in day care facilities and group homes, is routine. Some police organizations make a distinction between, on the one hand, government and voluntary agencies, who are not charged for the service, and on the other hand, for-profit agencies, who are. In one jurisdiction a prospective employee of a for-profit agency was required to pay the police eighteen dollars in exchange for a letter validating his or her good character. This fee was also charged to prospective employees of voluntary agencies if they were being hired for fund-raising activities, such as the running of lotteries or casinos.

Reflexivity with respect to security in risk society extends police jurisdiction over employment screening into new territories. In some places, for example, the police feel obligated to offer their screening services to householders who wish to scrutinize the records of prospective employees such as maids, nannies, and babysitters. A security clearance unit officer said that following the release of the Hollywood film *The Hand That Rocks the Cradle*, which portrayed a murderous nanny, 'Everybody got a little excited about it, worrying about their nannies or people who are looking after their kids. So they put it right in the paper that you could always get hold of security groups or the city police and have your nanny checked out. Well, we're busy, and it's been like that ever since!'

The police also contribute to the risk knowledge systems set up to regulate the unemployed. They enter into knowledge-exchange agreements with unemployment and welfare offices to check for welfare fraud, cheque fraud, outstanding warrants, and restraining orders (Skolnick and Woodworth 1967). A police officer who administered knowledge exchanges with welfare officers said that his role was to supply as much information as he could to assist them in their decisions about removing people from the rolls for noncompliance with welfare requirements.

Another area of police involvement is the volunteer sector. People who volunteer for work in programs that help the vulnerable are screened on applying, and periodically thereafter. As in other areas of employment screening, police 'intelligence' information that goes beyond routine CPIC checks is used by the volunteer sector in formulating judgments about prospective employees. A police officer involved in security screening explained that 'We will get requests from groups like Uncles at Large, Block Watch, and Big Brother for security clearances for applicants. Now there may be some intelligence information on that person's record and for that reason we may suggest that they not be hired. This is despite the fact that they have no criminal record. And we don't inform them what the intelligence information is.' A colleague of his elaborated with an example of a paedophile who chose victims in a manner that precluded successful criminal prosecution. The police nevertheless arranged for this person's exclusion from a volunteer position involving children by passing on the relevant knowledge to the agency concerned: 'There's some bad dudes and we know what they're up to ... we can usually kibosh it in a very clean fashion.'

People who apply to be police volunteers are similarly scrutinized. In one police organization, all the volunteers were security-screened on applying, and subject to further risk-profiling over the course of their volunteer work. In some areas of police volunteer work, security checks are done twice a year. A police officer involved in this process explained its uses:

> We're finding as the programs get larger, and the turnover with these programs, it's important for us to try and somehow track these individuals. We've had, of course, some negative experiences with volunteers and have had to terminate some. So what we can do in our database is flag those people so that, for example, if Victim Assistance has a problem and they terminate an individual and determine that the person should not be involved anywhere within the police, we can stop that person from going off to [another police] district and being hired on there because nobody was coordinating what was happening. So that's one of the roles that we try to take on here, is being a central registry.

In recent years the volunteer sector has become an increasingly important part of the labour force. It provides wage-free social capital for many social service needs. People who wish to obtain full-time paid employment in the social service industry can improve their chances by serving as enthusiastic and committed volunteers. As a result, police screening can have a significant impact on people's career prospects.

Health

As knowledge servants of institutions that manage risks to the people's health, the police are most active as regulators of drug use. Every major police organization has drug regulation specialists, although the bulk of drug-related arrests are made by patrol officers (Manning 1980; Ericson 1982). In 1992 the Royal Canadian Mounted Police had a Drug Enforcement Directorate with approximately one thousand investigators, as well as fifty experts at headquarters who specialized in areas such as the pharmaceutical industry and drug analysis. There were also three full-time educators or 'drug awareness officers.'

Drug enforcement by the police is accomplished within a compliance mode of regulation on behalf of the federal Ministry of Health and Welfare (Health and Welfare Canada), which is repsonsible for deciding which drugs are legal and which are not, and for their regulation through risk management strategies. Drug regulation and knowledge production by the police is constrained by the ministry's dictates and formulations. This interinstitutional relationship is systematized by way of a ministry form that the police must complete for each drug case. This form was designed jointly by the police and Health and Welfare Canada officials to serve as an investigation report, exhibit report, and source of risk profile data.

The recording of knowledge within the confines of the Health and Welfare Canada form is the police's contribution to the drug management industry, an industry composed of major research establishments such as Health and Welfare Canada and the Addiction Research Foundation of Ontario. The knowledge produced allows risk-profiling of substances and substance abusers the police wish to take action against. This knowledge is therefore an artefact of police organization, a portrait of what the police have decided are drug problems at particular times and in particular places (Manning 1980). As a police administrator and former narcotics detective said, 'When I was working narcotics and crack cocaine came out we concentrated all of our efforts on crack. We made lots of crack arrests and ignored other narcotics ... The Addiction Research Foundation was quick to call out a dramatic decline in the use of marijuana ... Well, they were using our statistics to show this decline and they did not look at how these statistics were created.'

The police also participate in the registration and regulation of mental health careers (Bittner 1967; Menzies 1987, 1989). This role has been expanded by the decarceration of mental health patients (Scull 1984). In most Canadian provinces, mental health is now regulated in the psychiatric wings of general hospitals and in community clinics, supported by a few specialized psychiatric hospitals. The system's goal is to minimize hospitalization and to help people function successfully in the community, but frequent patient lapses mean that the hospitals become revolving doors. Under these circumstances the police become responsible for dealing with the community and family troubles that ensue when mentally afflicted people cannot cope, and for facilitating patient entry into the hospitals.

Mental health work has become time-consuming and stressful for the police. As a result, in some jurisdictions the police are aided by experts who help them assess and make decisions for people who seem to be mentally ill. These experts perform a variety of functions beyond immediate assistance to police officers in mental health cases. They keep their own clinical notes, which can be of value to both the police and health professionals. One expert remarked that his clinical notes have been used to discredit mental patients who lodge complaints against the police or apply for firearms licences:

> If we've had contact with the person on something completely unrelated [to their current complaint] at some point, and recognize their mental illness – maybe have some background on that, have talked to the psychiatrist, those kinds of things, and we put that kind of information down into the system – when that person comes in to complain about a police officer and everything's very confused in the story and doesn't make sense, the person who's having to investigate this complaint has got some more information to go on ... [He recalled the case of a young person whom he diagnosed as schizophrenic, and whose diagnosis was confirmed by hospital doctors.] Within three months this youth had come in to apply for a firearms acquisition certificate. It was on file that my concern was that his danger level was increasing; his violence, his potential for violence was increasing. He didn't get his firearms acquisition certificate.

Hospital administrations are served in other ways by the police. In some jurisdictions the police collaborate with the ambulance service and other emergency services to develop vehicle-based computer links to hospital information systems so that patient data can be trasmitted to the facility before the patient arrives. One police jurisdiction we studied participated in the development of a computerized tracking system for Alzheimer's patients. In another jurisdiction the police gave hospitals reports on community facilities and organizations in specific areas of the city. A police interviewee said that all such cooperation entails reciprocity. For example, 'There are times when doctor/patient confidentiality goes by the wayside. When there is a problem like sexual assault, the doctor may let us know about one of his or her patients.'

Risk society is compelled to keep track of everyone. People who go missing even temporarily are registered, and the fact that they cannot be traced is in turn communicated to a variety of institutions. The police are at the fulcrum of the missing-persons knowledge system, once again serving as key brokers of knowledge to other institutions.

Because the vast majority of missing-persons are young people, many police organizations coordinate their missing-persons system through their youth services division (see also pp. 276–81). An urban police organization we looked at received approximately 3,200 missing-persons reports each year, almost 85 per cent of which concerned young people. It had a full-time missing-persons coordinator who, according to his supervisor, 'doesn't actually go out and search for people – he coordinates the files.' Indeed, apart from the rare occasion when foul play was suspected, or there was a request for information from the voluntary organization Child Find, the unit did not actually investigate disappearances.

If the initial missing-person report mentions that the person might be at a certain location, the police will on occasion check it out. Otherwise, all that happens is that a form is completed and filed. There is such a large volume of missing-persons cases from social service agencies and group homes for youths that their workers are bound by an agreement with the police not to report a missing-person case until eight hours have elapsed since the disappearance. An officer involved in administering the system said that this arrangement 'saves some paper headaches for us.' If the missing person has a record of disappearances, the responsibility for finding and dealing with the person is returned to the reporting agency. The officer also raised another point – police reluctance in some cases to simply return missing youths to the relatives or friends who report their disappearance: 'We have one very vocal parent who would like us to drag his daughter back by her toenails, but I guess my fear is that she's been sexually abused at home. And here, we, the police, dragging them back to the situation. What we'll do is recommend that social services get involved, you know, crisis unit.'

In missing-persons cases the police are almost exclusively knowledge brokers. They enter missing-persons data into the CPIC system; check other institutional data systems to which they have access, such as those maintained by hospitals; notify school and welfare organizations and volunteer agencies such as Child Find; and, in some cases, distribute photographs of and notices about missing persons.

In one jurisdiction a photoreproduction company had agreed to provide free copies of colour photographs of missing persons. A police interviewee praised the company as one that 'believes very much in community spirit and all this good stuff, and it's good PR for them too. They send out a little newsletter and talk about the fact that they work with us, and they provide us a real good service.' The RCMP maintains a central register of missing persons that is used for compiling monthly collective profiles of its subjects by age, gender, and 'cause' of disappearance. Also prepared is a monthly breakdown of parental abduction cases by age, gender, and location (see p. 277). Impelled by a risk management sensibility, the goal of police knowledge workers in the missing-persons field is to have no more than 3 per cent of the year's missing persons still missing at the end of the year. This national standard was set by the RCMP.

Policing the life-course continues up to the death of the subject, for the police serve as the investigative arm of their provincial coroner's office. This role ranges from the collection of detailed evidence for inquests to a cursory writing-off of people found dead. A police administrator recounted an example illustrating the more routine aspects of registering deaths for the coroner:

> You would have the situation where it's July and the coroner arrives at the scene where the corpse of a seventy-year-old male has been found. Now, it's hot and the body is up on the third floor. The coroner would ask the officer if there was any indication of violence or anything out of the ordinary. The officer would say, 'No, it just appears that the guy died.' The coroner would take the death certificate and write in 'coronary thrombosis' and leave. Not even bothering to go up and look at the body. Now this information is used by Statistics Canada and by health professionals. Ultimately, it impacts on all kinds of things. For all we know heart attacks aren't the leading cause of death ... we all develop our own prejudices and habits.

The main role of the police with respect to knowledge of death is to profile people who die in unusual circumstances. For instance, they prepare reports on fatal traffic accidents. They enter information into the provincial murder registers, which exist to provide a common source of murder-related data for police organizations. They prepare reports for coroners in various kinds of sudden-death cases, such as in deaths arising from alcohol, drugs, or poisons. They provide fine-grained detail on disaster victims using a form supplied by Interpol. They help to trace unidentified bodies by querying the CPIC data base and checking fingerprints and missing-persons registers.

Another police function is to remove the deceased from risk profile information systems. For example, when the owner of a restricted weapon dies, a form must be submitted to the police to verify the weapon's disposal. Other forms deregister deceased people with criminal records and serve to notify other police organizations of the change in official status.

One police organization in our study took the unusual step of offering solace to the bereaved. This service went beyond the usual police task of notifying next of kin in deaths due to accidents or crime, for it was believed the police could offer special expertise in helping the bereaved, and that the force's prominence in the community justified its outreach programs. Police employees and volunteers both took part. The service's rationale was described by a police participant as follows:

A: We have special outreach programs for people who are next of kin of people who have passed away suddenly. A woman may live with a man for fifty-two years or something and all of a sudden he passes away in their home and by the time we call her, which may be just after the funeral, it may be the first time that anyone has reached out to her and we'll supply her with some information on the grieving process and so forth. Generally, we seem to be calling these people about the same time as all their other friends have gotten tired of talking to them about it...

Q: But in a natural-death situation, why is that something which the police...

A: Because we consider it a major misfortune and we also reach out to people who are victims of major misfortune ... Our services in this unit are broken [down] into these three areas: *support*, which basically comes down to someone to talk to, someone who empathizes and, on occasion, sympathizes and who does care, gives you that kind of moral support. *Information* is the second prong which, people have a need for information about their case and generally most of these needs arise just after the police have driven away from the front curb and they don't know how to access information. We look after all of that for every victim in the city. And the third prong is *referral* and we, again, provide referrals to a number of agencies for a number of different reasons. Largely those reasons would be that they require some sort of professional approach to their situation that we aren't qualified to deal with.

Criminal Justice

The police have primary responsibility for registering people's careers within the criminal justice institution. They produce and manage data on criminals, victims, and informants, data that constitute each of these roles and the passage of people in and out of them.

Criminal Careers

The police produce and manage knowledge of suspect populations. Criminal careers are constituted by the contact card surveillance system, the CPIC system, various intelligence records on criminal organizations, and individual criminal records. The knowledge within these systems is police property. It is theirs to disclose, trade or restrict, as they see fit.

The Canadian criminal records system is vast. Each subnational police organization maintains its own criminal files and systems, while the RCMP manages the national criminal history system. The Records Analysis Section of the RCMP Criminal History Branch manages approximately 2,500,000 individual criminal records. In 1992 it had ten corporals as full-time analysts who handled problems related to the compilation of criminal records as they existed on the CPIC system. These officers were supported by sixty records-compilation clerks who were responsible for data entry and the checking of errors.

Criminal history knowledge workers are practical 'labelling theorists' (Schur 1971; Ericson 1975). That is, their actions are constantly reflexive because they understand that they deal in knowledge that can be used to destroy legitimate careers and sustain criminal ones. As a municipal police knowledge worker said in an interview, 'We're dealing with people's lives here, OK. We're dealing with accuracy that has to be beyond reproach ... If our record is found to be inaccurate constantly, we'll say, it becomes worthless ... If you speak to sentence in court, the judges accept the criminal record because of the integrity of the police ... We want to ensure that the integrity of the record is protected.'

Regarding criminals and criminality there are many layers of records and risk profiles. These range from the contact card surveillance of the merely suspicious, to the very detailed 'surveillance-subject' reports required to judge who might be a terrorist threat and therefore a target for continuous surveillance. There are different record and risk profiling systems for different types of criminality. For example, a databank on customs and excise seizures exists to help track repeat offenders. Bomb suspects, as we have seen, are profiled by a knowledge system managed by the Canadian Bomb Data Centre. Other systems are used to profile unsolved homicide cases and determine whether a serial killer might be at work.

Various types of organized crime are also subject to special approaches to record keeping. A police intelligence unit administrator whom we interviewed defined the term 'organized crime' as referring to 'a demonstrable group of people acting together in a criminal activity for financial gain ... on a regular basis, as a livelihood.' He qualified this statement, however, by stating that financial gain was not always the motive. Racist groups and bikers, two of his unit's prime targets, had other motives: '[They have] a group purpose ... That's why motorcycle groups are really good. They always seem to have a group purpose ... most of them have constitutions and sets of rules they live by.' Another view of organized crime is that it is any organized, purposeful activity that does not occur in a legitimate institutional context. Police efforts may be directed at terminating the group and its activities, or, alternatively, at institutionalizing the group through licensing, surveillance, and symbiotic relationships.

In some instances the municipal licensing of occupations (see pp. 236–7) is intended to regulate people who are assumed to be on the fringes of, or actually involved in, organized crime. A municipal police jurisdiction studied for this book subjected people applying for licences as strippers to an interview and also to background checks by headquarters staff, district staff, the detectives squad, the organized crime unit, and the special investigations unit.

The identities and careers of organized criminals such as bikers are recorded in surveillance files that map every significant detail of their lives. A file typically includes a photograph and full physical description, a description of the subject's vehicle, and details on associates and institutional memberships (clubs, unions, and so on). Information derived from visual surveillance, wire-taps, and interviews and other contacts is also kept on file. The intelligence units that create this knowledge also broker it to investigative units, where it may be used for further criminal investigation and possibly the laying of charges.

Records on organized criminals inevitably tie in with records on political criminals and terrorists. Much of the activity scrutinized by police intelligence units is explicitly political, racist meetings being one example. Many organized criminals are treated as potential terrorists. Of course, separate records are kept on suspected terrorists, the data files being similar to those for organized crime figures. In addition, 'VIP Surveillance Subject' files identify and risk-profile people who may pose a threat to figures 'of national or international importance.' A file will consist of a photograph; a biography, including the subject's employment history and family history; a record of the subject's travels; information on the threat posed; and an investigative narrative with recommendations regarding further surveillance.

As new social problems appear, or as old social problems attract increased public attention, new forms of criminal record are created. A recent example is the family violence form required by Health and Welfare Canada and by some provincial governments, which is used to risk-profile and regulate violence among cohabiting heterosexual couples.

The form begins with the following information for police officers: 'This report covers complaints to police alleging violence between a cohabiting couple. This includes those that did once cohabitate but are now estranged. Not included are parent/child, sibling, extended family or same-gender roommates.' It is not limited to recording activities that might be found criminal if prosecuted through the courts.

In one jurisdiction we studied, family violence reporting by the police was done with the assistance of social workers, who collaborated with the police to build records on domestic offenders and to coordinate forms of intervention beyond the criminal law. A police district administrator described the role of the social worker in his station:

> She has an office here, a desk in the parade room, as a matter of fact. And she works out here as often as she can spend her time out here between calls. And the officers that are working in the area on the problem-solving concept that we have – where we identify that there's repetition in the home – then they call upon her and she liaises with the family, with the agencies, be it social services or be it whoever is required to assist a particular family. She sits on the parades ... They're not at all reluctant to call her out to help them in these situations. And then she gets whatever agencies that are deemed necessary to assist from there ... [In turn, we will respond] if social services want to phone and check, 'We understand your officers were at this address and we have a concern there. What did your officers find? What's going on?'

The police subject people to a variety of ordeals to decide who to include and who to exclude from criminal career profiles, and to build their knowledge of criminal careers beyond the narrow parameters of registered convictions and CPIC records. As Nock (1993: 76) observes,

> Ordeals are today a conspicuous feature of modern society. Where ancients appealed to *God* to render a verdict when humans could not, modern ordeals appeal to *science* for a verdict. Both ancient and modern ordeals require a human to interpret the 'evidence.' As such, both are inherently subjective methods of verifying truth ... Ordeals are a form of surveillance. They establish or maintain reputations ... An ordeal is a ritual that determines whether an individual is telling the truth. It begins with a presumption of guilt or unresolvable doubt. A verdict is determined by an appeal to a nonhuman, sometimes supernatural power.

Although polygraph evidence is not admissible in Canadian courts, the police sometimes use this ordeal to sort out suspicions of criminality.

The polygraph examination is also useful in that it involves gathering details on the subject's personal history, including his or her health status. This additional information encompasses issues such as when the subject last had a headache or flu, or menstruated; drug use ('bad trips,' 'good trips,' 'no trips'); relationships with mother and father, and whether beaten as a child; like or dislike for animals; and whether the subject attended church during childhood. Such knowledge is used as a panoptic sorting that establishes the polygraph technology itself as a valid panoptic sorting. It is also potentially helpful as a contribution to the subject's career profile.

Fingerprint records, hypnosis, dental records, and DNA records are also produced through ordeals. As was noted in chapter 2 (pp. 52–66), the trend in risk society is towards the creation of laws and technologies that will facilitate rapid production of required knowledge without much fuss about due process (Ericson and Shearing 1986). For example, the Canadian Parliament has followed the lead of England and Wales in allowing the police to take body samples for DNA risk profiling purposes without consent. A device is under development that will allow police officers to routinely take fingerprints from people 'on the street.' On-line mug shot technology is also being readied for police use. An interviewee working on this technology spoke enthusiastically about how it would be used to rapidly sort suspect populations: '[You] hook a video camera up to a PC, take the mug shots that way, store them on the mainframe, and then if the guy in a district office wants to do a photo line-up ... he can enter the search criteria, call down all males that are over six feet tall between the ages of eighteen and twenty-four with beards, and you can go through them on the colour screen.'

The police also make substantial contributions to the correctional careers of criminals. They provide written recommendations on whether accused persons and offenders should be diverted into alternative programs. They enjoy systematized access to data on inmates in provincial and federal prisons. There are joint-force operations in prisons involving police and correctional branch law enforcement units. In one jurisdiction the police not only participated in law enforcement and in the laying of criminal charges within prisons but also reported regularly on the impact of their activity. They also participated in prison surveillance operations, which included intercepting telephone calls and determining which visitors should be barred from prison.

The police can also be found conducting joint operations with parole officers. A municipal police organization we studied had a parole officer working half-time in its crime analysis unit. A police colleague of his opined that 'This has been a useful arrangement because he is able to provide us immediate information on when people have been paroled and are back on the street. This is a sort of structured relationship that goes back and forth both ways. You see, he benefits from working closely with us because he knows when one of his parolees has been caught doing something.'

In this police organization parolees were required to report to district police stations and files were kept on them at the district level. There was also a police unit responsible for dealing with parole clearances. At the federal level, the RCMP have a unit that provides an automatic report to the National Parole Board on each parole applicant. This report includes the criminal history record, but the police also sometimes conduct an investigation for parole-hearing purposes.

The same RCMP unit conducts investigations into and makes recommendations on applications. In 1992, 28,000 of 31,000 pardon applications were granted. The investigation of pardon applications is allotted to police organizations across the country, based on where the applicant lives. At this local level of knowledge work, career factors other than the criminal record are salient. A police officer who worked on pardon applications explained,

> You're really seeing a lot of people that are really, really needing jobs. What I like is that we can do as much for the person coming in with the record, I think, as we do for the employer. When they come in, if they can apply for a pardon, we give them a pardon application. Most of them don't even know that you can do that ... If somebody [an employer] plain asks us, 'Well, what do you think?,' I'll give them my own personal feelings ... Just judging from the individual that is there and just how they're acting. Of course, everybody's fairly nice. They think you are part of the process that might gain them their job ... We've got dependable contact people in each organization ... if somebody's going to phone me and ask for a recommendation ... we make sure that we've got good contact to either the owner of the company or the director or this type of thing.

Victim Careers

The police also construct the criminal justice careers of victims. Many police organizations have victim-assistance units that keep detailed records on crime victims, provide a number of services for victims, and make referrals to other agencies. These units are a recent development fostered by the rise of the victims' rights movement (Rock 1986, 1990).

The risk management of victims' careers by the police is illustrated by the activities of one victim-assistance unit we examined. This unit was established to centralize and coordinate victim case management. It was staffed by two police officers, a civilian employee, a secretary, and sixty-six part-time volunteers, who each day received copies of all reports on criminal occurrences, fatal accidents, and sudden deaths. Crime victims were telephoned and given an occurrence number, and selected victims were offered special services (described below). A record of all services rendered was kept by a computerized knowledge system.

The unit's work was not confined merely to reacting to individual cases of victimization, however. There was also a proactive dimension that fed into the wider victims' rights movement and helped to create the need for the unit. Proactivity began with telephone calls to victims to offer expertise, counselling, and advice. As a unit member explained, 'Most people, unless you call them, they don't even know that you're there anyway ... Most people are shocked and amazed that their police department is contacting them to find out how they're feeling. After they ask us a few questions they just open up and out it comes. It's great.'

The unit also sought to promote itself and the good work it did. It published a monthly newsletter and had a display booth which it set up in shopping precincts and at fairs and festivals. A unit member described the booth as a means of making both police officers and citizens more aware of the unit, and of having people who thought of themselves as victims come forward even if they were not subject to an official police report: '[The booth was meant to] create interest in our unit ... If we pique their interest to the point where they want to ask questions of the guy on the street, the guy in the street's going to have to find out more about us ... [It generates] requests for our services from the field and from the citizenry out there. The trouble is a lot of people out there consider themselves victims, and unless their name is on the dotted line on the police report, we don't consider them victims.'

At the same time, not every putative victim was included in the unit's efforts. A risk profiling system was used to select victims eligible for services. If a person was attracted by the unit's promotional displays and telephoned for help, the first step was a validation procedure. Before services were offered an investigative unit was sent out to confirm that the person was a bona fide victim. Although all registered victims of crime were contacted and given a police occurrence number, only victims of selected offences – for example, robberies, child abuse, spousal assaults, other serious assaults, and residential (but not business) burglaries – were offered aid.

All victims were checked to ascertain whether they also had criminal careers. As was noted previously (pp. 229–30), the police are suspicious of victims' motives and frequently do as much work investigating their claims as they do probing the backgrounds of criminal suspects. Victims whose criminal careers were extensive or included especially serious incidents were excluded from police help in overcoming their victimization. The rationale for not helping people who have hurt others was explained by a member unit:

A: We do a criminal history check on every victim before we supply services, and if a person has suddenly been victimized but they're a person who has lived by crime, we don't provide services to them. We just don't contact them.

Q: Why is that?

A: Because we had to draw the line somewhere. We're very busy and we decided we would draw the line on people who had lived and survived and had a lifestyle of victimizing others. If we were going to leave anybody out, we decided it should be them. And we've had occasion to tell some that and they just seem to accept it ... They're usually looking for money from Crimes Compensation or money from us or something like that, and we usually just tell them the reason you had never been contacted is that our records indicate to us that you have actually victimized others on numerous occasions ... There are no strict criteria. It's up to the discretion of the supervisors in the unit. When a volunteer determines that somebody has a criminal record they come to us. For instance, if a person has been convicted of impaired driving and a minor shoplifting thing, we would provide services to them. If a person had committed two or three bodily assaults on other people, had maybe been convicted of trafficking in narcotics, those two teamed up, we wouldn't phone them. We wouldn't contact them at all ... We would only provide them with referral ... tell them who they could call to get information about what their...

Q: Because there might be a lot of people who are victimized who have records?

A: Oh yes. Oh yes ... to err is human. And we're quite divine, but not completely ... And it is very arbitrary and just at the discretion of whatever supervisor is looking at that person's record.

Victims deemed eligible were offered a range of services. A two-person team was sent out to the victim's home or place of work to do a 'needs assessment.' Depending on the results of the assessment, the victim might be offered advice on how to enhance his or her security and possibly psychological counselling. Where people had experienced considerable trauma, as in the case of bank tellers victimized by armed robbers, trauma management advice was given to both the victims and their work supervisors. Self-help literature was also distributed to those traumatized by crime. One booklet offered a check-list for signs of persistent trauma, which included being hyperalert and easily startled; being overcautious about safety; failing to deal with real violence or being upset by feigned violence on television; reducing communication with family and friends; and self-isolation. If these traits persisted, the victim was advised to seek further counselling, either from police social workers or the staff of other counselling agencies.

At the same time, the police discouraged the victims from asking for surveillance of their traumatizers as a preventive measure against further violence. Where appropriate, victims were informed that their traumatizers were no longer in custody. Otherwise, resources were allocated to providing lessons on self-help protection and to trauma management. As a unit member explained, 'Police don't have the time to keep an eye on anybody these days, except maybe international terrorists or bank robbers that they're following ... There has to be more than the concerns of the victim unless those concerns can be substantiated by some actual event.'

Victims were also helped to guide their case through the various institutions that had a stake in the crime. As mentioned previously, they were given the police file number for their insurance claims. Unit members helped them complete the paperwork for property loss claims. Those eligible for criminal injuries compensation from the provincial agency responsible for this form of insurance were also assisted by unit members. Assistance ranged from filling out the application form to checking with agency officials on the case's progress.

The unit also had a 'court accompaniment' program for victims who were called as witnesses, which helped them confront the anxiety of the court process. It also helped the police and court officials to manage cases and out-of-place witnesses more efficiently. Just as defence lawyers help to manage the passage of accused persons through the criminal process (Carlen 1976; Ericson and Baranek 1982; Rock 1993), so unit members helped to keep witnesses in order. One way this was done was by showing witnesses a video that explained the court's spatial arrangements and legal procedures, much like the in-flight video on airport procedures shown to airline passengers about to arrive at a foreign airport. A unit member would accompany the witness to court to ensure his or her security as a criminal justice commodity. The unit's victim/witness package was described by a unit member in this way:

> We will work with them from the time they're victimized right through until the end of court and keep them up to date on what's happening. Bring them in here and try to familiarize them with the court process, go to court with them, introduce them to the right people and make sure all the paperwork is in place and so forth. And then we sit in the front row and give them moral support when they give their evidence ... The investigating officers do turn ... the care of that victim [over to us] as a body of evidence. The victim is a piece of evidence basically, because they're a witness and they turn over the care of that piece of evidence to us.

Victims are as much a product and property of the criminal justice institution as are criminals. The police are custodians of this property, variously managing and discontinuing victim careers.

Informant Careers

Informants are also valuable 'pieces of evidence' protected by the police. Given the extremely limited capacity of the police to detect criminals, police forces rely heavily on informants and take extraordinary measures to protect their identities and interests. A police intelligence unit officer said informant security was the supreme goal, even at the cost of losing a case: 'We may wind up not prosecuting a case in order to protect an informant. It'd be extremely rare that we would jeopardize an informant. If you do that sort of thing your credibility as a police agency is more jeopardized than the informant is ... The informants are virtually sacred.'

Informants exist not only in the 'nudge-nudge' world of the individual officer working with his local 'source' (Ericson 1993: chap. 5) but also in the numerous police data systems that risk-profile informant careers. The most basic data system is the one that allows officers to register their informants. In one police jurisdiction each officer was permitted six registered informants. Registration established the officer's exclusive rights to the informant and provided a record of transactions, including cash payments for information. Another jurisdiction had a registration system that indicated which informants were available to every officer and which ones were exclusive to individual officers. A police interviewee explained that this system profiled

> all people within the police district area available to every investigator as informants. If the informant is a confidential source of the handler, the system will only code the handler and another officer has to speak to the handler, in order to obtain access to the informant ... [The system thwarts officers] wanting to keep it locked up, keep it away, keep it hidden ... Policemen ... are terrible for having their sources and keeping them all to themselves ... [we need to] spread the information around, spread it out, let everyone have access to it.

All major police jurisdictions operate a Crime Stoppers informant system (Carriere and Ericson 1989). A 'Crime of the Week' is publicized through the media as a means of encouraging people to call the police with information about that crime or any other crime they know about. A reward is offered using money supplied by local businesses, and anonymity is assured. The police maintain a coded registration system on all anonymous informants who reach them through Crime Stoppers. In one urban police organization we investigated, this system was operated by three full-time police officers and twenty part-time volunteers who took calls, developed informant and case dossiers, and decided which police unit would act on the information. An employee in the Crime Stoppers unit described for us the knowledge work involved in receiving and acting on informants' accounts:

> [We will] go to the computer and try to find the offence that the person's talking about ... do all the research ... It's all available on the same terminal. The bad guy: what's he got for a record? Where does he live? Where is the latest place he was checked? And put that in the package and send it out to the [police] district or to Robbery with a diary date, saying here's what we have ... And then there are times when the caller will phone back and say, 'I just saw him and he may be doing a robbery tomorrow at ———.' And so there's an ongoing kind of liaison ... One Friday afternoon ... [one of our workers] was on the phone and he said, 'OK, where is he now?' [The informant] said, 'Well, he's walking down ——— street.' It was an escapee and [our worker] said, 'Really? What's he wearing?' And he slid his chair over and there's ——— street and we watched him coming down here and we got the police cars out and we picked him up right there!

Informants are risk-profiled as much as are people in other careers.

The practices of one police organization offer a useful illustration of this point. People beginning careers as informants are subject to a 'Potential Source Assessment' investigation. During the course of employment, career profiles of the informant are kept, including a data set that risk-profiles and deselects 'treacherous sources,' and an annual review that summarizes work done and monies paid. For informants in important, lengthy cases, who may become eligible for entry into witness protection programs, a great deal of information is amassed on the person's life. There will be information, for example, on the following: marital status; whether others will be affected by the subject's work as an informant; next of kin; places of residence during the past two years; education; employment history; health, including alcohol and drug use; professional associates; financial assets and liabilities; home and property; vehicles owned; animals owned; wills; insurance policies; criminal record; and reasons for being an informant. These data are used to profile the police organization's own risks in using the informant, including the possibility of having eventually to pay for relocation under the witness protection program. Finally, when the informant is no longer needed, there is a debriefing report that reviews the informant's contributions and marks his passage, at least temporarily, out of the career.

In this chapter we have analysed the ways in which the police produce knowledge for various institutional career paths. The police are central to the efforts of institutions in risk society to register accomplishments and failures, credentials and demerits, routines and accidents, experienced throughout the life-course. Through this knowledge work the police help to regulate careers and construct peoples' career identities.

We now turn to an analysis of how police knowledge work creates population identities. Employing age-based, ethnic, and racial classifications, the police identify populations 'at risk' and therefore in need of special forms of regulation. In collaboration with other institutions, the police confirm people in their population identity categories and reproduce the identity structures of risk society.

12

Identities

Population Identities

A directory of social services produced and distributed by a police organization includes the following 'long range objective': 'To promote a professional police image by demonstrating impartial service to the law, and by offering service and friendship to all members of the public without regard to gender, race, religious beliefs, ancestry or place of origin.' This objective is proper for a public institution dedicated to consensus and order. However, it also represents one of the 'impossible mandates' (Manning 1977) typically set for the police, for it requires the police to be agents of a cultural coherence that does not exist. The police are no more able to sustain cultural coherence than were the anthropologists who originally devised that notion after studying the Zande. As it turned out, the Zande comprised twenty culturally distinct groups and spoke eight languages.

In risk society, impartial service to legal and community identities is impossible because the police are compelled to work within the identity categories of various risk institutions and to differentiate in terms of those categories. To effect their own forms of risk management, these institutions require, for example, that young people be treated differently from adults; that people of high financial standing be given insurance and credit privileges different from those given to people of low financial standing; that minority groups be given access to special institutional resources; and so on. Working within the identity categories of external risk institutions, the police inevitably reproduce the forms of differentiation created by those institutions.

Differentiation is the relentless product of the panoptic sorting process in risk society. It creates social-group identities for the purpose of differential treatment. While it thereby allows the legitimate needs of particular groups to be met, it also excludes others. Inclusion and exclusion do not necessarily entail prejudice (negative preconceptions) or discrimination (unjust selection), although prejudice and discrimination are often built into the classification schemes of differentiation and thereby become institutionalized.

Institutions are the authorial source of identities. People identify their selves with their institutional categories of risk and the differentiated needs those categories foster. Individual identity is confirmed within the classification schemes and expert knowledges of institutions. As Giddens (1990: 124) remarks, 'an individual must find her or his identity amid the strategies and notions provided by abstract systems' of risk. Thus individuals are 'inherently non-self-sufficient entities. The individuals so constituted must rely on forces they do not control to gain satisfactory control of themselves' (Bauman 1992a: 88).

The police author peoples' identities within the confines of institutional risk classifications and discourses. Through the routine work of checking-off boxes on forms, and through what happens to that knowledge as it moves into various risk management contexts and panoptic sorting processes, the police help to force people into particular institutional identities. Far from being original or creative authors in this work, the police merely tailor people to fit the identity characteristics available within police classification formats. Moreover, the texts created by the police escape their grasp and move into new contexts in which a person's institutionally relevant identity is sorted and imprinted. All police reporting on the actions they have taken offers 'a set of messages about the groups, selves and identities of participants. This is the case regardless of the self-conscious intentions of those involved' (Manning 1980: 96). These messages are 'the primary products of police organizations ... conveying statements to social groups about their moral well-being, their social position (horizontal and vertical rankings), identity, and status' (Manning 1988: 53–4).

Researchers who focus on structure argue that police involvement in processes of differentiation and identity construction goes beyond what can be observed by looking at routine police work. Differentiation is analysed by these researchers largely in terms of prejudice and discrimination, and inequality is said to be structured 'historically' and at a 'macro' level that transcends the minutiae of daily policing tasks. This view has been put forward, for example, by Brogden, Jefferson, and Walklate in *Introducing Police Work* (1988: 101):

> This sketch of the profane reality of policework – waiting, watching, serving, form filling, etc. – can obscure what the history chapter has so relentlessly revealed: the bias in police attention towards particular powerless groups ... The patterns of such bias will provide the key to understanding how policework relates to the wider structure of society – its role in relation to society's social divisions – in ways which attention to the most obviously visible and time-consuming feature of policework, the mundane, uncontroversial, routine matters, cannot.

We argue, to the contrary, that the most mundane aspects of police work – routine surveillance, form filling, and indeed the forms themselves – reveal a great deal about how the culture classifies people according to their identities and, through the power of risk classification, keeps them in their places.

In chapters 10 and 11 we dealt with achieved identities such as financial statuses and careers. In this chapter we focus on ascribed identities of age, race, and ethnicity. As Beck (1992a, 1992b) and Beck, Giddens, and Lash (1994) observe, ascribed identities have a new political significance in risk society. Risk expertise and technologies have both 'deterritorialized' and 'detraditionalized' culture. In turn, these effects have made social life increasingly individualized, privatized, and instrumental – in other words, not very sociable. In this context people search for social and personal meaning by looking to the fragmented identities presented to them by risk classifications. Risk classifications tell them not only what to do but also where they fit in the knowledge structure of society.

At the same time as risk classifications contribute to identity formation in this way, they also accentuate political differences and foster conflict. They do so because they make evident, with all the persuasion of actuarial science, the ascribed categories of social inequality. The new politics of risk identities is manifested in '*ascribed* differences and inequalities of race, ethnicity, nationality, gender, age and so on; second, in new and changing differentiations which arise from reflexivity in the domain of private social relations and private ways of living and identity. Thus, new social lifestyles and group identities inside persistent social inequalities begin to emerge' (Beck 1992a: 99).

One important manifestation of this politics of risk identities is the victims' rights movement. People in various ascribed identity categories – for example, women (spousal abuse), children (child abuse), the elderly (elder abuse), and ethnic and racial groups (discrimination) – give voice to their victimization with the assistance of the risk institutions of government (Rock 1986, 1990), science (Hacking 1995), and the mass media (Chermak 1995).

The police have become part of the victims' rights movement through the routine production of risk-relevant data on ascribed characteristics, data that are used by other institutions to address the movement's criteria and claims. In this work the police help other institutions determine which ascribed identities will be granted 'residence permits' and ultimately 'citizenship status' in the land of late modernity, and which ones will be deported (cf. Bauman 1992b). In other words, what is at stake is the policing of symbolic borders that make clear who is one of us and who is the other, and establish where people allowed to remain within those symbolic borders should be assigned so that they least disrupt the rational and efficient flow of institutional life. Bauman's (1992b: 678–9) observations on ethnic categories are instructive in this regard:

> we will accept, after Fredrik Barth, that 'ethnic categories provide an organizational vessel that may be given varying contents and forms in different sociocultural systems. They may be of great relevance to behaviour, but they need not be; they may pervade all social life, or they may be relevant only in limited sectors of activity'; that the continuous existence of an 'ethnic category' depends solely on the *maintenance of a boundary*, whatever are the changing cultural factors selected as the border posts; that it is in the end 'the ethnic *boundary* that defines the group, not the cultural stuff that it encloses'; that all having been said and done, the very identity of that cultural stuff (its 'unity,' 'totality') is an artefact of firmly drawn and well guarded boundary, though the designers and guardians of borders would as a rule insist on the opposite order of causality ... Identity stands and falls on the security of its borders, and the borders are ineffective unless guarded.

In what follows we examine the police role in patrolling the borders of identities. We focus initially on age-related identities, and in particular on youth. We then analyse the policing of racial and ethnic identities.

Age

Attending to Youth

There is substantial evidence that the police give 'overattention' (Brogden, Jefferson, and Walklate 1988: 112) to youths. For example, in a field study of police patrols in Ontario, Ericson (1982) found that youths in general, and young males of low socio-economic status in particular, were disproportionately subject to proactive stops, searches, questioning, and contact card reports. Within the police culture, young male's of low socio-economic status were referred to collectively as 'pukers,' signifying their status as a group outside the mainstream and therefore in need of extra surveillance. Similarly, a study of police patrols in London (England) revealed that 'younger people were much more likely to be stopped than older people, by a factor of about 11 to 1 in terms of the proportion of people stopped or about 30 to 1 in terms of the mean number of stops per person' (Policy Studies Institute 1983: 95).

There are many reasons for this overattention. First is the simple fact that young people are involved in more criminal and 'delinquent' activity than others, especially in public places.

Second, much of this activity is behaviour that would be deemed legal if engaged in by adults, for example drinking alcoholic beverages, being temporarily absent from an educational institution, driving automobiles, and congregating in public places. Consider, for example, the requirement in one police jurisdiction studied of a special application for a 'Teenage Dance Permit.' No similar application was required for adults. This application was a risk screening device whereby the police ascertained who was sponsoring and supervising an event, and whether music would be provided by a band known for inciting unruly behaviour.

Third, some of this criminal and delinquent activity is related to the fact that youth is a time when one acquires skill and experience in handling activities that adults are better acquainted with. For example, youths are a high-risk category as drivers and are targeted accordingly. As was explained to us by an accident data analyst, statistical categories are created to target particular problems such as impaired driving, and particular problem populations such as youths:

> drinking and driving is basically the young drivers. A lot of the statistics come ... from what you [decide to] collect. If you don't have it you don't even know [the] target groups that you've got to give this to. You don't just gear your advertising campaign, if you will, to everybody. Just like a private advertiser doesn't just send his money anywhere. He targets an audience ... You have to target people where you get results. And culture is sometimes as important in accidents as in statistics.

Fourth, the wider culture constitutes youth as a symbolic threat. Disorderly youths are an expression of 'respectable fears' (Pearson 1983) about disorder and decline in general. 'If the statistical involvement of youth in crime provides the justification for police attention to them, it would appear to be the *image* of "deviant" youth as *potential* trouble, or symbolic threat to authority, that structures much of police thinking and practice in this area' (Brogden, Jefferson, and Walklate 1988: 103). The reality of this image is recognized by the police in their efforts to proactively remove unsightly youths from sites where they pose a risk to people's sense of well-being and to the orderly conduct of business. In a document on downtown development prepared by a police crime prevention unit in collaboration with municipal officials and retail and other business representatives, it was stated that 'street youth' were '"abnormal" users of an environment (Newman 1972). They accentuate the differences between themselves and normal Downtown users. These differences may inspire uncertainty and a fear of the unknown in normal users. While these street youth/people may not increase the actual danger in the Downtown, there is a marked increase in the perception of danger. Social strategies to assist street youth/people are an important factor in improving the perception of Downtown public safety.'

The emphasis here is on *social* strategies. As we pointed out in chapter 2 (pp. 54–5), the result of police overattention is not heavy criminalization through prosecution and punishment, but further overattention, as knowledge of a youth's involvement with police is selectively transferred to health, education, and welfare institutions. With respect to the criminal justice institution, at least, the police usually underreact where young offenders are concerned. The vast majority of criminal cases involving youths are handled with informal warnings or formal cautions. In youth matters the police spend most of their time recording and risk-profiling behaviour in various ways – such as by contact card surveillance while on patrol, by setting up school liaison programs, and by criminal case diversion – and distributing this knowledge to other agencies that deal with youths more directly (Meehan 1993).

School Programs

An analysis of police programs in schools illustrates how the police join with other institutions in the regulation of youth.

The police have a long history of serving as expert educators in schools. In particular, they visit schools to provide instruction on traffic safety and personal security. Larger municipal police organizations usually have full-time officers dedicated to such education. Their role often extends to overseeing and evaluating school safety-patrol units.

Police educational efforts in the schools have broadened in recent years. Society's obsession with the risks of drugs has placed drug education on school curricula, and the police are brought in as experts. Some police organizations have full-time 'drug awareness' officers who lecture in schools and elsewhere. These officers have usually acquired their expertise by working as narcotics detectives, but they are expected to stay informed on the latest drug-use habits and risk analyses of those habits. A police drug specialist we interviewed said that full-time experts were needed because of the expert knowledge of their young audiences:

> the experience and background will add to the credibility. When you stand up in a high school with a bunch of kids in there they may be using drugs and they may be a lot more knowledgeable in drugs than that policeman standing up there. They can make it pretty hot and heavy for them if he doesn't know what he is talking about ... [Our instructors] are coming off of drug sections. They've been involved in drug enforcement in the past and it's a matter of taking their drug investigational knowledge, tying it into their presentational abilities and skills, and going out and selling a product.

The police also maintain a regular presence in the schools to help identify high-risk youths and to collaborate with the school authorities in their risk management. The following examination of school programs illustrates the fine-grained nature of the knowledge work involved.

A primary-school program was run by four full-time police officers and a social worker who was also a police employee. The social worker was initially hired to help the police gain acceptance in the schools. The original justification of the program was the need for education about the risks of delinquent activity, especially the use of illegal drugs, but the program rapidly expanded into other areas. A person involved with the program explained the place of the educational component in relation to broader concerns about risk and security:

> Drugs is the medium ... but we've got programs that talk about self-esteem, problem solving, peer pressure ... [Drugs are] something that's in the news and in the media and all that kind of stuff, so it's a good way to catch kids' attention

... There's this concern in school about violence now ... And I predict that pretty soon the people that make the videos will pick up on that as a medium and develop some good programs to deal with it ... [but] the underlying message is always the same ... to get the students familiar with the officer who will be in the school ... The real thing that we're trying to do is to be accessible to the students and to the parents and the teachers ... A kid blows up ... calm him down and get him back to the classroom. The teaching staff don't have time to do it.

This person estimated that the classroom teaching component took up 25 per cent to 30 per cent of an officer's time in the school. The rest of the time was devoted to the role of school security officer, whether the problem was disruptive children, trespassing by strangers, or aggressive parents. The key to fulfilling this mandate was risk knowledge production and management.

Risk assessment included an analysis of schools as organizations. 'High-needs' or high-risk schools were identified based on an epidemiological analysis of a wide range of population health problems such as truancy, poor nutrition, misbehaviour at school, and crime. This panoptic sorting of the population of school organizations was followed by a sorting, using the same criteria, of students as individuals. An official publication of the police organization was clear on this risk management approach, stating that the program offered 'outreach services to selected elementary schools ... identifying children (primarily in grades 4, 5 and 6) who are experiencing problems, and assisting with the coordination of a multi-agency effort to help these children and their families.'

High-risk children were identified by a wide range of informants. There was input from officials in health and welfare agencies, from teachers and school counsellors, and from parents. Home visits were sometimes deemed necessary. The children themselves were primary informants, often relating problems that were not school-specific. A program official stressed that 'students and their parents ... can access the officer about anything they want. And they don't necessarily have to let the school know. We've got disclosures of sexual abuse, physical abuse from kids. And we've got parents coming seeking information on marriage separation, wife battering, husband battering ... The officers can make referrals to any community agency ... We advise the [school] principal that we've done that.'

Members of the unit refrained from keeping formal intelligence files on children. However, they did keep notes on potential high-risk children, and used a student-profile form to rate welfare history, school history, special problems, contacts with other agencies, and family criminal history. As was explained to us by a program official, 'We've consciously tried to keep away from the officers starting to keep files on kids. That was one of the concerns that the schools have had about "Are you here to gather intelligence on students?" We can say that we don't keep files on kids, and we don't. The officers do, though, keep their notes on kids who they have a concern about ... so they get a picture of kids that they're trying to monitor.'

The various knowledges were brought together at case conference sessions involving the school's police officer and staff as well as representatives of other agencies. The school record was presented alongside records from other agencies. Higher-risk students were identified and marked down for counselling by outside agencies or the school police officer. One such officer remarked that counselling was provided

> in the sense of trying to find out what the problem is. And then get the student and the family to the resource that can best deal with the problem ... There's some students that are more behaviour problems. The student is taken out of class and actually spends time with them [a police officer] one-on-one, playing board games. We've got some officers doing, building models with groups of kids ... who have trouble interacting with their peers ... If these kids can be truly identified at the early stages, and if they can establish some sort of bond with a police officer, maybe they will think twice about the person they might be letting down if they go out and get in trouble.

The three dozen or so most risky individuals were placed in a risk management system set up to track them throughout their school careers.

The police saw their work in this program as exemplifying the interinstitutional partnership aspect of community policing. An official police statement on the program stated that one objective was 'To promote proactive police involvement in the community, and improve police relations through open communication and understanding.' A police officer echoed this statement by observing that '[we are] using the school as a base, it is true community-based policing, it's not reactive at all.'

The official statement also emphasized that 'the officer's effectiveness is enhanced if he/she is viewed as being a member of the school staff.' According to one police official, officers in the program were indeed viewed as school staff: '[officers are] part of the staff almost ... get consulted ... participate in the ... school resource group ... case conferencing

... the problems can be academic behaviour, whatever ... The officer might have a role to play, an equal role to play in the school. They really have worked their way into more of a, almost a staff position, an extra resource. The resource just happens to wear a uniform and has a different viewpoint.'

We also studied a police high-school program that was staffed by twelve full-time uniformed police officers and a sergeant. Unlike the primary-school program analysed above, schools were not selected on the basis of which were found to have the highest-risk populations. Selection of this kind was seen to be too 'political,' for the school board would have had to admit officially that some schools were especially troublesome, which in turn would have stigmatized those schools and affected students' school-choice decisions. Instead, school selection was based on the size of the student population. An officer would be stationed in each of the twelve largest high schools, but also visit a smaller high school and/or a junior high school in his or her area at least one day a week. The police office was usually next to the school guidance counsellor's office, and there was a close working relationship between the officer and the counsellor.

Before the implementation of this program, things were much different in the schools. No police officers had been stationed in the schools and problems had been dealt with reactively, not proactively. Uniformed patrol officers had been prohibited from entering the schools to conduct investigations, for only plainclothes juvenile bureau officers had been authorized by the school board to deal with problems.

This high-school program exemplified community policing as total involvement in an external institution. As one interviewee remarked, school-based officers are 'the only members of the department that face two thousand citizens day in and day out, all under [one] roof ... There's much more accountability in a school setting to follow up and do everything you possibly can to alleviate somebody's problems or stress level because you're going to see them in the hallway the next morning ... and they're going to be asking.' The program also demonstrated how community policing is set up to facilitate communications policing. The same respondent stated that 'the whole purpose of this program was to, in a kind of outreach way, obtain better communication, better attitudes, particularly among young people towards uniformed police officers.'

The program sought communication for the purpose of preventive security and enforcement. The classroom education component was explicitly oriented toward moral lessons about crime and related evils.

Eleven out of fifteen 'canned' talks focused on serious crimes and the law. One covered the Criminal Code, the Young Offenders Act, and the Charter of Rights and Freedoms. The others addressed provincial and municipal laws; impaired driving; theft and vandalism; sexual assault and date rape; organized crime and youth gangs; family violence; shoplifting; drugs and alcohol; runaways; and arrest and the court system. The remaining talks were on driver education, bicycle safety, anger management and suicide, and the role of the police (including the subject of police careers). In addition, the school police officer sought opportunities to integrate police instruction into courses in the academic curriculum. For example, a police traffic management specialist was brought into mathematics classes to show how formulas and measurements were part of practical police work. In keeping with their strong sense of what counts in risk society, the program staff kept accurate records of all of this activity. In a twelve-month period they recorded 812 presentations to a total of 27,009 students.

These presentations had several purposes and effects. They provided knowledge about legal institutions and processes, helped to promote the sensibility that the police are problem-solvers, and stimulated new problems for them to solve. A program officer related that after recent presentations on suicide prevention there were 'now four people we've identified with suicidal problems in those classes and I helped to set straight.'

The classroom was only one of many contexts in which the school police officers elicited knowledge about risks. The officers worked to establish trusting relationships with individual students in the hope that those relationships would eventually pay off in the currency the police value most – risk-relevant knowledge. An officer described his knowledge work in this way:

> I want to get involved with the new ones on a one-to-one basis so if they have a need then they'll come to me without being intimidated or scared, or [concerned] that I'm going to publicly announce what they come in to see me about. When they come in to see me I always have my window-blind down so nobody can see in. I have to give them that confidentiality when they're with me ... So there's always that stigma attached to it ... a student wants to see me behind [closed doors] in my office, confidential matters. I also provide that *service* to them. In fact, just this week I had one, was very startling actually. She had information on a major hydroponic operation in the city and we're dealing with that as an informant.

Another person involved in the program stressed the significance of having informants but indicated that there was a fine line between providing a reactive 'service' and proactively recruiting informants:

Our sole function wasn't to go there and develop informants in the school community ... However ... working in the school situation, working anywhere ... you get information. And then being policemen, we're in the information business, so we will take that information. We'll call it intelligence in many cases, and we will channel it to the proper department internally here, or to another agency if required. But we don't recruit informants at the high-school level or the junior high-school level. But on the other hand, if a kid comes in and wants to pass on some information, we will treat that as confidential information from a confidential informant basically, and then pass it on to the appropriate members or department or agency to deal with it.

At the time of the research there was tension between police and school officials over whether to make the information function more visible and explicit. From its inception the program was suspected by students of being a guise for a 'narcs' unit, and this suspicion lingered. Yet risk society is a knowledge society in which *informing* is promoted not only as legitimate but also as an act of good citizenship. The positive image of the informant is fostered by the police and mass media through televised wanted-poster shows such as *Crime Stoppers* (Carriere and Ericson 1989), *Crimewatch UK* (Schlesinger and Tumber 1994), and *America's Most Wanted* (Cavendar and Bond-Maupin 1993). People are strongly urged to join the police in their suppression of undesirable conduct by reporting anyone or anything suspicious.

Crime Stoppers had a limited presence in the school through wall posters. There was a desire by some, however, to have a full-time student-based Crime Stoppers operation. Others argued that this approach would make the informant-centred nature of the police presence too obvious. A compromise was reached by setting up a school watch program, which an interviewee described as helping to

make the students be responsible for the security of their school. It's similar but not the same as Crime Stoppers. There's no reward for it. If there's something going on in the school that somebody sees, then they'll report it. There's going to be a box set up where they can put the information in a box, slide [us anonymous tips] ... So they will look after the security of the school. And then, if there's something that we can grab and run with it, that's what we'll do. We'll charge somebody or have it ground out for investigation if it's in the community. One or two of the schools have started it. It started down in Florida and it seems to be working very well.

The community policing ideal of making everyone responsible for his or her own security permeated the school program. School staff were regarded as security agents, as an embodiment of Sir Robert Peel's notion that 'the police are the public and the public are the police' (Task Force on Policing in Ontario 1974). A school police officer said of school teachers, 'They're security guards also, not just me ... [and] I'm not just a uniform walking around there ... I am a staff member. We're all staff members ... I'm just like you or anybody else ... we all deal with the same problems.'

This conception of security collaboration allowed the police to naturalize their role in the educational institution. A school police officer said that his ability to maintain security depended on his ability to blend into the school environment and thereby to cultivate informants:

A: [Cultivating informants] depends on how much visibility you have in the school, and I make a point of walking around, constantly walking the hallways, dropping in on classes just so they know I'm there.
Q: You mean dropping in unannounced, even?
A: Yeah. Staff at the school I work with don't have a problem with that.

A close, regular police presence in the classroom was also sustained by surveillance cameras. The same interviewee continued:

If I need a particular problem solved, like camera work or something like that where you were monitoring, I'll go to [the school board security supervisor] because that's his job ... Say there was missing money from a classroom or a particular area and can't find it, or can't catch the person, we'll get a camera to monitor it, and just monitor it and see what happens. If the guy continues to show up – take the money out of the till – then we got our guy. But that would be in special circumstances. It's not normal procedure.

This high-school police program was clearly geared toward identifying and taking action against those who posed criminal risks. A police officer observed that the program was 'more into interaction with the zone [patrol officers] and with charging kids, and information sharing ... [from] the guys in the school to the guys in the street.' During school holidays the officers served as regular officers in the same zone as their school, to build information-sharing relations with other police officers. In a twelve-month period, high-school officers recorded 473 official occurrences and undertook 720 other school-based investigations. A school officer we interviewed estimated that he handled a monthly average of five criminal investigations, ten trespass warnings, and one or two trespass charges. He said that patrolling for trespass was a major part of his job:

If we have visitors from other schools, I'll call up the school and then tell the principal that Joe Blow from your school had visited our school, was seen on our property. They will then go to that student and serve a trespass warrant on him for our school and the next time he's there, I'll charge him under the School Act for trespassing. Or they're suspended ... The only time it's legitimate is when a student from another school walks in the door and goes directly to the office. If they're walking around the hallways, that's not legitimate. They're trespassing. If we allow that to happen, students would come to and fro ... Some people with the highjack boots and the shaved head, you know damned well they're not students. So I challenge them and take them down to the office, serve them. Tell them to get out, don't come back ... I do arrest them. I don't fool around at all. Neither does the staff ... The staff are the greatest because they know most of the students. If it's a nonstudent, usually they stand out like a sore thumb because they're looking around, they're aware that somebody's watching them. So they look suspicious right off the bat.

In criminal matters, the general orientation was to diffuse the problem and to handle it administratively by warnings rather than by criminal prosecution. School administrators were said to be very sensitive about crime-related publicity. There were stories about how school administrators went to great lengths to circumvent media coverage. Sometimes the police were not called at all about a major incident, or a school administrator reported an incident in person at a police station in order to avoid the possibility that the matter would be picked up by the media on their police scanners.

School officers said that students were very aware of the diversion practices of youth courts and that they were more concerned about how the school authorities would deal with their transgressions. As one officer explained, students

are more afraid of school punishment than they are of punishment from the police, so it works to my advantage ... In the court system, you take the person to court on assault, usually not much happens to them anyway. It's an inconvenience to get them to court with all the paperwork and the work involved. Is it really worth it? ... But being dismissed from school is very serious to the student and if they're sent to the area superintendent to either be placed in another school or suspended indefinitely, that's serious, and much further, long-range consequences than going to court.

Long-range consequences in the criminal justice institution are reserved for a select few. A primary orientation of school police officers, in collaboration with other police units, is, as we will now see, to identify and target the highest risks for more-intensive surveillance.

Targeting Highest-Risk Youth

In one jurisdiction we studied, youths aged fourteen to sixteen who had been identified through the school police system as being most at risk were candidates for a police risk management program. A police publication said that this program 'was initiated to efficiently control the activities of *high-risk* juvenile offenders,' based on the 'ideology' that 'today's young offenders may become tomorrow's hardened criminals.' The program involved up to two years of intensive, one-to-one contact with police officers, as well as surveillance of the youth's family and its involvement with health, educational, and welfare institutions. Each of the four officers in the program had a case-load of about a dozen youths. Support was also provided by a part-time social worker and citizen volunteers. The volunteers' handbook stressed that their role was not simply counselling but also surveillance and regular reporting: 'You may respect the confidentiality of your client, but you cannot condone the commission of an offence, whether it is a municipal bylaw, provincial, federal or criminal statute. You must report all offences committed by young persons under your care to police, preferably the youth unit members, so that the individual is held accountable for his actions ... you will be required to report your client's progress monthly in written form to the supervisor.'

This program was by no means the end-point of an already long process of panoptic sorting in the jurisdiction in question. People whose risk profiles were not lowered by being in this program – and apparent failure was likely, given the intensity of the program's surveillance – became candidates for yet another panoptic sorting process, known as the Police Attending Youth Program (PAY). As was stated by a police officer, 'If they're successful, great. If they're not successful then they move on to the other side of the wall with our PAYs.' According to an official statement, PAY 'Support[ed] increased efforts by the Youth Justice System to identify PAYs early in their criminal career; to work cooperatively together to investigate and record their activities; to actively disseminate this information on an inter-agency basis; to prosecute them using vertical prosecution techniques; to sentence them appropriately; and to supervise them intensively in institutions and in the community.'

About one hundred youths were identified as PAYs at any given time. Considering that the PAY program had a staff of nine full-time police officers and a full-time civilian analyst, as well as volunteer analysts, one hundred might seem a low number to have under intensive surveillance. However, the staff themselves were not actually responsible for direct surveillance. Instead, their job was to do the risk-profiling required to sort out who should be brought into the PAY program and subject to its more direct forms of surveillance. Direct surveillance was conducted by patrol officers and detectives and by officials in other agencies. A police manager described PAY officers as knowledge brokers who 'don't really investigate as much as they coordinate between investigators and constables out in the districts.' The PAY officers were fed information from the entire patrol force, who submitted contact cards when youths were deemed to be in the wrong place or in the right place at the wrong time. They also received information from health, educational, and welfare agencies, either directly or through related youth units such as the school police programs.

This targeting involved not guns but risk technologies. Candidates for the program were youths who received demerit points for their criminal activity, much like the system that operates for drivers in traffic offences. Once PAY officers had assigned a youth a designated number of demerit points he was subject to a special investigation. An officer explained that 'the investigator would go out and would look at the individual, talk to him, talk to the family, Mom and Dad if, in fact, there are two and most times there isn't. Talk to the school, talk to the probation people and so on, and understand who this kid is and decide, based on that investigation, whether or not they were actually serious habitual offenders.'

The decision to include a youth in the exclusive group of PAYs was made by an interinstitutional committee composed of representatives from the police, the provincial attorney general's office, the provincial solicitor general's office, provincial social service agencies, provincial community health agencies, the provincial alcohol and drug abuse commission, municipal social service agencies, the municipal public school board, the municipal Catholic school board, the John Howard Society, and the Canadian Bar Association. Although the risk profile generated by the points system provided a guide, the committee had the power to include or exclude youths from PAY regardless of their risk score. The main focus, according to a police officer we interviewed, was identifying the one hundred or so worst youths in the city to ensure that they were a target for every risk knowledge system available:

> We're interested in the kids who commit the most crime. If you listen to the numbers out of the States, they claim that 4 per cent of their youth commit up to 60 per cent of the crime. That may be [the case] here too, but we can't prove that. I wish we could. What we can say here is, at the moment, about 2 per cent of the young offenders [whom] we've identified as PAY offenders, are charged with probably between 15 per cent and 20 per cent of the crimes. And that's all we can go on is the charges that we lay. Now we're satisfied that they're responsible for a hell of a lot more than what we charge them for. Especially when you talk to some of them and [they] say, 'Look, you're catching me maybe 10 per cent of the time. The rest of the time I'm getting away with it.' We're confident that they're responsible for a heck of a lot more.

To raise their confidence levels, PAY officers devised an elaborate surveillance system aimed at a chosen few. The reach and intensity of this system is apparent from a police officer's enthusiastic description of how PAYs were traced into the urban geography he policed: 'We have a product called "Data Map" which runs on a PC. For one area of the city they plotted youth crime with red dots and they plotted known houses of PAYs in another coloured dot. It was incredible correlation. The red dot and two blue dots around it. A red dot, two blue dots. It shows where the problem is.'

Each district police station had a bulletin-board devoted to PAYs which had photographs of local PAYs and the following notice to police officers:

> Familiarize yourself with these offenders and check them whenever possible. The worst or most active offender in each zone has been selected as a 'target.' Make a special effort to:
> 1. Check them as often as possible.
> 2. Charge them as often as possible.

Let them know that we will continue until they change their criminal habits or they move.
Be polite, be professional, but be pressing.

In addition to such harassment by patrol officers, special surveillance projects were used to entrap particularly troublesome young offenders. For example, a decoy-car program was established in response to a rise in car thefts. The decoy car was a sports model chosen because of its popularity with thieves. Youths were enticed into it by leaving it running. When the youths seated themselves in the car, the ignition system shut down and a remote control was used to automatically lock the door. Arrests and charges followed.

PAYs were typically subject to various court orders, such as probation orders, which placed restrictions on their whereabouts and on whom they could associate with. Contact cards submitted by patrol officers were computer-searched to look for violations. According to one police officer, the policy with respect to any such violations was to 'charge them with breach and throw them back inside [prison] again.' A colleague confirmed this approach, stating that the purpose of the program was 'a pressure and a scare tactic to bring the full bear of the system against a habitual before they get that clean slate and turn eighteen.'

The PAY risk knowledge system was brought to bear most heavily at the point of prosecution. When a PAY was arrested, his or her prosecution file was stamped PAY. This signalled that one of four prosecutors designated to handle show-cause hearings for the program would be required. These prosecutors were assigned to PAY to help the police make the most thorough cases possible against accused PAYs and thereby achieve the most punitive outcomes. Prosecution was also supported by a special investigator who was a member of the PAY staff. According to a police interviewee, the investigator would have 'a copy of the show-cause in his hot little hands and we can provide the information on that kid from day one, from the first time he was reported missing when he was aged eight all the way through the gambit. There's often twenty or thirty pages of information that we can provide the court ... It almost becomes a police program as such in that we've gathered all this information and ... what we're getting is longer sentences and we're getting better terms of release when they are released.'

Criminal prosecution and punishment are only the very tip of the youth anticrime iceberg, but at least at those stages of the process the police in the PAY program were supported by the full knowledge resources of other institutions that risk-profiled youths. Another police interviewee emphasized PAY's maximum prosecution/maximum punishment orientation as follows:

> [We produce] complete and accurate packages for the court – who this person is, how many times they've breached probation ... It's very effective because, in the past, the system just could not keep track. A guy would come up and it would be his fifth charge. He's been on probation four times. What options has the court got? They don't know any background. They haven't heard what he's done, what the breaches [of probation] involve. Invariably they end up going off with the same thing every time. This and probation. And now what they're doing is they're to the point where some of these kids are being incarcerated almost to the limit of the Young Offenders Act. And they're starting to get a lot more reaction out of the courts. They're starting to get a little stiffer with some of them. They're starting to court-order a lot more treatment for them, as opposed to sending them somewhere and see if they can get treatment, that sort of thing. They target the young offenders, these habituals, so that they feel that when they go back out on the street eventually, that there's someone looking over their shoulder all the time.

Still, there were gaps. Plans were afoot for a reorganization of all police programs for youths at risk, the goal being better coordination of manpower. Under the plan, all police programs directed at schools and youths were to be combined under one inspector. Moreover, there was to be a new police program in the junior high schools, which had been served only part-time by the high-school police. A proponent of this plan said that the goal of the reorganization was 'targeting these kids in essence from day one, although in earlier years obviously we're talking intervention and education and so on, and then a natural progression to deal with the enforcement side of it.' But the ambition did not stop there. Fully committed to risk-profiling everyone's careers and identities from cradle to grave, the police envisioned a parallel unit for adult habituals:

> We're looking seriously at starting an adult recidivist unit which will take over where our program [PAY] ends ... At the moment when they reach eighteen they kind of get thrown back into the mainstream ... [There will be] better coordination of information and, quite frankly, I suspect it's going to be more kick-ass ... a couple of teams of five or six people with a supervisor who are going to be going out ... What we see is that when these [PAY] kids are on the street

they're committing crime. As we speak, probably 40 per cent to 45 per cent are behind bars. When they're [back] on the street, within a day or two they're back to a housebreak. So I guess our thought is that when they hit the street in the future we're going to have people following them around and wait for them to do it and we're going to throw them back inside again, you know, as adults at that point. I mean, you look at our statistics on house break-ins and car thefts, we're getting blown out of the water. We suggest that the youth is our problem.

The approach to youths taken by this police organization is consistent with our thesis that due process is disappearing in the face of system rights to knowledge for surveillance (see chap. 2; also Ericson 1994b). Due process does not even enter into the picture during the daily routines of surveillance in school police programs. On the rare occasions when the criminal process is invoked, as in PAY risk-profiling, every effort is made to emphasize the need for routine knowledge production over any procedural restrictions. A police document on PAY underscored this systemic orientation in no uncertain terms: 'The PAY process represents a system's effort ... PAY implementation leads to the creation of a system response ... The ultimate utility of the program is its ability to produce integrative methods and procedures.'

Ronald D. Stephens, the executive director of the National School Safety Center at Pepperdine University, was quoted in the document as a supporter of the free flow of confidential information as the key to system integration and procedural efficiency: 'Responding to the needs of children, particularly juvenile offenders, requires *not only good judgement* but also *good information* ... Confidential information should be shared on a routine, ongoing basis when specific needs warrant such sharing. Too often, juvenile agencies are unaware that they are serving the same at-risk youths. When information is shared appropriately, improved strategies for rehabilitating, educating, and better serving those youths – and for improving public safety – can be developed.' There was no mention of procedural propriety by Stephens, only procedural efficiency. It was efficiency in the production and distribution of risk knowledge that was said to hold the key to improving the system. Elsewhere in the document U.S. Justice Department marketing plans for PAY were cited to indicate that PAY was or should be, the wave of the future: 'Marketing activities and pro-training assessment for six additional PAY sites will begin in late 1989, with training at these sites to begin in the spring of 1990. By that time, the current 18 sites will have produced experienced prosecutors available for training and technical assistance assignments as PAY consultants. In the months and years ahead, an effort will be made to market [PAY] in a way that promotes fundamental change in the relationships among agencies that deal with justice.'

Youths at Risk of Being Unaccounted For

As we mentioned in chapter 11 (pp. 241–3), the police invest considerable knowledge resources in registering and tracing people who are reported missing. There are programs and knowledge systems for missing children and older youths, many of which are coordinated by the RCMP Missing Children's Registry in Ottawa, which was begun by the solicitor general of Canada in 1988 in response to interest group and mass-media concern over child abuse, child abduction, and runaways (Webber 1991; for parallels in the United States see Nelson 1984, Best 1990). The registry functions as a broker of knowledge. An official publication describes it as an operation that 'maintains and monitors files on missing children,' serves as 'an information and research centre,' and provides 'an investigative and consulting service' to other police organizations.

The registry is staffed by police officers, a research analyst, and statistical analysts, including one seconded to the registry by Statistics Canada. These people consult with other experts in the field of youth risk management at the Department of Justice, the Ministry of the Solicitor General, and Health and Welfare Canada. The heavy reliance on statistical expertise emphasizes the fact that the registry's primary tasks are indeed registration and the associated risk-profiling of youths who, however temporarily, cannot be accounted for.

At the investigative level, the registry is primarily committed to finding abducted youths whose risk was created by separated parents in conflict over child custody and property rights, that is, youths abducted by a parent. Registry employees are assisted in their investigations by three people seconded to the registry from Canada Customs and Canada Immigration, who act primarily as agents of the abducted child and its custodial parent by seeking to locate the child and return it to the place where the courts decide it is supposed to be. As is indicated by table 12.1, in 1991 the number of parental abduction cases recorded by the registry was 412. The *Annual Report on Canada's Missing Children* (Royal Canadian Mounted Police 1991) for that year states that

168 were abducted in contravention of an existing custody order while 244 had no custody order in effect at the time of abduction. Historically, we have seen a

TABLE 12.1 Missing-child registry cases, 1991

	Cases entered		Cases removed	
Reason	N	%	N	%
Stranger abduction	78	0.1	64	0.1
Accident	60	0.1	34	0.1
Wander off/Lost	783	1.3	746	1.4
Parental abduction	412	0.7	326	0.6
Runaway	43,786	74.0	40,426	74.1
Unknown	11,863	20.1	10,952	20.1
Other	2,153	3.7	1,967	3.6
Total	59,135	100.0	54,515	100.0

Source: Adapted from Royal Canadian Mounted Police (1991)

fairly constant level in parental abductions in Canada. This year shows a decline of 5 per cent from the 432 reported in 1990 ... there were a total of 246 reported cases from other countries in which assistance from the Canadian authorities was requested, and it was believed that there was a possibility that the children could be in Canada. The majority of the Registry's caseload is based on international cases such as these.

Table 12.1 shows that the vast majority (74 per cent) of unaccounted-for young people were runaways. Abduction by strangers was very rare indeed. Only 78 of 59,135, or 0.1 per cent, of recorded cases in 1991 were a result of 'stranger abduction.' And it must be noted, too, that the definition of 'stranger' used by the registry included close relatives (such as grandparents, aunts, and uncles) and friends who did not have legal custody of the child! The available data do not indicate how many of the 78 stranger abductions were in fact abductions by relatives or friends, but it is reasonable to assume that most fell into that category. Clearly, stranger abductions were not a substantial problem for the authorities, although they have great symbolic importance in our society.

Registry employees work mainly as knowledge system managers. The main knowledge system is provided by CPIC, which devised the categories listed in table 12.1. Police organizations across Canada file requests with the registry asking it to enter, alter, or remove missing-child cases. The data they supply are framed within the categories listed in table 12.1 and are used by the registry to continually profile Canada's missing-children problem, which includes producing and distributing a weekly overview to police, voluntary-sector agencies, and the media.

The registry brokers knowledge to police organizations in Canada and abroad. This function includes providing CPIC information on the status of young people reported missing, aiding in the investigation of parental abduction cases, and supplying advice on whether a case is a criminal or civil matter.

The registry enjoys a close relationship with voluntary-sector agencies such as the Missing Children Society of Canada, the Missing Children's Network, Child Find Canada, and the Missing Children Locate Centre. Cooperation includes providing these agencies with case-specific information and receiving information from them in exchange. The agencies supply the police with literature and with posters identifying high-profile missing children. They also distribute police-produced literature, including the *Annual Report on Canada's Missing Children.*

In addition to routinely supplying news releases to the media, the registry cooperated with the producers of *Missing Treasures,* a 'child find' version of police reality television. This show featured re-enactments of high-profile missing-child cases and solicited public assistance in supplying knowledge relevant to those cases. According to an interviewee, the police worked with the show's producers

> very closely in getting them the initial information so they could develop the program. And the 800 – number is answered by Canada Customs through their ... training academy ... [i]t depends on what you mean by success. It's been a success in that it's brought forward the information to the public. I don't know of any particular case that we can point to that we found the child because of that ... [but it helps people to] realize that things like this happen and they have to have some protection for their children ... tips for parents ... keep the problem of missing children there in the forefront to the public so they don't forget about it.

The sensibility expressed by this official is characteristic of policing in risk society. While the instrumental effectiveness of police programs is limited, there is an effort to promote a program's advertising value in order to induce reflexivity and make everyone his or her own risk manager. At the instrumental level of investigation work, missing-children programs have very little to do with the problem of stranger abductions, but at the symbolic level this problem remains the primary focus.

At the symbolic level the police unite with other institutions in promoting the education of parents, who are expected to educate their children about the problem of stranger abductions. Thus, despite its own evidence, the 1991 *Annual Report on Canada's Missing Children* stresses the need to be eternally vigilant about the risk of stranger abductions:

> because such high profile is given to any stranger abduction, the public's perception is that this phenomenon is common in Canada. This in fact is not the case. However, it is still prudent for parents to teach their children to be 'street smart' and to be aware of the dangers of our society. Street proofing of children is essential to preventing such tragedies. Many of Canada's police are actively involved in preventative policing and are able to provide tips on personal safety. It is important to remember that the legal definition of 'stranger' is anyone who does not have custody of the child. Therefore, children who are taken by a grandparent, aunt, uncle, or friend of the family would be entered into CPIC under the category of stranger abduction.

To prevent young people from being unaccounted for, police organizations include streetproofing as part of their tracing and mobilizing of territories. In some jurisdictions parents are asked to include their children in special registration systems. One police organization ran an 'Operation Child Identification Program' in which detailed written descriptions, photographs, and fingerprints were placed on file. A brochure produced by a provincial solicitor general's office and distributed by police throughout the province urged parents to maintain their own home-based knowledge system for mapping and tracing their children: 'Build a home information centre, which includes a map of your neighbourhood and its play areas, and have your child identify where he will be at all times, and when he will return ... Maintain up-to-date records which include a recent photograph of your child, his height and weight, medical and dental histories, and if you wish, a video tape and fingerprint record.'

A police officer we interviewed saw such urgings as part of the 'continual reinforcement' needed to persuade parents to maintain good records. In her view, these records would be important in the event of an apparent missing-child case, because parents are usually in an 'emotional state' at such times, which interferes with rational, efficient policework. In other words, families are to be like other institutions, providing data that are properly formatted and readily accessible: 'They have that information just there, they can hand it to the officer, it saves a hell of a lot of time in the police officer trying to calm them down enough to ask questions so they can get the information from them – details and description. The person wants the policeman to get out right now and go out and find their kid.'

Parents are not only to keep detailed records of their childrens' identities, they are also to remain perpetually reflexive with respect to risks. The aforementioned brochure stressed that the safety tips it offered 'will not completely protect your child, however they will increase the level of awareness.' Indeed parents were made aware by the brochure of imagined negative consequences that lurked behind the most mundane aspects of a child's everyday life: 'Avoid clothing and toys which personally display your child's name, because children are less likely to fear a stranger who knows their name ... Know all of your children's friends, their families and their phone numbers; insist that your child ask for permission to visit his friends ... accompany your child on door-to-door activities, such as Halloween or school fund-raising.'

As is suggested by the instruction to avoid labelling a child's property with his or her name for fear that that would give dangerous strangers a way of becoming friendly with the child, many of the lessons in the brochure focused on communication. In the brochure, community policing as communications policing extended into the home- and family-based education of the young. For example, children were expected to manipulate appearances and even lie in the interests of risk reduction: 'When children are home alone, [they are] to tell phone callers that you are there, but you are busy, and cannot come to the phone, and that the caller should call back later ... If a stranger is at the door, teach your child to tell the stranger that you are busy, and he should go away and come back later.' Like electronic home-security alarm systems, children were to be given a code that would help signal who were trusted insiders and who were to be excluded from contact: 'use a pre-selected code word with your child and those whom you may ask to give your child a ride; where necessary, change the code word with your child after it has been used for a period of time.' No mention was made of the confusion that might ensue for a mother trying to remember the codes of the six children being picked up in her station-wagon on the way to their Saturday morning hockey game. The parent was to know everything about the child's communications with other adults. In communications between children and adults who were not close family members confidentiality was to be breached: 'Some secrets – like surprise birthday presents – are fun, but a secret that another adult says only the two of you can know is not right – come and tell me.'

Seniors

Seniors are seen by the police as another especially vulnerable population, and are therefore singled out for special risk education programs. While the identity of 'youth' is primarily the basis for a panoptic sorting of a population of potential offenders, the identity of 'child' or 'senior' is almost exclusively the basis for designating potential victims and implementing risk-reduction strategies.

The focus with seniors, as with children, is on home-based risk knowledge systems and on how the vulnerable can streetproof themselves. A booklet on personal safety for seniors distributed by a police organization, for example, provides instruction on communications policing around the home. Seniors are told, among other things, to 'Turn your telephone bell down to its lowest level. A ringing telephone is an indication that you are not at home ... If you are at home, answer the door – you may prevent a housebreaker who thinks you're not at home.' Streetproofing is addressed in a section called 'Transfer the Risk.' Seniors are instructed to implement risk-reduction strategies such as carrying a bogus wallet in addition to their regular one, and adopting a buddy system for public outings.

A police crime prevention specialist we interviewed said that his organization was developing more programs for seniors because of their increasing numbers: 'Senior abuse is going to be a problem in the future. Seniors' problems are going to be a problem in the very near future. So we're just trying to get ahead of the times.' Efforts included instruction for seniors on risk management, by way of pamphlets, home visits, and lectures. The unit was also acquiring expertise in dealing with a wide range of seniors' problems, including suicide and other emotional and mental health issues. The goal here was eventually to set up counselling services. This police organization was already committed to such services through its bereavement unit (pp. 243–4), which provided seniors with empathetic home visits as well as a police-produced video on bereavement services available in the city.

Although the police in this jurisdiction helped seniors streetproof themselves against interpersonal violence and property crime, no attention was given to how they could suite-proof themselves against financial risks. A police officer remarked to us that there are obvious contradictions in the policing of age-related identities. For example, enormous resources are allocated to the problem of youths at risk from illicit drug use, but virtually no resources are devoted to protecting seniors from the substantial risks they face from financially marginal trust companies, aggressive mutual-fund promoters, shady marketing schemes, and the like: '[o]ur baby boomers are moving into the "over fifty" crew. We are going to pay a deadly price because of the emotional impacts all these frauds, advance-fee scams, and telemarketing scams are having on our elderly ... All these little nest eggs are being ripped off like you wouldn't believe and nobody really wants to take them to court.'

Race and Ethnicity

Just as the police think and act in ways that are responsive to the age-structure of the population, they also think and act in ways that are responsive to racial and ethnic classifications. Whether or not we judge the latter kinds of thought and behaviour to be prejudicial or discriminatory, it is clear that they are not merely a product of racial and ethnic stereotyping within police occupational culture (Chan 1996), but are embedded in the classification schemes employed by the police and the risk institutions the police report to. In these institutional classification schemes race and ethnicity are moral categories expressing dominant views of social hierarchy.

There is a long history of governments producing knowledge about race and ethnicity to discover statistical laws that allow policing of racial and ethnic groups (Hacking 1990; Goldberg 1995). One of the 'fathers' of probability statistics, Adolphe Quetelet (1835), advanced his 'average man' thesis by producing measurements of race-related physical and moral qualities. Hacking (1990: 17) notes that the racial classification structure of the U.S. census after 1840 made it appear 'that the North was full of mad blacks, while in the South blacks were sane and healthy – strong proof of what was good for them.' He (ibid.: 22) goes on to observe that biopolitics in all of its forms 'has the standard feature of a risk portfolio, namely that at almost the same time opposite extremes are presented as dire perils (today it is nuclear winter/greenhouse effect). The "population problem" denotes both the population explosion of other peoples and too low a birth rate of one's own people. During the nineteenth century in France, one's own people were French, the others German and British. In Prussia ... the others were Jewish. Today the others are the Third World. In late-Victorian England, the others were the laboring classes.'

Statistics are produced to discover laws of probability through which peoples' identities can be governed and changed. Another nineteenth-century statistician, William Farr, wrote in 1860 that 'Some races commit crimes of violence in greater proportion to other races. Some classes are more dangerous. [But] as men have the power to modify their race, they have the power to change the current of human actions within definite limits, which statistics can determine' (quoted in ibid.: 115).

Policing based on a connection between racial differentiation and risk assessment persists (Doob 1991). Most occurrence reports have a category for the racial and ethnic background of the people involved. Producing this knowledge is justified on the grounds that it is useful for identification purposes in subsequent investigations. However, such categorization is used more generally to influence how the police slot people into institutionally relevant identities.

Some police organizations that use computerized systems to map the incidence of crimes and other occurrences in their territories (chap. 7) include race as a datum. This plotting of the racial geography of trouble is justified on the grounds that it is an investigative aid. What this means in practice is that race is called up on the computer screen as an item to be considered when an officer responds to a call or proactively looks out for trouble. The officer is thereby always reminded to think of race as a relevant variable when dealing with people. If the officer should complete an occurrence report, which will note the subject's race, race becomes that much more heavily imprinted on the computer system.

Some police organizations record the race of people who make formal complaints against the police. One police organization categorized complainants as Caucasian, Oriental, East Indian, Native, Negroid, and Other. In this case it is difficult to imagine that the information was used to further identification for investigative purposes. It was used, however, in a statistical report on public complaints to identify the groups that caused the police the most officially recorded trouble.

Another police organization originally had an occurrence report that categorized people as White, Hispanic, Negro, Oriental, Arabic, Native Indian, and East Indian. However, as was explained to us by a police interviewee, this scheme was eventually abandoned. As the interviewee said, 'You can get people that speak Spanish and they can be from ten different countries, so that doesn't help. You can get Black, but Black comes from all kinds of countries, that doesn't help ... When you start naming like that then really the community involved says that that's being discriminatory and so we have to be very careful on that end of it. So when you come to records and try to bring up statistics that involve specific communities, it's almost impossible, so it really ties our hands to that.'

This police organization did not entirely abandon racial categorization, though. It decided to adopt a simple binary opposition in its occurrence reports between White and Other. This White/Other designation was used as a flag for further racial and ethnic panoptic sorting to ascertain whether there might be a 'multicultural' problem requiring attention. All cases involving people in the Other category were sent to the police organization's multicultural unit, where officers screened those cases for risk management purposes. We learned from a police officer that this unit received a daily 'printout of all people that are from a background other than Canadian and they go through it and it talks about victims and accused ... If they realize that they have a problem in a specific community then they will go to the area involved ... talk to the officers and the supervisors there and deal with the problem.' The screening was done by looking at the names of the Others to determine which racial and ethnic groups they belonged to and whether any of them were known to the police. If problem people, organizations, or territories were identified, an officer in the multicultural unit was notified, and in some circumstances other intelligence units were also mobilized.

The officer just quoted viewed the White/Other distinction as one between Canadians and 'people from a background other than Canadian.' This distinction is the key to understanding how officers in multicultural units think and act. Multicultural units are involved in identifying problem populations of racial and ethnic outsiders and developing risk profiles of them. This involvement allows the police to work with other institutions in tailoring racial and ethnic identities to fit the mainstream. An officer in a multicultural unit stated emphatically that his unit was 'dealing specifically not with the community at large but with the specific groups in the community that are of different cultures. We're not dealing with mainstream per se. We're going right out and dealing with another culture.'

An examination of the organizational structure of one multicultural unit reveals which groups were marked down for special attention. A police officer was assigned to each of the following seven 'portfolios':

Natives, Chinese, Vietnamese, Filipino and other Southeast Asian, Black and Hispanic, Middle Eastern, South Asian (India and Pakistan), and Minority Recruitment. It is noteworthy that there was no 'European' unit, although certain groups of European origin, such as Serbians and Croatians, were seen as sources of potential trouble.

The multicultural unit was staffed exclusively by white males. At one time there had been a Black officer, but he did not last long, apparently because he had difficulty being accepted by other members of the Black community. Although there were Chinese officers elsewhere in the organization, none were assigned to the multicultural unit. An interviewee said these officers did not speak Chinese and in any case would not be accepted by the Chinese community. No female officer had ever applied to join the unit. An interviewee believed that female officers would be unacceptable to some of the groups the unit dealt with:

> if you look at some of the cultural groups that we deal with, women are at the bottom of the scale or the low end of the hierarchy in the community ... I'm not sure how they would react to a policewoman coming and dealing with their community. I guess I don't want to put a policewoman into a position where she's not going to get the respect or the cooperation of the community. I think there's nothing worse than trying to deal with that and, as an individual, become so disillusioned that suddenly your will to do the job is affected or, in fact, just as a person is affected because of the treatment you get. I'm not saying that that's necessarily what happens, but obviously in some of the cultures that we're dealing with and looking at where the women in that culture are in the line of whatever, I would really be somewhat apprehensive to put a woman in that position only, you know, because I don't want to see a woman deterred or her own person be affected by something like that, and then she goes somewhere else and has to kind of live with that knowledge that this happened to me and she builds herself back up to where she was. That may not even be a problem or a concern but, you know, we've never had the opportunity to test it out.

The standard used by multicultural units to identify and protect the Canadian mainstream is the police culture itself. A basic goal is to have 'people from a background other than Canadian' understand the police and what they represent, as a way to have them understand Canada and what it represents. Given the long history of promoting Canadian identity through police symbolism, especially the symbolism of the RCMP (Walden 1982), this approach is not surprising. A multicultural unit officer we interviewed said that his unit's purpose was 'real educational. We're going to these people to bring to them the police culture.' His statement was echoed in an official police publication that defined the unit as a special type of foreign service: 'The Unit serves as a diplomatic corps for the Police Service, being extensively involved in helping new Canadians adjust to the police and law in Canada.'

This service was provided in various educational contexts. For example, unit members lectured to classes in English as a second language for new Canadians. A multicultural unit officer said that this instruction was 'so that they become comfortable with facing a police officer so that we bring down some of their fear and apprehension.' Instruction was also given during the handling of specific incidents. The following example provided by a police interviewee shows that cultural differences can run deep and lead to immigrant conflict with the police and the dominant culture:

> You get a family that comes to Canada, and particularly when the children are very young, Mom and Dad are still very strong culturally and traditionally and they are not changing ... Mom and Dad are very strict and they hold back the child. They don't allow the child to go out on dates and mix. You know, the child goes to school and comes home, doesn't partake in any extracurricular activities. So all of a sudden, now the child is starting to rebel, so the child runs away. The parents then come to us and they still do not understand that once the child reaches a certain age in Canada they are adults. And as adults they are able to do and make their own decisions and that we, as police, cannot go and force them to come back to the home environment ... Mom and Dad don't understand that. They get to the point, saying, 'You're not doing your job. Your job is to help us. You're not helping us.' So that's where they begin to use us as a scapegoat to say that it's our fault. Then we run into a number of situations here where they've gone to the media and really squawked and complained that the police aren't doing their job. And they will go as far, at times, to report a kidnapping when, in fact, their child has not been kidnapped, but they'll do that because they know that if their child, or the daughter in particular, is a missing person that we will tell them we can't do anything for them ... So they put the police service in a position of having to enter an investigation when, in fact, we know it's an investigation that isn't necessary, but nine out of ten times the police service will never go back and charge the people because they caused us to enter into an investigation. Charging them with mischief, it's a touchy thing. It doesn't enhance the interaction and communication between community and police.

Instruction is also given to the mainstream community. One police organization offered community groups the opportunity to engage in a play-acting exercise. People pretended to be high-ranking police officials who must make hard decisions and take action on a sensitive issue involving a racial group. An official police publication indicated that one goal of this exercise was to make civilians appreciate how difficult it is to police a multicultural society: 'Civilian participants will develop a closer bond to their Police Community by understanding the difficulties of providing a professional and effective Police Service to the community within a given framework.' Here, perhaps, was at least a partial admission that maintaining cultural coherence, other than through the constant articulation of how 'they' are different from 'us,' is an impossible mandate.

While the police are a central symbol of Canadian identity, and of what it means to be un-Canadian, they are not alone in their efforts. Their multicultural work is accomplished by networking with government institutions and community service agencies in the same business. The members of a police multicultural unit examined by us spent much of their time engaged in such networking. According to a report issued by the unit, police officers sat on the committees and boards of the following organizations: the immigrant aid society, the Catholic immigration society, the South Asian women's centre, the community college, the suicide prevention program, the suicide information and education centre, the aboriginal urban affairs committee, the board of education, the committee against racial and religious discrimination, the aboriginal health association, the property development project committee, the government cultural heritage unit, the board of the aboriginal alcohol recovery centres, the board of the aboriginal friendship centres, the board of the aboriginal awareness committees, the committee on race relations and crosscultural understanding, the foundation for youth, the youth minority achievement program, the Sikh youth development peer support project, the association for young immigrants, the committee of the secretary of state, human rights education council, the committee for good citizenship, the association for multicultural education, the society for intercultural education, training and research, and the metis child and family services agency.

In some cases the multicultural unit played a major role in developing programs for other institutions. For example, the police model for multicultural initiatives and in-service training was used by the board of education to develop teacher training programs. The police provided assistance in structuring the courses and in providing course content. At the same time, as was explained by a police interviewee, the members of the multicultural unit used their networking with other multicultural agencies to educate themselves about how to patrol the borders of racial and ethnic identities:

> We have contact with probably every government agency that works with community and/or immigrants and refugees. [There is also contact with] the other agencies like settlement agencies that are assisting the immigrants and refugees ... We sit on boards of directors, on advisory boards, act as resource people to any agency that is out there that requires our help. And one of the purposes of that is *they* are educators. I mean, that's where we go to get our hands-on information about what's happening in the communities and things like that ... So our continual interaction is where we gain the knowledge and information from. That's *our* teaching days ... We have a group called Interagency which I am directly involved with. It's a group of all the agencies that are in the city that, at one time or another, we all get together for a meeting ... [there is] representation from probably twenty [or] twenty-five agencies ... a networking situation ... so when we're dealing with people and we realize that these people have a certain need, we can channel them to the proper organization. You know, I think it's essential for us to do that because I would say that a lot of the times that we're involved with people it's because they're having a problem and they don't know where to go.

One consequence of this multicultural education and sensitivity is that police services are often tailored to particular racial and ethnic audiences. Police lectures and instructional materials on personal security, for example, are formulated and offered in this way. Thus a report on a police multicultural-liaison unit declares that 'In conjunction with the Crime Prevention Unit, crime prevention programs are presented to various minority communities. In particular, Ismaili Seniors and the Seniors in the Jewish community have participated in this program.'

Some races and ethnic groups are subject to criminalization by the police. In recent years, for example, Asian crime units have developed to identify problems originating in Asian countries or created by people of Asian origin. An administrator in a police criminal intelligence unit said that 'Asian organized crime' and 'Aboriginal organized crime' were priorities that year. When asked to specify what Asian organized crime consisted of, he replied, 'We use the term "Asian organized crime," and that's been a problem but only within the federal government, not anywhere else. Therefore, in the federal government context we call it the "Pacific Rim Organized Crime." Some people don't like using the term "Asian" because it blankets everybody and it's really just a small group and it's Asian organized crime.'

In a police organization we studied, the gang unit concentrated exclusively on two Asian gangs in the city. A gang analyst in another unit said that he also did 'a lot of work on Oriental crime. You don't just walk in and suddenly become familiar with Oriental names, identities ... there's a lot of cultural history you have to know to understand the crimes.' The intelligence unit of the same organization also assisted with racial and ethnic profiling. An interviewee who belonged to this unit said that its contribution to 'Asian Crime' was to ask, 'Do you think Group X is going to expand their operation either along this geographical location or through this ethnic community? ... It's a calculated guess ... There is a degree of subjectivity involved, but we try to remain objective in terms of correlating the information to knowns. It wouldn't be actuarial in nature ... It's not like [a large corporation] being able to say that because of this yield here, we'll be raising the price.'

Intelligence can get down to the most subtle details about how to deal with a suspect. The culturally aware police officer is one who knows the precise details of how people appear, interact, and deceive. A description of a multicultural unit's operations stated that when a mainstream Canadian suspect 'avoids eye contact with an officer it is often perceived to be a clear indication of the suspect's guilt or his attempt to mislead. However, in some cultures, this is in fact a gesture of respect and is more likely to indicate the suspect is telling the truth.'

Patrol officers and detectives, too, are sensitized to Asian crime. Some Canadian police stations display an American-produced '10 most wanted Asian criminals' poster. During our ride-alongs with patrol officers, the translation of this sensitization into action was evident. For example, during an otherwise uneventful patrol, two officers decided to visit two Vietnamese restaurants that featured poolhalls. The visits were punctuated by the officers making racist remarks to each other about 'slant-eyes.' During a check of 'flashy' cars parked outside these establishments, one officer had this to say about the security devices in some of the cars: 'These people have the best security devices to protect the things they worked so hard to steal.' In one establishment the officers stared down some youths who were playing pool, remarking to each other and to the researcher how 'bad' these youths were. In the other establishment an officer stood shaking his head and remarking to the researcher, 'It's a different world, it's a different world.' A woman at the front desk was asked whether there was any trouble in the establishment. When she replied, 'No,' the officer pointed at two men sitting quietly at a table and asked, 'What about them?' The woman replied that these men were very quiet. Even taking into account the fact that all police officers view their 'turf' with a suspicious eye and believe that there is usually something sinister going on (Sacks 1972; Shearing and Ericson 1991), these officers seemed oversensitive. To the researcher, the restaurant and pool-hall patrons were ordinary-looking people in ordinary establisments in an ordinary strip mall in an ordinary suburb. If these establishments were dens of inequity, then Durkheim was surely correct in his arguments about moral boundaries and deviance.

One police organization we looked at had a large command post vehicle equipped with electronic devices such as computer terminals, fax machines, wire-tapping cables, a television, and a VCR. When asked what this vehicle had been used for during the previous few months, the police officer said, 'You know, we have been lucky, we have never used this truck in a crisis situation. We have had it in Chinatown as a mobile community police station, but that's about it.'

In another jurisdiction, a patrol area that had only small numbers of people belonging to racial and ethnic minorities, a patrol officer told us about the knowledge-targeting of a minority family. He said that plain-clothes officers were producing as much knowledge as possible about this family strictly because its members were of a minority background and as such stood out in the community.

Special multicultural units and intelligence units seek to acquire knowledge of possible conflicts within selected racial and ethnic groups. This pursuit is accomplished by cultivating informants within the groups concerned. After giving an example of how informants were used to identify members of an ethnic group who were intimidating other members of the group, a multicultural unit officer observed, 'Now every area that these young people are running in, the police there are aware, they have pictures of them, they have a background on them, and they're going to take off after these people and that's the only way we're going to prevent the activity that they're involved with from happening.'

After an interracial homicide in the Chinatown area of the city, a squad of four officers was sent in to remove 'undesirable' members of the Chinese community from the area. As an interviewee remarked, 'the trash, if you want to call it that, the gangs, these kinds of people, disappeared because these guys were always on top of them ... so they went to other areas of the city.'

A multicultural unit officer indicated that such forms of proactivity were characteristic of policing in that city. Whether as educators, agents of crime prevention, or agents of law enforcement, the unit's members acted to imprint a Canadian identity on their subjects: 'We are not an intelligence unit, although we are a totally proactive unit. Whatever information does happen to come forward, or we are apprised of something, you know, we will directly bring that information to whatever unit should have it within the police service.'

The police are constantly risk-profiling populations with regard to ascribed identities that seem relevant to security provision. Police thought and action are guided by the risk classifications of the external institutions that they work with in risk management. In this chapter we have examined technologies that are used to produce and manage knowledge about youths and racial and ethnic groups at risk. We have also considered how these technologies frame police actions in relation to these populations and thereby serve to confirm peoples' places in a multiple-culture Canada. Along with police efforts in managing risks to territories, securities, and careers, this police identity work helps to sort out who is who in the risk knowledge structure of society.

PART V

Risks to Police Organization

13

Knowledge Risk Management

The police face the risk of having their organization overwhelmed by both externally derived risk criteria and the sheer volume of knowledge work. They have a strong sense of organizational risk and insecurity because of external demands for knowledge; a perpetual feeling of having insufficient knowledge; and a reflexive awareness that there are always systemic faults that can be corrected through better communication rules, formats, and technologies. As Manning (1982: 122) observes, organizations are 'resources for conceptualizing, assessing and coping strategically with perceived threats from the posited environment and in many respects therefore are *political* entities.'

In this chapter we examine the police perspective on the politics of knowledge. The police experience what they call a 'paper burden' that is largely attributable to the demands of external institutions. In chapters 14, 15, and 16 we analyse how the police respond to the paper burden through communication rules, formats, and technologies. Chapter 14 addresses the proliferation of rules and rule systems to regulate knowledge production and distribution. Chapter 15 considers the perpetual refinement of communication formats to better capture populations and events in risk-relevant terms and to distribute the captured knowledge more efficiently. Chapter 16 documents the rage to adopt new information technologies that will improve the production and distribution of knowledge both internally and to other risk institutions.

The police are undergoing rapid change in risk society. Chapters 14–16 are a study of the occupational changes brought about by the fact that the risk society is also a knowledge society. The police are knowledge workers who join other major institutions in believing that the world can be made more secure by ever more perfect knowledge of risk. This belief leads them to search incessantly for whatever rules, formats, and technologies will allow them to feel that they are closer to perfection. The problem is that they are constantly faced with imperfection in rules, formats, and technologies, which gives rise to both a sense of failure and a renewed sense that more such devices will work where fewer have not. At the same time they are faced with new demands from other institutions because those institutions are in precisely the same position with respect to knowledge risk management.

The Paper Burden

Police culture is permeated by what its members call the paper burden. 'Paper' symbolizes knowledge work in all its forms. Whether the knowledge is produced and distributed in hard copy or in electronic formats, it is seen as 'paper.' 'Burden' expresses the feeling of being overwhelmed by external demands for knowledge. Thus 'paper burden' articulates the prevailing sentiment that external knowledge demands are excessive and insatiable and detract from policework that somehow stands outside the communication process.

The sheer amount of time spent 'doing paper' gives every police officer a direct experience of the paper burden. In one municipal police organization, twelve officers we observed during ride-alongs each estimated that 30 per cent to 40 per cent of their time was spent on paperwork. We also went on many ride-alongs with members of a regional police organization, whose traffic patrol officers estimated that 30 per cent to 50 per cent of their time was spent on paperwork, while regular patrol officers estimated 60 per cent to 80 per cent. Their immediate supervisors (patrol sergeants) devoted at least 80 per cent of their time reviewing the reports submitted by patrol officers and 'scoring' those reports for data input purposes.

In the regional police jurisdiction, patrol officers remarked on how little they actually patrolled. They were largely office-bound, and went out 'on the road' only when responding to a call for service. Several officers likened their situation to that of a fireman who remains at the firehall until dispatched to a fire. The patrol officers were required to complete detailed reports on each incident, which is why they had to spend most of their time in the office. A patrol officer remarked, 'I would say at least 80 per cent of my time is in the office ... sitting at my desk doing files. The only time I usually go out in the car ... is when I get a call and go somewhere ... I get in my car, go to the complaint, and come back.' A colleague said, 'I'm dispatched out of my seat at the desk. That's the honest truth. Paperwork has always been the downfall of the force. There's just too much of it.' These officers also indicated that they worked many hours of unpaid overtime each week to catch up on their paperwork.

The paper burden is quite literally a burden. We observed police officers leaving their offices and proceeding to their patrol cars in the vehicle compound. On the way out were not only racks of shotguns but also racks of briefcases. Each officer had a numbered shotgun and a numbered briefcase, and the briefcases were as fully loaded as the shotguns. Unlike the shotguns, which most officers had never used, the briefcases were opened repeatedly during the shift.

There is a pervasive sentiment in police occupational culture that the paper burden is excessive and a source of alienation. The alienation arises because field officers are often unaware of why particular reports are required, where the knowledge goes, and how it is used. As such they are alienated from the products of their labours. Many police officers are concerned only with having 'clean' reports that are acceptable to their immediate supervisor. As one officer stated during a ride-along, after her sergeant has approved her paperwork, 'I don't give a shit what happens to it.' Police managers were also aware of this view of paperwork and of the alienation it caused among field officers: 'There has to be an effort to get relevant information to the officer on the street while freeing him from the requirements of providing unnecessary information. Often we hear complaints that other outside agencies are interfering in our work. The guys on the street collect the information but they have no idea what the information is being collected for. Often it is put to no meaningful purpose.'

An interviewee who specialized in accident data analysis pointed to what is perhaps the most salient reason for feeling alienated about knowledge production: 'There never is an end-product.' Even some police managers in knowledge brokerage positions were unaware of how knowledge moves and is used in particular cases. For example, an officer who worked full-time in a 'forms management' position was unaware of the origin, purpose, and use of most of the forms we asked him about. An officer in charge of the policy branch of a drug enforcement unit had no idea what Health and Welfare Canada did with the knowledge produced by the police for that ministry on a special form after each drug arrest.

On the other hand, many police managers were aware of how knowledge moves and gets used. An interviewee who had had over twenty years' experience as a police investigator before becoming an 'information manager' said that his new position gave him a better appreciation of knowledge production: 'I am so much in the records aspect of it, whereas before I just gave that to somebody to file, you know, not knowing where it ever went and what happened to it. I was always of the opinion that it's a lowly job, records ... and I never realized until I came here just how important it was. If you can't get the information, then you're lost ... And the same way, when I wanted something, it mysteriously appeared on my desk, not knowing where it came from.'

A senior police policy analyst, making a traditional distinction between information and knowledge, viewed field officers as producing formatted information, middle-managers as converting the information into risk data, and executive-level policy experts as converting the data into useful knowledge for decision making:

> In the field the officers are producing information. This information flows back in the different forms that they create and is entered into the [data] system. At this stage the information starts to resemble knowledge. This is more structured and is used to collect data and provide a range of frequency distributions ... At the corporate end of things, where we are located, we try to massage the knowledge that has been produced to create even more specialized and useful knowledge. It is more abstract at this third level. What this third level is trying to do is facilitate decision making.

Another concern is being asked to produce knowledge for external institutions that should be produced by the institutions themselves or by some other agency. There is no quarrel with the value of the knowledge being produced, but there is concern with the division of labour created in producing it. An exasperated police interviewee said, 'We are the garbage collectors of policing – we get responsibility for just about any new issue that comes along,' a responsibility that includes 'more paperwork.'

Underlying police culture talk about the paper burden is a belief that the police should be spending their time doing better things. If only the police had less paperwork and were more meaningfully involved in knowledge production, the story goes, they would do a better job of policing. This sentiment is grounded in the view that knowledge work is the secondary or residual reporting of events, not the 'real work' of dealing with the events themselves. A police interviewee observed,

'When you really get down to it, there is nothing that touches the officer more on a day-to-day basis than his computer, except for the police cruiser. There is still, however, the old mind-set among a lot of officers that this kind of work is secondary to normal policing activities. A lot of people have still not placed themselves into today's world.'

This mind-set of the police culture is also fostered at the administrative level. For example, specialized information management or 'informatics' police divisions justify their role by arguing that their technological solutions to the paper burden will free officers for more important activities. An interviewee employed as an information technology assessment officer for his police organization described his role as follows: 'The officer has to feed the information system ... If you really look at it closely a large amount of this is driven by weird provincial requirements for information. These are all making the officer less productive in doing their real police work ... [There is an] increasing burden of having to provide information to different agencies ... the repercussions of introducing one more form. The overall trend is to take officers off of policing duty and to make them information workers.'

During a presentation to his police commission, the chief of police of one police organization dramatized how the paper burden takes resources away from 'real police work.' Drawing on a type of dramatic imagery akin to that used in publicizing major drug busts (Manning 1980), he asked a patrol officer who had accompanied him to open her bulging briefcase and show the multitude of forms she took on routine patrol.

The referent for 'real' policework is crime work. During our field observations, police officers who sat doing paperwork complained about not being free to pursue crime. At the same time they recognized that most crimes were not something they could do anything about except create a record for risk management purposes. In some instances officers who complained about the paper burden also stated that there was very little crime in their area, but maintained nevertheless that real policework is crime work.

Officers were also sensitive to the fact that when the possibility of criminalizing an incident does arise, criminalization is largely a paper exercise. They sometimes avoided criminalizing an incident because of the paperwork involved. This avoidance was observed during ride-alongs, for example with respect to possible impaired-driving charges. It was also the subject of jokes among police officers. Sitting in a police station office, a police officer asked in jest, 'So we're going to come across some real crime tonight?' His colleague replied, 'God, I hope not, I don't want to do the paperwork.' Another patrol officer related 'a little saying that is probably right on the money: "ten minutes of fun on the street is two hours of paperwork."'

Complaints about paperwork abound in police culture. Complaints are often made with both a sense of humour and a sense of purpose. They frequently arise while officers are doing their paperwork, which suggests that they are in part a reflexive articulation of the meaning of classifications and their relevance. In one sense this articulation is no different from how people in general reflect on how they categorize and classify the world. However, in an occupation replete with the classifications of different institutions embedded in standardized forms, reflexivity is both formalized and relentless.

Police culture is a culture of forms. Many police officers, especially those in middle-management and administrative positions, appreciate that policing is literally formed through paperwork. A senior officer said that 'We kill a lot of trees in this organization. But seriously, the police department runs on its information abilities. People look at the police in terms of chasing and catching the bad guys. That's a very small part of our job. One of our main functions is to act as the processors of information for hundreds of agencies ... government or community agencies.'

A senior officer in another organization objected strongly to the use of the term paper burden, although it had wide currency at all levels of his organization:

> I tend to take issue with that. I think that the information is not a burden but an important part of what a police officer does. We recently had a [new data] system in here and it was set up in the middle of the floor. The guys came in and just learned the system. They did not find the system onerous in any way ... Policework is more than just working in the street. Intelligence analysts who sit down with a rack of paper and look for crime trends and develop hypotheses are just as much police officers as guys on the street.

A police organization hired a computer expert to develop a new system. This expert said that his mandate was based on the assumption that policing is a knowledge industry. Knowledge is produced, packaged, and sold to myriad consumers, and the purpose of the new multimillion-dollar system was to make it better for producers and consumers alike. In his words, 'The entire police force *is* simply one large information processing system ... [p]olicing is a generic function. No matter if you are talking about a large or a small force the information needs will be the same.'

The mentality of a police organization as 'one large information processing system' is not peculiar to computer experts interested in selling their wares. Rather, their expertise is called on because the police realize that they are in the knowledge business. Policing as an information processing system is a lived reality at all levels of the police organization. Two district police station administrators described their work as follows:

> In a nutshell, moving paper ... coordinating, making sure that the paper flows, the information flows ... My belief from way back is you get a piece of paper, do something with it. Delegate it. File it ... But keep it moving because if it comes to a stop it starts to build up and everybody's actions thereafter start to build up in a bottleneck.

> My role is to ensure that all the administrative paperflow, the systems are adhered to right down to the smallest, you know, the everyday mail ... a glorified secretary ... Systems and administrative paperflow, generating correspondence ... the funnel for the majority of paperwork coming in, and then it gets down, disseminated through me to other areas, I monitor our document-control log.

Field officers feed the funnel. They spend their time in what might be termed 'database policing.' That is, their mentalities, sensibilities, and practices revolve around augmenting, searching, and maintaining computer databases.

Although police officers know they cannot live without their knowledge systems, they constantly find it difficult to live with them. The basis of the difficulty is that the systems never reach stasis. Stasis is impossible because knowledge work has no boundaries or sense of place. As a police officer said, in knowledge work there 'Really ... is no limit ... It's the amount of time you want to spend on it.' An officer in charge of the records section of a large urban police organization observed that information technology was originally introduced to reduce salaried staff and increase efficiency. Over the years, however, staffing remained the same regardless of each technological innovation because knowledge demands grew and inefficiencies continued to be discovered: 'When we first started, this was a paper-driven unit. There were three hundred people employed in this office back then. I remember when CPIC was introduced, and the talk of the widespread use of technology, there was a good deal of fear that this would result in job loss. This has not happened. We still have the same amount of people as back when we were a paper-driven organization.'

Police information management specialists have an impossible mandate. On the one hand there are incessant demands for new communication rules, formats, and technologies to reduce the paper burden. On the other hand there are incessant demands for new forms of knowledge provision. Risk management of knowledge provision itself is elusive at best. As was expressed to us by a senior information management specialist, 'There is the *real* fear that we will just become a walking sponge of information. There are *irreconcilable* demands to produce more information and at the same time reduce the information burden.'

External Sources

In Parts III and IV we documented the elaborate networking between the police and external institutions and analysed the ways in which these interinstitutional entanglements are held together by webs of communication. In the light of this analysis, it is not surprising that police officers attribute much of the paper burden to the demands of external institutions. In this section we consider police views on external demands for knowledge and show that the police usually have no option but to meet the demands.

The perceived increase in the paper burden was attributed by our officers to a pervasive climate of accountability in the wider culture (see Stenning 1995). All institutions, including the police, are under an increasing obligation to publicize and explain their activities. To meet this demand for accountability they must continually develop and refine their 'account ability,' that is, the formats for communicating what they have done and the rules indicating that they have done it with procedural propriety (Ericson 1995a).

Our interviewees offered examples of how accountability demands are intensifying and leading to more-rigid communication rules and formats. They pointed to new reporting requirements regarding police practices (such as forms for reporting each incident in which guns are drawn), new social problems on the public political agenda (resulting, for instance, in new reporting requirements for domestic violence), and changes in legal procedure (such as new reporting requirements to facilitate defence counsel discovery in criminal cases). All of these have greatly intensified the paper burden.

The new forms of accountability were seen by the interviewees as an outgrowth of community policing, which requires the police to be more accountable to other institutions and to interest groups. Accountability includes having to format knowledge to suit the purposes of these consumers, as well police openness to receiving from them knowledge concerning specific incidents, issues, and policy directions. As one of our police interviewees said, 'As we move towards community-based policing the requests for statistics and information will increase ... There will be an increased need for information sharing ... This creates more and more work.' The same outlook can be found in many mission statements and academic analyses of community policing.

The accountability demands of community policing discourse were attributed by our informants to the success of interest groups and social movements in capturing the public stage. In particular, the advance of the victims' rights movement during the past two decades was seen as a reason for new reporting requirements. A policy analyst for a large urban police organization remarked that social movements have their own momentum, which is difficult for the police to resist:

> Whatever is on the political agenda affects the information that is collected ... Freedom of information ... women and violence, sexual assault, victims' groups ... You end up with different groups wanting different parts of an occurrence report. This causes more forms to be created. It is an escalating process. The more groups that are created, the more forms that are created ... [For example] the women's groups were putting pressure on the politicians to find out how come restraining orders were not on CPIC ... We tell them that restraining orders are part of the court's mandate and we aren't getting that information from the courts. So the chief told us to make sure that restraining orders got onto CPIC. There were meetings held on this topic with court officials, more forms created, more forms, more meetings. It was a lot of work.

Social movements and interest groups put pressure on the police, but so do individual complainants. Various mechanisms for supporting public complaints about and civilian reviews of police activity have become institutionalized in recent years (Goldsmith 1990; Landau 1994b). These mechanisms require officers to work with police complaints investigators to produce knowledge relevant to particular cases. New forms develop to meet the demands of civilian review agencies.

For example, an interviewee said, referring to a form being developed for incidents in which the police used physical coercion, 'that's probably driven by civilian oversight and those are the questions the [police] commission asks and those are the questions the community asks. We've operated for 125 years and we never ever were interested in knowing how many times we whacked people with a baton before.' Another interviewee said that the typical police responses to public dissatisfaction with policing are to produce new forms and revise classifications: 'Any time there has been a crisis in the police force, the force has responded by creating another form. If they were accused of not following a certain procedure they would draft a form that would enable them to demonstrate that they had followed the appropriate steps ... Every time there is a criticism of the police we get a new box on the forms to fill out.'

Complaints lead to new forms and classifications because forms and classifications provide standard accountability mechanisms through which procedural propriety can be demonstrated. Risk society is obsessed with procedural propriety (Habermas 1975), and procedural propriety is the key to sustaining accountability and to maintaining authority and legitimacy. A properly classified form allows an organization to show that it is following acceptable steps in dealing with incidents.

Police officers see the risk knowledge requirements of external institutions as the immediate source of the paper burden. While they appreciate that these requirements partly reflect societal demands for accountability, they know that they are also related to the panoptic sorting needs of specific institutions.

The demands of traffic accident reporting are one example of how the police have little effect on the risk knowledge sources of the paper burden. The reporting of traffic accidents to numerous institutions is a major component of police work. However, the police have very little control over the reporting requirements or the formats of communication. The accident report forms are put together by the provincial government and must be used by all police organizations in the province. They are formatted to meet the risk knowledge needs of external institutions and are of little relevance to police operations. A police manager said the following about a recent revision to the accident report form in his province: 'This form, we're stuck with it. We had two members on a committee, a province-wide committee, to determine what that form looked like. But essentially, that form ... the provincial government wasn't going to change it because we wanted it changed, unless every other police agency in the province wanted it changed ... That's the form we're *forced* to fill out, so that's the information the insurance company can have. That's all there is to it.'

Another interviewee said that health professionals 'have been very vocal' in influencing traffic accident data collection, so that 'as the police forces have been trying to reduce the data, they've been trying to increase it.' Transport Canada has been working with the provinces to establish uniformity in traffic accident data categories, the goal being to better serve its institutional constituencies. Among other things, there have been requests for better data to help regulate the automobile industry, improve traffic engineering, and ascertain the best standard for blood alcohol levels in determining impaired driving. An information technology specialist involved in this process explained that

> Transport Canada has approached the provinces and they're getting very good support from the solicitor generals across Canada to at least supply statistics that are good to meet their mandate ... They want to know certain areas that keep having accidents so that they can plan on redoing the roads, as an example. They want to know if one specific car keeps having the same accident and killing people. Therefore, they will turn around and insist that any cars manufactured should have this and that. So they establish standards. So in order to be able to establish that database, they are asking the municipal and provincial police force or province now to supply them with all that information ... They want to see if the blood alcohol count is too low and even people with 0.8 or less are having accidents all the time. So they want to make sure they can capture that ... They're going to request to the province to see if they can modify their form to have this thrown in. So when that's in, then that is added data which is going to be used to establish policy at the federal level which is going to be suggested to the province right down to the municipality ... [But that creates the problem that] you need to bring them [possibly impaired drivers] back to the detachment where he [the breathalyser operator] [can produce the] count [so] that ... [the officer] can fill the form out. Or you devise a mobile unit that has a count with possibly, assuming it has the proper interface, connect to the side of the [patrol officer's] laptop, it automatically puts it on the form.

Transport Canada, and its provincial counterparts, broker knowledge to a wide range of institutions. A partial list would include provincial and municipal traffic engineering departments (information on road conditions); provincial and federal regulatory agencies (information on vehicle- and operator-related deficiencies that contribute to accidents); the Canadian Council of Motor Transport; the National Accident Database group; the Traffic Injury Research Foundation; the Insurance Bureau of Canada; the Vehicle Information Centre of Canada; automobile manufacturers; issuers of drivers' licences; vehicle standards agencies; health care agencies; insurance companies; law firms specializing in accident litigation; and academics (see Pudifin 1991).

These institutions demand the fine-grained detail that appears on accident forms (see pp. 210–11). At the level of the patrol officer, this demand translates into meticulous knowledge work that seems, at times, all-consuming. In a police district station whose operations we observed, officers were required to attend all traffic accidents involving obstruction of a road, damage exceeding a minimum dollar amount, personal injury, death, or the possibility of an impaired-driving charge. These criteria were designed to curtail the amount of time officers spent responding to 'minor' traffic accidents. At the scene of accidents, officers attended to removing damaged vehicles from the road and sending passengers to hospital if necessary. They then proceeded to capture the accident within the required form.

The 8½-by-11-inch form directed officers to 'Please Press Firmly – You are Making 5 Copies.' These five carbon-paper copies were eventually distributed to a number of different agencies. There was also a noncirculating top sheet, which was almost entirely devoted to categories for officers to employ in describing various aspects of the accident, the vehicles, and the drivers. The top sheet was divided into twenty-five sections, with headings such as 'Light Conditions,' 'Road Surface Type,' 'Vehicle Identification,' 'Sequence of Events,' 'Major Contributing Factors,' and 'Location of Damage.' Each section included classifications that limited the officer's communication possibilities. These ranged from as few as three options under the heading 'Ejected from Vehicle' ('not ejected,' 'ejected, 'partially ejected'), to twenty-seven options for 'Major Contributing Factors.' Alongside each set of classifications was a series of numbered boxes where the officer recorded the most appropriate code. In most classifications the officer had a box to fill in for each vehicle involved in the accident. For more-elaborate classifications additional boxes were available. For example, officers could check off up to four 'Major Contributing Factors' for each vehicle and three chronological incidents under 'Sequence of Events.' In total, there were 310 classifications. Additional reporting was required for each person directly involved in the accident.

Because accidents were to be known only through risk classifications of relevance to other institutions, officers were given no opportunity to provide classifications beyond those on the form, let alone offer interpretations or provide a narrative. The classifications were immutable. Weather was reduced to one of eight possibilities ('clear,' 'cloudy,' 'drifting snow,' and so on). Road conditions were also limited to one of eight possibilities ('wet,' 'dry,' 'muddy,' and so on). Diversity of conditions was eliminated with one stroke of the pen, and that act in turn facilitated the keystroking of data entry and the subsequent stroking of data for statistical analysis.

The form asked for 'General' information on the severity of the accident and for the date, the time, the number of injured or killed, the speed limit on that portion of the road, and information on damage to property other than the vehicles. Stylized arrows were checked off to indicate the directions the vehicles were travelling when the accident occurred, and there were further boxes to check off for 'Location,' 'Driver,' 'Vehicle,' 'Owner,' 'Insurance,' 'Persons,' and 'Additional.' This last classification allowed the officer to note the charges laid and provide a visual sketch of the accident. If more than two vehicles were involved in the accident, the officer was required to complete another form for each additional vehicle.

The completion of traffic accident paperwork places an enormous burden on police time. A Transport Canada study observed that 'In 1987, there were 203,431 accidents in Ontario alone involving 381,929 vehicles. Assuming (on average) that two officers spend two hours at each accident scene, and approximately 25 per cent of this time is spent recording accident data, the total time spent recording data would be 203,431 man-hours' (Pudifin 1991: 1). And in addition to the knowledge work of Ontario's on-the-scene investigating officers, the reports are reviewed by a police supervisor and then by the provincial motor vehicles registry. The registry enters the data into its computer system, a task which takes six minutes for each of the thousands of forms it receives weekly.

In a police organization we studied, the initial entry of data from traffic accident report forms was completed by clerical employees. A recent change in the form had generated a great deal of additional reported knowledge and had placed a significant burden on clerical resources. A supervisor of the clerical staff remarked, 'Before ... we only entered limited data ... my girls can enter an abstract of that. They can enter forty an hour. The new system, and I'll be generous, I'd say they'll be typing four an hour. That's the difference in the kind of information that's being collected again.'

Police officers emphasized that the traffic accident knowledge they produced was of little or no use in policework. A district police station manager observed that

> I've been in [the police service] for sixteen years and we've never been able to use traffic data effectively. And I've been an analyst at one time up in this district. And we couldn't get the traffic data from the ... accident forms and use them effectively to solve traffic problems or even identify them ... Because our computer system never got its [improvements] in order to be able to do it. The whole thing is kind of confusing. You write out reams of forms and nobody ever knows what happens to the information ... The accident forms changed three times since I've been on the job and it makes as little sense as it did when we started. They just ask for more boxes to be filled out ... It all goes down to the government and who knows what they do with it because we never get any feedback from them.

Although he was very senior and experienced, this officer knew little about where traffic report data went and how they were used. His focus was on possible police uses of the data, without appreciating the significance of the data for external institutions. This limited vision was typical of operational officers. In another jurisdiction, the police destroyed their copy of the accident report after one month, retaining only a computerized record of date, location, type, and cause. This act indicated that accident reporting was for the benefit of external institutions, not the police. However, the officers we spoke to believed that external institutions also had little use for the knowledge. A police interviewee observed that 'The original and one copy gets tossed in the basket under the front counter and every two weeks or so gets bundled up and shipped to the registrar of motor vehicles, where they take and compile all kinds of weird and wonderful statistics that nobody ever uses.' A colleague in the same office said that at the registrar's office 'they just file them and do whatever they do with them. They create paper. I know there is a room ... that is just filled with accident reports. They employ people to categorize them, to check up on insurance policies and shit like that.'

The demands of criminal occurrence reporting also lead to a situation in which the police have little influence over external sources of the paper burden. Several external institutions, which vary depending on the crime and the outcome of the investigation, demand knowledge of criminal cases. Moreover, because the demands from these institutions are framed within their own communication formats, the police find themselves having to provide similar knowledge in a different form to each of them. This redundancy obviously creates extra knowledge work for the police. Referring to Health and Welfare Canada's need for information to be recorded on a special form in drug cases, a police interviewee said, '*All* of the information available in this form is available in other forms used by us.'

The use of special forms for reporting domestic violence provides another example (see also pp. 246–7). Both the federal government and the provinces require special reporting on family violence. Police officers viewed this reporting as an external demand created by political considerations over which they had no influence. One interviewee said about a new form that her police organization was 'told that they were going to be using this form every time there was an incident involving family violence. They did not ask us about doing this, they just told us that it was going to be done.' This new reporting requirement created an additional paper burden for a number of reasons. First, the new form produced knowledge identical to some of the knowledge produced by other forms. Second, the new form introduced new knowledge requirements, and therefore additional information to record. Third, and most fundamentally, the police were required to think in terms of a new discourse of violence which, in their minds, did not fit their understanding of criminal violence. They found the new definitions of 'violence' and 'abuse' to be too diffuse, forcing them to incorporate into their thinking on criminality cases that previously would have been treated as unfounded or as symptoms of some other problem.

Playing loosely with 'violence' himself, an interviewee in another jurisdiction said of a new family violence form, 'It's certainly created violence around this office a few times':

> If I'm going to do something, it has to be meaningful and if it isn't meaningful and purposeful and accurate then I'm not going to do it at all. They want us to do these family violence reports, statistical information. In my mind, it's politically driven. So what we're doing is we're going to capture all this information ... for all circumstances alleging violence. So what's going to happen is the wife picks up the phone, calls the police and says, 'My husband hit me.' Stop right there because, according to this, we need one of these reports. But when we actually get there, nothing of the sort occurred. So what we've done now is

we've built a humongous base of information to say we've got this big problem with family violence but, in reality, when you sit down and you start to go through some of the actual complaints like I did last week – there were twenty-nine domestic situations reported and most of those were alleging violence – so for argument's sake, we had twenty-nine situations alleging violence, we needed twenty-nine reports. But when you start to look at the actual circumstances and the history, you find that there was only one violent situation out of twenty-nine ... So there was a couple in here that were between mother and daughter ... it's a mother-daughter fight. Another was just like a standby or somebody's coming in to collect their debt. Another was an unwanted guest: 'I don't want him here anymore. Get him out!' And in order to get the police there, they allege violence ... Now if you do this big number, let's say we have twenty-nine circumstances, so we got this hue and cry from particular movements to say, 'Family violence is a serious problem in our community. What are we going to do about it? We want more money for these programs' ... I say it should be actual violence where there's evidence to support a charge, a charge is laid.

This interviewee made a conventional distinction between information and knowledge, and complained that this reporting requirement forced police officers to produce disinformation. He also believed this disinformation was nevertheless used by external institutions to produce knowledge in the form of policies and aggregate data on family violence. This knowledge in turn pressured the police to read family violence in ways that in their view were unproductive. In the interviewee's eyes, the family violence forms, and the routine reproduction of disinformation they compelled, provided a reading of the family violence problem that made the problem more difficult for the police to deal with.

One police interviewee complained that Health and Welfare Canada's 'domestic violence initiative has created a range of information to be collected that is not of interest to the police.' Equally blunt was another interviewee who told us that 'from a policing perspective all of this increased [family violence] information is unproductive. It is of little use to the police.' Typically, however, police officers knew little about how family violence data were used for risk analysis in other institutions. A police station administrator said that 'The opinion of most officers on the street is that all we're doing is collecting statistics for the government which, in essence, is pretty well accurate ... I don't know the exact route up there, how it gets funnelled through.'

The police also face a mandatory reporting requirement from Statistics Canada in criminal cases. This requirement is significant both because it is time-consuming and because it affects the crime classification process.

In a district station of one police organization, the 'scoring' of Statistics Canada Uniform Crime Reports (UCR) was the responsibility of the officer in charge of each shift, although the officer sometimes assigned the duty to a patrol supervisor. An officer who worked on this scoring said that 'You spend a lot of your time on each file doing something for another organization, something that is broken down into minute and painstaking great detail.' A colleague complained that the work was 'taking a supervisor, a man off the street to just do that for Stats Canada. What other organization would have a supervisor – a person of high rank who is accountable if we screw up – doing that?'

These officers pointed to several reasons why UCR reporting was seen as a burden: it was time-consuming, took police officers away from other work, and was largely in the service of an external institution whose needs were in many respects different from those of police. Much of the knowledge demanded was about matters which the police did not regard as important. One police interviewee estimated that only one-third of the sixty-five elements addressed by the UCR dealt with matters of operational relevance to the police. A senior officer in an information management unit offered as an example of irrelevance the requirement to classify weapons used in crimes: 'If you have the example of assault with weapons, we are now required to list if the weapon used was a baseball bat or a lead pipe or whatever. I don't know who would use that information or what good it would do anyone. The information demands were not really assessed before these pieces of legislation were implemented.'

That Statistics Canada and the police have different views on how crime should be classified results in a dual system of classification and an additional paper burden for the police. A police supervisor in a municipal police organization that ran a dual system said that 'one thousand man-hours [had been needed] just to define the rules to implement Statistics Canada's new reporting requirements.' On the other hand, some police organizations had developed their information technology to the point where their central database on crime can interface with Statistics Canada's database to allow many offence codes to be used by police.

Statistics Canada also requires additional reports when particular kinds of crime occur. For example, homicide is deemed important enough to require a separate, detailed report. The 'Homicide Return' process is typically overseen by police information management supervisors who ensure that each homicide in their jurisdiction is accounted for and properly scored. One such information manager described his role in this way:

> In addition to the very basic scoring that appears on the statistical database for a murder, there's a lot more related information they want to know about in that murder: relationships, type of weapon used, things of that nature that don't get scored on [the general] statistical database. As a result each [police division] has a homicide coordinator that is a liaison person like I am with Stats Canada. I have a number of those forms on my desk. When a murder happens at a location, we're responsible for investigating. I send the chief investigator that form, saying, 'Please complete and return to me.' And then I forward it on to Stats Canada.

The paper burden of UCR reporting to Statistics Canada was typically seen not only as a drain on police resources but also as a constraint on police authorship, for reports had to conform to formats provided by Statistics Canada, and Statistics Canada's subsequent use of the knowledge meant that the police lost control of the texts. As a crime analysis unit supervisor told us, 'Most of the audience for the UCR stats is [the] public, private interest groups, [and] politicians ... When they release a study, they don't even release it to us before. So our first thing ... is that we get phone calls from the media ... It goes out to the [House of] Commons, it goes out to the interest groups on their lists and it goes out to the media, but it doesn't go out to the police. So what's UCR for?'

The criminal courts were seen by the police as another significant contributor to the paper burden. Although the role of the courts in creating rule-based responses to police organization is considered in more detail in chapter 14, it is worthwhile at this juncture to introduce the subject of how court requirements can increase the paper burden.

It is important to note that because the administration of criminal justice is a provincial matter, court forms are standardized province-wide, with little variation for local policing requirements. Every police organization in a province uses the same forms from the attorney general's office for warrants, summonses, informations, recognizances, and subpoenas. Moreover, because these forms are created within the framework of federal criminal law, they are more or less the same across Canada. The police can only proceed on their terms.

Large police organizations must run substantial units whose responsibility is the registering and securing of such documents. In one large urban police organization, the court documents unit was staffed by twenty full-time employees – a civilian supervisor, three clerks, and sixteen summons officers – who among other things coordinated police officers and civilian volunteers that assisted in the serving of the documents. There was also a separate court unit, which coordinated the police dossiers compiled for prosecution purposes and had thirteen full-time employees.

Particular judicial decisions were viewed by the police as having a major impact on the paper burden. *R. v. Stinchcombe* ([1991] 3 SCR 326, 8 CR (4th) 277) was singled out as a major contributor to extra knowledge work and thus the cause of a considerable drain on police resources. This case required the police to prepare documents that would permit disclosure of the prosecution case to defence counsel more fully than had been done in the past. We consider this case in detail in chapter 14, but for the moment police perceptions of its impact on the paper burden are relevant to our analysis.

According to the crown attorney's office in one jurisdiction we studied, *Stinchcombe* required crown attorneys to alter their practices with regard to disclosure to the defence. The result was that the police were now compelled to provide a very detailed written account of the evidence in every criminal case. The crown attorney's office thus collaborated with the police in producing a highly formatted 'Report to Prosecutor' check-list and procedural manual that gave police officers elaborate document production guidelines. The check-list required the police to report procedurally sensitive details of their dealings with the accused, as well as to supply their notebooks, written statements from all relevant parties, and other documentary evidence well beyond what had been required before *Stinchcombe*. The additional paperwork was seen by the police as especially burdensome because they knew that most cases result in guilty pleas and that files are usually not read in detail by crown attorneys (cf. Ericson and Baranek 1982; McConville, Sanders, and Leng 1991).

Stinchcombe required 'just-in-case knowledge.' That is, extensive documentation had to be made available to the prosecutor just in case the defence decided to contest the matter and ask for full disclosure. Previously, extra documentation had been produced only when it was believed a trial was likely, something that would not have been known until well after the initial case file had been prepared. Now extra documentation had to be produced for every case at the point of arrest. As a police administrator who managed a district station said,

> Under *Stinchcombe* you have to have what they call full disclosure. So now you have to basically provide copies of everything and a statement of everything that everybody does, absolutely everybody ... You have to have copies of all of the statements. You have to have copies of all of the original notes for the officers that investigated the original complaint. You have to have all of that documentation. You have to have everything that links that person [the accused] right through the entire case. You have to basically rewrite all of the reports so that everything falls into categories so the prosecutor can take it and say, 'This is all the evidence that I have and this is where it is going to go' ... And the demands being placed on [investigating officers] by the Crown prosecutor's office saying that if you want the person charged, then you have to do this and this and this and this prior to laying the charge when, in fact ... you don't need to do all that prior to laying the charge because the guy's going to plead guilty. Why should I waste all the time doing stuff that's never going to be utilized? And rightfully or wrongfully so, the old system was the fellow went to court ... if he pled not guilty or he got a lawyer and the lawyer said I want this information, then they come back and say provide the lawyer with this information, provide us with this information so we can give it to the lawyer. So basically, what you used to be able to put off and do until the required time, now you've got to do it. It's added probably five hours to an arrest. If you arrest a person at four o'clock [in the afternoon] you can be pretty well sure that you're not going to be done the paperwork until midnight. It's a fair amount of time. And a lot of the time, it's like I say, the guys sit down and they say, well, it's kind of ridiculous.

Some interviewees chose less kind words. A police officer who managed another district station complained at length about the *Stinchcombe* burden, describing it as 'one of the intellectual masturbation things that the Supreme Court comes out with.' We found, moreover, that the extra burden created by *Stinchcombe* was not limited to investigating officers. In another urban police organization, *Stinchcombe* paperwork was said to have required two new clerks, a new photocopying machine, and an additional $90,000 a year in paper for photocopies.

Stinchcombe was also pointed to by our police interviewees as an example of how the courts remain creatures of a print culture, while other institutions have moved into the electronic age. At the same time as the police struggle to reduce their paper burden by adopting document reproduction technologies and 'paperless' computer systems (see chapter 16), the courts prefer the traditional authority of print. As a police information system manager remarked, 'The courts are slow to change, and we are facing issues about the validity of photocopies before the courts. Some judges demand the original. As we move to a system that does not use paper, that is becoming more difficult. I think the courts are going to recognize that they cannot have the original, simply because there is no original ... As long as there are security provisions and an audit trail ... I think the courts are going to have to accept it.'

The police believe they have no option but to comply with external demands for knowledge of risk. While they can debate the meaning and practicality of particular classifications, they know that in general they must provide the knowledge required within the established formats of the external institutions concerned. Respondents saw this subordinate, reactive position as a consequence of the fact that the police are a government agency in the service of government. They get paid to do knowledge work for government and therefore must work within the framework laid down by their government 'clients.' As one police officer commented, 'We are at the mercy of government agencies for funding. If they want specific information we pretty well have to provide it. If we don't play ball we don't get any money.' A police information management specialist said that he could not recall ever having refused a demand from an external institution for systematic reporting. He observed that the police are a convenient source of knowledge production for those external institutions that can lay claim to police time because of their role in government:

> The [police organization] tries to be cost-efficient in its operation, has to be careful that they don't end up gathering extra statistics for other agencies when those other agencies should gather it themselves or get it in some other manner ... Our officers every year fill out thousands of these forms for the motor vehicles branch. It's an assistance to the provincial motor vehicles branch. That's a fair workload and if our people weren't doing that they'd have lots more time to do more important things. But we do that because we're working for the province. They're paying part of our salary and we are assisting one of their agencies in doing this.

The division of political jurisdiction in Canada among municipal and provincial governments and the federal government has a major impact on the range of police reports required and on how they are formatted. Having to report to institutions at all three levels of government is a problem for all police organizations, but in particular for provincial police forces (such as the Ontario Provincial Police and Sûreté de Québec) and the RCMP. The provincial forces must meet the requirements that arise not only in regular municipal and provincial policing but also in special services and regulatory policing for various provincial government institutions. The RCMP must perform a wide range of municipal and provincial policing functions and collaborate with federal government institutions in specialized compliance and regulatory functions.

The RCMP, for example, engages in compliance-based law enforcement on behalf of a number of 'host' federal agencies. Among other things, it works on behalf of the Customs and Excise Branch and Revenue Canada by acting against smugglers. In this work the RCMP files reports using forms supplied by Revenue Canada, and its policy follows a format established by Revenue Canada. And because the RCMP has a greater geographical reach than other federal institutions, it is often called on by those institutions to act as an inspectorate, in matters ranging from checking on migratory birds and protected species for the Ministry of the Environment, to mines inspections under the Explosives Act for the Ministry of Energy, Mines and Resources. Performing inspectorate functions for numerous government bodies is a major reason why, at the time of our research in 1993, the RCMP used over two thousand operational forms and required six hundred employees for its Ottawa 'Informatics' Division.

The police are situated as a 'centre of calculation' (Latour 1987) amidst institutions at all three levels of government. They produce, broker, analyse, and distribute knowledge at the behest of these institutions. As an information manager for a police organization pointed out, this situation is a prime contributor to the paper burden: 'There is certainly a range of different groups who are interested in the information collected by police. We become their agent ... We become the reporting agent for all three levels of government. All three levels of government want their forms filled out in a specific manner ... These different levels of government have their own information concerns and these just become translated into a different form.'

Internal Sources

While the paper burden is largely created by external institutional sources, it is also a product of how the police themselves respond to external demands for knowledge. In the very process of creating communication rules, formats, and technologies to manage the paper burden, the police sometimes amplify it. The sources and dynamics of internal efforts to manage the paper burden, and how these efforts sometimes compound rather than alleviate the burden, are analysed in chapters 14, 15, and 16. At this juncture we provide an overview of some of the internal dimensions of the paper burden.

The police contribute to the paper burden in four main ways. First, police administrators – who are themselves responding to the external pressures documented in the previous section – demand greater internal accountability. This has the effect of creating new kinds of accountability, as well as an overproduction of knowledge that might be needed for accountability. Second, working in a culture where knowledge is power, there is a tendency by the police to overproduce knowledge that might be useful to them in the future for purposes other than accountability. Third, police administrations are obsessed with full and accurate reporting. This leads to a proliferation of monitoring devices and auditing systems aimed at maintaining the quality of reports. Fourth, there is redundancy in reporting systems, including overlap between electronic and paper systems. This redundancy leads to a duplication of effort that also drains resources.

These four internal sources of the paper burden operate in tandem. For example, greater demands for accountability increase the overproduction of knowledge, intensify the administrative obsession with detail and the attendant monitoring of reports, and foster redundancy in the knowledge systems.

The police officers we interviewed pointed to signs that the internal demands for accountability were intensifying. They also enumerated the ways in which information technologies created to assist their work also provided a means of monitoring it. We were told, for example, how computer-aided dispatch systems were able to register every use of those systems by patrol officers, thus allowing instantaneous or after-the-fact monitoring by supervisors. Laptop computer terminals in police vehicles allowed supervisors to check filed reports instantly and to demand immediate corrections.

Administrative rule systems and reporting formats were also being tightened up in response to accountability requirements, our interviewees said. During our observation of a patrol supervisor's work at a police station, a woman came into the station and turned in a wallet she had found. The patrol supervisor returned to his desk and said to the researcher, 'This is the kind of thing that police officers hate.' He explained that in the past, if someone returned a wallet the police officer could telephone the owner and have him come to the station to retrieve it, without any paperwork. Now, he continued, the police officer must prepare an occurrence report as well as an exhibit report that lists the wallet's contents. If the owner cannot be contacted immediately, the wallet must be secured in an overnight locker, and another form must be completed and signed by the owner if the wallet is eventually claimed. When the wallet is removed from the locker, a supervisory officer must be present to ensure continuity of evidence. The patrol supervisor concluded his comments by muttering, 'Just what I need, another twenty minutes of paperwork.'

These intensified accountability requirements were attributed by the officers we interviewed to new possibilities for supervision created by new information technologies, and to increased legalism. Information technologies and legalism were not only seen as sources of new paperwork requirements but also as creating an *aura of accountability* that led to a production of knowledge beyond what was actually required. There was a pervasive feeling among the officers that it is best to produce detailed knowledge, and to keep complete records of it, just in case one is called to account. A district police station administrator drew our attention to his patrol officers' obsession with detail and tendency to photocopy and keep records of things that were already recorded in several filing systems within the organization. He attributed this obsession to what might be regarded as the trinity of accountability in risk society: 'part of it, I think, is *fear*, part of it is a lack of *trust*, part of it is a *technology* problem.' A supervisor in an investigative unit did not mention these key words, but his account of the overproduction of knowledge in his unit speaks to the same trinity at work:

> Some of what we do may be speculative in nature, but if we fail to at least do a basic background check into some of these things and something occurs, the obvious question is, 'Well, why didn't you know?' So they do an awful lot of information gathering ... Everything that anybody does here generates a report. It may be an information report saying we can't find anything about that person or organization, but everything we do generates a report so that when we are asked questions about our activities or about the activities of somebody that we should or may know about, we'll be able to refer back to that report.

Police administrative *systems* are equally obsessed with registering minutiae for accountability purposes. As we document in the following chapters of this book, elaborate systems and procedures exist to ensure that the knowledge police officers produce is properly formatted, 'clean,' and ready for direct access by external institutions.

Overproduction of knowledge is not solely the result of police officers fearing the wrath of administrators who may call them to account. It also results from a strong belief that knowledge should be produced and stored in case it may come in handy for investigative purposes. In this respect, as well, police officers are authors of their own paper burden.

In interviews and during our fieldwork, police officers repeatedly justified the production of knowledge on the grounds that such knowledge might be useful in the future. There was an appreciation that meanings change with contexts, and this led to the conclusion that it is worthwhile to produce knowledge that appears irrelevant in the present context because it may prove useful in future contexts. An officer remarked, 'We were taught no information is really useless, but there is that information that you take that you don't really need. But the thing is, the scenario can change from now to two weeks from now, where something you thought was not important today turns into being very important two weeks from now, so I don't think there is anything that is unimportant.' A colleague of his expressed a similar sentiment: 'Accurate reporting would be to take the time where others wouldn't listen to *drain that person of everything you can think of* with regards to a matter. No matter how trivial ... somewhere down the road that trivial information is worth its weight in gold.'

This sentiment translates into police officers taking every opportunity to produce populations-related knowledge that may help to trace those populations in the future. This knowledge opportunism was bluntly described by a police officer who stated that 'The more people that the police encounter then the more we have for our information purposes.' Another police officer provided an elaboration of this notion: 'Everybody and anybody that calls in we try to get as much information from them as we can. Because you never know if next week they are a suspect in something else, so that we can go to our computer system and punch them up, and we know where to go, we know who they are, we've got a date of birth.' A third officer said that people not directly involved in an incident sometimes object to being asked for their date of birth: '"I just saw the car accident, why do you want my date of birth?" But who says that a few weeks down the road something comes up where the person is involved in a crime or was a witness in something else? Name, address, and telephone numbers are a big one; with that sort of thing you can find them. It may play a role somewhere down the road. You've got it on file.'

Police officers also emphasized that once they have captured a piece of information on file, there is a tendency to keep it there because, again, one never knows when it might be useful, and it can be embarrassing to have had it and then destroyed it. An officer said, 'I know if I file something away I can go back and get it at a later date. I'm terrified to throw something away that I may need later.' Another officer, in charge of records for a large urban police organization, said, 'We're pack rats. We store everything. Just as one example, occurrence reports must be cross-referenced fifty different ways. This creates more and more work.' His colleague, an administrator of computer and telecommunication systems, added that 'There are a number of different regulations about storing different types of information. We have a retention schedule that is outlined in the Police Services Act. Mostly, however, we tend to keep the information forever ... I think it is a "just-in-case" mentality. The notion that it may be useful some day.'

The overproduction of knowledge not only exacerbates the paper burden but also fosters new needs to protect the knowledge from unauthorized users. Elaborate systems of data access and protection are created, as are additional forms of accountability. This link between overproduction and overprotection was pointed out by a police officer who had moved to a private company specializing in police information technology. In her opinion, police organizations 'are tremendously heavy on the administrative side. It's scandalous when you look at the administration that supports police forces, especially uniformed people ... It's this paranoia about policing and information ... we're the only people that are cleared and we're the only people that are in confidence. It's a paranoia.'

The security of having knowledge that is potentially useful for investigative or accountability purposes, and the need to keep that knowledge secure, contribute to redundancy in knowledge systems, which in turn adds to the paper burden. Redundancy also occurs because new knowledge systems are developed but the previous ones are not always replaced. The old systems are kept because they are seen as having additional uses or as functioning as a back-up. Another source of redundancy, common to all organizations, is the desire to have hard copies of what is otherwise available in computerized 'paperless systems.' This desire relates to employees' failure to adjust to new information technologies. Employees distrust the retrieval capacities of the new technologies and want to keep hard copies just in case.

14

Communication Rules

One response to the paper burden is the elaboration of rules to rationalize and regulate it. Communication rules emanate from numerous sources, are embodied in various texts, and become embedded in particular institutional contexts of police action. The development and enforcement of rules pertaining to knowledge production leads to additional paperwork and in turn to more rules, in an amplifying spiral. The managerial response is always to administer more doses of the same, as rules are perpetually refined, revised, and elaborated in an effort to stem a tide of paper that never ebbs.

In this chapter we first consider the regulation of knowledge work associated with the legal institution. Law not only places enormous knowledge demands on the police, but does so according to particular regulatory and format requirements. The police respond by developing their own communication rules and procedures. While this response routinizes paperwork, it also augments it.

We also consider police administrative efforts to regulate the minutiae of knowledge production. Police knowledge work is structured, guided, and rationalized by various regulatory texts: policy manuals, step-by-step instructions for particular types of knowledge work, rules regarding release of knowledge to external institutions, and systems for auditing communication practices. Each of these communication rule systems inevitably falls short of the task and therefore is constantly under revision, which of course adds to the paper burden.

This chapter is a study in police bureaucratization. It shows how the elaboration of rule systems is the result of new accountability requirements and the knowledge work associated with them. At the same time, the rationalization and regulation of knowledge work creates more work, which in turn gives rise to the need for more rules to help manage the work. A managerial class of knowledge regulators has arisen in police organizations. In what follows we study the work of this class by analysing how they classify knowledge.

Criminal Procedure

The law of criminal procedure is a continual elaboration of the ways of producing legally acceptable knowledge for the courts. As was first mentioned in chapter 2, the tendency in criminal procedure is towards giving the criminal justice system the right to access whatever knowledge is required to obtain evidence and achieve an expeditious outcome. As part of this effort, the police are provided with precise communication rules regarding how to format their requests for knowledge from informants, witnesses, and suspects, and how to formulate this knowledge for the courts. Indeed, Part 28 of the Criminal Code provides the precise legal wording for each form of police knowledge work related to criminal court jurisdiction. Fifty-one models are provided, for registering of informants, summonses, promises to appear in court, indictments, reporting to justices, recognizances, certificates and writs of default, registering convictions, sentencing and acquittal orders, custody orders and discharges from custody orders, statements of fitness to stand trial, challenges to arraignment and for cause, production of fingerprint records, income tax disclosure, subpoenas to witnesses, depositions of witnesses, and warrants (for searches, arrests, committals to trial, remands, conveyances of the accused from place to place, production of witnesses, and endorsements by justices). In one police jurisdiction the police 'package' prepared for the crown attorney in criminal cases contained on average seventeen different forms.

The rules of criminal procedure are embodied and embedded in these forms. As such, they become the means by which the law is translated into police action. The communication rules of criminal procedure are fitted into established legal forms and these forms affect how the police think and act. Having to meet the formal legal rationality of these forms, the police form their actions accordingly and are thereby able to show that they conform.

The rules of criminal procedure are also imprinted on other police forms and documents. For example, the legal rights of suspects are specified on cards that police officers can read to suspects when necessary. In some instances the same wording is found in forms that are used in asking suspects to waive their rights or to acknowledge that they have been read their rights. Such forms remind police officers about what they must say, and remind the accused that they are entitled to have their rights read to them. One police organization we examined had a 'Charter Consent/Waiver Search' form that provided great detail on suspects' rights regarding access to lawyers and the execution of search warrants. Suspects could waive these rights by signing the form.

Another species of forms is used to document that the police have established the veracity of the technologies they use to measure the behaviour of miscreants. For example, one police organization had a 'Certificate of Stop Watch Test' form to register the accuracy of stopwatches used during aircraft checks on highway speeding. It also had a three-page 'Blood Sample by Warrant' form, tightly formatted to produce procedural regularity in the taking of blood to measure alcohol levels. When breathalysers were used for the same purpose, there was a 'Breathalyser Operational Check Sheet' with thirteen steps for the technician to follow. Where breathalyser technology was unavailable, there was a very tightly formatted and detailed form entitled 'Investigative Guide and Report – Alcohol Impairment,' whose purpose was to show the police officer how to test a driver for impairment. All of these forms are evidence of the extent to which impaired driving has been an especially contested area of criminal procedure, requiring a perpetual elaboration of communication rules and formats to demonstrate procedural correctness.

The courts regularly bring down decisions that reject police forms. When rejection occurs, new rules and procedures must be developed, and knowledge work increases. An interviewee working in the court document unit of her police organization described what ensued when the court decided that it was illegal to serve the third rather than the second copy of a form:

> [The court said] we had to start serving the second copy. There was different wording on it [different from the third copy] so we had to recall all the [forms] that were out, reissue them ... Our officers would pull the second copy because it was just in the way, so we didn't have a second copy to serve! There would be a first and a third; the subject would get the third copy. The first would come back to us for paperwork ... Now our computer department's pulling off the third copy and the summons officers have to issue the second.

The impact of court decisions on police communication rules can be illustrated by examining in detail how one police organization responded to the Supreme Court of Canada decision in *Stinchcombe* (see also pp. 313–14). A special committee made up of representatives of the crown attorney's office and police decided that *Stinchcombe* required the crown to alter its practices with regard to disclosure to the defence. In a nineteen-page training bulletin setting out rules on how to produce and format knowledge post-*Stinchcombe,* it was stated that disclosure needed to occur before the accused was asked to elect the mode of trial or to plead. The crown would have to disclose all relevant knowledge, whether or not it intended to introduce such knowledge into evidence. This disclosure would include, for example, both inculpatory and exculpatory evidence, evidence obtained from people who were not going to be crown witnesses, and police notes. The bulletin said that the obligation to disclose would arise when the accused or someone acting on his or her behalf asked for disclosure.

Discretion with respect to the timing of disclosure and what to disclose, the bulletin continued, resided with the crown, not the police. The crown would be responsible for assessing the relevance of knowledge; deciding whether the identity of witnesses should be withheld to protect them from possible harassment or injury; deciding how to apply the rules of privilege for informants, including protection of identity; and making determinations about the effects of early disclosure on completion of an investigation. The bulletin emphasized that '*Disclosure is the responsibility of the Crown – <u>not</u> the police! It is the investigator's responsibility to get the information to the Crown* ... You will *not* provide any information directly to either the defence or the accused, other than the standard documents for impaired driving cases or other statutory requirements which have always been served upon the accused.'

In summary, the police were now required to treat every case in which someone was charged as if it was going to proceed to trial. This requirement may seem obvious and unexceptional: surely, when the police decide that someone should be charged and prosecuted, they should provide full documentation to support their decision. But the typical practice had been to do everything possible to obtain guilty pleas and thereby avoid the paper burden of going to trial. This practice was followed in the dual-defendant plea bargaining case cited in chapter 2 (pp. 61–2), where, in spite of the crown attorney's urging, the detective simply refused to do the paperwork for what he saw as an obvious case for guilty pleas.

A senior officer in the same police organization said that his officers in the pre-*Stinchcombe* era had had minimal paperwork to complete in the 80 per cent of cases that resulted in guilty pleas without trial. However, following *Stinchcombe*, they were required to treat those cases in the same way as the 20 per cent that went to trial, that is, by preparing dossiers detailing each and every piece of evidence, in legally acceptable formats:

With respect to *Stinchcombe*, the difference between where we were and where we are now arises from the fact that we provide information to the crown in preparation for a court case. We generally didn't do so until the accused had made their first appearance and had entered a not guilty plea. If they made their first appearance and pleaded guilty, there was a short arrest report completed at the time of arrest which was a sort of overview of the charges and gave the crown prosecutor something to relate to the court, the nature of the offence, which the accused or his representatives would either agree to or make some sort of addendum to. Then the judge would deal with it from there. *Stinchcombe* has caused us to do ... what we used to do when we received a not guilty plea, which was a more elaborate court presentation outlining in greater detail what every witness would contribute to the prosecution and, in addition, a greater burden to provide information that the prosecution may not call but could be deemed as relevant to the defence's side of the process. And the significant difference is that now we have to do that prior to the indication of plea ... 80 per cent of the cases, according to the crown, are dealt with through some other mechanism other than trial. So, when we were doing 20 per cent of the more in-depth court preparation, now we're doing 20 plus 80 which has put a huge burden on the paper process ... In the past ... if it didn't go guilty, there'd be the next notification level where you would go back and review it and shore it up. Now every case has to be assumed as being a not guilty plea in the first instance. And all that information, by law, has to be provided to the defence at their request before they even get around to entering that plea. So they have to scrutinize every case, and every case has to be prepared like a full court presentation at the time of arrest, essentially.

Because the same procedure had to be followed in all criminal cases – no matter whether summary conviction, indictable, or dual procedure offences were involved – fine-grained documentation was required even in the most routine cases. In commercial crime investigations and other major cases that focused on following paper trails and knowledge traces, the evidentiary burden became overwhelming. A commercial crime investigator described how *Stinchcombe* had fundamentally changed the way he managed his knowledge work. He offered the example of a case involving a waste management company charged with dumping illegal waste and forging documents:

> Before we even lay the charge, when we phone the lawyer and say, 'OK, we're ready, bring down your client,' we have to have volumes of paperwork ready to turn over to the lawyer right at that time, and we find that that really ties our hands ... Previously, we'd call the lawyer and we'd go through it. We'd certainly give them copies of the guts of our file, OK ... [But the crown attorney's] interpretation goes beyond the guts of the file, goes beyond what we're going to present in court. We will go to a place and we may seize twenty-seven boxes of exhibits, OK ... [The crown attorney] says you don't give him the guts of the file, you give him all twenty-seven boxes ... copy the full twenty-seven boxes of stuff and give them to the fellow when we're laying the charge ... [In the waste management company case] all of a sudden they wanted copies of absolutely every picture we had taken of these barrels being exhumed. I had, *myself*, to go and use a colour photocopier for three days solid copying pictures to give to them. Well, there was three days of useless work. So that's how it [*Stinchcombe*] has been so devastating on us in that it ties up manpower.

The crown attorney's office and the police tried to control the added paperwork by establishing tight communication rules embedded in a new form, the 'Report to Prosecutor.' This had been created by a 'Docket Congestion Disclosure Committee' that had also produced a twenty-five-minute training video and a detailed manual on how to fill out the form. As was stated in the manual, 'The Report to Prosecutor format is designed to: instill Case Ownership with the "Primary Investigator"; assist the investigating officer in preparing a thorough and chronological sequence of events; allow the Crown to evaluate the evidence supporting the charge; and provide a means to facilitate disclosure as mandated by the Supreme Court of Canada.'

The 'Report to Prosecutor' form required assignment of responsibility for a case to a named investigator, who was expected to indicate his or her availability during the two weeks following the date of the form on a calendar grid at the top. This was followed by a long check-list of documents that had to be attached. The offence had to be reported according to a detailed format set out on the back of the form and elaborated on in a code-book. The format called for various items: a synopsis of the case, a description of the evidence linking the accused to the crime, a witness list, an informants list. Also required was information on the following:

police concerns about disclosure by the crown, witnesses' evidence, the examination of the crime scene, neighbourhood inquiries, preventive action or advice regarding witnesses, special-unit involvement, the officer's opinions, and follow-up investigations. The check-list also alerted officers to the need to attach, as required, witness statements, statements of others possessing relevant information, police notes and/ or statements, statements of the accused, photographs, the notice to the parent of a young offender, a waiver of rights of a young offender, driving offence documents (such as a driver suspension notice, breath analysis certificate, second offence notice, vehicle examination report, and diagram of the scene), a list of seized items, CPIC and criminal record checks, and other required documentation. This check-list was followed by a space in which the officer was asked to explain any missing documentation. The officer was required to sign the form, and it would also be signed by a supervisor to indicate that the latter had reviewed the 'content of attachments,' 'report content and format,' and 'legibility.' The court unit of the police organization reviewed the entire package. If the unit deemed it acceptable, an 'information' was produced and the package was forwarded to the crown's office. If the crown, however, determined that the package was unacceptable, it was returned to the commander of the primary investigator's district or section.

The instructional booklet for completing this documentation included communication rules regarding what had to be reported and how it was to be reported. It also included rules about exceptions to rules (Edgerton 1985) and what could be omitted. For example:

> The focus of this decision is to complete disclosure of all relevant information so that the accused is able to 'make full answer and defence' as provided for in Section 7 of the Charter. Any relevant information that an investigator decides to withhold is likely to result in the dismissal of the charge. It certainly will *not* be admissible at trial. This is the law and we are duty bound to adhere. The *only* exception relates to the Information Privilege previously discussed.

> Boxes will not be left blank. If an applicable section is marked 'No' then an explanation is required in the section titled 'EXPLAIN ANY MISSING DOCUMENTATION.'

> With respect to informants, investigating officers do not have to provide this information to the Crown. If an arrest is made as a result of informant information, the elements of the offence must be provable, independent of the infor-

mant. If not, the informant becomes a witness and is subject to disclosure. The informant may fall within the protection of the witness exemption, thereby impacting on the timing of the disclosure.

In *most* cases the Crown has decided that a copy of the 'synopsis' will not be provided as part of the disclosure process. Therefore it is important to ensure that sensitive information such as informant or Crime Stoppers involvement is not mentioned in this section.

Stinchcombe was a landmark decision in three respects *vis-à-vis* the knowledge structure of arrest, charge, and prosecution. First, it was the culmination of a long process in which the knowledge requirements for criminal cases had expanded. An officer in charge of a specialized investigative unit remarked, 'When I was a detective in here, I needed a straight one-page report, often a paragraph or so. Today, when we prepare a charge to a prosecutor, you have to do probably thirty or forty pages. It is radically changed. The time spent in the office doing the paperwork is increased dramatically. And from that perspective, administratively here, the paperwork is mind-boggling ... We used to give a brief narrative and hide information ... We have property sheets now. We never used to have those. They used to be included in the original report.'

Second, *Stinchcombe* entailed a great deal of new classification work and formatting to meet the demands of the crown attorney's office and the demands of the police for efficient production of relevant knowledge. Communication rules had to be built into various forms, including the general occurrence report. In turn, these changes had ramifications for various criminal information systems and for Statistics Canada reporting. An administrator involved in forms revision noted that with *Stinchcombe*, 'What the crown requires now is a fuller report initially, up front. And just the way we have to summarize a lot of stuff for them and provide a witness list ... A lot of the information is repeated because the crown wanted it in a different format. It lengthened the whole occurrence report.' A police manager also involved in forms revision added:

As a committee we modified what the [crown's initial] demands were because they were, logistically, basically impossible for us to meet. It would have meant developing two separate records systems – one for the crown and one for our own computer database of police information management system, which would have been extremely duplicitous. You would never have known which file to go to to get a complete file ... There's certain things that the crown just didn't require that we need for statistical purposes to report – Uniform Crime Reports, Stats Canada. They don't need those kind of offence category numbers. It's not got anything to do with prosecution. But for us to delete that and make a separate report for them at this point in time would require two separate systems. So what we eventually agreed upon was to modify our system, in particular the narrative text part of it, to address their rules so they could just get essentially, from that narrative, text in an organizational format that met their requirements. And that's what we did, and developed a check-list to go with it to make sure that all of the documents were appended to the police report, such as witness statements or certificate to evidence or things that may be introduced of that nature would be included. Somebody could review it quickly and see that no stone had been left unturned.

Third, the new rules that resulted from *Stinchcombe* had a significant influence on how the police thought and acted in producing knowledge. While doing paperwork on a case, officers would frequently say that they were doing the work 'for *Stinchcombe*.' By this they meant that the work was not so much an internal requirement of their supervisors, but an external legal accountability requirement of the court institution. Although they knew that their work was of no direct use in the majority of cases – because, for example, a case was an 'obvious' one for a guilty plea, or one the crown might decide not to proceed with – they rationalized their work as the provision of just-in-case knowledge. One officer remarked, after completing his 'Report to Prosecutor,' 'Report to Prosecutor' check-list, occurrence report, notes, witness statement, arrest report, and family violence report, 'In all likelihood he will go back to her. She won't show up in court. But later on when he kills her we can say that we did our job.' The job was to fully account for what happened and for police decisions, and then leave it up to the crown and other institutions to use that knowledge for their own risk management purposes.

Police officers said that *Stinchcombe* altered the timing of when arrests were made and charges laid. Before *Stinchcombe,* the police would first arrest and charge, and produce detailed evidence only if it was required at some later stage of the legal process. With *Stinchcombe,* when to arrest and lay charges became a matter of deciding when all the knowledge was in place to meet the tightly formatted requirements of the criminal justice knowledge system. A police middle-manager said that with *Stinchcombe,*

The thrust of it is not to charge until you've got just about everything you can possibly get done because ... the reality is that it doesn't really matter what you're charged with nowadays ... Maybe other than first-degree murder, people aren't held in custody ... You're just deciding when you're going to process that individual through the system by whether or not you've got your information back ... Don't arrest because you don't have that link of the accused to the crime. You've got a lot of other indicators but you don't have the link ... whereas in the past we probably would have arrested ... and we would have charged them and, because we didn't have to do disclosure at that point in time, we didn't almost have to have prima facie at the point of arrest. We could wait for that test to come back, have him processed, say we've got reasonable and probable grounds, continue with the investigation ... So that's the different mind-set and that was a difficult thing for the policeman to get used to. And they're not fully used to it.

The production of case knowledge was also affected by the disclosure requirements of *Stinchcombe*. The requirement to disclose the names of witnesses to the defence at an early point was said to make witnesses reluctant to cooperate because they might be subject to retaliation by the accused or others. More fundamentally, established practices in cultivating and dealing with informants were affected. A police interviewee told us, for example, about the problems *Stinchcombe* created for protecting 'agents,' 'the guy that's in between being an informant and being a party to the offence.' The local crown's interpretation of *Stinchcombe* was that the police's agents – who had been especially helpful in orchestrating a series of drug busts – now had to be identified at the outset of the first case in which someone was charged on the basis of their information:

In the past we could keep them concealed until court ... It's a transient criminal, is essentially what they are in many respects, who's involved in the culture and gets caught by us and decides to roll over and save his skin. He's in town and we're going to use him to patch off his half-ounce possession charge. He has to do five or six things for us which is five or six other people. Well, as soon as we do one and reveal who he is, life expectancy and usefulness gets real short ... *Stinchcombe* has now caused us to have to reveal the identity of that agent right away ... and there's guys playing games with that. They're saying, well, he's an informant, and try to protect his identity as an informant. Or it's an ongoing investigation; well, I guess it could be ongoing except it's not the same investigation in real terms. It's a drug investigation and this guy's going to do five or six operations within it.

Stinchcombe exemplifies the trend in criminal law towards system rights to knowledge that facilitate risk management practices. The court institution and its key actors – especially the crown attorney and defence lawyer – are given more-routine access to knowledge that eases their disposition of the case. In the past, ad hoc requests for knowledge after a person had been charged led to sporadic extra work, delays, and uneven quality of results. Since *Stinchcombe*, the job of the police is more explicitly one of producing uniform knowledge that makes the job of others more efficient. For the police, criminal court work has become similar to the work they do for other external institutions. Such work is tightly governed by the communication rules of external institutions, and these rules frame how the police think and act.

Information Law

The legalization of rights to information is another development that has led to an elaboration of communication rules and to more knowledge work. Special units within police organizations deal with requirements under the federal Access to Information Act, Freedom of Information Act, and Privacy Act, and their provincial equivalents. The police manager of one such unit described the changes he had witnessed with the introduction of new information laws:

> Things have changed a lot from the early days when there was more of a reliance on 'gentlemen's agreements.' We would find out what groups needed information and we would enter into an informal gentleman's agreement to provide them with certain types of information. Today, with the influence of federal and provincial freedom of information acts and human rights commissions, things have changed drastically ... There is now an emphasis on accountability on both sides ... We have ten people working in the Freedom of Information Unit alone. This is concerned with citizens who want to get their hands on some information that we might have on them ... We may have to go through all of the files and occurrence reports looking for this information. It is a very labour-intensive process.

In one large police organization we studied, thirty-two employees worked in a unit devoted to access to information requests. Most of the staff were experienced police officers rather than civilian experts, for the organization had decided that experienced police officers were the people most qualified to interpret 'sensitive information' and to decide whether it should be kept confidential. However, outside experts, especially lawyers, were consulted on a regular basis about individual cases and communication rules.

The unit was the key vehicle within the organization for regulating access to information. A unit member said, 'We've got 99.9 per cent tracking [of requests for access to information]. We're totally centralized.' The unit developed communication rules to guide decisions made throughout the organization concerning release of information. If a police officer who was authorized to release certain information needed guidance, he or she could consult a district specialist, who might contact a unit member. Unit members regularly appeared at district stations to give lectures and offer individual consultations. They also provided their expertise to other government departments that were developing their own communication rule systems and procedures with respect to access to information. In the opinion of a unit member, 'I would say, by a long shot, more people consult us than we consult them in terms of expertise and interpretation and application ... It's a rarefied and specialized field.'

Each year the unit dealt with approximately 3,500 privacy-related requests and requests for access to information. Almost two-thirds of the requests were from institutions rather than individuals, primarily the media, businesses, and universities. The unit worked closely with a number of other government agencies that had access to police information, especially regarding questions about whether those agencies could release police information to others.

The unit was in a compliance relationship with the Information and Privacy Commission, whose officers had the power to review complaints about the way in which a request for information directed at the police was handled. They could also independently initiate their own investigations of police abuses of privacy. There were about one hundred investigations initiated by complaints each year, the vast majority of which resulted in the complaint being judged 'not well founded.' An interviewee gave the example of a district station that had posted in its cell block photographs of four AIDS carriers. The complainant said that a prisoner who had seen this poster was later released and confronted him in the street, exclaiming that the complainant was an AIDS carrier. The Privacy Commissioner's Office was called in to investigate and the police were required to discontinue the practice.

The police organization's administrative manual included a copious set of communication rules regarding mandatory and discretionary exemptions to access to information and privacy regulations. It pointed out that confidential information obtained by the police from government institutions, and information produced by the police in the performance of contract duties for provincial or municipal governments, are exempted from the application of both the Access to Information Act and the Privacy Act. The acts also allow discretionary exemptions related to risks to territory (such as intelligence information on subversive or hostile activities, or information that would reveal the vulnerability of buildings); risks to securities (such as information that would reveal the vulnerability of computers or communication systems); risks to careers (such as information that would threaten the safety of an individual); risks to identities (such as information of a personal nature); risks to professional organization (such as information subject to Solicitor-client privilege); risks to government organizations (such as records of government plans that cannot not be made public); and risks to police organizations (such as information collected during lawful investigations that might reveal investigative techniques, details of ongoing investigations, plans for future investigations, or confidential sources).

In Canada an information bank exempt from Access to Information Act and Privacy Act requirements can be created by an order in council. Especially sensitive information is 'deposited' in the bank and is inaccessible even when formal legal requests for it are made. The police organization we have been discussing had one such bank, for 'criminal intelligence.' According to a report prepared by the organization, 'There were 131 requests in 1991/92 for access to the exempt bank, Criminal Operational Intelligence Records. Pursuant to Section 16(2), all such requesters are advised that the [police organization] neither confirms nor denies the existence of records in this bank and, if any did exist, they would be subject to exemption under subsection 18(2) and sections 21 and 22 of the Privacy Act.' Decisions to bank information were made according to a risk calculus set out in the organization's manual:

More than 50 percent of the personal information must be such that its disclosure would result in a failure to:

1. maintain the confidentiality of an ongoing criminal investigation
2. protect 'third-party rule' information
3. ensure the physical or economic well-being of confidential police sources, informants, or witnesses, or
4. safeguard confidential police enforcement techniques, strategies and procedures.

An audit by the privacy commissioner concluded that the bank was improperly constituted because the police were unable to 'identify exactly which files were reviewed for the purpose of initially constituting the exempt bank.' The police responded by proposing to have the existing order in council revoked and a new bank created by a fresh order in council. Their official justification for this proposal reveals how important they thought it was to have a blanket exemption to rules about access to information and privacy: 'Disclosure of information contained in this bank could result in a disruption in the flow of criminal intelligence information, the fragmentation of law enforcement systems, the identification of information sources and investigative techniques, and the termination of the recruitment and development of confidential human sources.'

A document prepared by another privacy and access to information unit maintained by a police organization declared that information law had helped the police to further structure their knowledge systems in a way that was helpful to police. It made the point that the law articulates with communication technologies to strengthen the regulation of knowledge. The privacy and access to information legislation was viewed by the document's authors as having no harmful implications for their organization's ability to patrol its own knowledge boundaries:

> To date, there is no evidence that the Canadian data protection legislation has had any negative effect on police operations. Certainly, no investigations have been jeopardized due to the release of information under the terms of the legislation. Possible reasons for this relatively smooth transition lie in a changing view of the role and importance of information assets in the modern police organization ... Prior to the enactment of ... [such] legislation in Canada, information management in large organizations was an emerging issue in its own right as a characteristic of the new 'information age.' Many organizations in both the private and public sectors, including police departments, are recognizing that improved information management practices are desirable from a business standpoint. For example, it is unlikely that any police organization can fully exploit rapidly emerging information technology without taking a structured approach to management of its information assets. Thus, the measures required to implement data protection rules are often the same measures necessary to manage information systems and services effectively ... As it turns out, the principles of *Access to Information* and *Privacy* Act reinforced these objectives by providing a regulatory incentive for good information management practices ... In conclusion, the Canadian police experience with national data protection legisla-

tion to date has not been as troublesome as we may have predicted. Improved departmental information management practices, more professional police reporting and increased sensitivity at all levels to issues of personal privacy and information security have resulted.

This assessment of information law is consistent with our thesis regarding system rights to knowledge that is useful for administrative purposes. The communication rules that resulted from the Access to Information Act and Privacy Act were seen by the police as helping to structure the efficiency of their knowledge system. Moreover, the structuring effects of information law were not received passively. The police played an active role in structuring the legislation in relation to their own communication rules, formats, and technologies. For example, they acted as advisers to provincial governments that were formulating their own information laws. A senior officer in information systems management said that 'The police are involved in almost every level of legislation,' including the assessment of legislation's bearing on police forms and reporting requirements. A colleague in a special investigation unit said that his unit employed analysts who monitored court cases to gather systematic knowledge about the need for law reform: 'If there's shortcomings ... with our laws and statutes, the way they're worded now ... if they lose cases in courts, they monitor dispositions and so on and so forth as well. So if there's a problem in a certain area, they will make recommendations through to this department or through the channels of government in order to have legislation amended or changed as need be.'

Police organizations also manage risks to their knowledge assets by developing communication rules about who can have their knowledge and under what conditions. While many of these rules articulate with legal rules regarding privacy and access to information, they remain relatively autonomous from direct legal regulation.

In the remainder of this chapter we examine four types of police communication rules. First, we consider police administrative efforts to centralize the regulation of access to their knowledge assets. Second, we analyse the commodification of police knowledge assets – the rules and conditions under which knowledge is sold to external institutions. Third, we address the role of administrative manuals that set out rules for communication. Finally, we look at the development of audit systems for the risk management of police communications.

Centralized Regulation of Access

All police organizations centralize the processes by which external institutions gain access to their knowledge. Special correspondence units manage inquiries, and all responses are subject to restrictions. All general correspondence is sent out in the name of the chief of police, symbolizing that what is said is officially authored by *the* authority in the organization rather than by those who actually do the writing. The chief's authority marks the death of the author and the life of highly institutionalized communication rules.

The correspondence unit in a police organization we studied was staffed by ten employees whose job was handling requests for knowledge for external institutions. Table 14.1 shows that the unit recorded 7,196 knowledge transactions during one month in 1992. The meanings of most of the categories in table 14.1 are self-evident. 'Request for Report Information Forms Added to PIMS' refers to the act of entering into the 'Police Information Management System' database a notation that a request for police report information was processed. 'Miscellaneous Correspondence' refers to correspondence replying to nonroutine queries directed towards individual police officers or the administration, which had to be responded to within the format of a 'Letter Request Form.' 'Outside Agency Requests' refers to special requests for institutional access from outside agencies. 'Special Projects' refers to requests for police reports, such as data analyses concerning a particular problem. 'Notice for Missing Traffic Reports' and 'Incomplete Accident Forms Checks' relate to the correspondence unit's role in policing police officers whose reports were not adequate for sending on to external users.

Correspondence unit employees followed detailed guidelines for disclosure of knowledge. Some of these guidelines were found in a nine-page document entitled 'Access to Information: Agencies Authorized to Access Information.' This document listed the 'authorization level' ('copy,' 'read only,' 'limited access,' and 'restricted access') and 'conditions' of access granted to thirty-seven external institutions in the areas of health, social service provision, criminal justice, civil litigation, public trusteeship, transportation, national security and intelligence, national defence, military security enforcement, private security enforcement, education, municipal by-law enforcement, private insurance, public insurance (such as the provincial workers' compensation board), and animal regulation. The provincial family and social services department, for example, was given 'restricted access/read only' status with respect

TABLE 14.1
Police correspondence unit activity during one month in 1992

Activity	N
General	
Request for Report Information Forms Sold	1303
Request for Report Information Forms Completed and Mailed	518
Request for Report Information Forms Added to PIMS	613
Insurance Letters	85
Property Letters	132
Miscellaneous Correspondence	111
New Outside Agency Requests	3
Outside Agency Requests Completed	2
Restraining Orders and Letters	32
Occurrence Reports	11
Special Projects	8
Traffic Accidents	
Request for Report Information Forms Processed	1301
Request for Report Information Forms Added to PIMS	92
Correspondence (Letters)	104
Reports Sent to Attorney General	91
Out-of-Town Traffic Collision Reports Sent Out	64
Notice for Missing Traffic Reports	135
Incomplete Accident Forms Checks	2591
Total	7196

to police occurrence reports, with a condition that all 'Requests will be directed to the Correspondence Supervisor for authorization.' In civil law cases involving traffic occurrences, the provincial attorney general was authorized to obtain copies of police reports, subject to the following conditions: 'Upon written request, traffic occurrence report copies, A-Forms and Witness Statements may be released; associated criminal report will be included on discretion of Correspondence Supervisor (e.g., traffic matter involving a stolen vehicle); form letter in response.' Distinctions were made in the privileges granted to the various branches of the provincial correctional service. Correctional institutions received 'restricted access/copy – direct all requests to [named person].' The parole authorities had 'limited access – all requests directed to [named person].' The probation authorities had 'restricted access/read only – upon request, access to read occurrence report available to probation officer.' Insurance companies were given two kinds of 'restricted access,' one for traffic reports and the other for criminal reports:

Traffic Collision Reports

i) Upon written request, copies of 'A-Forms' *only* for those persons they represent ($15.00 fee).
ii) Traffic report reconstruction to be directed to the Correspondence Supervisor (structured fee schedule, must be a civil matter, no outstanding court dates).
iii) Witness statement requests must be accompanied by a letter of authorization to release said statement and signed by the writer of the statement (signatures must match that on the original witness statement).

All Criminal Reports

i) Request for information forms may be obtained ($15.00 fee). See Sample.
ii) 'Suspect' names are not released, but 'Charged' names, addresses and charges laid can be released upon request.
iii) Damage values are not given as these are merely estimates done by either the submitting officer or the victim.
iv) Highlighted officers' names; contact this officer as there are extenuating circumstances which the insurance company may want to know about.
v) Court disposition information not available through our department.
vi) Please *type* your return address on request form.
vii) In the case of your subrogated interest; a letter stating same may be written to the [police organization]. Your interest will then be noted and you will be notified in the event of a recovery or arrest.
viii) For stolen property updates, there is no need to submit a second request form. A telephone call to the Insurance Coordinator [telephone number] will suffice.
ix) Please return request form complete – do not separate pages. Also, the bottom portion of form is for police use only. Please do not write in this area.

Many of the communication rules were embedded in the forms. For example, the request for report information form referred to in the above instructions regarding insurance companies stated the fee and included statements such as 'We do not release copies of criminal files/ witness statements/officer's notes.'

This existence of a specialized unit for regulating knowledge brokering to external institutions was justified on numerous grounds. First, there was the view, again symbolized by having all general correspondence sent out in the name of the chief of police, that the knowledge being requested was corporate knowledge that had to be centralized in the corporate interest.

Second, an important component of corporate centralization, it was argued, was the need to reduce an investigator's report to *the* authoritative police version of the incident in question. Despite all the formality police reports were subject to, they were viewed as too open to alternative interpretations, and as possible sources of embarrassing contradictions, if released without being circumscribed even further. An interviewee working in a police correspondence unit described a time when the disclosure of report information to insurance companies had been much less centralized:

> You would have the situation where they [insurance adjusters] would contact two [police officer] partners and get them to provide completely different accounts of a situation. When you actually looked at it, the officers were actually talking about completely different incidents. So now all the requests for interviews come through this office and we schedule them and the insurance company pays for them ...
>
> ... [Police] investigators usually guard their information much more loosely than we ever would ... They're real funny ... sometimes they would just really give everything ... So it's actually addressed in our manual ... and ... our reports come with printing right across it that it's to be released only from the [correspondence unit] ... I have examples where a constable has given his mother a copy of an occurrence report and then she'd phone up complaining that her son says the report isn't done well enough and the constable [who wrote the report] should have done this and this and this. So you can't maintain any level of security on information if you give everybody a free hand.

Third, centralization was seen as necessary for informed judgments about what an outside institution should have access to. There was a perceived need to have a central decision maker who was aware of interinstitutional knowledge needs and thus able to review rules and exercise discretion in individual cases. The central decision maker in one police organization had several rules under review. One rule under review concerned the full release to the telephone company of occurrence reports on telecommunications offences. There was considerable information in such occurrence reports, for instance the identity of witnesses, that the police believed the telephone company did not need. In another instance, a rule that allowed full disclosure of case details to forensic scientists was replaced. The new rule required the provision of only an edited version of the case, excluding, for example, the identity of victims and witnesses. The central decision maker also dealt with requests that did not conform to established communication rules:

> We get queries ... every day, and all those queries are kind of examined at face value and then they determine from there whether they're going to comply with exactly what they're asking for ... Actually I have one right here that is odd. It's a woman writing to us who is saying she is ... left out of her father's will ... So now she wants us to provide documentation on two motor vehicle accidents he had when he was alive. But he didn't die as a result of the motor vehicle accident and it makes absolutely no sense what she's looking for ... what the connection is. So this initially went to correspondence and then, because it made no sense to them, and because we wouldn't normally just supply copies of occurrence reports to relatives, it comes to me to kind of handle and sort out what she wants and what she's really after. A normal thing would be, 'My garden hose was stolen in September and I want to put a claim in to my insurance company. Can I have a copy of the report?' That's usual.

Fourth, centralization was seen as necessary to produce 'clean' external communications. It allowed for the verification of reports. It also allowed for tight editing to ensure that external communications were expressed properly. For example, any member of the police organization who wanted to write a letter to an external recipient had to ask permission by submitting a Letter Request Form. The draft letter was scrutinized by the correspondence unit and edited to make it fit the organization's rules. The Letter Request Form carried the warning, 'This letter is subject to editing if it fails to meet departmental standards. When completed, please obtain approval and forward to ...'

Fifth, centralized regulation of external communication was justified on the grounds that it allowed the tracing of what knowledge was released to whom. A log of transactions was kept, and request for report information forms were entered into the computerized police information management system (see table 14.1).

Commodification of Police Knowledge

Centralized regulation of external communication is also necessary because police knowledge is commodified and sold to others. A police information system manager said, 'I think that information is increasingly seen as a resource. We are really trying to establish information as an asset.'

There is nothing new about police commodification of knowledge. The police have always relied on a barter system in their dealings with informants. They also barter knowledge by offering risk and security expertise to external institutions in exchange for access to external institutional resources. One urban police organization, for example, obtained routine access to a telephone company's customer database in exchange for allowing the company to use the organization's graphical maps of the city and materials created for an equal opportunities program. In another jurisdiction the local school board allowed the police to use a vacant school building for a training academy in exchange for cooperation in staffing a school-based police officer program.

Police informant programs are also funded by external institutions. The Crime Stoppers program receives money and services from businesses to finance rewards for information about criminals and to support its infrastructure (Carriere and Ericson 1989). A police organization we studied supported its Crime Stoppers program by obtaining sponsorships from major private corporations, which financed rewards and the production of crime-of-the-week television spots. Special arrangements were also entered into from time to time, involving, for instance, Crime Stoppers posters being put up in a large chain of retail outlets, and Crime Stoppers receiving a generous donation. Donations were also solicited from small businesses that had been helped by Crime Stoppers.

The police also sell their knowledge to external institutions in accordance with a fee schedule. Such selling is justified as a means of cost recovery and, to a lesser extent, as a deterrent to those who might make frivolous requests. But the practice is followed only in dealings with certain external users, especially for-profit institutions; government agencies and nonprofit or voluntary sector organizations usually get their knowledge free of charge. Whether a charge for knowledge is levied also depends on how the police value the uses to which the knowledge will be put.

A police manager involved in commodification decisions offered a number of examples of how the police value their knowledge depending on the user and uses. Government institutions and community policing groups were not charged, whereas for-profit agencies and individuals without an institutional affiliation were:

A: We produce a monthly stat book and, based on why the request has been made, we may provide that free of charge. If it's a security company wanting everything broken down by every zone in the city so he can base his marketing attacks on our information, we'll charge them. And we will tell them, and let them know how many hours it will take to produce what they want, and then we'll figure out what our hourly programming and retrieval fee is and if they want to pay ... We do the same thing with, you get a lot of private interest groups like these people that are against impaired driving. We have a maniac ... that wants the strippers outlawed, and she believes every sex crime happens as a result of a man having seen a stripper, and so she is always phoning and wanting extraordinary searches of all our data done to provide her that information. And so she's told the same thing, like to pull all that type of information out would be costly and this is the cost and this is the hours ...

Q: But ostensibly, if she was willing to pay in the thousands of dollars?

A: We'd pull what we could ... to do something that explicit and that specific we would have to be able to develop a program and then run the program against all our data and pull out what we could.

Q: So it might be a five-figure amount or something?

A: Yeah, that would be an ugly one. And a very timely topic right now is crime on the train stations ... Well, [that's] city hall's concern and we provide the data to city hall. But then Mary Smith that catches the train at station X and thinks it's not safe and she phones and wants all the stats on weapons, or attacks on persons that ever happened at station X, we would explain the deal to her ... pay ... and we'll do it.

Q: What about a community association that's connected with a community policing program?

A: They usually have a very good liaison with the district analyst in the specific zones and districts. And if they're addressing a problem and it's a community policing issue, they would get that information free of cost through the district analyst.

We were confronted with police knowledge commodification in negotiating access for our research. A police manager who interviewed us about what we wished to accomplish and its value, said that a major objection to the research was its cost to his police organization. He said that the knowledge work required of police employees to access documents, and to serve as interviewees, would be a drain on resources. When the researcher replied by suggesting that the interviews could be conducted outside regular working hours, he retorted, 'Yeah, at overtime wages.' We were not granted systematic access to this police organization.

The police sell knowledge in a variety of formats to external institutions. Occurrence report information is often sold for a fee (to which is added Canada's Goods and Services Tax). In one police jurisdiction, external institutions that wanted knowledge drawn from police occurrence reports were required to submit a request for information form together with a fifteen-dollar processing fee. In another jurisdiction, traffic accident reports could be obtained from the provincial ministry of transportation for five dollars, but the insurance companies were willing to pay ten dollars to the police for the same report because the police service was more efficient.

The time police officers spent in interviews with insurance adjusters and lawyers was also commodified in some cases. In one jurisdiction the charge was seventy-five dollars for each hour of an officer's time. (The police association wanted to increase the proportion of this fee that was paid to police officers, arguing that officers should receive the higher rate they were entitled to when on paid duty as private security guards at sports stadiums, shopping malls, and so on.) Insurance adjusters and lawyers were said to be content with the arrangement because they could simply pass on the cost to their clients. Moreover, it was more efficient to have established procedures, including scheduled appointments with officers, rather than having to make ad hoc arrangements in each case.

Some police organizations also charged for time spent searching files for and copying civil law documents. One organization had a twenty-five-dollar filing fee for civil enforcement orders such as restraining orders, access orders, custody orders, and orders for exclusive possession of property. An interviewee who had been involved in setting the fee described its cost-recovery rationale:

> All of our systems were set up for criminal enforcement and all of a sudden the demand upon us for civil enforcement became greater and greater and greater. And we had to sort of develop sort of little substructures and subsystems within the criminal enforcement systems that we already had in place. When you examine the whole civil proceedings, there are exorbitant fees at every step of the way and we just felt, because we had to develop new tracking systems, because we had to provide additional training to several people within here so they'd have the expertise to review the orders, and be able to write directions to the constables on the orders, that it would offset the cost of doing it.

A number of other routine knowledge brokering tasks are subject to commodification. For example, in municipalities where the police are involved in investigating applicants for business licences, they receive a portion of the licence fee for their work. Police security clearance units that conduct checks for private sector institutions sometimes charge a fee for their services. One such unit charged eighteen dollars for a letter to a prospective employee about a person's criminal record.

A police organization we examined decided to charge for traffic accident reconstruction reports. Previously, no information from these reports had been released. The new rule was that the report could be released in its entirety for a fee of $1,500. The high fee was justified on the grounds that the reports were used by 'reconstruction engineers' who in turn sold the knowledge at a much higher rate to lawyers involved in accident litigation. As we were told by an officer who helped sell this knowledge,

> There's a little bit of a difference when you're providing something to a person that wants to get a pardon and needs his exact date of conviction so he can deal with the clerk of the court. To me, that person is not going out to make a profit out of it ... [The reconstruction engineers] use it to prepare a number of other explanations than what our explanation of the accident is and then base civil litigation on the other explanations they've been able to provide. And so then they would sell that to the lawyer, usually acting on behalf of the insurance company or the estate ... [Previously they would] get notes through the back door ... It needed a written policy and it needed a procedure and it needed a fee attached to close those back doors.

There are other types of commodification agreements. One police organization was working with municipal government employees to develop better computerized maps of the city. The municipal government planned to recover its costs by selling the maps to private sector institutions. Perhaps the most significant recent example of police commodification in Canada is the agreement signed between the Disney Corporation and the RCMP to market toys and other products incorporating the image of the Mountie. After a long history of difficulty in regulating its own imagery (Walden 1982), the RCMP has sold its symbolic identity to a world leader in profit-based image management.

In the process of commodification, the police change their ways of doing things to fit the formats of the external institutions involved. This is not limited to dramatic examples such as the Disney commodification of RCMP imagery. It is also evident in the routine commodity exchanges between the police and risk institutions such as insurance companies. A police interviewee described how an employee in his organization had redesigned the form for brokering knowledge to insurance companies once the decision was made to charge them for the knowledge they required. This employee argued that 'insurance companies [now] pay to get their form and so the form should look more like something that they are buying rather than just a photocopy of something we're providing them ... how to put it so that it would be more logical for insurance companies because they're actually the external customer.'

Policy Manuals

Another regulatory response to the paper burden is the creation of policy manuals that address how police knowledge production and distribution should be managed. Policy manuals spell out the rules by which knowledge is to be communicated, including the rules governing reporting structures and selective disclosure to different audiences.

Police organizations vary in the extent to which they formalize their communication rules in policy manuals. The extreme case among the police organizations we studied was one organization that had four thick volumes of rules for information management. The index alone was twenty-two pages long. These volumes, which were officially declared to provide an 'integrated information management policy,' addressed, for example, the organization and functions of the information management operations; telecommunications; electronic data processing; records management; occurrence reporting procedures; statistical reporting procedures; information retrieval system options; and communications risk and security. In well over a thousand pages of rules, one could discover, for example, how to complete different types of forms; create, classify, index, file, store, deactivate, and destroy records; file things alphabetically; rate the importance of files; prepare monthly returns on the level of 'message traffic' in the communication centre; prevent, investigate, and report violations of communication security; pay for and catalogue library books; handle and distribute mail; score data for statistical reporting; ensure the safety of telecommunications technicians; maintain equipment such as radar guns; make and report modifications to communications systems hardware; and communicate using secret codes.

The rules were both prescriptive and proscriptive. For example, on the subject of files risk management there were detailed instructions on how to open a file, label it, and track where it moved and how it was used. There were also warnings on what not to include, such as 'Do not include matters of internal administration or criticism of another department and/or its officials in investigational reports,' and 'If adverse comments and/or criticism is necessary and warranted, report it separately through channels' (described in another section of the rules).

One could also find rules about exceptions to rules (see Edgerton 1985). For example, regarding police requests to other government institutions for personal information on specific individuals, the rule was, 'When information is required urgently, contact the applicable institution and request the information you require under Sec 8(2)(e) Privacy Act be provided informally. If you require the information, as soon as possible, complete form ——— and send it with a covering memorandum to the applicable federal institutions explaining the circumstances of your informal request.' This rule was apparently needed to cover situations where the police desire for personal information as a basis for action would be impeded by the time taken to make a formal legal request. This was, therefore, a formal rule about how to circumvent a formal rule that prohibited the informal acquisition of information, and about how to formally justify the practice after the fact.

The fact that there were multiple layers of communication rules and exceptions was also evident from this police organization's rules about public access to its policy manuals. The public had access to one set of policy manuals, but this set had been vetted for rules the police organization had decided should not be made public. Eventually the vetted copies themselves were withdrawn. According to one of the organization's annual reports, 'vetted manuals were removed effective April 1st, 1991, from reading rooms at [district stations] ... because of a lack of use ... No degradation of service has been experienced and a substantial saving in cost has been realized.' Elsewhere, policy manuals instructed police officers how to avoid public disclosure of the rules if called on to do so by the courts: 'If applicable, have [the police organization's] counsel notify other counsel involved, that the member is not an expert witness or interpreter of [the police organization's] policy, but is a manager and administrator of [the police organization's] policy.'

Rules provide a communicative framework for action, a way of prospectively and retrospectively rationalizing and accounting for what is done. As we saw with respect to *Stinchcombe*, new rules lead to changes in communication frameworks, including changes in the classification formats and reporting procedures that shape how police officers think and act. It is the articulation of rules within communication frameworks that is the key to understanding the relationship between rules, interpretations, and actions.

It is in the context of these frameworks that one must interpret the well-established finding that police officers pay little or no attention to policy manuals and administrative rules (Ericson 1981; Shearing and Ericson 1991). It was common for the officers we studied to admit that they had not read the policy manual except for promotional examination purposes or to seek post hoc legitimacy for a decision. Even officers in charge of administrative rule production and manual distribution made it clear that the rules were not regularly a basis for police action. A police officer who participated in drafting administrative rules and maintaining the policy manual said that the rules were irrelevant as a guide for police decisions:

> The purpose of the manual, in all honesty ... I can't really say it's to provide direction to members and I'll tell you why – this is a kind of strange thing – is that the manual, each person, each member does not have a manual. And so on the one hand, I guess the party line would be that's a handbook, a day-to-day handbook and it's to guide you and provide direction on policies and procedures. But I was a police officer for seven years before I saw it ... Our manual is distributed to people for study material ... [for] a promotional exam ... When I got the manual the year I decided to study for [the] promotional exam I was absolutely amazed ... Everything I ever wanted to know about everything was in there, [even] hairstyles ... [We'd learn policing with] officer coaches and some partners, more-experienced partners. And so often what I learned was wrong. It was just the opposite of what the manual was prescribing ... I never had the opportunity nor the need to go look something up. And I wouldn't have known even where to look.

A police manager who specialized in information technology said that even when police officers were required to consult the manual, they found it too large, complex, and confusing. For example, 'candidates for becoming [ranking] officers must pass a test where they have to find the appropriate authority in the manual for a given scenario. Approximately half of the people who take this test fail it ... They are talking about computerizing this system, so that may help a little.' The policy manual manager in another police organization said that his organization had computerized the manual three years earlier, but without any apparent effect: 'No one knows how to access it ... They don't have the training. They don't even know it exists ... My secretary and I do the manuals. We only found out a year ago it was on-line!'

This manager also believed the administrative rules were not central to police management. He said that many management-level officers preferred 'crisis management rather than long-term planning,' and that he was often left to decide on policy 'because no one else is interested.' His view was confirmed by the officer in charge of a district station, who said that he received so many change-of-policy statements that 'it [the manual] loses its meaning ... Nobody can possibly expect to remember what they're about ... they kind of get lost in the shuffle because of the volume ... You might as well put them into the shredder ... the manual system is used only if you're studying it for promotion.'

These views led to various proposals for reform. A manager of the manual for one police organization said that he had once proposed distributing the manual to all police officers in the organization, but the proposal had been rejected. Another time he had suggested, following the lead of the Strathclyde police in Scotland, that the manual should be scrapped, but this suggestion had not been taken seriously. Some police organizations required every officer to sign a copy of each new policy issued, indicating that the policy had at least been read. The police organization with the four-volume manual setting out communication rules (pp. 345–6) had, in total, twenty-two volumes' worth of manuals of administrative rules. At one point it initiated a program aimed at reducing the total number of administrative-manual pages in circulation. Success was claimed on the basis that a more economical use of page space, a reduction in the number of rules, and, especially, the taking of some sets of manuals out of circulation, had lessened the number of pages in circulation from about twenty-eight million to about twenty-one million. However, at the time of our research the number of pages was beginning to increase again. An information manager for this police organization said, 'We just did our statistics on the directives and our paper has gone up instead of down ... [because] they're wanting more policy basically.'

If administrative rules are not directly related to action, why do they proliferate? Our interviewees offered a number of answers. First, police organizations need the imagery of rationality provided by voluminous manuals full of administrative rules. That policy manuals are a matter of external form, rather than generated by internal need, is suggested by the extent to which their wording and the areas covered are identical across police organizations. A manuals manager for a large urban police organization said that smaller police organizations across the country

> Just call up and pick up our policies to fit their needs ... If they are regular requesters, rather than sending them stuff weekly, after a while I just say, 'Take the whole thing, use what you can ... [a small city] is tailoring itself or will be a shadow of [our police organization] ... Their new manual is probably exactly like ours, which is kind of strange because they're so small ... But you know we did it too. We went on a road trip across North America to look at other models and came back and built ours based on other models. It certainly wasn't a grass roots, and it certainly didn't come from the community. I deal with the [federal] solicitor general [and] the Ministry [of the Solicitor General] in Ontario probably more than anywhere else. It's strange, we never deal with [our province's] cops ... I don't even talk to ... [our province's] solicitor [general], I get nothing from them ... Ontario [Ministry of the Solicitor General], I know all the numbers and so I deal with them. And they always seem to be ahead of the game anyway.

Second, policy manuals are directed towards liability considerations. If something goes wrong, it is easier to claim administrative control and accountability if rule-governed procedures are in place. A police manual manager said that 'We write policy with an eye towards liability and discipline.'

Third, as the manager's comment indicates, administrative manuals are a means of discipline when the need arises. Every officer violates administrative rules every day, so the question becomes one of using the rules selectively to discipline an officer who is found wanting on other grounds (Ericson 1981).

Fourth, administrative manuals are part of the ritual of promotional examinations. In this respect they are used to show who is disciplined enough to memorize and adopt the discourse of rule-based administrative rationality. Against a background of increasingly intense competition for promotion in police organizations, they are therefore useful for deselecting those who have difficulty with the formats and thinking associated with administrative rules.

Fifth, policy manuals are useful at the administrative level in providing communicative frameworks for action. They articulate the structure of reporting, the audiences, and the formats of communication to those audiences. It is the translation of the communication rules into formats and technologies that has a bearing on police action, as we document in greater detail in chapters 15 and 16. Thus a district police station administrator was able to say that at least at his level, the manual served as a tool of governance: 'Most companies have a little Bible. We have a bookcase of them ... Everything that we do is governed by these manuals ... Any scenario that you come across, there is going to be a portion ... to tell you how to do it. You can go to these books and they tell you, 'Do this, do this, and if you can't, then get this guy to do it for you.' You can effectively do a complete investigation without having any training, just by using these books.'

A colleague in the same organization offered a similar view. He said that his administrative responsibility as the officer in charge of records was to find and interpret policies for members who couldn't possibly know all of them. As an adviser to field-level officers on communication rules, he had a greater responsibility than they to be aware of the contents of the manuals: 'Most of it is in the manual anyway, it's all how you read it ... I had a district call me the other day about some security checks they were doing for a certain company. I said it doesn't sound right to me ... I checked into it and I found that they were doing it wrong.'

Audits

Internal auditing systems are a fourth mechanism through which communication rules are developed. Auditing procedures are used to manage communications in major cases, address critical incidents, and ensure overall communication efficiency in the police organization.

The auditing of major cases is achieved by having investigators submit detailed reports on case plans, practices, and outcomes. Reporting is done by way of forms that prospectively format the steps to be taken in the investigation as well as retrospectively review what has been achieved. One police organization we studied had a heavily formatted six-page form for the prospective auditing of major drug investigations. It required details on the suspects chosen as 'targets'; informants; investigational strategy (methods and how they were to be employed, objectives and how they were to be achieved, and the duration of the operation); support units (undercover operators, cover-team members, and the participation of other agencies); organized crime involvement (use of legitimate businesses as covers); predicted outcomes (estimates of success in terms of subjects arrested, subjects disrupted, money flow, items seized); and authorization (level of authorization required and operational budget plan). Such forms structure investigations by articulating communication rules that reflexively enter into case decision making at each step.

The police also engage in systematic auditing of particular types of critical incidents. This form of auditing provides communication rules that have the dual purpose of, first, making officers highly reflexive with respect to the risks involved, and second, making the police organization appear publicly accountable for the risks its officers take.

An example is provided by the auditing of high-speed pursuits. In one police organization the auditing of high-speed pursuits was initiated by having the officer or officers involved submit a five-page form. Other required documentation included the audiotape of the officers' communications with the police communications centre and a report from the centre itself. Another report was required from the officers' immediate supervisor. The district commander was required to review all of this documentation to ascertain whether the incident would be counted as an official pursuit and sent to a coordinating inspector for further review.

A district commander we spoke to said that he was at once an editor and an adjudicator of such incidents. If he decided not to treat an incident as an official case, he still had to prepare an elaborate written justification in support of his decision: 'I find myself generating three-page memos to say here's why it isn't a pursuit.' And when he decided to formalize a pursuit as an official case and forward the documentation to the inspector, he spent a great deal of time editing and adjusting the material to fit the communication rules. 'Usually I have to interview the officers to clarify any little particulars. I tell them not to do the chronological narrative ... [because] when they start to do the chronological narrative, I have to redo it all anyway and put it into the third person and not the first person and this type of thing. Plus I add details usually. And then I'll go in with comments and recommendations. Usually I'll adjudicate the whole pursuit and then give it to the inspector.'

The inspector's first task was to review all of the documentation in light of the rules pertaining to high-speed pursuits. He was also required to develop and maintain a computerized risk profiling system, 'so we can do database searches on the types and nature of pursuits ... [and] make sure ... discipline is appropriate and consistent throughout the organization with various commanders, to various areas.' This risk management system also allowed him to complete the monthly report on pursuits required by the police commission.

Pursuit auditing stood as an icon of the paper burden in this police organization. A senior officer involved in pursuit auditing said that the knowledge work involved was yet another reason why 'We're not in the street dealing with problems because they're in the office dealing with paperwork ... For your standard fifteen-second pursuit, that's ten hours' worth of labour ... documenting ... just so they can say that it's been done.' She thought this mechanism of system surveillance was ineffective because it was based on the wrong assumptions: 'Building a system to make people accountable is a real problem. It doesn't work. People have to make people accountable.' She believed regulation through the systematic elaboration of communication rules was unreasonable because high-speed pursuit decisions are inevitably situation-bound and therefore cannot be accounted for in terms of abstract rule systems:

> There isn't one [pursuit] that I could probably not find some fault with on a technical basis, based upon the way the policy is laid out. Technically, I could find that the officers involved did something wrong because there is just so much to do in that situation. I mean, you're expected, in the first instance ... the primary officer, to announce that you're involved in a pursuit, a description of the vehicle, the licence plate, number of occupants, age of the occupants, description of the occupants, direction of travel, environmental conditions, traffic conditions – all of this as you're driving at whatever speed, often a one-man car [being driven] with one hand, talking on the radio, trying to coordinate a secondary unit, listening to the dispatcher, listening to the district sergeant giving you directions and asking you questions. Very few guys can do that. I don't care how much training you have. And maintain it as a running dialogue through a two- to five-minute activity ... At two minutes [the officer] is supposed to be thinking about cutting it off now because statistics indicate that at two minutes the likelihood of the guy ever stopping is, unless he crashes, is really remote. At that point in time you'd resolve to get away regardless. Your pursuing him isn't going to change that result. However, I've got tapes where policemen have been shot at as they're chasing them and there's a whole lot of things going through your mind other than how much traffic is on the road and how slippery it is when the shotgun [round] goes bouncing off your windshield. And you should hear these guys' voices. They could sing their highest octave in the choir. There's that much excitement running through them.

This officer expressed concern that the focus in the auditing was on technical and procedural risk criteria, to support the need to appear publicly accountable. She believed this focus led officers into an excessive technical reflexivity that interfered with their decision making and, ironically, increased the risk of pursuit driving:

> We get technical ... We get what you call semantic violations ... If you can get people to think safety more, and justify their activities based on safety terms and not on technical terms like, 'Did I have this siren on at this particular instant?' ... I can't measure it no matter how many reports you give me because I'm not there at the time. To my way of thinking we have to teach people judgment skills and give them the background and experience to deal with those situations. We pay them a lot of money to make those decisions as they're occurring on the spot. I could Monday-morning quarterback it forever and I can write another policy that says you won't do it if the guy's only got three tires – one's flat – because in this particular case that car's going to swerve into a fire hydrant and kill two people. But in ten other cases it may not have. Who knows? ... There's nothing ever static enough to measure.

In spite of these concerns, she saw benefits flowing from the auditing of pursuits. Communication rules, she believed, promote reflexivity with respect to risk, which has a positive effect on police actions: 'I think, as a policy itself, [it] probably is good in that it certainly generates a lot of chat over coffee about pursuits. Keeps them in the forefront of everyone's mind as to what their responsibilities are in pursuit. And they know that, generally speaking, that [when] they're 'out to lunch' they're going to get it. So they guard their actions accordingly.'

Many police organizations have special units to perform regular audits of internal operations. A medium-sized municipal police organization we examined staffed its audit unit with an inspector, another full-time officer, and twenty-one part-time officers. The largest police organization in our study maintained an audit department with forty full-time employees. This department stood at the apex of an audit system that encompassed auditing at the unit, station, district, and divisional levels. Nongovernmental auditing and technical experts were brought in for some tasks. On occasion the unit also worked with other government auditing operations. Affinity with the auditing profession was expressed through membership in the Institute of Internal Auditors of North America, and officers sought professional certification by taking courses offered by this body.

Auditing units are a way to maintain an ongoing process of standard setting and of reflexivity with respect to standards. Because they affiliate with the Institute of Internal Auditors of North America, the auditing units of other government departments, and other police auditing systems, there is a tendency to set standards by using external criteria, which leads to a homogenization of standards. The auditing unit of one police organization we visited, for example, used an American standards manual. A unit member said that this manual had been adopted because 'There is no other standard ... It is just nice to evaluate yourself like the dental or medical profession ... It is a generic guideline for policing. While it was designed in the American context, almost all of it applies directly to Canadian forces.' When asked how the standards were adjusted to account for Canada's different legal regime, he replied that 'we apply the Canadian equivalent. For example, if the standards talked about the American Bill of Rights we substituted the Charter [of Rights and Freedoms] for it.' This officer noted that some provinces had developed their own standards to guide their police organizations, but 'You can see that they simply plagiarized this accreditation manual.'

The primary goals of standard setting are the articulation of communication rules and the establishment of processes for ensuring compliance with those rules. For example, standards manuals are used to review the quality of record keeping. An auditor described a recent audit in which he had examined 900 files pertaining to 878 separate standards, covering 'everything from reporting practices to janitorial and technical services.'

Audits of police district stations or specialized units focus on the security of evidence, of knowledge assets, and of communication systems, for lax security in these areas poses risks to the police organization's need to appear accountable. An auditor described for us this form of compliance auditing and its rationale. He said that as a member of a centralized auditing team, his first task was to scrutinize audits conducted by division-level auditors, to ascertain 'whether one division is starting to deviate ... And all of those things will enter our risk analysis picture ... [indicating] that maybe we should go there as opposed to somewhere else.' Once a high-risk division was selected, the team focused on areas of greatest threat to the accountability claims of the police organization:

> We like to test something operational and high-risk as opposed to only going in there and looking at administrative areas because – where are you going to get the most sensitivity? where are you going to get the most trouble? – is in the operational areas, the sensitive operational areas. And search warrants would be an area. Exhibits, if some unit seizes a ton of cannabis ... is that secure? Is it

secure to a point where it's going to stand up in court? Is somebody going to break into their exhibit locker and steal it? ... And we could actually view the exhibit to make sure it's there and to make sure it's labelled properly and certainly check the paperwork. And a lot of that sort of auditing is compliance auditing. It's checking the checks and balances ... Are the exhibits being handled properly, and if not, let's clean it up so we don't have an embarrassment ... When some parent calls and says their twelve-year-old daughter was sexually assaulted, is that investigation getting adequate attention? That sort of thing. High-risk operational things ... If you don't have checks and balances, people steal ... So there's lots of room for embarrassment, there's lots of room for error ... we go in and jump on those things.

Internal audits also focus on efficiency, and in particular communication efficiency. An auditor defined his job as 'the three "e"s – economy, efficiency, effectiveness.' When asked to discuss recent examples of auditing, he said that typically they had focused on communication systems. There had been an audit of the 911 system; an audit which dealt with the problem that 'not all the paper ... [made] it back' after court documents were sent to police district offices; and a time-and-motion audit of the resources expended on preparing arrest documentation following the *Stinchcombe* decision. This officer said that such efficiency audits were vehicles for justifying procedural changes and calls for additional resources. For example,

In [the] communication [unit] ... one of the recommendations over there was to redesign the shift schedule so they are in a better position where they'd have enough people to handle the various peaks in their call, in their call-load. As a result of that, they're a lot more effective, a lot more efficient ... Certainly, our communication audit impacted on the budget. Usually you think of auditors going in to save money, but sometimes you spend money. You recognize that in order to enhance the area ... you're going to have to spend some money.

Audits were also conducted by the organizations we studied in anticipation of accountability requirements, and led in turn to a perpetual elaboration of standards. Indeed, auditing units were privately justified by the police as a buffer against what would occur otherwise, namely public investigations following a crisis or in response to pressure from external bodies with a political agenda. An auditor said that his unit's existence could be justified because it institutionalized the auditing process and made it predictable, thus heading off externally driven audits initiated 'out of ignorance or from political pressure.' As an extra precaution, his organization identified risks and anticipated trouble by including two annual surveys as part of the auditing unit's responsibilities. Police officers were surveyed regarding job satisfaction, and members of the public were surveyed regarding satisfaction with police service.

As we have said before, risk society is characterized by a perpetual elaboration of communication rules that are used both to assess risks to knowledge and to better regulate how knowledge is communicated and used. In this context the police are increasingly subject to external institutional pressures to produce and disclose knowledge within the confines of rule-governed formats. The criminal law dictates forms of disclosure, as do various areas of information law that touch on privacy and access to information. The need to appear publicly accountable also leads the police to establish their own communication rule systems. Rules develop to centralize the access of other institutions to police knowledge, to commodify police knowledge that is bartered or sold to external institutions, and to regulate internal knowledge production and distribution systems. These rules protect police organizations from the risk of appearing irresponsible in the handling of their knowledge assets.

Communication rules are a response to the paper burden, but also lead to that burden's being compounded. They make communication more efficient, yet undercut efficiency by requiring continual elaboration and the creation of auditing mechanisms. They do not, in any case, have a direct bearing on police action. Their contribution to police action is mediated by the formats through which communication occurs. The rules become embedded in the communication formats through which the police report knowledge of risk. As we will now see, these formats are crucial to managing the volume and content of risk communications.

15

Communication Formats

Communication formats are incorporated into the medium of official police forms. Forms vary from being blank and thus open for a narrative report, to being entirely restricted to fixed-choice categories that are predetermined by requirements for risk analysis. The knowledge available in a report depends on the format used and therefore is always secondary to the format. Formats provide for the selection, transmission, and reception of knowledge. They govern how knowledge is conceived, recognized, and communicated as a capacity for action.

In this chapter we first consider negotiation processes through which police communication formats are decided on. There is a politics of formats whereby the police negotiate with other institutions regarding the risk classifications to be incorporated into forms. There is also a politics of formats internal to the police that relates to how things are to be classified and for what purposes.

We next consider police efforts to regulate forms internally. Some forms are created for the sole purpose of regulating other forms. There is also a need to regulate the volume of forms. Aided by personal computers, police managers in various decentralized divisions and units create their own forms to meet their particular needs. These 'bootleg' forms increase the paper burden and create new formats and risk logics that are then subject to regulation. There is also a need to regulate *how* particular forms are formatted, and an effort to reduce the police officer's ability to construct independent narratives by confining him or her to fixed-choice formats. The policing of narratives is also accomplished by direct supervision and by auditing procedures that are designed to ensure that officers adhere to the format requirements of the forms they use.

Finally, we examine some of the effects of changes in police communication formats. Police work has become more 'scientized' (Ericson and Shearing 1986) in terms of risk management criteria. This scientization entails fixed-choice reporting formats that allow the police to state the facts. Factuality is the means by which the police effect closure and express authoritative certainty about what they know and the decisions they have taken. At the same time there is resistance to scientization and to its consequence of a perpetual barrage of new forms and classifications. This resistance is the mechanism whereby reflexivity with respect to classifications is ensured, and thus reflexivity feeds into the ongoing internal politics of communication formats.

The Politics of Forms

The external institutions that demand knowledge from the police operate according to risk logics different from those of the police, and therefore require different classifications. In response, the police develop communication formats that are comprehensive enough to meet the needs of external institutions as well as their own requirements. Full-time police knowledge workers and special police committees negotiate with external institutions over appropriate classifications and formats. This work is ongoing because any communication formats settled on inevitably require adjustment, and because the risk knowledge needs of external institutions are always in flux.

An information systems unit officer described how he was trying to make some of the classifications in a provincial traffic collision report form compatible with the classifications in a criminal occurrence report form. This effort was directed at reducing the paper burden faced by officers investigating traffic accidents that also involved criminal offences, for in such cases the officers needed to use two formats to report similar knowledge. He said that his starting points were, first, the criminal occurrence classifications laid down by Statistics Canada, and second, the classifications laid down by the provincial traffic collision report form. It was beyond his power to change either set of classifications. Concerning the provincial form, the officer said that 'we're stuck with it. We had two members on a committee, a province-wide committee, to determine what that form looked like. But essentially, that form has been here for three years, in use for three years, and the provincial government wasn't going to change it because we wanted it changed.' Given the rigid Statistics Canada and traffic collision formats, his task was to have them mesh with the occurrence system that we're putting together. Essentially, a policeman could go out and investigate a traffic accident where it's an impaired driver. So we have an occurrence of an impaired driver in which we [also] have to meet Statistics Canada codes, and we also have a collision in trying to meet provincial things. To give you an example, Statistics Canada, here, under when they're describing a person, has one of ... 'apparently normal,' 'impaired by alcohol,' 'impaired by drugs,' or 'impaired by both.' This [provincial] form doesn't. Things like that, just little irritating things like that.

Knowledge workers assigned format-integration tasks were faced with many such irritations. An expert in accident data collection and automation for the federal government said that her task was overwhelming because even the most basic classifications varied from province to province. For example, in some provinces a traffic 'fatality' was defined as death within a week of the accident, but in others as death within a month. She observed that even the definition of what constituted a motor vehicle was inconsistent, indicating that 'for a small country, we have a host of ... fiefdoms.'

Formats useful to external institutions may be of little value to the police, and in some instances may even produce knowledge that operates against police interests. The head of an auto theft investigative unit said that he had been successful in convincing his organization that it should not use the Statistics Canada Uniform Crime Report system for reporting vehicle thefts, because that system results in inflated crime figures. He contended that the UCR system included what the police would classify as 'attempted theft' and 'unfounded' incidents, so that 'you're increasing the [public] alarm and the overreacting to something that isn't quite right [accurate] ... You're erroneously reporting, in actual fact distorting, the true picture to the public ... I said [to the deputy chief], "I am not going to inform the police commission that there are ... 11,800 stolen cars this year. I've got that down to 7,800. You've got 3,000 attempted and unfounded thefts in that."'

This interviewee indicated that the politics of formats involving external institutions sometimes intersected with the politics of law and order. The police, he said, make their judgments about which formats and classifications are appropriate in terms of how the resultant knowledge will make them appear and how it will legitimate their interests.

Communication formats designed to enhance the police stake in the politics of law and order are especially evident in the reporting of drug seizures (Manning 1980). An interviewee offered insight into his work as a classifier and valuator of seized drugs. At the time of the interview he was involved in altering his organization's drug classifications to make them compatible with the classifications used by Health and Welfare Canada and by the national police information retrieval system:

We requested to have it [his organization's drug classifications] amended ... to make it compatible with our police information retrieval reporting system reporting as well, but also it sort of gives a false impression ... If analysis shows that street-level purity is higher than normal, the estimated value is the value for which it would be sold locally if diluted to normal street purchase. So really if you seize a kilo of heroin at 100 per cent purity, they say don't report the wholesale price ... because the thinking of course – and not trying to inflate the seizure at all – the thinking is that if you seize a kilo of heroin it's not going to be sold at 100 per cent purity. Of course, it would kill anybody that took a sniff of it actually. So it's broken down, say to 5, 10 per cent purity ... But when it's broken down to, say, 10 per cent purity, it may actually be ten pounds and then that's sold at the ounce level ... whereas the wholesale price may be $2,000, when retail on the street may be $2,000,000 ... So we're trying to change that because really it does give a false impression ... What we're saying is don't break it down. If it's seized as wholesale, then quote price. If it's seized at the street, then retail price ... We just changed the marijuana reporting not that long ago, marijuana plants. Now the weight system, how do you get seedlings? They're this high. Now I bet you these are going to grow to this big and each plant may be a pound of marijuana. But we don't seize that. We seize this much. Initially, the police said we will get the estimated value and weight when it's sold. But we're just seizing this [seedlings]; all of a sudden you've seized a million of these little plants. On the same token, maybe you go out and you seize a field of the plants this time, but do you seize it just as it's time to rain? They're all weighed down with water so you weigh them, [but] they weigh twice as much as they should. Or some people maybe seize them and they got a ball of earth on them like this. Now you weigh all that. Well, we solved that, or hopefully we solved that by saying don't report any weight, don't report any value. Report the number of plants if they're this big or if they're this big. A plant is a plant. Forget about size. I guess, really, when you're talking to the ordinary layman, I seize 100 plants. Well, you see in your own mind, you see 100 plants. Some of them may be this size maybe, but there's still 100 plants.

Such calibrations vary according to the interests and institutional audiences involved. For example, when the goal is to dramatize the risk and the efficiency of law enforcement in managing it, an inflated maximum value of the contraband seized will be publicized. This approach is routine in law enforcement activities involving the mass media and business interests such as Crime Stoppers (Carriere and Ericson 1989; Schlesinger and Tumber 1994). A police officer involved in a Crime Stoppers operation said that 'The drugs that we're coding in here would be absolute maximum value of the drugs. If we seize a pound, we ask the drug squad to tell us how much it would have sold for if it had broken right down to the smallest denomination and sold. So that figure of $2,900,000 [seized last year through Crime Stoppers] is open to interpretation. It might have been a pound, but a pound might be $25,000 [and] ... when it's broken down might be worth $50,000.'

Drug calibration work shows that classifications for risk management are political acts reflecting knowledge/power relations. The classifications used make a political difference not only for the external institutions involved but also for the police. In devising classification formats, the police are always half-watching in terms of another show, namely, the value of the knowledge produced as symbolic capital that may enhance or detract from police resources.

The Crime Stoppers officer quoted above emphasized that his drug calibrations were part of a more general effort to symbolize the risk management efficiency of the program. The strategy was to play on the popular penchant for statistical trivia – evident, for example, in sports reporting, health promotion talk, and business news – to dramatize the efficiency of law enforcement programs. Thus, Crime Stoppers' role in the recovery of stolen property was premised on the need to 'always put in some trivia here. [For instance], for every dollar we paid out, we recovered nineteen dollars in property and [it] cost us about $66.95 to solve every case. Now that's just money paid out [in rewards to informants]. That doesn't include investigative time and all that thing. We're solving one crime every fifteen hours and we're recovering about $345 every hour of operation. They like trivia.'

When classification formats are open to negotiation or to changes imposed by external institutions, the police are sensitive to how knowledge produced within a new format will affect the appearance of police efficiency and, therefore, their access to resources. Thus one of our police officers, who worked on the Child Find registry system, fretted about the implications of moving to a child-based rather than incident-based data system. Because some children become 'runaways' more than once a year, the apparent magnitude of the 'missing children problem' (Best 1990) would be lessened by a move to a child-based data system: 'The only thing that bothers me is we've been reporting fifty-five-thousand to sixty-thousand cases and if this system shows us – because there are so many multiple runaways – that we're only dealing with twenty-thousand children, suddenly ... maybe I shouldn't [publicize this] ... We're going to have to be awful careful when we produce our first report based on our own, the information coming off our database ... [it is] going to have to be so well written and explain[ed].'

As we saw in the case of the auto theft unit that changed how auto theft crimes were counted (p. 359), classifications may be rejected because they show the police to be less efficient than they want to appear. There is always a tension between dramatizing the risk and showing that the police are efficient risk managers. Thus, classifications may also be rejected because they show too much of a decrease in a threat, thereby posing a risk to police resources. A communication format expert described to us how his organization decided to reject a classification that would have captured 'drug-related' crimes. It was feared that the data would show less of a danger to the public than had been imagined, and therefore adversely affect police claims on resources:

> We [could] score a survey code to show how many times this happened in each file to indicate the drug-related crime. In other words, here's theft from a vehicle. Somebody stole a stereo out of a car. Did the person steal that stereo so they could take it to the tavern and sell it for money and then buy drugs with the money? That would be drug-related crime. Did they do an armed robbery because they wanted money for drugs? How many different offence files could you have officers reading and scoring on a statistical system that, because of what you might call drug-related in a definition, they'd say, 'Oh yeah, that applies in this file,' and they'll score it as a drug crime ... on line two or three ... So at the end of the year, this guy in headquarters could say compared to last year, compared with this year, our drug-related crime has gone way up. Therefore, the province or Ottawa, we need more money to help us fight drugs because our drug-related crime is going up. Now, we examined all the sides of that request and I didn't make a unilateral decision by myself. I went to all of the different subdivisions, talked to the people who were doing the managerial quality reviews. I talked to a division audit officer. I talked to many different people who would have an interest in this issue and I would say, 'What do you think about this situation? Is it feasible? We could do this. What would you call a definition of drug-related crime?' And that became an issue. Different interpretations. What is drug-related crime? Then if you come up with a suitable definition for this group out there reading files day in and day out, when they read

a file, how could you really know if it's drug-related crime? ... you can't, really. Policemen might know full well that drugs are a real problem in the area and chances are those stereos are stolen for drug money, but that's only speculation. Therefore, even with our good definition, we really can't score drug crimes ... on line three. Other times you might find somebody committing an armed robbery, you question him, you interview him, and he admits, 'Yeah, I was doing this because I need to pay off a drug debt.' Great, no problem there. Drug crime ... on line three. Directly related. So, because of the problems in defining and the problems in knowing whether to use it or not and, even if they are thinking about using it – because they might read a file and they even forget it is drug-related – but they forget there is a survey code because there is so many of them out there now. Quite honestly, they forget to use it. So for all those reasons, the yearly statistics, when you get those numbers out there at the end of the year, the numbers might be far lower in that report than they should be. Now, how would it look if you went to the province or to Ottawa and said, 'I really need more money to enforce drugs.' But then the statistics show drug-related crime is way down this year compared to last year. You're not going to get your money, are you? So therefore, trying to gather statistics in that way, using a survey code, setting up policy that says how we're going to use it, would work against you. So we're better off not to do it. Just leave things as they are. Say we use the main codes that report how many drug offences are being reported. They've gone up significantly this year; therefore, there's more drug activity, we need more money, and let it go at that.

The politics of formats means that the police are themselves constituted within formats of efficiency. In the eyes of police employees, it seems that just about everything is measured in terms of risks to police organization and how those risks can be better managed. One police organization we looked at even had forms that required officers giving public lectures on risks and security to risk-profile their presentations in great detail, including not only data on audience size and reactions but also on technical failures in the use of audiovisual equipment. As one officer remarked, data were even kept on whether 'we screwed up because the VCR was broken.'

The politics of formats reflects the simultaneous impact of different risk logics in police work. These different risk logics emanate from both external institutions and from the internal requirements of police organization. The police try to mobilize particular classifications and specific formats that will minimize risks to their organization, but they are not always successful in face of competing logics from other institutions. An interviewee observed that 'Most policing activities are not easily transferable to a standard format. Sometimes when you try and fit things into that format it may even work against you.' Another interviewee, involved in the creation of a general occurrence report for his police organization, described the process as a 'political nightmare' because of the competing risk logics of 'a really diverse user-group.'

The inability to work within unified formats reflecting a singular risk logic means that policing inevitably lacks uniformity and is fragmented. As a police officer employed full-time as a forms manager explained, 'Police work is police work no matter where you do it, and it *should be* done in a uniform manner. And reporting *should be* uniform. The problem is, of course, that sometimes other government agencies ... may have requirements and, because we're under contract with these people, we have requirements to meet those demands.' The best the police can do in this discursive field of competing risk logics is to develop mechanisms for the regulation of communication formats as an integral part of their daily tasks.

Patrolling the Facts

The regulation of formats consumes a great deal of administrative and supervisory resources. There are four major means by which regulation is accomplished. First, there are forms about forms, that is, formats used to trace the whereabouts of other forms, monitor their uses, and risk-profile the 'population' of forms. Second, there are mechanisms for tracing 'bootleg' forms – forms created by police divisions or units without central authorization – in order to either recognize them officially or eradicate them from the knowledge system. Third, there are efforts to reduce knowledge production to fixed-choice responses, in other words to police narratives to the point of virtually eliminating them. Finally, there is direct supervision, as supervisors at various levels edit the reports of their subordinates to ensure uniformity in format.

Forms about Forms

Some forms are devised to regulate the formats and uses of other forms. The fact that there often are many institutional users of the knowledge produced through a police form, combined with the fact that the police try to use a single form to satisfy as many users as possible, means that some forms have become extremely complex. As a result, new forms are devised to simplify the production of the knowledge that is recorded on the main form. For example, a police organization had an 'Accident Investigation Field Note' form for guiding officers in taking notes at traffic accident scenes for later use in completing the main report. We also encountered police officers who devised their own formats to ensure that they produced adequate knowledge in the format of the official form. An officer we observed said that he found impaired driving reporting so complicated that he prepared his own flow chart of forms and procedures to ensure that he followed all of the required steps.

There are also forms that trigger the correction of knowledge contained in other forms. One police organization had an 'Attention Chit' form to send out to police officers who had filled out reports incorrectly. This form included a check-list of the items requiring attention. Correction forms are especially common in connection with police inspectorate functions. The Canadian weapons registration system has a correction form that is sent to weapons dealers who have filled out the original form incorrectly. Another example is provided by a police organization that devised nine new forms 'to replace unofficial forms being used in the Records Compilation Section. They serve to collect data concerning questionable information obtained from fingerprint forms received from police departments and detachments. This data is then inputed into a computer which has an identical format thereby generating a message to the department, detachment or institution requesting the clarification of the information on [a specific form].'

Another group of forms is designed to summarize what is available in more complex forms and files. These forms allow quick scans without one having to read the more detailed form. As in the case of the 'Report to Prosecutor' form analysed in chapter 14 (pp. 326–8), the scan format allows systematic checking of whether proper reporting procedures have been followed and of whether forms have been correctly completed. It also directs the person looking for relevant knowledge to particular parts of forms or files. One police organization, for instance, had a form that was officially described as designed 'to brief information on intelligence files so members may quickly supply information without reading entire file.' It also had an 'Intercept Monitor Form' on which a person listening to a tape of wire-tapped conversations could flag for investigators what was worth listening to and transcribing. Another type of form used by police organizations to activate the production of knowledge was termed a 'powerfile.' In one organization, for example, there was a 'Powerfile Statistics' form for ensuring the collection and distribution of selected statistics on a daily basis.

Various forms exist to risk-profile other forms and their uses. An entire form or file may be used for assessing the nature and complexity of a case. The assessment is used to judge how that case should be managed given the resources of the police unit concerned. For example, a police commercial crime unit that worked on long and detailed investigations devised a 'Complexity Form' to assist case management. This form was designed to rate the complexity of various investigative activities. As we were told by a unit member,

> You have a complexity form which rates the file as to complexity. We have basically an action plan for each investigator which the investigator continually updates. And that provides some accountability and control – accountability for the investigators, control for the supervisors. We rely on that a lot, on the progress of the investigation. The investigations here are long; some take up to a year to develop and get before the courts. So the whole thing could get lost very easily, but if it's detailed as to the action steps then you're in a better position of control.

There are also forms to risk-profile the whereabouts of forms. In keeping track of the population of forms, these forms risk-profile, for example, the movement of knowledge. A police organization we studied had a 'District/Section Document Control Form,' a 'Unit/Zone Document Control Form,' an 'Overdue Document Notification,' a 'Document Control Card,' and so on. Another police organization had an 'Information Release' form to trace the release of knowledge from files. It also had a 'Notice of Destruction' form as a kind of death register to mark the demise of records no longer required.

These forms are designed to indicate the availability of other forms and files and to trace the movement of knowledge for risk management purposes. There are also forms designed to secure specific forms of knowledge. These range from forms that instruct other police officials, for example those at airports, to exempt police officers from normal searches, to forms for reporting unauthorized access to police knowledge. The simplest of the latter variety we encountered was a 'Security Bulletin' form that was blank except for a logo of a key at the top, inside of which were 'signs' representing a video screen, a desk, a file, and a filing cabinet, which together symbolized security concerns about police knowledge.

Forms also exist to flag a high-risk file for scrutiny by senior officers. In a police organization where all officers' reports were examined by a field supervisor, a report reviewer, and a data entry clerk, there was also a form that triggered further reviews by three levels of supervisors.

Another type of form about forms is designed to authorize and centrally regulate all forms in use within a police organization. One police organization we studied had a form that had to be completed when seeking approval for a new form, and another form that initiated a review for determining whether an existing form was still needed. The 'Forms Coordinator' for this organization described the work:

> If a division or unit requests a form, they send the request in to me and it's profiled by Sergeant X. And then I design the form and we sort of agree back and forth on whether it's suitable or not. And then we send a copy of that up to headquarters, distribute it ... There's a lot of units that are using forms that are not approved, but basically they're for the same thing, only they are designed differently. So [in each case] we're going to try and make one form for everybody ... There's a lot of paper around and to try to cut down, you really don't know where to start.

Containing Bootleg Forms

The interviewee just quoted pointed to a problem with what the police term bootleg forms. New forms and formats proliferate in the microcontexts of everyday police work. The reasons for this proliferation include the need to further rationalize complex procedures, the problems posed by unique local circumstances, administrative peculiarities concerning what should be reported, and the ease with which forms can be created using personal computers.

Particular units are faced with complex reporting requirements that necessitate the creation of unique formats to manage their work. Forms are created that address only the peculiar requirements of a specific police task. A police interviewee described how new forms and formats are created during a commercial crime investigation: 'An average search warrant from my section is probably fifty pages. You're probably working on them for three months because they have to be so precise and accurate and they have to show the complexity of the scheme ... So what they have is the computers used to build these things and to cross-correlate data and information and build forms into the machine.'

The belief that knowledge formatted in risk management terms will enhance regulatory capability means that new forms become an 'obvious' response to novel situations or problems. An information manager for a police division said that he had initiated a program whereby administrators in each police station were asked to identify bootleg forms. At the beginning it had been thought 'there were [only] a few' bootleg forms, but 'It turns out there was hundreds ... You name it ... [from] keeping track of the tires for police cars ... [to] check the ferry for a [suspect] vehicle coming off.'

These unique risk management forms often reflect local administrative peculiarities regarding what should be reported. At one police station the administrator decided that he wanted night-shift patrol officers to report on their checks of commercial properties. A thirteen-page form was created, listing all commercial properties to be checked and asking patrol officers to 'check off' that they had inspected each property at a particular time. A police forms management specialist described the inspectorial process activated by this form:

> And when the constable on patrol would check that property at night, he'd write down the time that he checked it ... Every doorknob that he shook he wrote it down. There are two purposes ... an investigative tool ... keeps the investigating constable on his toes. He has to sign that he checked these properties, therefore he better be right. He'd better check them. But then that becomes, you see, in a sense a kind of 'cover your ass' kind of form ... If the place is broken into, you say, 'Well, my constable checked this at three o'clock this morning and it was fine.'

This interviewee described other police stations where similar forms were created to, for example, record all bars checked, suspected impaired drivers stopped, and private residences patrolled. He said that with such forms, 'There's always a case of overkill.'

Overkill is made easy by the availability of personal computers. A police officer specializing in forms management expressed frustration that 'The computer has become a big toy in a sense. When a guy's got nothing better to do, he sits down and starts designing forms on the damn thing when he should be out doing policework ... they're not experts in form design to start with. The forms that came in from [a police station], when we went over them, there are all kinds of typographical errors, missing data, data on them that weren't on the original, and so on. It's a real problem and I think it's going to get worse before it gets better.' A colleague in forms management did think that things were getting worse, in the sense that the proliferation of bootleg forms created on personal computers was increasing the paper burden faced by officers: 'While automation is going to be used to solve some problems, it also creates its own problems. People are now creating their own forms at the divisional level using their PCs. Now it's not a big problem to create a form. The burden is for the guys who have to fill them out. All of our effort goes out the window because of the computers. For everything that you do on the computer, more information is produced.'

As is indicated by these comments, forms managers fret a great deal about the illicit circulation of unauthorized forms. The very term bootleg suggests that these forms are seen in a climate of communication format prohibition requiring tough policing. A forms risk manager for a large municipal police organization said that 'all the different divisions are creating little databases all over the place.' His solution was to crack down hard: 'What we want to do is *eliminate* this ... This is not easy. There is an inertia that we have to *break*. Each group also wants to create their own priorities by keeping certain types of information.' His counterpart in another police organization offered a more restrained approach: 'One is trying to look at the paper and trying to reduce the number of forms, rationalize the number of forms, who's the owner of them, combine them, eliminate them, whatever.'

The techniques for policing bootleg forms vary. There are routine audits to ferret out unauthorized forms and to decide which ones might be officially accepted or integrated into existing official forms. A forms manager involved in a paper reduction project for her police organization said that 'One of the first things that we had to do was simply identify the forms that were in use. Just by asking the question there was a 40 per cent reduction in forms.' A colleague in the same organization was working on computer surveillance mechanisms that would signal the illicit creation of forms and prevent units and officers from altering existing forms: 'The problem is going to magnify until [we have] some kind of controls, locking mechanisms. If we don't have a locking mechanism on a [computerized] form that we create on there, some guy sitting in a [police station] could change what we've already created, sort of thing. That's another fear that we have.'

Police officers resist giving up to centralized systems the forms they have created. Their resistance is based on the belief that a form is created to meet a local need, and that the response to that need is compromised by any effort to centralize it. Centralization entails format standardization for all police stations and units at the expense of classifications that are sensitive to the needs associated with local contexts, particular units, and particular procedures. An information manager for a police division described the opinions of police officers on this point: '[Their view is], "I still have to use a piece of paper. What the hell difference if it's an 'X' Division form or a 'Y' Division form, or there's nothing [officially designated] on it? I'm still going to have to use a piece of paper to control whatever I want." And sometimes they're right. And if they already had the form done up and it really works, then what's the point in changing it if they have to use a form anyway?'

In geographically dispersed police organizations, officers try to maintain as low a profile for their idiosyncratic forms as they do for the investigative aspects of their knowledge work. A forms manager said that even if bootleg forms are creative and may be of benefit to other units, officers might not make them more widely available, out of a fear of sanctions: 'From their point of view it is a risky business just to give us the forms because they may get a medal for recognizing an important information need or they may get shit on for developing a form without authorization.'

Some of the administrators and forms managers we spoke to were pessimistic about forms reduction efforts because the trend in policing is towards meeting more and more risk knowledge demands. Although bootleg forms are continually being eliminated, others are incorporated into official formats at an even faster rate, and therefore the corpus of official forms continues to grow. An administrator in the enforcement branch of a police organization said that a forms review project in her unit did not result in a reduction of forms – 'We had to keep just about all of them.' A senior police information system administrator indicated that forms management had an iatrogenic effect: 'We have a section in my department called "Forms Management," but this is a bit of a misnomer. What they actually do is produce forms. They were not concerned with managing forms because they were evaluated on how quickly and efficiently they could produce new forms.'

The Policing of Narratives

In addition to regulating the number of forms, the 'forms police' work hard to restrict the narrative capacity of police officers. This restriction has evolved through successive changes to the communication formats of reports. Reports have been increasingly formatted in fixed-choice or fill-in-the-blank terms, to the point where free-form narratives are highly circumscribed or eliminated.

Changes in the occurrence report forms of one municipal police organization we examined illustrate the shift from an open narrative to fixed-choice risk classifications. Before 1939 the occurrence report was simply a blank sheet of paper. The reporting officer was required to compose a narrative of his investigation without the aid of any classification format. The first step in form-alization occurred in 1939 (figure 15.1). The new form was headed 'Occurrence Report' and had spaces for the date, subject, occurrence number, file number, and inspector's signature indicating approval of the narrative. But the investigating officer was still required to compose a narrative of the 'once upon a time there was a theft' variety, as is illustrated by the narrative from 1939 reproduced in figure 15.1. This form remained in place until the 1960s.

Figure 15.2 reproduces the offence report as it appeared in 1964. Here we see the beginning of enclosed formatting. There are twenty-eight items in addition to the narrative. These relate to investigative details such as the victim's profile and how the crime was carried out. Apparently safe-cracking was a problem at the time, as it is given its own section. Vehicular information is also singled out as relevant to investigations. In addition, there are classifications related to the nascent effort to risk-manage police officers' activities and efficiency. For example, knowledge must be provided about how the matter came to police attention ('How Received': 'Radio,' 'Station,' 'Citizen,' 'On View'), and about its disposition ('Case Declared': 'Unfounded,' 'Cleared by Arrest,' 'Cleared Otherwise,' 'Inactive Not Cleared,' 'Investigation Continuing'). The narrative space is now reduced to half the page.

Figure 15.3 reproduces the occurrence report in use in 1981. While officers could add a 'continuation report' that included a space for a narrative, figure 15.3 is entirely formatted in fixed-choice terms. It calls for precise detail on the offence and when it occurred, and on the *modus operandi* ('M.O.'). It requires a detailed population-profiling of victims, and an even more detailed population-profiling of accused persons, suspects, and missing-person 'subjects.' The population of vehicles is also subject to extensive classification and valuation. The population of investigating police officers is profiled by recording how they were notified about the occurrence, how they processed the case (for instance by applying for a warrant, issuing an appearance notice to the accused, serving a subpoena, issuing a victim services card, or entering informa-

FIGURE 15.1

OCCURRENCE REPORT

City Police Headquarters
Province, May 31st. 1939

Chief Constable

Subject: Re Theft of dresses

Occ. No._____
File No._____

I beg to report that on March 23rd, 1939, Mrs [Victim] reported the theft of three dresses to the value of $5.94, from the soft drink counter at Woolworth's Store, these dresses were taken on Saturday the 11th of March.

About a week after they were taken one of the dresses was exchanged at the dress shop where they had been purchased by [the Victim].

On interviewing the Clerk that had sold the dresses I learned that a girl from Woolworth's had exchanged this dress, I took the Clerk to Woolworth's store and she pointed out [Miss X] who was in charge of the soft drink counter as the girl that had exchanged it.

[Miss X] stated that on the date the dresses were stolen a foreign woman who was described as about 35 to 40 yrs. old, dark comp. slim build and wearing winter clothing had spoken to her, she asked her for her address and she said that she would send her something from the farm, a few days later this woman sent the dress to her asking her to return it to the dress shop, get a refund of the money and return it to her, she sent a letter with the parcel which [Miss X] produced when she returned the dress, this letter was destroyed when it served it's purpose and [Miss X] stated that she was not sure of the name but it started with P and ended with uik, this woman lived on a farm in the district.

[Miss X] promised to get in touch with the police when she saw this woman again in the City, she was discharged from Woolworth's on account of this matter and stated that she did not get a chance to see her again.

As [the victim] called at this Office a few days ago, Miss X was again interviewed and gave the same story as previously mentioned, she is living above a store, 4th Ave. and 1st St. E., she is working in the Restaurant on the corner of 6th Ave. and 4th St. E.

Miss X appears very anxious to get this matter cleared and if she ever sees this woman she will notify this Dept., Mr. Y was looking after her interests in regard to this matter.

Examined and forwarded Respectfully submitted,

..................................Inspector Detective.

FIGURE 15.2

CASE NO.		

OFFENCE REPORT

1. OFFENCE	2. DIVISION	3. DATE AND TIME OF THIS REPORT

4. PLACE OF OCCURRENCE	PATROL AREA	REPORT ZONE

5. TIME OF OCCURRENCE	DAY	DATE	MONTH	YEAR	HOUR	RELIEF

6. VICTIM (IF FIRM, NAME AND TYPE OF BUSINESS)	7. HOME ADDRESS	8. HOME PHONE
	9. BUSINESS ADDRESS	10. BUS. PHONE

11. DESCRIPTION OF VICTIM	SEX	AGE	RACE OR NATIONALITY	OCCUPATION	MARITAL STATUS

12. REPORTED BY (NAME AND RELATIONSHIP TO VICTIM)	ADDRESS	PHONE

13. TYPE OF PREMISES (PREMISES USED FOR)	14. HOW ATTACKED (HOW COMMITED—ENTRANCE GAINED)
15. MEANS OF ATTACK (WEAPONS—TOOLS USED)	16. OBJECT OF ATTACK (MOTIVE—TYPE OF PROPERTY STOLEN)

17. SAFE ATTACKED YES ☐ NO ☐	EXPLOSIVES	TORCH	PUNCH	PEEL	WORKED COMB	CARRIED AWAY	OTHER (DESCRIBE)

18. TRADE MARKS

19. DESC. OF VEHICLE USED	YEAR	MAKE	MODEL	COLOR	LICENSE	UNUSUAL FEATURES

20. DETAILS AND WITNESSES:

21. REPORT BY				22. ACCOMPANIED BY		23. C.I.B. PERSONNEL IN ATTENDANCE	
24. HOW RECEIVED	RADIO	STATION	CITIZEN	ON VIEW DATE AND TIME REPORTED		APPROVED BY	
CASE DECLARED	UNFOUNDED		CLRD BY ARREST	CLRD OTHERWISE	IN-ACTIVE NOT CLRD	INVSTGN. CONT.	SIGNATURE
BULLENTIN NO.	CANCELLED		CIRCULAR NO.	CANCELLED	TABULATED		TYPED BY

FIGURE 15.3

Occurrence Report

Case No.

1 ☐ Committed | 2 ☐ Attempted | 3 ☐ Conspiracy

OCCURRENCE

How Received	R ☐ Radio	S ☐ Station	V ☐ On View	Date & Time Reported to Invest.	Date & Time Report Submitted by Invest.
Type of Offence				Damage Value $	For Data Entry Use Only
Place of Occurrence		Zone		DAY	DATE .... MONTH .... YEAR .... HOUR ....

VICTIM

Victim(s)	LEGAL NAME				
Business Address		Phone	Postal Code	WEAPONS USED IN ATTACK: 1 2 3 4	
Home Address		Phone	Postal Code		
Description of Victim	Sex · Age or Date of Birth · Race: W/C	Occupation	Marital Status	Drunk · Impaired	Sober
Reported by	Address		Phone		

M.O.

Type of Premise or Location	Exact Location at Premise	How Attacked
Means of Attack (tool/weapon)	Object of Attack	Trademark/Type of Drug

VEHICLE

C ☐ Crime Vehicle | S ☐ Stolen Vehicle | L ☐ Lost (for license plates and validation tags)

Type: 01 ☐ Auto · 02 ☐ Bus · 03 ☐ Truck · 04 ☐ M/Cycle · 05 ☐ Snowmobile · 06 ☐ Aircraft · 07 ☐ Watercraft · 08 ☐ Motorized Recreation · 09 ☐ Trailer Recreation · 10 ☐ Trailer Utility · 11 ☐ Other · 12 ☐ Lic. Plate · 13 ☐ Val. tag · 14 ☐ Motor · 15 ☐ Transmission · 16 ☐ Vin. plate

Year	Make	Model	Style	Color	License #	Province	Lic. Year	Value $
Vin #/Valtag # motor transm				Distinguishing Interior Features				
Exterior					Insurance Co.			Policy #

SUBJECT INFORMATION

C ☐ Charged S ☐ Suspected M ☐ Missing	C ☐ Charged S ☐ Suspected M ☐ Missing	C ☐ Charged S ☐ Suspected M ☐ Missing
Name # 1	Name # 2	Name # 3
Address	Address	Address
Postal Code · Phone	Postal Code · Phone	Postal Code · Phone
Sex · DOB · Ht. · Wt. · Race W/C	Sex · DOB · Ht. · Wt. · Race W/C	Sex · DOB · Ht. · Wt. · Race W/C
Eye · Hair · Occupation	Eye · Hair · Occupation	Eye · Hair · Occupation
Marks, Physical Peculiarities, Clothing	Marks, Physical Peculiarities, Clothing	Marks, Physical Peculiarities, Clothing
Alias or Nickname	Alias or Nickname	Alias or Nickname
Photo # · F.P.S. #	Photo # · F.P.S. #	Photo # · F.P.S. #
Charges	Charges	Charges
Relation to Victim · Fingerprint Date	Relation to Victim · Fingerprint Date	Relation to Victim · Fingerprint Date
App. Notice # · Appearance Date	App. Notice # · Appearance Date	App. Notice # · Appearance Date
Warrant Applied For ☐ Summons ☐ Arrested ☐	Warrant Applied For ☐ Summons ☐ Arrested ☐	Warrant Applied For ☐ Summons ☐ Arrested ☐

CONCLUSION

Report by	Reg. No.	Accompanied by Reg. No.	Zone	IDENT. SECTION	Reg. No.
Case Declared	U ☐ Unfounded · C ☐ Cleared by Charge · O ☐ Cleared Otherwise · I ☐ Inactive · A ☐ Investigation Continuing		C.P.I.C. ☐	Approved	Reg. #
DO YOU WISH TO SERVE THE CIVILIAN SUBPOENAS: ☐					
Victim Services Card Issued ☐		Assigned to Zone		No Approval unless all facts embodied. Approving Officer will be held Responsible.	

tion on CPIC), and what the outcome of the case was. This profiling is also furthered by providing space for supervisory checks.

As will be discussed in more detail later, by the early 1990s this police organization had moved into a 'paperless' computerized occurrence report system. Officers are no longer required to fill out occurrence reports by hand, but rather do so electronically using highly specific categories and codes. Fully printed out, the present occurrence report runs to twelve pages of fixed-choice classifications.

A veteran member of this police organization discussed the changes in report formatting over time. He attributed the changes to the combined effects of computerization and the demands for knowledge from external institutions:

> When I joined, the [general occurrence] report was one 8.5 by 11 [page] that was folded into three, and the boxed information would then be on that much. That much was boxed. And now we're up to twelve pages ... Computers are driving it. The fact that we *can* now collect vast amounts of data ... The more information you have, the more information people want, so you gather more, so they want more, and you just keep going and going and going ... See! What are *you* doing out here? You're collecting statistical data! The demand is there, but I think we also fuel the demand by saying, 'Well, we'll collect that information for you.'

A forms manager in another police organization, commenting on the same development in his organization, said that the expansion within given forms was of even greater magnitude than the expansion of the number of forms. He believed that the change towards closed formats occurred because of internal risk management efforts to police narratives: 'I would say that is where the main growth has taken place. There is much more detail on the forms now. Some of this is designed to ensure that the officer does not forget certain things. If it is just there as a box to tick off they are much less likely to forget it.'

In this man's organization, the narrative space in the general occurrence report not only was restricted to a tiny fraction of the report but also was regulated by an official limit of 229 character spaces. Another forms police officer in this organization said that 'We just simply encourage being brief, concise, and to the point.' A station-level supervisor added that this limit helped to encourage police officers to write their narratives in a concise, factual manner, similar to what was required in a brief to a crown attorney. The goal was to 'kill two birds with one stone' by formatting the general occurrence report in a manner that was consistent with the format of reports to the crown attorney.

The movement towards communication formats that express factuality was policed by other mechanisms as well. There was a policing of language that limited the officer's interpretations to his or her own narrow expertise. For example, a police information systems specialist discussed efforts to prohibit sex crime investigators from using the language of clinical psychology and psychiatry in their reports because that language connoted an interpretive capacity they did not in fact have: '[The] Sex Crimes [unit] wanted the officer to be ... able to put on the form whether he thought this person was a paedophile and we said no, that's more like intelligence information. If a doctor says this is a schizophrenic, well yeah, we'll believe him that he's a schizophrenic, but we don't want policemen making that determination on, essentially, what we're considering a factual document that's going to be used by everybody ... little things that seem to go more into the intelligence field than fact reporting.'

An interviewee involved in revising the format for collecting national data on bombs and bomb threats said that an important part of the process was the elimination of the potential to incorporate value judgments into narratives. This effort extended to the fixed-choice classifications themselves, which in the interests of technical efficiency were to be made more value-neutral:

> [The present] form asks them to make a lot of value judgments. Like with this, an 'attempted bombing' or an 'accident' ... 'was this initiated by a victim or was this for a human goal?' You know, like a bomb went off on a guy ... Motivation doesn't really mean a whole lot to us. We're technical ... It's always a guess anyway. How do you know whether the guy was trying to commit suicide or his bomb blew up accidentally? Maybe from the police investigation it may bear that out, but from the technical side of the bomb, who cares? I don't really care. And so we've tried to go more technical, get a better description of components ... [For example] the important point for us is to know there's a clock in there and what kind of clock it was because, then, if we find another one with a clock in there, has the same type, then maybe you can start drawing parallels. Then you can look a little bit further. So we're going down more to the technical aspects and a little less on the side of value judgments.

For the narratives police, the goals are factuality and efficiency. A police station administrator said that writing a report should be 'like taking an exam where you get true-and-false and short-answer-type questions, where there's a process to take to get the needed information in a more expedient manner.' This sensibility extended to the policing of continuation reports. In some jurisdictions continuation reports were discouraged on the grounds that, because they contained narratives, they augmented the paper burden and could not easily be converted into useful computer-formatted knowledge. From the perspective of police officers, however, continuation report narratives allow one to include additional relevant context and to show one's supervisor that one has been thorough. A police supervisor described the tensions this gives rise to:

> What we find officers are doing is often being somewhat verbose, saying a lot on this form. If they do create it then we've got to open a paper file in the station ... So the records management people are saying, 'No, no, no. Tell them *not* to generate the continuation. We're taking the view that a number of us want to say those things. It's cover your ass, it's tell the supervisor ... to do the right things ... I just think I need to record some dealings. So you've got the supervisor liking to see this sort of information because there may be something there that benefits somebody in the future. You've got the policy people saying, 'Oh, no, no. That's just another piece of paper.'

One police organization was developing information technology that would scan narratives to convert them into closed formats. An information systems operative said that this technology would mean that 'A lot of the narratives are going to be pre-canned. They fill in the blanks on a lot of them ... [which, it is hoped, means] fewer mistakes, faster time to get it into the system. It's a ... traffic accident, the girl calls up the narrative, fills in three blanks, hits "answer" and she's done.' However, the main effort in this organization was still to close off the narrative at the outset. A colleague of this interviewee said that in the past, when some narrative leeway was allowed,

> We couldn't extract the information because there's no format to it. So we've gone to a lot of boxes in the report form and, essentially, it's now, I believe, an eleven–page report, but essentially it's not made to capture any more detail than what we captured before, just in a different format ... The data typist can say, 'No, I can't put that in my box. It's not a valid option. Which of these options would you like? ... Definitely it is going to take a lot of the freedom [away from

the reporting officer] but we haven't taken the narrative away from them ... It's like going to court and watching them give radar evidence trial after trial after trial where the guy's been at the same location. Even the judge gets tired of it ... You do lose some of your freedom of expression.

Supervision

Communication formats are also sustained by direct supervision. Supervision of communication formats includes systematic editing of reports, periodic auditing of reporting systems, and training on how to classify knowledge. As one interviewee expressed it, these supervisory mechanisms produce a collective notion that 'If you are putting out good paperwork then you are doing good work.'

Training in this context is a process of learning how incidents encountered relate to relevant forms and their communication formats. For example, part of the training of police recruits sees a more senior 'training officer' accompany the new officer to teach him or her how to fit events into the communication formats of the police organization (Shearing and Ericson 1991). Some training courses also have the learning of communication formats at their core. An interviewee described a two-week training course in his area of specialization as one 'where they're instructed on procedure and how to fill out forms.' In all contexts, training in communication formats is a perpetual process, not only because the incidents encountered in the course of policing present a kaleidoscopic variety of human behaviour and interpretive possibilities, but also because the formats are in a constant state of flux as a result of the fact that they must be adjusted to new institutional demands and situational needs. As was said to us by a patrol officer during a ride-along, 'You go to a briefing one time and they tell you to fill it out one way, and then a couple of months later they tell you to fill it out another way. By the time you actually have a case like that you can't remember how to fill out the bloody form.'

Memory is managed by editorial control systems designed to patrol the facts. These systems detect any interpretive leakage that has occurred in spite of the use of closed formats. We observed a station-level operation in which patrol officers' reports were initially reviewed by their supervisor for completeness and accuracy. The supervisor would also assign a 'diary date,' usually set for two weeks after the initial review, for reviewing the file again. At the time of the second review the supervisor could keep the file open by assigning a new diary date, or close it. When a file was closed, the supervisor 'scored' it in terms of fixed-choice classifications that satisfied various users within the police organization and in external institutions. An internal report on patrol supervisors' responsibilities estimated that 70–80 per cent of their time was spent checking reports. A patrol officer provided this perspective on the process: 'your supervisor is sitting there reading your file and that's a full-time job. ... he is in here on his days off reading the files. He is not on the scene. He does not know what happened. All he knows is what the members report.' A supervisor had this to say: 'You basically control filling out all of the forms. When you sign the bottom of that you are basically saying the form is filled in correctly.'

Once a supervisor completed the scoring, the file would be passed on to a 'reader' for further editorial scrutiny. The reader was a full-time police officer whose sole function was to review files once again to ensure that everything was filled out completely and accurately, and that the scoring was also correct. He was simply a data-checker and could not, for example, reject a file and ask for further investigation. From the reader a file would go to a data entry clerk, who would again check the completeness of the file and competence of the scoring and seek clarification of any slippage.

In selected cases there was further cleansing of the data. For example, all sexual assault, domestic violence, and major crime files were sent to the second-in-command at the station for additional scrutiny. This officer also conducted random checks on other files. A police officer described this task as one that was 'concerned with how the files are taken care of. He [the second-in-command] is also concerned on the administrative side with how the file is scored, because if it is not scored properly then it is going to reflect back on him at audit time.'

Some of the reports reviewed by the second-in-command had to be reviewed further by forms managers at the divisional level. In such cases a form was filled out to flag the fact that a file needed further review and data cleansing. This was designed to ensure the appearance of uniform reporting across the police organization, especially in high-profile cases. A police officer observed that in such instances 'Your supervisor reads your work, the sergeant checks his work, staff sergeant looks after him, the commanding officer inspects all of it. Now it goes to another group of people and they inspect it. If they find anything they send it back. You have so many people checking up on what I do on the street it makes it kind of repetitive all of the time.'

A colleague elaborated on the fine-tuning involved and on how it was perceived by police officers. He described the role of two readers at divisional headquarters as follows:

> [The readers] read these reports to ensure the policy. Most members believe that it is ludicrous that an inspector in a station this size hasn't got the ability – and the staff sergeant – to tell me when I submit a report to them that I've filled it out correctly. There is something wrong with the system. And the girls have to type this up, so there is man hours lost in the typing. [The forms used to transmit a report to the division for checking] are the most time-consuming things going. You have to follow a special format and because you do it infrequently, quite often they are running to the books looking for the format that has to be followed.

In addition to this complex system for case-by-case editing and data cleansing, this police organization had a coterie of communication format auditors. There were, for example, division-level auditing teams that spent a week in each station reviewing the quality of data entry. A division-level officer involved in this process said that the main task was a random audit of files 'to make sure they have all the necessary information fields they're supposed to have, compared to the computer printout'; a 5 per cent margin of error was allowed. The process included a written report by the auditing team and a debriefing session on the mistakes that had been found. The officer we have just quoted said that there were plans to intensify the process, including extending station visits beyond one week, 'because we're finding more stuff and we have to be a little more vigilant.'

The division also had file auditors in its field-support information unit, who on a three-year cycle audited every record-keeper in every station. They served, in effect, as supervisors of station-level coders with respect to the reliability and validity of the coders' data collection. As an inspectorate, they followed a compliance model that emphasized cooperation and expert advice. One of the auditors said that it was not difficult to motivate station-level officers to score reports accurately because accurate scoring was what brought them recognition for a job well done: 'You usually don't have any real problems motivating people in terms of accuracy when it comes to statistical scoring because the station commander knows full well that he has to be accountable again, to his supervisor and to other people at upper levels, in terms of how these files are being scored.'

The written protocol for station-level quality reviews reveals the extensive reach of the auditing process. The auditors were to

1. Perform quality reviews ... based on a representative sample of the previous or current years' files.
2. Examine file flow (e.g., 'who first reviews files'; 'how many baskets and how long to reach data entry level').
3. Special File Review (e.g., 'how often reviewed and diary dated').
4. File Content.
5. Determine Use of Paperless or Bulk Files.
6. Review Use of Street Check function.
7. Other information system applications (e.g., regarding security inspections, watch programs).
8. Review proper use of codes.
9. Review of monitoring procedures.
10. Ascertain who needs information system training.
11. Check the information section of the rules manual to ensure that it is updated and promote the use of it.
12. Discuss quality review procedures with the commander.
13. Review the file system maintenance guide and procedure.

The notion held by the police that they are data cleansers is reflected in the following description by an auditor of the quality review process. Referring to a station-level audit he had just completed, he said that

At the end of the week I had my memos all structured and my laptop so that I could print a copy for Inspector X ... I did a rough copy, a draft for them and I sat Friday morning and had a debriefing with all the members, the stenos, subdivision personnel, and so on. I reviewed everything that I found in the quality review. In other words, the strict statistical review ... here's where our rates are ... not over the 5 per cent. That's good. I then went into other areas that I checked into – the file flow, into specific types of scoring, certain groups of files that need to be looked at in addition to the standard review. I looked at all the drug files. I looked at all the missing-persons files, all the stolen-vehicle files, to see if they were scoring them correctly, using some of these other lines of scoring on the information system. And I looked at their file records keeping system. They were using one central file storage area for the whole building, sequentially ... If the section in the building takes the file out, they put a charge-out card in its place with the file number on it, saying who's got it. And that's permitted. They keep it in their office for a while, but eventually it should come back into sequential storage. I examined that. I examined how well they're complying with records-keeping policy. In other words, once a file's concluded, there's a certain retention period attached to that code. At the end of that retention period, whether it's two years or five years, that electronic file must be purged off of the database. If it's a physical file, then it must be physically destroyed. We must keep complying with standard, set records-keeping policy. And that reflects, you know, if we were violating that it would have implications, I think, in the Access to Information [Act] and Privacy Act and so on ... Reading certain strips of files to tick on the sheets, percentage error rate, you get that done in the first two days ... I sat with the stenos and reviewed how to use email because they weren't familiar totally, so I brought them up to date on that. I also showed them how to submit these data system reports to get these detailed ... other data reports. I sat with the station commander and showed him how I did my review on these sheets so that, when he has to do his, maybe he'll do a little better job.

Format Effects

These intensive efforts to format police communications have a number of significant effects. They result in enclosure and certainty in police thinking, resistance and reflexivity in police actions, and a scientization of policework .

The communication formats developed to manage the paper burden constitute police officers as social science fieldworkers. They are sent into the field with forms, manuals, and coding instructions, to be consulted as the need arises.

A police administrator observed that officers rarely use coding manuals to guide them in their field reporting. For example, a traffic accident coding manual was seen as 'too big, too complicated.' Faced with an accident, officers '[are] going to grab that form and they're going to start filling it out, and they're not going to refer to a book ... of how to fill out this form.' A colleague, who served as the administrative head of a police station, said that the traffic accident reporting format is taken for granted to the point where officers accept that they are producing scientific knowledge for external institutional purposes without direct relevance to immediate investigative needs:

The majority of what you're putting down there isn't necessarily relevant to an investigation, whether it's fatal or whatever it is. It's for statistical purposes ... for [Ministry of] Transport ... insurance ... Police agencies have traditionally been used for that type of thing because they're right there and that's the only way we can collect a lot of that data ... It's instructed from day one when they join the job that they do that ... So why not do it? It's a given. You don't really hear guys grumbling. They know the paperwork involved ... [but they wouldn't] necessarily bring it up as a point of contention. It's just been there all the time through their whole career ... It's the job.

Police supervisors are, in effect, 'research associates' who as part of a 'research team' cleanse data to ensure that it is reliable and valid. As we were told by a supervisor in a full-time 'information field-support' position, 'We identify inconsistencies or lack of uniformity in our statistical system and then attempt to act as coordinator and say everyone will do it the same way.'

The scientization of policework goes beyond the reporting of incidents during the course of routine patrols. As we have already discussed, the police conduct inspections for compliance-based law enforcement systems in other government institutions and for private sector organizations, to meet their needs in the area of preventive security. These inspections are guided by check-list formats that ensure that risk management knowledge is profiled in useful ways.

Social science techniques are also used to mobilize data to argue for organizational change. As we mentioned in chapter 11 (p. 232), an automobile theft unit wanted to shift more responsibility onto the insurance industry for dealing with the problem of fraudulent claims. To this end it conducted a systematic survey of automobile theft complainants, promising them immunity from prosecution in exchange for information. The goal was to show the extent to which the insurance industry itself should be investigating complaints.

Scientization within established communication formats has the intended consequence of effecting closure and certainty in policework. It allows the police officer to prospectively decide whether something should be subject to policework (whether it fits an established format), and if so, to complete the task in concrete and discrete risk management terms. The effect, however, is that police officers inevitably must think and act according to the concrete and discrete terms of the formats within which they communicate. Their thinking itself becomes characterized by closure and certainty. This effect was discussed by a police special unit employee who, as part of his responsibilities, offered instruction to police officers on the social-psychological aspects of crisis management. He expressed his frustration at police officers' 'linear thinking ... Abstract thinking is not a strong point of traditional police officers. They're very concrete. And it's very interesting to just even watch their learning styles within classrooms or whatever it is. There's a real need to completely tailor information in the teaching ... It's critical, absolutely critical.'

We observed that whenever a police officer encountered something new, the first question asked was whether a form was available to cover it. In one case, a patrol officer was asked to notify a family of the death of a relative. His immediate response was, 'I've never done one of these, is there a form I'm supposed to fill out?' The form is *the* prospective means of working towards certainty and closure, providing the basis for taking action and at the same time accounting for the action taken. A police officer commented, 'It doesn't take too long before you know what has to be there and what doesn't. Of course, they don't have to tell you every day.' Another police officer observed that 'The mandatory fields are there and you are kind of prompted, whereas if you have the old traditional notebook and are asking some questions and there are two or three other people all giving their points of view at the same time, it's chaotic, so you don't think to get all of this information.'

The way in which classifications help to effect closure is illustrated by the example of a police organization that built Statistics Canada scoring requirements into its communication formats. If a category to be scored is built into the communication format, police officers know the preferred institutional meanings that have to be communicated, and these in turn affect how they approach the case. When it came to reporting how a crime was solved, Statistics Canada said that the 'cleared otherwise' option should be scored only in cases where an arrest had been made and charges could have been laid but were not. According to a police supervisor, building this requirement into the communication format meant that officers took it into account simply because

> they feel they have to. The block is there ... Most members never understood scoring before. Like, why did the supervisor want to know if you had enough evidence to take it to court? Well, he wanted to 'clear it otherwise,' and it is a prerequisite of scoring 'cleared otherwise' for Statistics Canada. And members know that now and are starting to put it down and justify it. They start to think, 'Well, if I want to clear this, at least I have to have enough evidence. I'm not going to charge him but at least I have to have enough evidence to go to court so maybe I will take a statement from the young fellow about ripping-off his mother.'

Effecting closure and certainty becomes simply a matter of completing whatever administrative knowledge requirement is demanded by the communication format. A year after we completed our field research, a police officer working in the forms unit of her police organization called one of the researchers to ask about our progress. The researcher answered that a report would be available in a year or so and offered the caller a copy of a preliminary article that addressed some of the issues (Ericson 1994a). It was immediately evident that the officer was not in the least interested. She said that she had been given the organization's file on the research, noted that a report was supposed to be forthcoming, and needed to record the date for the submission of the report. When the researcher asked who the research report should be submitted to, the police officer hesitated. The researcher then suggested that the recipient could be the person in charge of information systems, who had helped with the research. The officer replied that this person had left the police organization. When asked where he had gone, she answered, 'I think to another part of government. Frankly I don't care. As long as I don't have to report to him I don't care where he is.' She reiterated that she only needed a projected date for submission of the research report that she could enter in her file, and added that the report could be sent to the new head of information systems.

Resistance

The fact that communication formats are scientized to effect closure and certainty does not mean that they are always fully understood and accepted by the police officers who use them. In spite of tight formatting and editorial control by supervisors, there are problems in the use of communication formats, including resistance by police officers.

Health and Welfare Canada introduced a new family violence form that was supposed to be completed by police officers for each family violence incident they encountered, regardless of outcome (see pp. 246–7). Police officers resisted this mandatory reporting requirement on a number of grounds. For one thing, it placed an additional paper burden on officers, who did not appreciate how the knowledge they were producing for external agencies might be useful to them. An officer working in the policy and planning division of his organization observed that 'There was some backlash because guys were saying, "Don't tell me how to write an assault case, I know how to," without perhaps the understanding of why [Health and Welfare Canada] might want a dollar figure for how much damage you saw when you were there, how many children were in the house, how many other times you've been at the house.'

The family violence form was also seen as intruding on police officers' discretion because it required them to account for any decisions not to lay a charge. As such, the form was an externally driven surveillance technology based on an outlook of distrust. As the administrative head of a police station remarked, 'Before, the guys had discretion. Then they weren't accountable to anybody. We trusted their judgment. Now what we're saying is we don't trust your judgment because, if you're not laying a charge, according to policy, we want to know why. "Do you think I'm going to fill out that sheet? No! You're not trusting me" ... and taking away discretion ... [Thus] we don't get as many of these reports as we should.'

Another police station administrator said that in his district resistance was effected by construing violent incidents as nonviolent, thereby avoiding having to complete the family violence form and possibly other paperwork if a criminal charge was advised by a supervisor:

> With domestics [it] used to be, 'Go, advise – want to lay charges? No? OK, fine.' Now they go and there's a booklet of information to give them, and a family violence report, and put it on your computer terminal, and you'll be plagued to death if you don't have that family violence report in, and then, especially, you better lay charges. So they know they're going to get a ton of paperwork at each call. What is really happening at the calls is debatable. Again, you wonder if the officer's interpretation of everything isn't kind of, he's trying to taint it the other way, like, 'That's not so bad, so they really didn't complain about violence' – you know, because of what's required and all ... They know that the great majority of statistics are not for our service's use at all. It's a number-one problem. Number two, they know that the majority of the charges they book... in our district ... almost 50 per cent of those charges are gone [not proceeded with] ... Their perception now [is], 'Why should I do this?' ... With the *Stinchcombe* ruling and everything, that paperwork has escalated ... the cost now is just incredible ... They perceive that a lot of their discretion has been taken away from them, and in essence it has.

Some patrol officers answer the question, 'Why should I do this?,' by deciding not to do it. A patrol officer we accompanied on a ride-along said that he simply refused to submit the family violence form:

> I don't fill it out. It is just a waste of time. That's a good example of some outside

agency placing demands on the police for information. All of those statistics are available from other places. Why should they want the police to fill out another special form? ... So I'm not going to just go around laying charges if they are not going to be proceeded on or if there is no chance of conviction. And that is what they are trying to do to us. We have to justify when we don't lay charges ... so I just don't fill out the form. Now if I was going to lose my job over it, sure I'd fill out the form. But until then I don't see the need to fill it out.

Supervisors and administrators said that they had continuing problems with police officers who failed to submit reports according to format. An administrator responsible for brokering police knowledge of risk to external institutions said that she dealt with such problems as a routine part of her work. Inadequate reports were returned to officers daily, 'And I would say daily I get various obscene little notes sent back to me.' At one juncture a senior officer became upset with the extent to which administrative clerks were correcting occurrence report errors and omissions, and ordered that all such reports should be sent back to the officers themselves for correction. But approximately 70 per cent of reports had to be sent back, which impeded the efficiency of the knowledge system to the point where 'it's like you grind to a halt.'

Another response to resistance, and to the concomitant need to be more efficient in risk knowledge production, is the revision of communication formats. Revision is complicated because it must be negotiated with the external institutions that require knowledge of risk to be formatted in their terms. Moreover, changes to classifications that reduce the resistance of officers may also create inefficiencies because the knowledge resulting from the streamlined format is of little use. A police interviewee described one such effort at format reduction as being motivated by the fact that officers 'were getting bogged down filling out the whole form, so they just shortened it.' In his view the resultant 'information being entered into the system ... [is] garbage information. It can't really be used.'

The revision of communication formats is increasingly influenced by the use of computers and other communication technologies in policework. We now turn to an analysis of how these technologies form part of the knowledge risk management system maintained by the police.

16

Communication Technologies

Despite the pervasiveness of communication technologies in policing, there is little academic research on the subject. Manning (1992a: 373; see also Manning 1992b) concludes a recent review article on police and information technology by stating that 'It is not possible to evaluate interactions between technology and social organization and practices because little has been written about the practices, constraints, and opportunities associated with the use of new information technologies.'

In this chapter we rectify the lacuna in the literature by analysing the ways in which communication technologies relate to police organization and action. We initially consider how communication technologies are conceived of as *the* solution to police problems, especially problems of knowledge management. We then examine how communication technologies alter regulatory regimes within police organizations by framing how police officers think and act and by creating the possibility of routine surveillance of police activities. The surveillance capacity of communication technologies intensifies the administrative urge to risk-manage almost every conceivable aspect of police officers' lives. It constitutes the population of police in biopower terms, governing their work activity, competence levels, health, and security. Communication technologies also radically alter the structure of police organization by levelling hierarchies, blurring traditional divisions of labour, dispersing supervisory capacities, and limiting individual discretion. In the process, traditional rank structures of command and control are displaced by system surveillance mechanisms for regulating police conduct.

We also examine the problems involved in trying to introduce new communication technologies. Our analysis reveals that communication technologies have negative effects, leading to resistance by police officers and to the amplification of inefficiencies, including an acceleration of paper burden growth. The very success of communication technologies in creating useful knowledge of risk means that paper continues to weigh heavily.

Technological Solutions

While all large-scale organizations must stay abreast of computer technologies, the police have been among the leaders in technological adaptation and development. The proprietor of a computer systems company said that 'I really see the police as being way out ahead of business in these areas. They were using information systems in the early 1970s that business firms did not have for years later ... My background is in business ... I worked with large banks and brokers. I firmly believe that the police have been way out ahead in some of these areas.'

The police infuse their organizations with sophisticated electronic technologies and telecommunications infrastructures, and search constantly for improved computer-based solutions. Larger police organizations have full-time staff in the business of finding new computer solutions to meet changing needs. At the time of our research a municipal police organization had a plan to invest $35 million in a new computerized information system. Several police organizations were experimenting with ways to make the police vehicle a 'mobile office' that would allow officers to spend more time on the street, even if only to do their paperwork there rather than in the police station. For example, some jurisdictions were experimenting with having police officers use laptop computers for direct entry of occurrence reports and other field reports. A computer expert informed us that the RCMP was considering this new mode of electronic connection for its officers, and estimated that the cost of implementing it for all detachments across the country would be between $250 million and $360 million.

Police organizations buy computer technology for several reasons. They see it as the most obvious way of addressing the difficulties and desperation they encounter in making a discernable impact on the paper burden. They believe it will help them produce knowledge of risk more efficiently, in face of expanding demands from external institutions. They appreciate that some of this efficiency is accomplished through the capacity of computer technology to conduct surveillance on the knowledge production activities of police officers. Computers are also embraced because they offer a sense of organizational security. Security stems from their ability to structure knowledge within predictable, apparently fact-based formats, and to transmit this knowledge rapidly to members of the organization in various locations. Computers are a source of organizational legitimacy. They symbolize the competence of organizations, an attribute that is associated with the values of rational coordination and efficiency (Altheide 1995: chap. 2).

A police communication technology specialist said that in her experience computer technology is embraced because it is important to be seen to be embracing it. How else can one appear progressive? 'You almost design through [the latest computer] magazines to be able to stay ahead. Technology is changing that fast.' She said that this outlook is entwined with the view that the latest communication technology is one more thing to throw at organizational 'fires' in the hope that they at least will be damped. By this she meant that communication technologies are adopted to deal with particular crises because they are an incarnation of legitimacy in our culture and therefore seem to be an obvious solution to a crisis: 'One of the problems with this whole thing is the chicken or the egg – technology or corporate plan re information flow. It's very difficult, and we're seeing it more and more, to take technology and apply it to policework unless you have a first run at the information flow ... You just can't take technology and throw it into the mixing bowl and have something come out. There has to be corporate planning.'

Many technological innovations are a result of deliberations about the existing knowledge system and how it can be made more efficient. Consideration of several recent technological innovations in policework indicates that communication technologies solve some problems even as they create others.

Computer-Aided Dispatch (CAD) systems are now commonplace in policework. These systems include a computer terminal in police vehicles that allows dispatch messages and other centralized communications to be transmitted on screens rather than by voice radio. The terminal also allows officers to communicate interactively with each other without using the radio system and to run information-system checks on vehicles and people without going through the dispatcher.

We found that CAD terminals were seen by police officers to have many benefits. The terminals were used frequently during routine patrols to run checks on licence plates to learn whether there were irregularities in the registration and insurance of vehicles. Licence plate checks were also used to identify vehicle owners so their names could be run through the CPIC system for information on criminal history, outstanding warrants, and so on. Such checks were executed rapidly and efficiently compared to the former system whereby each check request had been radioed to the dispatcher, who would run the check and then report back to the officer (Jorgensen 1981; Ericson 1982). CAD terminals were also used by officers to communicate with each other without having to worry about their conversations being intercepted by journalists or others using scanner radios (Ericson, Baranek, and Chan 1987). As such, the terminals were often used as toys to communicate jokes, the names of places to meet for coffee, gossip, and other aspects of occupational culture. They were also used to run random checks on unsuspecting people, a task that helped to relieve boredom. At the same time, CAD terminals enhanced the capacity of administrators to risk-profile police officers regarding, for example, their times in and out of the vehicle and the volume and nature of the information-system checks they ran.

We also spent time observing patrol officers in jurisdictions that were using laptop computers. These computers incorporated the aforementioned features of CAD terminals but had a number of other features that made them acceptable to most of the police officers we studied. The main feature was that the general occurrence report could be completed electronically in the field. This feature facilitated entry of the final report at the point of interviewing the people involved, completing the remainder of the report while still in the field, and immediate electronic transmission of it to supervisors. Reports could therefore be created closer in time to the events being reported, and thus there was the potential for an improvement in quality. Disseminating reports to other members of the organization and to external institutions could also potentially be done more rapidly. Of particular importance was the fact that the laptop reporting system was part of an effort to move towards 'paperlessness.' In one jurisdiction we examined, minor occurrences were recorded only in electronic form, and such reports amounted to 47 per cent of all general occurrence reports.

The laptop computer also facilitated the production of other reports. For example, it allowed CPIC reports to be provided by copying information already entered in the main occurrence report. It facilitated the routine production of contact card surveillance reports on suspects questioned during street checks. It allowed victims to immediately be given the occurrence report identification number, thus eliminating the previous practice of having to telephone them later or report the number to the victim's insurance company. Last but not least, it incorporated an element of reflexivity, for officers had the capacity to instantly send messages about problems in using the system back to the information system designers. This capacity to talk back to the system was seen as especially significant in gaining the consent of officers to this technological innovation. Many said that it was the first time they had even been consulted about an innovation of any type in their organization.

Another police organization we looked at was introducing a voice-entry occurrence report system. All patrol officers were to be issued portable cellular telephones to call in their reports to clerks specially trained in the required reporting formats. The electronics were developed in conjunction with a new occurrence report format that was more tightly classified than the old one. Tight classification was designed to reduce narrative capacity, to overcome the problem of missing information, and to provide 'automatic' scoring of data for immediate entry in other risk analysis systems. The voice-entry system was also designed to involve one basic data input for multiple users, who could each take off the basic classified knowledge they required. Because police officers would be relieved of the mechanics of form-filling, the designers believed that there would be a marked improvement in the quality of reports, an increase in the quantity of data produced, and greater efficiency overall.

Police organizations are constantly developing new technologies for moving knowledge internally and externally. Police units that are required to produce specialized knowledge of risk for internal purposes adopt new computer technologies and formats that allow them to be more efficient. A police manager responsible for risk-profiling bombs and bomb threats described a new computerized system for producing and transmitting data in a 'paperless' format by saying that 'We'll just have this on a CPIC, and a revised format, so that the bomb tech, when he comes in, afterwards he sits down [at] the computer, fills in the various blanks, it's flashed to us electronically, and then we can take it out of our electronic mailbox, electronically flash all the same information out to all the bomb techs, and then take it electronically and dump it into our databank.'

The police also seek to design computerized reporting formats that are interchangeable, so that data produced for one report can be copied automatically and used for other reports. This method, referred to as 'distribution processing,' can take knowledge, including narratives, from one report and insert it into related reports and files. It also allows authorized persons in one part of a police organization to query the databases of units in other locations.

Police organizations are also working on their telecommunications infrastructures and knowledge systems to achieve better interorganizational communications. In many cases this task is made difficult because of the high cost of harmonizing incompatible telecommunication systems. Moreover, police officers resist this form of integration because of a belief that amalgamated communication technologies ultimately entail amalgamated police organizations, in that communications amalgamation breaks down both territorial and formal organizational boundaries. In one province, small-town police organizations were resisting a request from the provincial attorney general that they open their databanks to the RCMP, because the RCMP was not required to reciprocate. An information system expert described a case in which his police organization was developing improved electronic connections among its own police stations and units, but had failed to convince a large municipal police organization in the region to join the new electronic system: 'We've already got a communication line that runs into [one of our police stations]. It wouldn't be very costly to run a line all the way down to [the large municipal organization] ... using the same database. They're dealing with the same types of criminal element, they got access to the rest of Canada. It's a real system. Why didn't they go that way? Probably because they wanted their own system, their own control.'

There are, however, examples of substantial integration of telecommunication and knowledge systems across police organizations. One region we studied had a system-integration project that involved twenty-three police organizations and several external institutions such as the department of motor vehicles, the courts, and the correctional services.

Internal and external technological innovations are designed to enhance police data-matching capacities. The manual of one police organization defined data-matching as 'the collecting and comparing of personal information that has been obtained from a variety of sources by electronic means, i.e. by computer modem or an interface between computer systems, for the purpose of making a decision about the person to whom the data pertains.' Data-matching is built into knowledge systems, so that in the routine movement of knowledge between the police and other institutions an electronic panoptic sorting takes place. This process is both automatic and invisible. A police interviewee involved in data-matching with government consumer and corporate regulators said that 'Our relationship is so smooth I can't say that our accounting practices are that visible ... It has been in place for years. There is a *system* of reporting that we never see.'

Police System Surveillance

Supervisory Formats

In the very process of using communication technologies to accomplish their work, police officers are subject to the surveillance capacities of those technologies, which are able to monitor and risk-profile officer conduct in greater detail than human supervisors can. As we argue in a later section (pp. 406–12), the supervisory formats of communication technologies alter the police hierarchy of supervision and make some traditional supervisory functions redundant.

Communication technologies are designed to compel police officers to use them. When basic occurrence reporting is built into the communication technology, the police officer simply cannot do his or her work without using the technology. Communication technology accentuates the fact that paperwork *is* the work and cannot be avoided (Altheide 1995: chap. 2). Resistance, such as that described in relation to the family violence form (pp. 385–7), becomes increasingly difficult and sometimes impossible.

In a police organization that was introducing a voice-entry reporting system, police officers who failed to file reports properly were subject to immediate demands for correction. Any errors or omissions were registered immediately, sent back to the officer electronically, and remained on his or her screen until corrected. A police interviewee outlined the disciplinary dimensions of this mechanism:

> If the officer does not give us information that is mandatory, the person that's doing the data entry will press a button which will create an error message for the constable on the street. When he comes into work, he signs onto the system, he will have either nothing or he'll have twenty or thirty messages of errors that he created when he submitted his [report] ... He is going to have to be accountable to ensure that the errors are corrected, otherwise they will continue to come up on his screen under his regimental number ... It'll be right on his car, his CAD terminal.

As this example suggests, communication technologies are also designed to compel quality in knowledge work. They force the officer to produce knowledge that is complete, reliable, and valid according to the data expectations of the system itself. This supervisory quality-control is largely accomplished by way of the formatting of forms (see chap. 15) within computer logic. The fit between computer logic and communication formats is based on three features of how computers must be used. According to Altheide (1995: 39),

> *Determinate connectedness of procedures* refers to the integration of steps that must be followed to achieve an outcome. Shortcuts are not easily arranged within computer logic. Moreover, what is done at one point in the procedure will have implications for what is to follow. *Serial progression* means that step 7 cannot be achieved without first passing steps 1–6. *Constant form* refers to the orderly execution of procedures and the objective appearance of displays and output; combinations of bivariate switches are set in motion.

A police supervisor observed that under his organization's former paper-based system an officer 'may [have] forget[ten] to fill one box out and it [was] the job of their supervisor to catch that. Now, with some of these computer programs there are provisions to ensure that the officer acknowledges all the specific boxes or he or she cannot go on.' In a police organization that was implementing a new computerized reporting system, officers said that previously they had had the tacit approval of their supervisors to not always complete all of the forms officially required. However, the compulsory nature of computerized reporting formats meant that such avoidance of paperwork was no longer possible. If they chose not to enter certain pieces of the data the system either would not let them proceed or it would 'publish' the fact that there were omissions. At times the system would activate both strategies.

Walking the beat is now a matter of 'walking' through the reporting process with a keyboard rather than nightstick in hand. The necessary classifications are all there. Every keystroke on the keyboard types or classifies the population policed for institutional risk management purposes. The mind-set to which this gives rise was described by a number of police officers who had recently been introduced to a new computerized system for reporting occurrences:

> When you tab through the screen it tabs to each individual block and it makes you just a little bit more aware [that] that block is there. It just triggers something in your mind.

You can fill in the blanks. Some of these just jump out and hit you over the head. It makes you conscious of it ... there are so many blanks, so let's fill them in.

[It is] basically idiot-proof. It tells you everything you have to do. If you punch in the wrong numbers, the wrong question, or the wrong answer, you just *can't* frig it up.

There are pick-lists in there, so you can get very specific and use the proper ... codes that are there and required, as opposed to throwing just any old thing in. So it's more efficient that way, less room for error.

Now you make the effort to fill in all the blocks; before, when you were doing the paper, you were doing as little as you could.

[It] forms exactly what is needed. It's *making* you get all the necessary details ... you *have to* report it.

In addition to compelling the production of better-quality reports, computer technology provides precise calibrations of the quantity of knowledge produced. In being used to produce knowledge of risk for other institutions, computer technology simultaneously registers and profiles the knowledge production of its users. As such it is an important vehicle for policing the police. It disciplines in the Foucauldian sense of producing docile and useful workers without the need for direct supervisory intervention (Foucault 1977).

The computer terminal in the patrol car serves as a time-and-motion study that never ends. A police communications unit specialist described the surveillance capacities of the CAD system used by his organization: 'The CAD system then creates and starts a unit history for that car and for those personnel for that time period ... Build this chronological record of the officer until he books off ... All of the calls ... Your status changes and relative scene and clearing ... If you go for coffee, if you go for a follow-up, no matter what you're doing and when you do so.' An officer in another police organization was more succinct about the supervisory capacity of the computerized dispatch system: 'Every time you fart this system records it.'

The centralized communication systems of police organizations monitor officers' movements in other ways. In many police organizations all telephone and radio conversations are recorded. In one police organization we studied, the officers' activities in the patrol car were monitored by a computer system and their time in the office was monitored by another reporting system. Officers who spent more than the average amount of time in the office were summoned by their supervisors to account for their deviance.

Computer technology increases some kinds of work activity, and this activity in turn spawns additional knowledge about what police officers are doing. For example, the introduction of laptop computers in one jurisdiction increased the number of street checks carried out and contact cards produced. This additional knowledge production then increased the surveillance to which officers were subject, not only with respect to their level of knowledge production but also with respect to knowledge about the areas where they were concentrating their patrol efforts.

The new technologies are also able to register all acts of data entry. Telecommunications systems employ audit trails that measure, for example, the use of telephones, radios, and computers. Each computer keystroke can be counted. For the patrol officer this might mean there is a record of the number of CPIC checks he or she has undertaken on a shift. For the data entry clerk this might mean surveillance by way of a keystroke-per-minute count to ascertain whether he or she is keeping up with production norms. An administrative supervisor said that in his view data entry staff were the most scrutinized members of the police organization: 'I know, to the minute, how much work these guys produce – to the minute. I don't know anybody or anywhere else in the department [where this is the case], whether they go by quota systems or no quota systems.'

These practices of calibrating knowledge production give the police the sense that they are being disciplined by technologies. A police officer working on policy said that '*Everything's* documented, so it seems like there's more discipline ... [We are] documented *for* discipline.' Our interviewees used the police officer's traditional military language to describe how they felt structured by communication technologies. For example, they said that they were more 'regimented' by computer technology than by the supervision of officers of higher rank. The sense of regimentation was reinforced in some police organizations that regulated access to databanks according to rank and specialization. The computer access-code was the officer's regimental or official number.

When an officer is permitted to access a data system he faces other procedural restrictions. For example, police officers entering the CPIC system do so on a read-only basis. CPIC data entry and alteration are strictly controlled by a section of the RCMP in Ottawa. In other criminal record systems, police officers enter the initial data, but cannot make changes without central authorization. Thus, if an accused's status changes from 'charged' to 'convicted,' the change has to be made by specially authorized staff.

As we discuss at greater length later in this chapter, in the section entitled 'Dispersing Hierarchy,' no one escapes the supervisory formats of communication technologies. The supervisors themselves are supervised. In a police organization that introduced new computer technology into patrol cars for direct entry of occurrence reports, supervisors said that they themselves felt compelled to produce more and better knowledge. In the words of one police supervisor,

> The information quality that is going on [the system] now is much better than it was. If the block is there, people are being told to fill them out – fill out every possible block that you can. Whereas if you were writing it up it's one more block that you have to fill in by hand and it just wasn't being done all the time. The quality of information that's going on is being monitored more closely. When I do a file on there I'll check the details and if it's not adequate I'll send it back to the member and ask him to fix it up. Whereas if he wrote it on a handwritten form I have a tendency to overlook it more.

In addition to the regulation of production norms, communication technologies allow for the detection of police officers who stray from procedural requirements. Among other things, computerized knowledge systems are used to trace and audit the issuance of traffic summonses. One jurisdiction had a system for monitoring the traffic-tag books given to officers. This was done to ensure that all the summonses written up were actually issued to violators, rather than being destroyed by officers. Under the traffic-tag audit system officers were required to use a special format to report any irregularities. In such situations their instructions included the following statement: 'The tags mentioned above were signed out under your name. The original copies of these tags have not been received by the Traffic Tag Accounting Office. Forward the Traffic Tags to my attention immediately. If you are unable to locate some, submit a Departmental Report for auditing purposes.' The same police organization also had a 'courtesy ticket' that was issued to traffic violators who were being warned rather than charged. Officers were required to indicate the reason for their decision not to issue a summons. This requirement facilitated not only further profiling of the violator but also surveillance of the officer's exercise of discretion. For example, the police copy of the courtesy ticket contained the reminder that 'A copy of this ticket will be placed on file to trace residents of the City who may be illegally using out-of-province licence plates. Should this ticket be issued for this purpose only, it will be so indicated.'

Computer technology also permits the creation of data-matching systems to police the police. One of the police organizations we researched was having difficulty with officers who were seeking illegitimate double payments for their informants. The officers would submit a claim through regular police channels for payment of informants, and then encourage their informants to repeat their information to Crime Stoppers in exchange for an additional cash payment. Crime Stoppers, of course, would not be told that the police had already received the information. As an investigative unit supervisor told us, this practice led his organization to begin matching data on informant payments from the two sources:

> We're always careful that we're not getting burnt by our own people – in other words, we're not having detectives who might be going to the superintendent and saying one hundred dollars for informant 178, and then having this informant come through Crime Stoppers and give the same information. So there's a process built into our reporting system that we get a tip and we pull that report, we get an indication that the informant might be paid and that keys us to go up and check the nature of the information against what we got from the Crime Stoppers tips, just to make sure that the detective isn't making sure his man or girl gets a lot of money. Crime Stoppers might have five hundred dollars, and if the detective gets information, pays for it, [he also] gets another five out of the separate system.

Officer misuse of the electronic communication system is itself subject to surveillance. In one instance, the information security branch of a large urban police organization created a software-piracy unit that was designed to ensure that the organization's members were all using legally sanctioned software and therefore were not in violation of copyright law. This unit was established because the problem of software piracy was widespread in the organization and underpinned by what one interviewee called a 'Who cares?' attitude among police.

The fact that communication technology serves supervisory functions does not mean that it inevitably is constraining. The use of communication technology to produce and analyse data allows creativity and innovation as well as regulation and discipline. A commercial crime unit of an urban police organization decided to use detectives rather than civilian clerical staff to enter routine case investigation data. This decision was justified on the grounds that entering data helps detectives think creatively about classifications and patterns of evidence, which in turn fosters novel discoveries. As a unit supervisor explained:

> All of a sudden you come on one [fraudulent document] that has different information on it and ... it opens up a whole new avenue of investigation for the fellow. He knows what he's looking for in the case. By examining every cheque that he's putting in on the computer he is more aware of the information that he needs, that he wants; if something peculiar comes along, he's ready to grab it. Plus it helps him to organize his exhibits, gives him more-intimate knowledge of the case ... If they hadn't done that themselves, they wouldn't be that familiar with the file, they would lose some of that working knowledge.

The creative process is even more evident in major investigations that involve full-time communication technology experts working with the police to develop novel classifications and analyses as a case proceeds. The new communication programs and formats in turn prove useful in subsequent investigations of the same type. One police organization we studied had an 'Automatic Reporting Information System' that flagged whether the organization already had a computer program to handle a particular knowledge production need.

Police Populations

The police are routinely measured and sorted in terms of their capacities as human resources. This risk profiling makes them into members of police populations that embrace a variety of performance ratings and career potentials. In this section we consider four main risk profiling mechanisms through which police populations are constituted: employment screening, competence rating, work activity reporting, and occupational health and safety monitoring.

People seeking employment in police organizations must submit to a number of screening technologies. For the prospective police officer there is a lengthy interview process involving several sessions and different technologies. One police organization had an intensive screening process that delved into nearly every aspect of the applicant's background: associates, relatives, neighbours, residences past and present;

military service, education, reputation, loyalty, local police record, credit status, driving history, and criminal and security history. This process was repeated on a lesser scale with up to five friends and associates of the applicant. Applicants who survived this panoptic sorting and went on to be hired were given the security classification 'reliable,' which was reviewed every five years, or whenever an upgrade in classification was required. Upgrades included 'enhanced reliability' and 'clearance' ('confidential,' 'secret,' 'top secret,' and 'special activity').

Many police organizations use lie detectors in employment screening. A police organization we studied subjected all new recruits to this 'ordeal' (Nock 1993). Selected civilian employees, such as those responsible for the safe keeping of drugs or for wire-tap interceptions, were also given lie detector tests.

Auxiliary officers, volunteers, and temporary employees such as paid informants are also screened thoroughly. One of the police organizations we looked at assessed its auxiliaries-in-training for proper attitudes, comprehension of the training material, communication skills, ability to comply with instructions, initiative, 'potential,' and appearance in uniform and in civilian clothing. This, combined with criminal background checks, led to the production of a rating of how the auxiliary would uphold the 'prestige of the force.'

Police employees are continually subject to competence ratings. One force conducted regular audits of officers' competence, which included interviews. These audits focused on an officer's overall expertise and competence as a record-keeper. The organization wanted to know, for instance, 'Whether member has sufficient knowledge, expertise, and training to perform his/her job' and 'Are entries being made in notebook?'

Another police organization kept a 'noteworthy events' record on each officer, which included assessments of areas of competence and incompetence and overall career development. This record was very detailed, for example giving information on the officer's behaviour under the headings 'Date/time observed,' 'Observed behaviour above or below expected performance,' 'Supervisor's name and number,' and 'Member's initial.' It fed into related systems for risk-profiling careers, such as the 'Performance Management and Development Plan' for each police officer in the organization.

Career-risk management records of this type are linked with other information systems that indicate problems with police behaviour. For example, there are systems for recording and dealing with complaints against the police by the public (Goldsmith 1990; Landau 1994b). Information from these systems is incorporated into the career-risk management profiles of police officers. A police organization we studied had information systems for recording a number of indicators of possible police misbehaviour: vehicular accidents, 'service offences' (violations of internal regulations and the Police Act), and criminal offences during police service for which they had been pardoned. The form for criminal offences was designed to register the 'criminal' record of the officer even though all other records of the matter had been expunged. Thus the form included the instruction 'Do not reproduce this form,' and a requirement that the person submitting it sign a statement that 'To the best of my knowledge there are no documents left at this location [the investigator's unit] referring to the above-noted conviction.'

The rating of some police credentials is mandatory and continual. For example, competence in the use of firearms is required of all police officers, who are rated at regular intervals. One of our police organizations had a 'Revolver Classification Shoots' system that was described by an interviewee as 'an automated system to pick out the highest score, the average, break it down by subdivision, things like that, so they can kind of analyse where they need to do their training.'

Mandatory checking of credentials also occurs when one is transferred to specialized units or operations, which normally require the transferee to undergo additional screening or training, or both. One police organization conducted a training assessment of officers being assigned to general investigation detective work. Given the knowledge-based nature of this work (Ericson 1993), it is not surprising that all of the eight areas assessed were related to knowledge production and communication: evaluation of evidence; presentation of evidence; ability to interview complainants, witnesses, and suspects; ability to use information technologies; court case preparation; public relations; quality of police reports; and quality of notebook use. Another police organization had an elaborate screening and training process for officers being assigned to undercover investigations, including a profiling of an officer's personal background; police career record; motivation for undercover work; undercover experience; role-playing abilities; interpersonal skills in general and as background for blending into the target 'criminal milieu,' including his or her potential for adapting to the milieu's speech and jargon; types of drugs most suited to; and notetaking abilities.

Regardless of their assignment, police officers are subject to routine surveillance of their work. The regulation of time worked is itself a time-consuming and elaborate knowledge system activity. We researched a police organization that had forms and information systems that tracked shift time and payment for shift work, court time, overtime, and total hours worked over the course of a year, the latter system also noting overtime, irregularities in attendance, and so on.

Patrol officers must also submit reports on how they spend their shift time. These are usually monthly reports and are used to establish production quotas and to identify officers who are either overproducing or underproducing (Ericson 1982). In one police organization we studied, patrol officers were calibrated in terms of their monthly output in responding to alarms, on-view calls, on-zone calls, and off-zone calls; issuing appearance notices, warning tags, traffic tags, subpoenas, warrants, and check-up slips; making arrests; laying charges; conducting accident investigations; conducting follow-up investigations; attending community engagements; and writing reports.

Similar activity reports are required of officers in specialized units, with the form being tailored to the particular tasks deemed important to the unit in question. While some of these reports are as detailed as those required of patrol officers, others are more open. One organization, taking into account the fact that detectives are given a great deal of autonomy and may produce little in the way of tangible results in the short term (Ericson 1993), constructed an activity report for its general investigation detectives that employed an open format. The detectives were asked simply to list up to five 'Investigations/Assignments: Include Name of Persons Charged or Suspected,' as well as 'General Duties: Meetings, Reports, Courts, etc.' A form in the same organization for tracking the activities of crime prevention and police-community relations officers was similarly open, although it was designed to check matters of importance in these areas of policing, such as the officer's clothing (working uniform, dress uniform, civilian clothing), the officer's audience (size, characteristics), whether the event being reported on was police-initiated or requested by an outside group, and news media coverage.

Since policework is knowledge work, a lot of the work activity reported on pertains to knowledge production and the use of communication technologies. The organized crime unit in one police organization was required to report on the technologies it used, for example surveillance vehicles, radios, binoculars, polaroid cameras, 35 mm cameras, lenses, trackers, body packs, receivers, earpieces, and tape recorders. Members also had to report on hours spent on specific knowledge tasks, including direct surveillance, watching video screens, making computer-assisted inquiries, operating radios, serving as cover-team members, preparing search warrants, conducting interviews of applicants for municipal licences, conducting 'vice street-counts' (monitoring prostitutes), making general inquires, conducting street checks, meeting with informants, preparing cases, writing reports, and performing general office duties.

The administrative unit for the detective division of the same police organization was required to report on the most mundane features of its knowledge work. Day in and day out its members measured their occupational selves in terms of the number and nature of telephone calls, tapes transcribed, pages typed, front-counter enquiries handled, messages written, pager calls taken, and general office duties performed.

When such routine reporting on police activities does not provide enough detail about what employees are doing, time-and-motion studies are conducted. A police officer we observed and interviewed complained about being 'studied to death.' He had participated in a time-and-motion study whose questionnaire, which had to be completed for each shift, took two hours to complete. He said that in frustration some officers added a new classification to the questionnaire which indicated the time it took them to complete it. The regressive reality of a job that requires knowledge work about knowledge work was not lost on this officer.

Police officers also have their careers monitored and profiled in terms of occupational health and safety. Large police organizations have specialized accident investigation and prevention branches for vehicular accidents involving their own members. The accident prevention branch of a municipal police organization operated under the following mandate: 'Reviews and verifies all police vehicle accidents, compensation injuries, and claims to the City Claims Department, coordinates Accident Appeal Board Meetings and notifies personnel of the Board's findings. Investigates safety concerns identified by field personnel, provides safety training for supervisors and ensures that senior management are kept informed of new safety legislation.'

Police vehicle accident reports are even more detailed than those prepared according to the formats provided by provincial motor vehicle branches (see pp. 210–11). In one police organization the report was five pages long. There was a particular focus on the officer's work habits and on his or her physical condition at the time of the accident – whether the officer was tired, the number of hours he or she had worked during the previous twenty-four hours, whether he or she was in uniform or civilian clothing at the time of the accident, and so on. A check-list of causal factors related to the accident included twenty-two items, sixteen of which pertained to the officer.

Equally detailed profiles are created for any personal injuries sustained by police officers while on duty. In one police organization the 'Personal Injury Investigation Report' format was designed to analyse whether unsafe conditions or unsafe acts by police officers had been responsible for an injury. There was also an 'Exposure Report' for injuries sustained as a result of exposure to hazardous substances, smoke, blood, needles, noise, or extreme temperatures. Members were also required to file provincial workers' compensation reports.

In addition to having their accident and injury careers profiled, police officers must conform to biopower norms for healthy bodies. Membership in the population of police bodies is made compulsory by regular technological assessments of bodily shape and function. For example, one police organization had a 'Cardiac Health and Lifestyle Appraisal Report' system that risk-profiled officers' 'body composition,' 'aerobic fitness,' 'bicycle heart rate,' 'treadmill heart rate,' and so on. Officers who failed to meet the standard were directed to a section of the policy manual which read as follows:

> A minimum acceptable level will be the 40th percentile in four of the five parameters measured by CHALA. The parameter, Maximum Volume of Oxygen, must always measure at or above the 40th percentile to meet the minimum acceptable level. A probationary member who fails to meet the minimum acceptable level thirty days prior to completion of probation will be subject to dismissal.
>
> A member not on probation who fails to meet the minimum acceptable level during any one appraisal, will be retested within six (6) months and expected to meet the minimum acceptable level.
>
> A member not on probation who fails to meet the minimum acceptable level after the six-month extension will be issued with a departmental warning and given a further ninety (90) days to meet the minimum acceptable level.
>
> A member not on probation who again fails to meet the minimum acceptable level after his ninety (90) day extension, will be suspended without pay and given a further ninety (90) days to meet the minimum acceptable level. The testing will be conducted by an independent agency.
>
> Failure to meet the minimum acceptable level after being tested by an independent agency, will be grounds for dismissal.

Police organizations also require healthy minds. Accordingly, risk communication technologies are devised for imagining norms of police mental health. A police organization we examined had a detailed two-page guide for supervisors on employee stress. Police officers' stress levels were calibrated according to various 'cognitive,' 'interpersonal/affective,' 'at-work,' and 'physical' indicators. The physical indicators included, for example, 'over-eating' and 'poor posture.' Observations of signs of stress at work were to focus on, among other things, 'expression of pessimism, negativism or inappropriate elation,' 'deterioration in penmanship,' 'errors/omissions in statements or reports,' 'increase in risk-taking behaviours,' 'bragging about accomplishments at work,' and 'excess in all forms.'

Large police organizations also monitor and foster healthy minds by providing psychological services units staffed by full-time psychologists, though there is sometimes a considerable gulf between what the psychologists want to accomplish and what police officers are willing to participate in. This gulf stems from officers' knowledge that if they do bring their problems to the psychologists they may find their actions registered in the police career profiling system, with possible negative consequences. In one police organization, some officers avoided the psychological services unit and set up their own self-help groups, such as a chapter of Alcoholics Anonymous, in its place.

Dispersing Hierarchy

Through supervisory formats and police population construction, communication technologies alter the traditional police structure of command and control. New hierarchies of expertise are formed, including an enhanced place for computer specialists. At the same time, some existing hierarchies of supervision and accountability are deconstructed. Communication technologies blur the division of labour between police officers and their supervisors and among specialized units. The levelling of hierarchy and blurring of responsibilities do not mean that the individual police officer's discretion is enhanced. Discretion is curtailed, taken away from the individual officer and dispersed into the embedded knowledge systems – the supervisory formats and police population mechanisms – that provide routine surveillance of the police.

The levelling of hierarchy and blurring of the division of labour was evident in a police station we studied, where direct computer entry of occurrence reports had been introduced. Patrol officers, civilian clerical staff, and police supervisors all ended up doing each other's work, and some positions became redundant. Computerization of occurrence reporting turned patrol officers into data clerks, and made obsolete much of what the civilian clerical staff had done in the past. At the point of initial entry, the patrol officer classified knowledge, keyed it into the knowledge system, and scored it for later statistical analysis. Ironically, while computerization was justified to police officers as a tool for reducing the paper burden, it actually increased their knowledge workload because many of these functions had previously been performed by supervisors and clerical staff. This irony was not lost on patrol officers, whose collective sentiment was expressed by one officer as 'We shouldn't be doing what some girl should be doing.' Another patrol officer observed that officers were now 'stenos,' and clerks were their 'editors': 'Now we are the stenos, we are doing all the typing, we are putting all the information in. All she does is proofread it after it has been proofread twice before, and then she does her thing with it and puts it into the information retrieval system.' Meanwhile, a clerical staff member we interviewed worried about her job: 'Slow we've been before – this is downright dead.'

Some supervisory functions also were usurped by information technology. For example, the previous division of labour had included an officer who reviewed all reports after they had been completed by the patrol officer and the officer's supervisor. However, the new information technology had made this role nearly obsolete. Patrol supervisors also had their checking and data-scoring workload reduced because of the new supervisory formats made possible by information technology.

The clerical staff were allotted new responsibilities that gave them additional supervisory discretion. For example, they could now decide whether an occurrence was minor enough to remain 'paperless' or required a hard copy report and file. They also checked further on the work of patrol officers and supervisors, thus effecting an additional level of quality control. Meanwhile, supervisors bore some of the workload previously assigned to clerical staff, and had some new forms of clerical work thrust on them by the new system. For example, they were constantly comparing computer records and paper file records in those instances where both existed. Scoring functions were also duplicated when the two kinds of records were present. This situation gave new meaning to the 'civilianization' of police work, for patrol supervisors joined patrol officers in being civilianized in their work tasks.

In another police organization there was an effort to increase the telephone recording of occurrences without dispatching a patrol officer. In 1991, 21 per cent of all reports (39,917 of 192,000) were taken by communications section employees without dispatching a patrol officer. The clerical staff who took the reports worked within tight supervisory formats. An information system supervisor remarked that 'Because the girls are experienced coders they know the types of questions to ask to ensure that they're getting the proper information ... Basically what we [the coders] do is we go through this format and ask questions, which means filling in the blanks.' A communications unit supervisor observed that while telephone report taking was not new, it had increased greatly both in volume and in the types of complaints handled: 'The primary reason [for taking reports over the telephone has always been] ... to gather information quickly and get it on the national system, on the CPIC system. And then, through the years, whenever we get into resource crunches you found more ... routine types of offences where there is no particular benefit to be at the scene, we would take those by telephone ... [mentions thefts, break-and-enters, stolen vehicles, missing persons]. No suspects. No real information. Nothing to be gained by attending the scene.'

This organization also maintained a voicemail system for those times when operators were not available: 'You go into this voice-response unit and perhaps get routine answers or answers to routine questions that way and, in fact, not even involve interaction with a real live person. Those kinds of things, I think, they just get ... better ... You will still have situations where people are really in need and they really have to talk to somebody and they really need assistance. So I think the heart and soul won't change but maybe some of the more routine or less critical elements continue to be impacted by technology.'

Some police organizations we studied were considering the adoption of an American system for bridging the gap between, on the one hand, the virtual reality of communication technology reporting, and on the other, face-to-face contact with police officers when 'people are really in need and they really have to talk to somebody and they really need assistance.' An information system supervisor in a large urban police organization said that with this system

> The person calling the police will start to fill out the report over the telephone. They say what was stolen, et cetera, and the officer is dispatched to the scene. After the officer arrives at the scene he simply verifies the information ... We will start recording more and more information over the telephone ... If your crite-

rion is that a report is filled out for insurance purposes, that criterion is met. If it is for VISA or Mastercard, that criterion is met. They are currently talking about user-friendly reporting where the victim would fill out a form that they could then use for reporting to the insurance company.

These visions not only suggest that the police officer is increasingly subject to the supervisory formats of communication technology but also that communication technology itself is to become the police officer. This virtual reality is symbolized by police acronyms for communication technology. One police organization, for instance, dubbed its new computerized knowledge system 'CONSTABLE,' which stood for 'Centralized On-Line System to Achieve Better Law Enforcement.'

A police information system officer's imaginings extended to having instabank-like terminals in police stations and shopping malls. These terminals would have 'the exact same software as a police officer [employs], except that depending on who you are, you have access to certain things and other people don't ... The system automatically recognizes that, yes, you're the person and accepts that you're that person, or the system will print the whole thing out after you complete it, you bring it over to the clerk, he signs it, checks your identification, he signs that you've been there, and your job is done.'

The vision goes beyond having the officer as supervisor and clerk, the clerk as officer and supervisor, and the supervisor as officer and clerk. The communication technology itself is to form *part of* the constabulary, and the citizen as police knowledge worker is to be brought within its orbit as well. This vision is becoming reality, and it has enormous implications for the dispersal of hierarchy within the police organization and beyond. As in all other organizations now governed by communication technologies and knowledge systems,

The concentration of data and information is accomplished by the *dismantling* of hierarchically organized mega-bureaucracies and administrative apparatus based on the division of labour. The centralization of functions and information interpenetrates with *de*bureaucratization ... Irrespective of distances, the 'middle' level of bureaucratic organizations ... is fused together in direct interaction via video display terminals made possible by information technology. Numerous tasks of the welfare state and the state administration – but also of customer service, jobbing, and repair shops – can be transformed into a type of electronic self-service store, even if all this means is that the 'chaos of administration' is transmitted into objectified form by electronic means directly to the 'mature citizen.' In this case the person entitled to a service no longer interacts directly with an administrative official, customer adviser or the like, but rather chooses the desired treatment, service or authorization according to a procedure whose rules can be looked up electronically (Beck 1992a: 218–19).

Anyone who knows the operative communication rules, formats, and technologies can participate in the culture and social organization they give rise to. However, participants must also be aware that communication technologies not only format the reality of particular tasks but also put *the participants* into the surveillance system. System surveillance means that each person connected to the communication technology loses autonomy in decision making because his or her decision is immediately available to others to scrutinize and to keep on record for subsequent profiling. As such, no one person is the decision maker per se. A communication technology specialist made this point with reference to his previous employment as a police officer: 'A police officer on the street would never make a decision. They investigate everything, *every possible thing,* they investigate ... Everything has got to go to the next level, so it's *mistrust ... structured into it* ... They can't get anybody to make a decision, so it just gets recorded.'

In such a system, hierarchy and the division of labour are further complicated by the ascendant power of communication technology specialists. Status and influence are transferred away from those who claim traditional distinctions such as length of service, loyalty, rank, and public service, and onto those who demonstrate technical skills. Thus a deep division was created when a police organization started a new information systems branch in the 1980s by hiring a team of civilian technical specialists and cancelling its recruitment of new police officers for one year. In speaking to us several years after that decision was taken, the organization's officers still expressed their animosity toward it.

Information systems units have developed at some distance from policework 'on the ground,' and there remains a significant divide between communication technology specialists and street-level police officers. As an information systems branch administrator informed us, 'I largely talk with people in information systems. I don't talk with many police people ... There is a real distinction in the police culture between civilians and officers. I think one of the things that upsets the officers is that they are used to having the power. But here I don't have to defer to a police officer. I don't think they really like that. There is a real move in this force to civilianize those jobs where a sworn constable is not required.'

Another civilian communication technology specialist said that he had been employed by his police organization for nineteen years, but until the past year had never been 'Out in the field ... [encountering] policing. What I did realize, when you got out there, is that there's a real world out there. There's police out there and they're doing day-to-day work and it's something that we don't always look at in here. We come in here, work from nine to five, whatever it is, see how we can feed the machines downstairs, and then leave. And very little thought is given, from what I've seen in the past, to the actual policeman in the field, what he's doing, and his problems.'

This interviewee added that the strain is compounded when outside communication technology experts are used, because they leave the police organization 'holding the bag' after they have put a system in place.

Our data indicate that knowledge, power, authority, and hierarchy are being transformed in police organizations by the infusion of communication technologies. However, this transformation is neither unidirectional nor deterministic. The material technology of computers, cellular telephones, video, radio, and telecommunications infrastructures determines nothing. It does provide new technical means for sensing and representing the environment, which vary according to the specific communication formats they enable. However, it is only its particular uses within culturally specific interpretive frameworks and visions of social organization that result in cultural and social effects. As Beck (1992a: 216) observes, '[m]icroelectronics is introducing a stage of technological development which *refutes technically* the myth of technological determinism ... Computers and control devices are programmable ... One must know what type of social organization in its horizontal and vertical dimensions one *wants* in order to use the networking possibilities of electronic control and information technologies at all.'

Neither the communication technologies themselves, nor the cultural frameworks and visions that inform them, exist as structures for ordering the world independent of their uses. There is not first a world ordered by technology and culture and then communication about it. The world is constituted in the communication processes of its articulation and reception using whatever rules, formats, and technologies are at hand and deemed appropriate for the task. Things can always be different.

Police decisions to adopt new communication technologies are made with the realization that cultural and social organization is changing, but also with the intention of altering police organization and creating new cultures of policework. Their decisions do have the intended effects. They create knowledge systems in which it is difficult to decipher who is in control. They create new systems of rule in which orders to act and deference to hierarchical authority are replaced by more self-regulation according to the principle of efficiency. Concomitantly, they make the organization more transparent because so many knowledge system users can access its 'data points.' Although there is a hierarchy of controlled access, anyone with access can sense myriad components of the organization simply by sitting with the computer *command* key at one's fingertips and casting one's eyes at the *display* terminal. Back regions become front regions. Front regions merge into the communicative regions of other organizations. The regionalization of institutions is the result.

Police organizations try to use the discourse of community policing to create cultural coherence out of the dispersal of hierarchy. Community policing discourse is a way of enacting the external environment, preparing it for new forms of communications policing involving dispersed institutions of risk. But it is also a way of enabling the police organization to address internally the significant changes that are occurring in its communication rules, formats, and technologies. The academic literature depicts community policing as a response to problems with the 'professional' model of policing, including that model's emphasis on the relation between communication technology and professionalism (see, for example, Leighton 1991: 497). It claims that the community policing model is an important and necessary means to deconstruct the professional model, resulting in organizational changes such as delayering of the authority structure, geographical decentralization of management and resource deployment, and temporal decentralization. But the literature misses the crucial point that communication technology itself is the thing that permits the dispersal of police hierarchy, and of policing tasks more generally, into myriad microcentres of knowledge and power in risk society.

Problems and Resistance

Our analysis of police system surveillance shows that police employees, using communication technologies to see better and be more efficient, have a coterminous sense of being efficiently seen through. This fosters dis-ease, and is a significant reason for the strain between communication technology specialists and the police officers being introduced to their ways of seeing. It is also the basis for wider conflicts within police organizations and beyond because it triggers instant reflexivity with respect to who is conducting surveillance on whom and for what purposes. As Beck (1992a: 218) predicts,

> The microelectronics metamorphosis of the control structure will make the direction and monopolization of information flows a central problem ... [The organization will] become 'transparent' for the employees and interested environment. To the extent that the localization of production becomes worn and frayed, information becomes the central means that enables the connection and coherence of the production unit. Thus it becomes a key question who gets what information, by what means, and in what order, about whom and what, and for what purposes. It is not difficult to predict that in the organizational disputes of the future these power struggles over the distribution coefficient of information flows will become an important source of conflict.

We have documented how new communication technologies become structured into the working environment to the point where police officers are compelled to use them. However, compulsion does not mean that implementation is always straightforward and successful. Police officers actively resist some uses of communication technology. Many planned uses fail to materialize because of peculiarities in the working environment and the dehumanizing effects of communication technology. There are also unintended consequences of introducing new communication technology that create further inefficiencies.

In a police station we studied, the head of a patrol unit refused to participate in a project that involved direct computer entry of occurrence reports by patrol officers and the creation of 'paperless' files. He rejected training in the use of computers and would not allow a computer terminal to be installed in his office. As a result, his subordinates were required to print out the 'paperless' files for him to read and sign, and a specially assigned officer had to check that the paper files matched what was on the 'paperless' system. A patrol officer in the same police station began to use the new computer system but found it too difficult. He said that using the system was taking him longer than simply filling out forms by hand, and refused to use it any longer.

In another police organization there were many instances in which police officers resisted computer technology. During a ride-along a patrol officer was asked about the most significant changes he had seen over his twenty-year career. The conversation went as follows:

A: The technology. No doubt about it. The radios and computer systems have been a real boon.
Q: So I guess you use the police information management system fairly regularly?
A: Well, to speak the honest truth, I have been having some problems with my password for the past four months.
Q: So you have not been able to use the system for the past four months?
A: No.
Q: Doesn't that affect your work?
A: It hasn't really yet, but I have to get that sorted out.

An information systems manager in the same organization said that resistance or simple aversion were ongoing problems, but were about to be corrected by a technological solution: 'There are guys out there that I know for a fact that haven't logged on for two years, because we just put in a new payroll system and now they have to log on to put in their overtime, and I've seen guys in there that have not logged onto the system for over six hundred days! We keep track every time they log on ... [Our new system will correct this because] any errors that are discovered in the report, we're sending them an electronic mail message back to their user-base so they will have to log onto the computer every day.'

Complete refusal or failure to use computer technology is rare. More common are techniques to subtly resist some of its uses by police supervisors as a surveillance tool. For example, patrol officers collaborate with dispatchers to overcome computer-aided dispatch systems that record their whereabouts. The patrol officer enters the designation for a legitimate activity into the computer system, then calls the dispatcher by radio to let him or her know where he or she is actually going. If a supervisor uses the computer system to its full surveillance capacity, the avoidance can turn into subversion. A patrol officer commented during a ride-along that the computerized police information management system used by his organization was a problem because

Cops don't like surveillance. I guess it's like any other job. You don't like your boss looking over your shoulder ... Police officers are a resourceful bunch. A little bit of graphite into the keyboard ... will completely shut down this terminal.

Things like that might happen if you had a supervisor who was too gung-ho about knowing where you are all the time. Or let's say that you are going for a break. You type into the terminal that you are going for a break and don't send the message. That way if your supervisor is driving by and sees your car at the donut shop he might come in and ask why you didn't log off. You then say that you did log off and bring him out to the car and show him the message that will still be on the screen. You then tell him you sent it and the computer must not have taken it. Little things like that help you out.

Some systems are only partially effective, or eventually fail altogether. An effort to introduce a computerized direct entry occurrence reporting system was judged to be more efficient for the 60–70 per cent of cases concluded without further investigations, but not for the remaining cases when there was a major follow-up investigation or people were charged. In another police organization, there was an effort to make voice-radio communications among detectives secure. As a telecommunications specialist told us, 'When you have a voice-security system like that, one of the things that you have is a numerical key that has to be changed. We provided them with a very secure system and the key had to be changed on a weekly basis. One of the problems was that you had to plug in all of the radios being used on that system at the same time to change the keys. This was just too much for them to bother with, so they don't use the system.'

A police organization introduced a laptop computer system into one of its patrol divisions, but the system quickly failed. As soon as the system was in place the officers began to complain about several negative features of the technology. The computers were difficult to carry and use, especially on foot patrol. Many of the officers were not computer-literate, nor even good typists, and they were therefore reluctant to use the computers in interviews with complainants for fear of embarrassment. Officers had difficulty adjusting to the reporting format presented on the computer screen, and complaints continued despite efforts to make the format more like the printed forms they were used to.

Another police organization rejected the idea of introducing laptop computers for direct entry of occurrence reports. It was believed there would be too many of the aforementioned problems with implementation, and that the technology would be dehumanizing.

We found a pervasive concern among police officers about the dehumanizing effects of some of the communication technologies being used. For example, computer-aided dispatch terminals in patrol cars and the communication formats they employed were seen as too mechanical, to the point where patrol officers were made to feel that they themselves were little more than machines. A records system supervisor in one police organization complained, 'Those CAD terminals ... you're sitting there at three o'clock in the morning, all you have is this terminal to talk to ... There's no more human intervention ... too machine-oriented.' The planning unit of the same organization surveyed officers about the CAD system and 'found out people were lonely, basically. They are used to radio dispatch and now you just get a beep, beep, beep, beep on the car and the computer telling you what to do, and people were getting upset ... So they did change the dispatching methods somewhat to allow for more radio dispatching ... just trying to give the whole thing a more human face.' An interviewee in the organization's communications unit said that the CAD system's dehumanizing effects affected the quality of policework. Reality became that which appeared on the computer screen, and observations outside of that reality became distorted: 'I use the terminology "terminally oriented"; in other words, the officer becomes so engrossed in his machine that he stops his observation. He stops seeing what goes on around him and if it's not happening in the machine, then it's not happening because he's not seeing it. All he is seeing is the machine.'

Existing in a state of 'simulacra' (Baudrillard 1983), many police officers prefer the 'unreal' yet familiar world of the screen to the 'real' yet less familiar world of people and territories. Just as the television viewer recognizes the outside world through the familiar formats of television (Altheide and Snow 1991), so the police officer sees the territory policed through the extraterritorial yet familiar formats of his computer terminal.

A police organization introduced computers into patrol cars to permit direct entry of occurrence reports on the assumption that officers would no longer have to return to the office to complete their reports, meaning that they could spend more time on the street. However, many officers preferred to prepare their reports using computer terminals in the office and, according to office staff, actually spent more time than ever there. Ironically, the effect of the new technology was less visibility to and more distance from the public.

Police-public relations are inevitably affected by computer technology. An information technology specialist with extensive experience as a police officer said bluntly that computer terminals yield 'an impersonal approach to people. People don't mean anything.' People are seen merely as members of populations. Moreover, many police officers, like television viewers, clearly prefer the familiarity of sitting in front of their screens to the intense daily pressure of settings where ongoing face-to-face contact is demanded. A police organization we studied had a great deal of difficulty recruiting officers to serve in schools. When vacancies arose for a school position there were usually only two or three applicants among a police force of several hundred. At least some officers, it is possible, may have preferred being under CAD terminal surveillance to the prospect of being under surveillance by a large population at close quarters day in and day out.

A fundamental problem is that by the time a new information system is up and running it is inevitably seen as inefficient when compared to newer systems coming onto the market. On the other hand, once a familiar technology is in place there is a reluctance to change even in face of evidence that it is not the best available technology. This reluctance derives from the fact that employees like the technologies, formats, and rules they are familiar with, but also because there are many system users inside and outside the organization who have learned to routinize their relations through the existing information system arrangements (cf. Powell 1991).

In large police organizations internal competition over preferred information systems yields inefficiencies. One police organization we researched was simultaneously developing two expensive yet incompatible computerized reporting systems in two different divisions. In another police organization, incompatibility between the auto theft unit's computer system and the main police information management system meant that all auto theft data had to be entered twice.

There is also no guarantee that computerized systems can make information available more speedily. In a police organization that introduced new computer technology for direct entry of occurrence reports by police officers, information from the new system still had to be transferred to the existing computerized information retrieval system before it was available to other officers for reference. This process meant that basic case information actually took longer to reach other officers than under the former ledger-based system.

Inefficiencies in police information management were seen by officers and other police employees as an inevitable result of having to serve so many users from external risk institutions. Making the risk management systems of external institutions more efficient was done at the cost of inefficiency in police information systems. As the head of a police records unit observed, with computerization comes more work in the service of other institutions: 'You have to do everything every which way, to card and to query, to go in if you can't find something ... On the computer you [always have new] detail so you have to sit there and type in a whole paragraph of details ... Much more efficient for everybody outside, but it's a lot more work doing the entry.'

More Paper Burdens

The greatest inefficiency is the fact that computerization has in many respects amplified rather than diminished the paper burden. Amplification is the inevitable result of the ways in which communication technology fosters the production of more knowledge. The new knowledge so produced is often useful to the police, and more particularly to the various risk institutions they serve, but there is also a lot of knowledge that is of tangential or dubious value. Nevertheless, police organizations become more burdened with paper and more bureaucratized (for parallels in social security administration see Adler et al. 1991).

The administrative head of a police station observed that while police work has always been knowledge work, the communication processes involved in that work have changed dramatically. Computerization has not meant a shift away from print culture but the reverse. Although computerized communications are produced, carried, and stored electronically in order to create 'paperless' files, they have actually fostered an increase in printed communications:

> We've always had need for information. That's how we function, how we survive. But ... with the advent of the computer a lot that was just spoken words is now printed word or the terminal word ... We worked on the street. When I was a constable on the street, you'd get a radio-call and that's how you responded. If you had a parade before the shift, you got a certain amount of information. Now the information is all sitting on the terminal and you're expected to punch it up and check into it. You've got terminals everywhere you turn. So there's more information.

A police organization that introduced direct computer entry of occurrence reports discovered that officers were soon imagining new uses for the technology. Computerization of the reporting process was not experienced as technological determinism but rather as a creative device leading to new discoveries about how to classify the world. A police administrator involved in the introduction of this technology observed that 'Its development could go on forever. As you develop one thing, you get an idea about something else ... [Officers have become] tremendously eager and enthusiastic ... the people that weren't interested in EDP [electronic data processing] bought computers for Christmas.'

In the process of discovery, new classifications are added that augment the knowledge work and consequently the paper burden. A feature of menu-driven computer programs is that new classifications can readily be added without changing the entire form. As new classification needs are discovered, they can be met immediately with a minor change to the computer program. Police officers working with a new computerized system for direct entry of occurrence reports began to realize the extra work involved, and on occasion misclassified information to lessen the workload. They sometimes, for example, placed a person involved in an occurrence in the category 'other,' even though the category 'suspect' was more appropriate. If they had placed the person in the category 'suspect' they would have been required to enter a great deal of extra information. Such practices confirm that additional knowledge work results from computerized reporting. Work avoidance provides only minor relief from the new burdens.

The formats of computerized reporting systems also compel more knowledge production. They feature 'pick-lists' of appropriate responses for each category, which force police officers to pick something in each case. The officers we observed and interviewed identified the ways in which this feature amplified their knowledge production. One officer said, 'Basically we're entering the details now on the system, and because of the layout of the terminal, and certain fields are required, we're getting – and we're making sure that we get – certain information that maybe six months ago, or before we had the new system, that we weren't worried about getting.'

We have previously analysed how communication technologies permit the production of entirely new classificatory schemes or 'bootleg' forms to meet local knowledge management needs (pp. 367–70). A police computer specialist, who helped to develop a computerized direct reporting system, observed that it had led to greater workloads for police officers and to a more extreme overload of information within his organization. He said that the prevailing view was, 'We like the system, start adding a million new forms to it.'

The additional knowledge production that resulted from this system was also related to the ease with which basic information could be downloaded and used on another form. A police officer described how the system allowed production of a CPIC form from the information that had already been inputted for the main occurrence report: 'You used to have to get a CPIC form, get it down, fill it out. Now it's there. You print it off and it's done. Even if you want it or not.' A colleague added, 'A lot of times [in the past] you might bypass that step just because it is a time-consumer, and you would say, "Well, he's only a shoplifter so I'm not going to bother putting him on CPIC." But if the machine is going to give you the form, then why not use it? Because it only takes one or two minutes to fill in another line and then you can ship it off.'

This capacity to expand the number of subforms leads in turn to expectations that such forms can be produced routinely during the preparation of case materials. What appears initially as an interesting feature and convenience of the technology quickly becomes an expectation of superiors and a part of system surveillance. A senior information systems officer observed that

> Through automation ... you can pull out stuff that you would never find manually. So now these expectations have been placed there ... Management expect more answers and faster answers ... In manual systems, they know that if they rode out to a distant police station and asked for some information, they knew it was not reasonable to expect an answer for a couple of weeks ... or not to ask at all ... They're so accustomed now to getting an answer in a timely manner that if they call out this morning, they wonder why that answer isn't in this afternoon.

Always working in an environment of risk – of uncertainty and probability – the police compulsively produce knowledge in the belief that it will give them greater powers to reduce risk. Thus it is predictable that computerized systems for the direct entry of occurrence reports result in more police surveillance aimed at the collection of potentially useful details about the minutiae of people's lives. The police sensibility in this regard was articulated by a crime analysis unit officer in a police organization that was adopting a new direct entry reporting system: 'We have a huge electronic file cabinet being built that, if you know enough elements, you're going to be able to give all the information out ... Electronically we don't throw anything away. There's no tidbit that can't, or might not, some day, be of use.'

The direct entry reporting system introduced into another police organization clearly led to increased collection of 'tidbits' that might come in handy in the future. During ride-alongs we observed patrol officers regularly submitting street-check reports, and they invariably said that this reporting had increased dramatically because the work had been made much easier by the new computer system. One time, for example, a patrol officer saw a man lying at the side of a road in a snowbank next to the man's car. Although he confirmed that the man was in reasonable condition and able to care for himself, he nevertheless decided to submit a street-check report on the encounter. The patrol officer's supervisor said that this report would not have been filed in the days before the new computer system was adopted. The ease of reporting, however, made it worthwhile to submit the report in the belief that it might assist future knowledge work down the road:

> Well, we're probably going to find that guy dead sometime – you know, a corpse. So he took the trouble to do one of these street checks and put in the colour of hair and the guy's name and the fact that I picked him up at such and such a location ... If we [find] him as a body, we can go and check and see if there's somebody like his description by height and weight and apparent age and whatnot on the new information system ... So we have some idea of next of kin and what location to search for next. He probably wouldn't have if it had just been paper. But because he had this technology he took the trouble.

Officers also used the technology to develop new surveillance classifications. For example, they added descriptive details about the hair colour, height, and weight of complainants. The main justification for this addition was that it is always useful to have more detailed knowledge of the population. Today's complainant may be tomorrow's suspect, and anything that helps to trace and identify people is worth registering.

The supervisors we interviewed were dubious about the investigative value of such information, but they suggested some possible latent functions. One supervisor said that the production of such information was a result of the ease with which new classifications could be added: 'There is an increased amount of information, such as the description of the complainant and so on, that they didn't do before, that they really shouldn't do, but it is convenient for them to do.' Another supervisor saw production of such information as a useful device to discipline officers regarding completeness of reporting: 'If you can establish input patterns they can get in the habit of doing it with suspects.' An information system specialist working on the design of a new computerized reporting system said that he was sympathetic towards officers who made creative additions to the knowledge produced, because he did the same thing. He said that he had decided to include a classification for 'subjects with alias. That's not really useful information but we put it on ... I happened to have the number available when I was going to the screen, and it looked as though it was a nice thing to put on.'

Security of communication technologies and information systems is a source of additional knowledge work that again expands the enterprise. Large police organizations have established special branches for electronic and data security. In some cases security extends to maintaining duplicate data systems. A data analyst said that he did not trust the main data system in his police organization and therefore kept his own duplicate system as a backup.

Needing a sense of security is behind the urge to print out paper copies of computerized knowledge rather than to leave it in its paperless form. Officers we observed said that they were printing out copies of reports as 'insurance.' A senior officer in a criminal intelligence operation described this as 'the lost blanket syndrome. You work twenty years with a file and paper and now somebody says we're not going to do that any more and people go through ... a period of withdrawal ... You still get people that print off a copy and ... they want to read it. So there's a natural resistance and it takes time.' A supervisory officer working in an information systems branch said that she had concluded that 'Technology will not resolve all of the issues. The members still have to see and touch information. This creates a lot of hard copy.' Security derives from familiarity, and the current generation of police officers is more familiar with the formats of print than those of computers. Paper files are easier to follow because of their linear and chronological order, and this in turn gives a feeling of things being in order.

Paper is also generated for a number of reasons internal to police organization. While a case may be reported by direct computer entry and initially kept paperless, subsequent developments may require the filing of paper and thus the defeat of the paperless system. For example, a police officer who was using a computerized direct entry occurrence reporting system said that as soon as a request was made to another part of the organization a paper file system became necessary. He mentioned a recent case in which he had made a routine request to the identification branch, and the response came back in paper form stating 'no matches.' Because he now had paper on the case he had to open a new file jacket and also put the once-paperless occurrence report into the file in printed form.

One of our police organizations that introduced a computerized direct entry occurrence reporting system nevertheless kept *two* complete paper files on all major cases and on cases subject to follow-up investigations. One file was to be kept by the investigator and the other file was to be kept in the office at all times for immediate access by supervisors. This system, designed for the benefit of supervisors, gave them access to information on the progress of a case when accountability demands were made, allowed ongoing case supervision, and served as backup security if information went missing from the investigator's file. Maintaining reports under this system was estimated to take up about 20 per cent of an officer's time. A complaint about the workload involved led to a proposal that officers keep only selected information in their own files, with the office file being the main repository. This proposal was not adopted, however, because it went against police officers' own proclivity to hoard every piece of potentially relevant information, and because it implied that supervisors, rather than investigating officers, were the ones who truly needed to have all the relevant knowledge at their fingertips for accountability purposes. A police officer who complained about the two-file system pointed to the irony of its co-existing with a computerized direct entry reporting system that was designed to foster a paperless office environment: 'The man-hours that I spend at the photocopy machine making a copy for myself! This police organization and paper seem to go hand-in-hand. Somebody must have shares in MacMillan Bloedel.'

Investigative work has always been measured by the volume of knowledge produced about cases (Mann and Lee 1979; Ericson 1993). Investigative efforts are judged not only in terms of case outcomes but also by the process of knowledge production. As a police information system specialist told us, a thick file shows that the job is done even if the case remains unsolved: 'A lot of members don't like to move to paperless. Where before you used to have a big pile of paper to show for all of your work, with paperless it now looks like the requirements for the job are less. The complexity of the job could be symbolized by the amount of paper that you produced.'

Another police officer, who specialized in information systems and forms management, said that computers have not, despite the efforts of large police information system bureaucracies such as the one he worked for, 'reduced the paperwork burden ... Paperwork burden is the amount of effort that's required to use and handle paper. Computers need paper to feed them and they spit paper out at the end. And it takes just as much effort in between, or more if you're not a very good typist, than to write the damn thing by hand. So what advantage?'

Other interviewees held this view, and to substantiate it they pointed to the fact that paper file storage capacity was increasing in tandem with the advent of new communication technologies. The head of a records section for a large police organization said that the only effective effort to reduce paper comes when the existing file storage capacity has reached its limit. He pointed with pride to a recent purge of old files that had been spurred by the need for space for files from the current year.

A more differentiated division of labour in police knowledge production has not provided patrol officers with relief from the paper burden. A police organization we examined developed a complaint response system to allow more complaints to be handled over the telephone or at the front desk of the police station. While the hope had been to free police officers for more 'real police work' such as crime work, the actual effect was that officers now had more time to prepare good reports. In the words of a station administrator, the main effect was that 'the quality of reports has increased ... [there is] more detail, more information on the reports that are coming out.'

The complex division of labour between the police and external risk institutions has also failed to bring relief from the paper burden. As knowledge brokers to external institutions, the police feel the impact of how those institutions develop and use new communication technologies. An information systems manager for a police organization said that technological innovations in external institutions were the main driving force behind both his own technological efforts and the inevitability of the paper burden:

> The demands for service grow daily ... Our user-community is becoming more and more computer-literate and they see more and more uses for technology. And there's just an increasing demand for information ... Our ability to provide the information easily and faster will also increase. We will always lag behind what's required, just because of the time it takes to build it. We will always be understaffed here. There's no way we will ever be able to meet all the requests that are put upon us. That's no different than any other information system shop that I've ever worked in.

The feeling of being 'put upon' by those who demand knowledge is omnipresent in police work. This feeling results from the fact that the police are reactive agents *vis-à-vis* the risk knowledge requirements of external institutions. It also expresses the fact that the police are not only entangled in a seamless web of system surveillance but are actually part of its very fibre. The system, consisting of communication rules, formats, and technologies, is the real autonomous police force.

Summary and Conclusions

In this final chapter, we move beyond a close analysis of the research literature and the data to provide a succinct summary of our findings and draw conclusions. Subheadings and literature citations are eschewed so that readers can experience our thesis as a unified whole. Readers who find this approach too breathless are invited to return to the detailed documentation presented in earlier chapters.

We have claimed that both policing and the society in which it takes place are best understood in terms of a paradigm of risk. We have backed up this claim with empirical research on how the police organize within risk communication systems. This research has provided the basis for the first major study of the administrative apparatus of policing. It has focused in particular on the supervisory and management levels in police organizations and on the communication systems that operate at these levels. These levels and systems are enormous in size and scope, and crucial to operations, because they coordinate the central policing task of risk communication to and from external institutions. Given the enormity and importance of these levels and systems, it is curious that other researchers have ignored them.

In reacting to the demands of external institutions for knowledge of risk, the police are governed by the communication systems of those institutions. All institutions develop communication systems – rules, formats, and technologies – to deal with uncertainty. These systems are inscribed in institutional practices, and this inscription represents and visualizes what the institution does. Institutionalization itself is a process of devising risk communication systems that foster certainty and effect routine decisions. Institutionalized risk communication systems form the foundation of contemporary society and provide the governing basis of social life.

The possibilities of contemporary neoliberal market society depend on the probabilities of institutionalized risk management regarding territories, securities, careers, identities, and organizations. The police help to make possibilities probabilities by reacting to institutional demands for knowledge of risk. They make up events and populations through classifications provided by other institutions that want to count people into being for their own risk management needs.

Risk society is characterized by a perpetual elaboration of communication rules to govern how knowledge is communicated and used. In this context, the police are increasingly subject to external institutional pressures to produce and distribute knowledge in rule-governed frameworks. For example, the criminal law dictates conditions and criteria of disclosure, as do various areas of information law regarding privacy and access to information. The need to be publicly accountable also leads the police to elaborate internal communication rule systems. Rules develop to centralize the access of other institutions to police knowledge, to commodify police knowledge that is bartered or sold to external institutions, and to regulate internal knowledge production and distribution systems. These rules protect police organizations from appearing irresponsible in the use of their knowledge assets.

The external origin of communication rules is exemplified by the law of criminal procedure, which continually articulates how to produce legally acceptable knowledge of risk for the courts. The rules of criminal procedure are embedded in police forms to govern how the police think and act. Part 28 of the Criminal Code of Canada incorporates over fifty forms designed to embed procedural propriety into police actions. Having to meet the formal legal rationality embedded in these forms, the police form their actions accordingly and are thereby able to show that they conform.

The procedural law pertaining to impaired driving also illustrates this phenomenon. Because impaired driving has been an especially contested area of the law, the procedural rules have become more and more elaborate, and in turn have been embedded in reporting formats. The fine-grained classifications of blood samples by warrant reports, breathalyser reports, and investigative guides and reports on alcohol impairment are all designed to ensure that the police have evidently established the veracity of the risk technologies they use to make their case.

The Supreme Court of Canada decision in *R. v. Stinchcombe* is another example. This decision, premised on the need for more thorough disclosure to the defence, resulted in new requirements for police reporting to the prosecutor's office. In one police organization we studied in depth, this ruling had a profound impact on the internal communication rule system and on the level of knowledge work required. An elaborate set of new communication rules was developed and then put in place using a tightly crafted reporting format. These rules had a significant effect on police action, for example changing the point at which officers made arrests and laid charges, and the ways in which they handled informants whose identity might be exposed in the courts.

The effects of *Stinchcombe* also show how external rule changes can ramify through the police communication rule system. We found, for example, that the rules, formats, and knowledge requirements resulting from the case affected Uniform Crime Reports classification procedures as well as a police organization's own classification procedures.

Various legislative enactments pertaining to freedom of information have also permeated police communication rule systems. The police have created large specialist units for handling freedom of information matters, and these units have added to and adjusted internal rules concerning disclosure of knowledge to external users. This elaboration has necessarily given rise to new rules about exceptions to rules. For example, one police organization created a formal rule about how to circumvent a formal rule that prohibited the informal acquisition of knowledge from another institution, and about how to formally justify the practice after the fact. Communication rules are used to centralize and regulate the release of police-produced knowledge to external institutions. These rules define all police knowledge in corporate terms, make it unified and authoritative, regulate access to and distribution of it, and commodify it as a resource that can be bartered or sold to external institutions.

Our analysis of how external communication rules relate to police action is not a claim that these rules have direct effects on police behaviour. Rather, the effects of new external communication rules are always mediated by the elaboration of internal police rules and by how both the internal and external rules become embedded in the classifications the police use to report on their own activities. As such, communication rules have multiple functions. They provide an image of rationality, suggesting that the police are indeed organized within a communication system. This rationality becomes a framework for accountability and for offsetting liability claims regarding risks caused by the police. The police have implemented auditing arrangements for scrutinizing particular types of incidents (such as high-speed chases) as well as for scrutinizing police communication systems (such as those that relate to standards and information security) in order to preventively patrol the facts that might affect their liability and accountability. As such, auditing arrangements structure police account ability to ensure that accountability will result.

Communication rules provide a communicative framework for action at the administrative level. They address communication system needs about what knowledge is to be communicated to what audiences in what forms. This is exemplified by the detailed policy manuals pertaining to police communications, which provide a means of prospectively and retrospectively rationalizing and accounting for what is communicated, especially at the managerial and administrative levels. As we discovered, neither these manuals, nor the external rules that affect them (such as freedom of information legislation), are seen by the police as constraining. Rather, they are welcomed as enabling devices for structuring the police knowledge system and facilitating the wider interinstitutional mandate of system surveillance.

Communication rules also provide communicative frameworks for action by police officers in the field. Police officers' decisions in the field are not governed primarily by the informal rules prevalent in the local occupational subculture, but they are constituted by the communication rules embedded in reporting formats. Legal and administrative rule changes are peculiarly ineffective until they are made part of the police communication system and its rules, formats, and technologies.

The immediate loci of police work are the risk communication formats that shape the thinking of police officers and through which police officers inscribe their actions in reports. The knowledge conceived, recognized, and communicated through a report depends on the format used and is therefore always secondary to the format. Formats provide the means by which police officers prefigure their actions, are able to act reflexively as they take action, and regulate actions taken.

While the proliferation of communication rules signifies the extent to which the police have been subject to legalization, the acceleration of communication formats is also one dimension of police scientization. The police are now deployed in a manner similar to social science researchers. They are equipped with extensive closed-ended systematic observation reports along with coding instructions. These communication formats serve the dual purpose of effecting certainty and closure in police work and of providing the requisite knowledge of risk to external institutions.

Risk communication formats do not stand apart from the police and other institutions but rather participate in their formation and change. They establish the criteria through which institutional participants understand risks and articulate their preferred courses of action. Alternative meanings are either seen as unrealistic or not seen at all. As such, communication formats are the focal points for an institution's selection and definition of risks. To know an institutions is to know how its communication formats are used to select and define risks in ways that support and stabilize the institution. Communication formats provide the sinews that connect institutions and that allow the perpetual articulation of risks as reality. They broker consciousness and social existence, defining what should be taken as objective reality with respect to risks. They organize social relations in terms of risk population categories, of who should relate to whom, on what terms, and for what purposes. They create knowledge structures based on who knows what, about whom, and compared to whom, and thus create institutional environments of inclusion and exclusion.

The police orchestrate a cacophony of communication formats designed to meet the risk management needs of external institutions as well as their own. This orchestration occurs through the tireless elaboration and refinement of reporting forms. Forms management is perpetual because the communication formats settled on always require adjustment and change, and because the risk knowledge needs of external institutions are always in flux. Furthermore, the police classify with an eye towards symbolic politics and implications for police resources. The police paradox of efficiency requires communication formats that dramatize risks (dangers) but at the same time show the police to be efficient risk managers (probability calculators).

A substantial proportion of police resources is dedicated to the regressive task of risk-managing the forms themselves. This task is necessary because it is the only way of guaranteeing that the proper communication formats are in place to produce the knowledge of risk required. We documented a tough police crack down on 'bootleg' forms, that is, on forms created by police officers for local practical uses but without official sanction. In an era of communication format prohibition, only forms that meet the risk criteria of centralized institutions are acceptable. We also documented that the trend in policing is towards more-tightly formatted, fixed-choice risk classifications to meet surveillance system needs. The policing of narratives extends to limiting written accounts of occurrences to 229 characters, circumscribing the use of abstract and interpretive language, and searching for scanner technologies that will convert the written accounts into closed-ended formats.

The search for formats that stray from procedures or that require narrative policing is backed up by elaborate supervisory systems. Police training is a process of learning how incidents encountered relate to relevant forms and their communication formats. The process is ongoing because the incidents encountered represent a kaleidoscope of human behaviour and interpretive possibilities and because the formats are in constant flux as they are adjusted to new institutional demands and situational needs. In consequence, police supervisors function as incident report editors, patrolling the facts to detect and correct interpretive leakage that has occurred despite the closed formats. They are supported by forms about forms: forms that trace other forms to ensure that they are correct, subject to appropriate review, secure, and so on. They are also supported by the electronic infrastructure of communication technologies that further enhance the overall surveillance system.

Communication technologies have transformed risk communication systems and radically altered social organization. The fact that computer technologies allow rapid transmission of written texts collapses time and space among institutional actors. Institutional actors become disembedded from their traditional territorial spaces and social places and operate instead from microcentres of inscription such as computer terminals in vehicles, home offices, and satellite organizational offices. So positioned, actors contribute to interinstitutional communication systems that know no boundaries except those posited by the computer's formats and by telecommunication infrastructures. The boundaries of institutional jurisdiction are blurred and organizational hierarchies are reconfigured.

At the same time, the surveillance capacities of computer technology allow 'remote control.' Supervisors can use remote terminals to access, review, and convert knowledge production. Moreover, communication rules can be embedded in communication formats to reduce complexity and effect efficient knowledge production in accordance with administrative needs. The result is system surveillance, a capacity to simultaneously produce and scrutinize knowledge.

These features of computer technology are evident in police organizations. For example, computer terminals in patrol cars permit immediate and efficient knowledge production about populations and incidents encountered. The centrality of computers in police communication systems, combined with the ways in which they are formatted to meet system surveillance needs, means that police officers are compelled to use them. Computers compel the production of knowledge that is complete, valid, and reliable according to the data expectations of the system itself.

Computer technology is used to accelerate surveillance of the population for risk management purposes. Some of these purposes are internal to the police. For example, computer terminals in patrol cars increase the use of contact card surveillance, allowing the police to trace more people who appear out of place. Some of these purposes are external to the police. For example, police computer formats are made compatible with those of external institutions in order to increase the efficiency of risk communications to such institutions. The needs of external institutions are also met by 'distribution processing,' the electronic creation of specialized subreports by taking data from main reports.

Every keystroke on the keyboard also 'types' the police officer in terms of the quality and quantity of his or her knowledge production and thereby disciplines the officer as a useful worker, without the need for direct supervisory intervention. At the very point of registering who and what he or she observes, the police officer is also registering the time, place, conditions, and circumstances of his or her observations. Computer technology thereby automates the routine profiling of the population of police, constituting their work activity, competence, and occupational health in biopower terms. The computer terminal in the patrol car is a time-and-motion study that never ends. The police officer is routinely measured and sorted in terms of his or her capacity as a human resource. This risk-profiling makes the officer a member of the population of police, with finely calibrated performance ratings and career potentials.

Computer technology also permits the development of paperless reporting for minor occurrences that do not require further investigation, and thereby reduces the paper burden and enhances efficiency. It enriches the occupational culture by allowing police officers, isolated from each other in their patrol cars, to communicate jokes, gossip, and trivia without fear of interception by outsiders. It provides for immediate reflexive feedback from police officers to communication system designers, allowing both technological refinement as well as a sense of participation and agency in the process of technological change.

At the same time, the introduction of computer technology in police organizations encounters problems. Computer technologies and the communication systems they embody seem chronically obsolete. New technologies take a long time to implement, and by the time they are in place they have been superseded by something that seems even better. Moreover, there is typically a reluctance to change to a new technology because change means a new communication system. Under existing technology, the communication rules and formats are familiar. Moreover, there are many other users, internal and external to the police organization, who have learned to routinize their communications within the existing arrangements and who must also adjust to the new technology.

There is outright resistance to computer technology among some police officers. Some officers are simply against innovation because of their unfamiliarity with a new technology's capabilities and their fear that it will affect how their competence is assessed. Others try to use new computer technology but find that they are not competent and thus argue against it. The fear of appearing incompetent is increased when portable computers are used in interviewing members of the public, for whom two-finger typing does not signify efficiency. As for computer terminals in patrol cars, they create a collective sense of dehumanization through mechanization. Dehumanization is accentuated because police officers using computers to see better, and to be more efficient in knowledge production, have at the same time a sense of being seen through. This sense leads to resistance to, and conflicts over, the distribution and uses of computerized knowledge.

The most fundamental problem for police officers – and another source of dehumanization and resistance – is the fact that most of their efforts to use computers for efficient knowledge production are driven by the needs of external institutions over which they have little or no control. Despite the efficiencies in knowledge production provided by communication technologies, the paper burden continues to weigh heavily because external institutions demand more and more knowledge. In addition to the accountability requirements and risk management needs peculiar to these institutions, this knowledge is demanded because of the increased capacity to provide it through computer technology. Computer technology makes new classifications imaginable and eases the task of altering communication formats to meet new classification needs. It allows subreports to be 'stripped' from main reports for the purposes of specialized users. In easing knowledge production and distribution it accelerates the volume of knowledge work.

The external demand for more knowledge, and the ease of computerized knowledge production, feed into the police compulsion to produce internal knowledge in case it might come in handy in the future. What appears initially as an interesting feature and convenience of the technology quickly becomes an expectation of supervisors and of police officers themselves. It becomes structured into system surveillance and takes on an autonomy of its own. Furthermore, given the strong print culture that has dominated police organizations – as well as some of their primary institutional constituencies, such as the criminal courts – there remains the tendency to provide paper copies of reports even when they are unnecessary. Paper files signify security. They are easier to follow because of their linear and chronological order, and this in turn provides a feeling of things being in order. Computerization has not meant a shift away from print culture, but an augmentation of it.

The most fundamental change brought about by computer technology in policework is that it creates a new communication environment which transforms traditional structures of command and control. The division of labour among police officers, clerks, specialized units, and supervisors becomes less distinct, and hierarchies of supervision and accountability are blurred. In one police jurisdiction a new computerized system for direct entry of occurrence reports meant that officers were doing the data-entry work formerly assigned to clerks and supervisors, supervisors were doing the report checking formerly assigned to clerks, and clerks were largely redundant, except for checking the work of supervisors. Patrol officers and their supervisors were effectively 'civilianized' by this new computer system.

In another jurisdiction computer technology was being developed to make the public direct participants in the reporting process. For example, voice-mail and remote computer terminal systems were devised for direct entry of complaints by citizens without the need to dispatch an officer. These electronic self-service units were made possible because the police were confident that the reporting format itself was all that was necessary to elicit relevant knowledge of risk, to the point where face-to-face encounters were unnecessary.

The traditional structure of command and control is further blurred by the introduction into police organizations of civilian computer technology specialists. These specialists have the power of abstract knowledge and technical skill on their side, which conflict with traditional hierarchical distinctions based on length of service, loyalty, rank, and public service. Computer technology specialists create the communication system architectures that either make the police officer-as-reporter redundant or make him report within highly restricted formats.

The blurring of roles and reconfiguring of organizational hierarchy mean that no one person is the decision maker. Decision making occurs within the communication formats, which have their own autonomy, and indeed reality, at the system level. Hence the role ambiguity and alteration of hierarchy does not enhance the discretion of field-level police officers. Rather, discretion is at once circumscribed and dispersed into the communication systems that provide for routine surveillance of both the population of citizens and the population of police.

While computer technologies are determinative, they are not deterministic. They are used within culturally specific interpretive frameworks and visions of social organization, and their effects are always related to these frameworks and visions. They are used to enact particular horizontal and vertical dimensions of social organization, and they are also resisted in these terms. For example, we learned about police organizations that were not eager to pursue telecommunications compatibility because of a fear that such compatibility would result in intrusions on each other's autonomy. There is not first a world ordered by technology and culture and then communication about it. The world is constituted by the communication processes of its articulation and reception using whatever rules, formats, and technologies are deemed appropriate for the task. Things can always be different.

The police adopt computer technologies with the intention of bringing about change in their culture and social organization. They create knowledge systems that make it difficult to ascertain who is in control. These systems foster self-regulation according to the principle of efficiency. They also make the organization increasingly transparent to members in different roles, who are able to see through its data points, command keys, and display terminals.

At least for the purposes of risk communication, police back regions become front regions, and police front regions merge into the communicative regions of other organizations. The regionalization of institutions is the result. Communication technology permits the dispersal of policing structures and tasks into myriad microcentres of knowledge and power in risk society. Communications policing is the result.

Our analysis of how the administrative apparatus of policing is constituted by communication systems has important consequences for how we should think about police. Our paradigm transforms existing research on police in seven key areas: mobilization, the locus of knowledge work, visibility, the role of criminal law enforcement, the role of compliance-based law enforcement, the types of security offered, and the basis of community policing.

Police mobilization has been conceived of almost entirely at the level of individual demands for service by citizens (reactive), and individual interventions by suspicious police officers (proactive). However, embedded in each individual police-citizen encounter is institutional mobilization for the production of knowledge of risk. Something only becomes mobilized as policework if it fits the risk knowledge requirements of external institutions. It is the communication systems – regulatory regimes, knowledge formats, and electronic infrastructures – of these external institutions that govern police mobilization.

In addition to individual mobilization that meets the risk knowledge needs of external institutions, the police mobilize their own communication systems for territorial surveillance and protection. These communication systems are used to literally make the territories and communities they police. They use the electronic infrastructures in police vehicles – computer terminals, mapping systems, video cameras, voice-radio systems, still cameras, and so on – to trace their territories and those who populate them. They develop expertise on and offer advice concerning spatial infrastructures. As agents of architectural and semiotic policing, they help to make environmental designs that are pleasing to people who consume normally and discouraging to those who do not. They also use various inspection devices to trace the security of people into their spaces: contact card surveillance, registration of vice practitioners, special events security registration, business security review, residential security review, special properties analysis, house-to-house inquiries, and so on. When people are mobile, vehicle registration and driver credentials are used to trace ownership, insurance, and identity, and thereby to give assurance that obligations are being fulfilled and risk of loss protected against.

In the aggregate, what one sees concentrated in private security settings such as shopping malls and entertainment complexes exists more diffusely in the wider urban landscape. A focus on population categories, precise movement through territories, pervasive surveillance devices, and aesthetically pleasing design makes coercion embedded, cooperative, and subtle, and therefore not experienced as coercion at all.

The police also participate in the mobilization of private property and the generating of territorial protection. Through community policing mandates, they encourage private security operatives to develop their own electronic surveillance infrastructures, design expertise, and inspection devices. Encouragement comes in various forms, including police security inspections of private property and the generating of crime trend data and other horror stories that feed the communality of fear.

We discovered a rich variety of police programs in this regard. Watch programs encourage organizations and individuals to monitor their own risks and to feed relevant knowledge of risk to the police. Relevance is shaped by the formats of forms that instruct watch program participants on what to look for. Inspection programs include, for example, the Shield of Confidence Home Security Program, through which the police, developers, insurance companies, and contractors establish acceptable standards with respect to security devices for the home. The PCCOPS automated telephone warning system mobilizes people in specific territorial settings to conduct surveillance and be defensive, thus sparing the police the trouble of more-direct involvement. PCCOPS exemplifies the sensibility that a primary police task is to warn people to routinely look after their own security needs. The police also serve as experts and risk monitors for private electronic security systems and form partnerships with the private sector for commodifying and marketing private security products.

These observations on mobilization suggest a different locus of police knowledge work than that presented in the existing research, which depicts knowledge production as being mainly related to needs internal to police organization. We have shown that considerable demand originates from external institutional sources and that many knowledge requirements that appear to be internally derived are actually related to external sources of regulation and accountability. External sources include, for example, legal demands for police procedural propriety (as in *R. v. Stinchcombe*), formal mechanisms for civilian complaints against the police, new public issues (such as calls for family violence reporting), and local community movements (such as community policing). There is a perpetual dialectic between external knowledge demands from these sources and adjustments to police communication systems to meet these demands, all of which affect mobilization patterns.

Existing research also concentrates on the ways in which the police try to obtain knowledge from individuals and organizations to meet investigative needs but are frustrated in their endeavours because of the institution of privacy. But there has not been a parallel emphasis on how external organizations routinely access the police for knowledge useful for their own risk management systems. The loci of police knowledge work in this regard are expert systems of risk that are of little or no direct relevance internally. In many contexts, people and events are to be known only through risk classifications that are relevant to other institutions. Police officers are given no opportunity to classify things otherwise, nor to provide a narrative or offer alternative interpretations. The rich kaleidoscopic image of an event is telescoped into external risk management needs. Diversity is eliminated with a stroke of the pen, an act that facilitates the keystroking of data entry and the subsequent stroking of data for risk analysis.

Police knowledge work is located in communication systems over which individuals and subunits have little or no control. Moreover, these systems are designed to make policework highly visible to interested institutional audiences. The research literature has exaggerated the low visibility of policework. It suggests that police officers have a repertoire of covert and manipulative devices to keep knowledge from others and thereby maintain discretionary space for their activities. The research focus on how officers escape the supervisory grasp has led to a neglect of how communication rules, formats, and technologies make officers more visible to police supervisors and managers and to external institutions for whom relevant knowledge is routinely produced.

Our research also reconfigures the place of criminal law in policing. The criminal law is but one of many institutions that demand police-produced knowledge of risk. Like other institutions of risk, the criminal law is organized around its own peculiar knowledge requirements and system surveillance needs. Knowledge of criminal activity is produced for a range of purposes, only one of which is criminal prosecution and disposition. Knowledge of crime and criminality is produced for dissemination to interested institutions outside the criminal justice system, in particular those concerned with insurance, health, education, and welfare. Also common is police overproduction of 'just-in-case' knowledge about crime and criminals, a relentless surveillance to feed the police's own sense of being in control.

The criminal law is compelled to obey the 'social laws' of risk that shape all branches of law and all institutions in risk society. These social laws are embedded in the communication systems that the criminal law participates in, and it is these systems that govern how criminal justice operates. The criminal law is part of system surveillance for actuarial justice.

The emphasis on crime control is displaced in favour of crime risk management. As a system whose principal coordinating mechanism is knowledge, criminal justice seeks suspects to make into objects of knowledge for risk management purposes. The focus on efficiency in punishment gives way to efficient production and distribution of knowledge useful for the management of suspect populations. Knowledge is preferred to coercion where practical, although coercion is sometimes necessary to obtain knowledge.

The law of criminal procedure provides the coercion necessary to meet the system's knowledge needs. In place of suspects' due process rights we find the surveillance system's rights to knowledge that is useful for its own risk management needs. The search for uncluttered actuarial justice means that some of the basic principles of criminal law – and their basis in morality, procedure, and hierarchy – recede. Consensual norms are displaced by security wants. Morally based deterrence and punishment are displaced by deselection and exclusion. Criminal law becomes compliance-oriented, serving the fragmented risk, surveillance, and security objectives of various institutions in risk society.

The research literature depicts compliance-based law enforcement by the police as a function of informal decisions not to invoke the criminal process. Potential offenders and minor offenders are made compliant by being given a second chance or by being diverted to other agencies that are ostensibly more benevolent than the criminal process. We have shown, however, that compliance-based law enforcement operates through police communication systems in much more pervasive and fundamental ways. Many of the rules, formats, and technologies that form the police communication system are shaped by the knowledge requirements of external institutions that operate within a compliance-based mode of regulation. The police relation to the insurance industry is a case in point. The police are knowledge brokers for insurance risk management systems that seek compliance from their clients to maintain proper standards of security and self-regulation. These standards are backed up by contractual requirements stating that if they are not met insurance claims may be denied and policies cancelled. Criminal law enforcement mainly enters to underwrite the integrity of the insurance institution itself, for example with respect to the prosecution of fraudulent claims.

The emphasis on producing knowledge for the compliance-based law enforcement needs of other institutions points to a different conception of security than that which prevails in existing research. Most police researchers define security as territorial protection of people and property. However, the police also deal with many extraterritorial forms of security directed at securities, careers, and identities. In these forms of security the police are in touch with much more than what is on the ground. They deal in abstract systems of trust and risk that require sophisticated surveillance mechanisms not tied to territorial boundaries. They represent institutional boundaries that traverse time and space but still manage to keep people in their place. The intangibility of trust and acceptable risk, and the always precarious balance between them, mean that there is a perpetual thrust for more and better knowledge about them.

Securities such as financial instruments, certificates, and credentials attest to credit, ownership, identity, and achievements. They provide security in the form of a promise to fulfil obligations and to guarantee against any loss, damage, or default that might ensue. They are backed by institutions which warrant that obligations will be met and guarantees honoured. The trust thus created facilitates communication and freedom of action among people who are strangers except for their identities within the risk knowledge systems of institutions. Institutions also organize around distrust, for example to minimize risks in fiduciary relationships and to collectivize risks more generally.

The police are an important component of how institutions establish trust and efficiency through their security instruments. Their main tasks are interinstitutional knowledge coordination, risk profiling, and auditing to verify the integrity of securities data, products, and markets. This involves the constant appropriation and redistribution of the security symbols that have been developed by other institutions, and of the risk criteria relevant to those symbols. This work is often intangible and involves the police in interinstitutional networks without clear boundaries or borders. In addition to front-loading the securities risk knowledge system and serving as the hub of interinstitutional coordination, the police underpin the institutional obligations and guarantees associated with securities. They help to maintain public confidence in markets by maintaining registry systems (for example of stolen art and vehicles), financial instrument verification services (for example with respect to counterfeit currency and bad cheques), and financial market auditing services (providing, for example, equity market risk analysis).

The police also help other institutions to construct the careers of those who populate them. In the most mundane aspects of their work – reporting on accidents, submitting a contact card, conducting an employment screening check, and so on – police officers register people's significant accomplishments and failures, credentials and demerits, routines and accidents.

For example, the police contribute to knowledge about careers of insurable risk. Insurance deterritorializes regulation into classes of populations and their respective insurable careers. The world of insurance is not only mapped and plotted in terms of physical space, but also in relation to abstract classifications of populations exposed to danger, harm, premiums, and indemnifications. Working *within* the institution of insurance, the police de-emphasize territorial surveillance. In traffic regulation and property protection, for example, they conduct at best minimal and highly selective surveillance. The focus is on compliance and regulation within insurance logics, helping insurance companies to constitute the insurance-relevant victimization and accident careers of individuals. The help extends to allowing insurance company investigators routine access to police reports and files, diverting cases to insurance companies for alternative justice within their compliance-based law enforcement mechanisms, and joint investigations when the integrity of the insurance institution itself appears threatened.

Careers are also policed with regard to credentials. A credential is something that gives access to legitimate performance of a role or function; in other words, a socially ascribed confidence that someone is qualified for the performance of a particular task. Examples include licences to drive vehicles of different classifications, business licences, awards of merit, and educational qualifications. The police examine credentials for authenticity, vetting people's claims about accomplishments and rights of access to a role or function. That is, they help institutions to guarantee the security of their credentials as securities *vis-à-vis* individual careers. Credentials are also a means of tracing populations and regulating them beyond the specific role or function for which the credentials are issued. For example, driver's licences are used for a variety of identification purposes, and municipal business licences include risk profiling systems for tracking business integrity and the movements of practitioners.

The police also provide career-relevant knowledge to specific institutional arenas of population management. For example, they offer a variety of knowledge services regarding the health of populations. They operate enormous drug regulation bureaucracies that routinely report cases to other bureaucracies such as Health and Welfare Canada. They handle mental health cases, regularly delivering ill people and reports about them to local hospitals. They make similar efforts in relation to personal injury accidents, feeding knowledge to hospital information systems every time an accident victim is delivered to the emergency room. They maintain large-scale missing-persons registries, helping to ensure that as few people as possible are unaccounted for. The same mandate informs their participation in the registration of death. In one police organization, the end of the life-course was dealt with not only in the usual ways but also through bereavement services offered to close relatives of the deceased.

The police have the primary responsibility for maintaining the career profiles of people targeted by the criminal justice system. They maintain criminal career records that can destroy positive careers and sustain marginalized ones. They organize and manage criminal careers through contact card surveillance systems, licensing of vice operation, and symbiotic relationships with organized crime. They are gatekeepers of criminal careers through the use of ordeals such as polygraph testing, fingerprinting, hypnosis, and DNA testing. They also open the gate to criminal-free identities by maintaining the record system for criminal pardons.

The police also maintain a parallel knowledge system for recording the careers of victims in the criminal justice system. Victim assistance units have arisen to manage victim involvement in the criminal justice system. Assistance is contingent on particular criteria, and therefore a special knowledge system is used to select those who qualify. Assistance takes the form of providing knowledge to the victim concerning how to deal with insurance and other institutions that have a stake in the case. There is also a court accompaniment service that ensures the victim's security as a commodified piece of evidence until case disposition.

Informants are also valuable police property. They are subject in the first instance to detailed risk profiling regarding their general suitability for employment as informants. Profiling also occurs when specific informant career paths are being considered, for instance when assessing a person's potential to be a police officer's operative or a participant in a program such as Crime Stoppers. Other profiling systems come into play when special protection of an informant is required, and for career exit debriefing exercises.

The police are also involved in the construction of institutionally relevant identities. Through the routine work of checking off identity boxes on forms – regarding age, race, gender, ethnicity, and so on – and through what happens to that knowledge as it moves through various panoptic sorting processes, the police help to force people into particular institutional identities. Far from being original or creative authors in this work, the police merely tailor the person to the available identity characteristics.

The police are compelled to work within the identity categories of external institutions and to differentiate according to the criteria laid down by those institutions. As a result, the police necessarily reproduce those institutions' forms of identity differentiation as well as any prejudice (negative preconceptions) and discrimination (unjust selection) that results from such differentiation. As such, police prejudice and discrimination are grounded not only in the police occupational culture but also in the external institutional knowledge systems within which the police are required to think and act. In turn, those knowledge systems are structured by the wider culture of difference and differentiation.

Institutions are the authorial source of identities. Institutional identity classifications are moral categories expressing dominant views of preferred places in the social structure. Institutions confirm identities. People identify their selves with their institutional categories of risk and the differential needs those categories create. In producing risk-relevant data on identity characteristics for other institutions, the police help them to determine which favoured identities will be granted 'residence permits' and 'citizen status,' and which ones will be deported.

Patrolling the symbolic borders of institutions through the routine production of facts about identity, the police help to clarify who is one of us and who is the other, and, within acceptable boundaries, where people should be assigned so that they least disrupt the rational and efficient flow of institutional life. Identity categories only exist through this border patrolling. The border, rather than the cultural ingredients it circumscribes, defines the institutional group. By accentuating differences, identities policing makes evident, with all the precision of actuarial science, the ascribed categories of social inequality.

To document police participation in institutionalized identity construction, we focused on their work in governing the young. The young receive police 'overattention' as a risk category for a number of reasons. For one thing, young people are more likely than adults to be victims of interpersonal crime. They also commit more crime, including some behaviours that would be legal if engaged in by adults. They are subject to demonization as a symbolic threat, stereotyped and reacted to because of the respectable fears of older people more than the malevolence of their conduct. For all of these reasons the police devote considerable resources to patrolling the borders of youthful identities.

Police overattention to the young does not entail overcriminalization.

If anything, there is undercriminalization. There is typically an interinstitutional social response to youthful misbehaviour and the risks it poses: registering conduct through contact card surveillance, administering school police programs, and participating in criminal case diversion. In all such activities the basic police task is risk communication to other institutions that deal with youths more closely.

The police also help to secure the social boundaries of youth by working within the interstices that separate the institutions that deal more closely with young people. Our analysis of police programs in schools revealed that police officers function simultaneously as security officers, risk educators, informant system operators, and counsellors, and that they mobilize school staff and students to fill these roles as well. Through these school programs and other interinstitutional connections, the police also operate more-intensive surveillance systems for the deselected few. In one jurisdiction we studied, high-risk youths aged fourteen to sixteen were placed in a two-year intensive program involving collaboration on the part of the police, the school, the youth's family, and health and welfare agencies. The youths who failed this program were further deselected for a habitual offenders program, which was clearly based on system rights for surveillance: full interagency exchange of whatever knowledge is necessary to trace the select few and keep them in their institutionally designated places. The police alone dedicated ten full-time staff to this program, who spent their time deselecting the 'top of the charts' 100-worst youth in the city – a who's who of the troublesome that was used to demarcate the institutional borders of youth more sharply than ever.

We also examined police involvement in the governance of racial and ethnic groups. Urged on by other institutions, the police use racial and ethnic classifications to understand trouble and to risk-profile populations. These classifications appear on various occurrence reports and sometimes are embedded in computerized mapping systems that profile the racial geography of trouble. Police multicultural units deselect those who are in the category 'other' (that is, other than 'white') for more-intensive scrutiny of the troubles they experience or pose. Multicultural units also engage in extensive interagency networking to better understand different racial and ethnic groups and to make those groups understand who it is the police stand for. Police standing is also enunciated in lectures and educational programs directed at racial and ethnic groups. These programs propagate the longstanding tradition of using the police to symbolize what it means to be Canadian.

The final area in which our paradigm transforms existing research is community policing. Community policing is a discourse that captures and articulates the policing of risk society. This discourse is entwined with the communication systems that provide the context for how the police think, feel, speak, write, design their buildings, mobilize, and so on. Community policing is communications policing. It explains and organizes the ways in which community networks have become communication networks with more and more lines of 'publicity' to and from the police. As one of our interviewees described it, community policing is like a satellite orbiting around social institutions, functioning as a conduit of knowledge and facilitator of activity. It performs these functions in many ways, for example by providing routine risk profiling based on incident reports, through police station architecture, by selling of security technologies and programs, by the operation of Crime Stoppers and PCCOPS programs, by inspectorate and regulatory work on behalf of compliance-oriented institutions, and by 'problem solving.'

At the same time, community policing discourse is a way of creating cultural coherence out of the material forms and practices in which it is embedded. It defines community as a construct of institutional methodologies for risk communication and thereby constitutes the community of risk institutions that govern communal life. This constitution makes new forms of risk communication both visible and possible, and making visible helps police organizations confront, first, the significant changes that are occurring in their own communication rules, formats, and technologies, and second, the implications of those changes for the blurring of roles and dispersal of command hierarchies the police are experiencing.

In communications policing the traditional community of interpersonal relations and direct action gets lost. This loss is symbolized by police efforts to fit definitions of what *the* community means into computer formats. These efforts prove troublesome because *the* community inevitably fragments into multiple, differentiated communities and multiple forms of policing. These efforts expose how risk management efforts create the reality of segmented communities of interest: the policing of public spaces in collaboration with special interest watch programs, the policing of private securities in collaboration with corporate entities, the policing of careers in collaboration with the maintainers of institutionalized credentialism, and the policing of identities in collaboration with the maintainers of the institutional boundaries that define the social place of those identities.

Communications policing also reveals the shift in responsibility for governance to dispersed risk institutions with their devices for self-governance. Police 'problem solving' usually means an outcome effected through the offices of other institutions, one that the police deem just and reasonable. In community policing we see a dissipation of the community as a network of interpersonal communications with a defined locus and a tradition of immediate reaction to events by responsible policing agents.

To summarize, our findings direct researchers to new ways of thinking about seven key areas of policing. Police mobilization is not only a matter of intervention in the lives of individuals but also a response to institutional demands for knowledge of risk. As a result, the loci of police activity are the communication systems – the rules, formats, and technologies – shaped by external institutions. Through these communication systems, external institutions are able to routinely access the police for knowledge useful for their own risk management. This routine access makes policework highly visible and circumscribes the discretion of individual police officers. Criminal law is no different from other institutions in organizing itself through risk communication systems. Most of the crime-related knowledge produced by the police is disseminated to other institutions (such as health, insurance, welfare, and educational agencies) for their risk management needs, rather than used for criminal prosecution and punishment. Although the police have considerable coercive power to produce knowledge of risk, the police mainly use this knowledge to feed risk communication systems of institutions that regulate within a compliance-based mode of law enforcement. Compliance policing is effected not only through territorial surveillance but also at the extraterritorial level of abstract knowledge of risk and trust with respect to securities, careers, and identities. Community policing has arisen as a discourse to capture all of the above dimensions of policing the risk society. It accounts for the fact that our communities are based on risk communications that provide no sense of place or identity beyond institutionalized risk classifications.

In addition to changing the ways in which we think about police, our research offers a number of contributions to sociology. In relation to the sociology of organizations and institutions it provides new perspectives on organizational communication. Organizations and institutions are constituted by risk communication systems that enmesh them in complex webs of internal and external expectations. Each organization's internal communication rules, formats, and technologies are intrainstitutionally and interinstitutionally woven together with other organizations' communication rules, formats, and technologies. The result of this entanglement is a perpetual sense on everyone's part of being out of control. The organization is experienced as a juggernaut. There is an endemic feeling of insecurity that is derived from a feeling of never having enough knowledge and from a reflexive awareness that there are always systemic faults that can be ameliorated by better communication rules, formats, and technologies. This situation is accentuated in police organizations because they enter into transactions with a wide range of organizations and institutions that are also experiencing knowledge insecurity and that translate their insecurity into demands on the police for more and better knowledge.

In relation to the sociology of occupations and professions, we have shown how professions and their working environments are changing in a society governed by knowledge of risk. A risk profession is an occupational group that claims some exclusive abstract knowledge concerning how to address particular risks, and some unique ability to provide expert services of risk management. Risk professions make risks visible, rationalize them through the use of processes of assessment and validation, and then offer an interpretation to constitute and enforce standards. Each risk profession exists within a system of professions defined by abstract knowledge of risk. The success of each profession, including the police, depends as much on the structure of the system itself as it does on the specialized knowledge and efforts of a given profession within it. Each risk profession in the system tries to colonize new jurisdictions by employing the strategies of abstract knowledge production, competition, regulation, bureaucratization, and collaboration, but these same efforts also mean that the profession may be destabilized and assimilated and lose jurisdiction.

Within the system of professions, professional knowledge of risk becomes embedded in communication rules, formats, and technologies. The result is that professional work gets done at a systemic level above that of the individual professional. We found in the case of the police that the profession is literally 'formed' by paperwork. Moreover, abstract systems of risk professions and institutions deskill labour to the point where workers feel alienated. Workers often do not know where the knowledge they produce moves, let alone how it gets used by other professions. With the development of computer technology, this alienation is accompanied by dehumanization. In 'data policing' the entire work day revolves around maintaining, augmenting, and searching databases for other users. While professionals know they cannot live without such communication systems, they experience constant difficulty in living with them. One part of the difficulty is that the systems never reach a point of stasis. Stasis is ever-elusive because risk knowledge work has shifting boundaries and no limits or sense of place.

The above observations also point to the ways in which our research contributes to the sociology of science and technology. We have scrutinized the practical contexts in which technologies are used, and their influence on how work is accomplished. Communication technologies permeate the social structure and organization of work and are integral to the ways in which workers think and act. In particular, they facilitate immediate production of and access to precise risk communications from dispersed locations. This power of immediate, dispersed risk communication has reconfigured organizational hierarchies, roles, and relations. It has fostered decentralization and fragmentation in organizations as well as an organizational politics that focuses on who regulates knowledge of risk.

Our research also addresses, and moves beyond, traditional approaches to the sociology of deviance and control. We have contributed to the demise of the sociology of deviance and control as a field that focuses narrowly on the problem of order. We argue that society is organized less in terms of deviance, control, and order, and more in terms of risk, surveillance, and security.

Risk communication systems turn the moral discourse of deviance into a utilitarian morality of probability calculus. The systems make up people more according to the former's internally referential systems of rationality than in terms of extrinsic moral questions of deviance. People are panoptically sorted according to utilitarian criteria – as more or less stable, bright, strong, efficient, useful, and so on – creating the 'transmission society' of risk career tracks. Gutted of moral wrongdoing, deviance is treated as a normal accident. That is, deviance is treated as a contingency for which there are risk technologies to spread the loss and prevent recurrence. Deviance becomes a technical problem that requires an administrative solution, rather than an occasion for expressing collective sentiments and moral solidarity, which are relegated to mass media morality plays through which people remember values that are increasingly at odds with those of other institutions.

Risk communication systems require surveillance. Surveillance provides knowledge for the selection of thresholds that define acceptable risks and justify inclusion and exclusion. Surveillance agents such as the police front-load the system with relevant knowledge that is later sorted for distribution to interested institutional audiences. Coercive control gives way to contingent categorization. Knowledge of risk is more important than moral culpability and punishment. Innocence declines, as everyone is assumed to be 'guilty' until the risk communication system reveals otherwise and one is admitted to the institution for the purpose of a specific transaction.

The rise of risk communication systems marks a shift away from order as morality, procedure, hierarchy, and territorial protection. The result is a movement towards security, defined by each social institution in terms of its peculiar definitions of risk and logics for dealing with risks. Security is accomplished by extraterritorial communication technologies that address concerns over securities, careers, and identities. People are no longer bound by consensual order but by communication rules, formats, and technologies that connect them in time and space and provide them with immediate knowledge for action. The phenomenal world of the police, and of the policing agents in other institutions, changes. All of these are unified not only by a correspondence of territorial settings but also by an ability to move through any place as members of expert systems of risk and security. They police from microcentres of inscription that render people, events, processes, and states of affairs into discourse, the discourse of knowledge, risk, and security.

Beyond supplying fresh insights on organizations, institutions, occupations, professions, science, technology, deviance, and control, we have contributed to new ways of thinking about society. All of us live in a risk society governed by institutions that organize themselves through the production and distribution of knowledge of risk. These institutions channel their actions through communication systems for imagining and coping with danger. The representational frameworks and techniques of these communication systems provide the institutional foundations of risk society.

The institutions that make up risk society share a number of common elements. Risk society operates within a negative logic that focuses on fear and the social distribution of 'bads' rather than on progress and the social distribution of 'goods'. It is characterized by a foreboding that is reflexively connected to its reliance on probabilistic thinking. Collective fear and foreboding underpin the value system of the unsafe society, perpetuate insecurity, and feed demands for more knowledge of risk. Knowledge of risk is directed towards the control of the irrational by rational means. Life is to be made both real and liveable by risk technologies that tame chance in the landscape of fear.

The negative logic of risk society produces positive results. The sciences of risk join the law in providing orderly accounts of danger. They help people and their institutions to take risks, to take enough chance out of chance that a course of action seems worthwhile. However, the negative always creeps back in. Modernity is not only the promise of emancipation from danger but also a source of danger. Danger results from knowledge. Knowledge of risk is a producer of risk. This paradox creates space for other knowledges to seep into risk discourse, including the aesthetic, moral, political, and ethical. The science and technology of risk communication does not have a monopoly on rationality. However, even when the science and technology of risks is resisted, the resisters are forced to rely on what they are arguing against. Scientized risk communication systems frame discourse, and when fear and foreboding exceed knowledge these systems are turned to for new forms of surveillance.

Risk society is fuelled by surveillance, by the routine production of knowledge of populations useful for their administration. Surveillance provides biopower, the power to make biographical profiles of human populations to determine what is probable and possible for them. Surveillance fabricates people around institutionally established norms – risk is always somewhere on the continuum of imprecise normality. These norms are never static. They emerge from the interinstitutional politics of risk in which rules for classifying populations are negotiated, the formats for communicating these classifications are devised, and the ways of acting on the knowledge so formatted are considered. Surveillance is systemic, providing both the condition and the product of an institution's knowledge of itself and of other institutions. Surveillance bolsters bureaucracy, helping it to form its authority and govern at a distance.

The surveillance systems of risk society are entwined with privacy and trust. The more that foreboding and fear lead people to withdraw from public involvement, the more privacy is valued and people withdraw into privatized lifestyles. The greater the privacy, the greater the need for surveillance mechanisms to produce the knowledge necessary to trust people in institutional transactions. These surveillance mechanisms, paradoxically, intrude on privacy and are a constant reminder that trust is doubtful or absent. Yet it is only in a framework of trust that patterns of risk can be properly institutionalized and form the basis of decisions. Privacy, trust, surveillance, and risk management go hand in hand in providing the probabilities and possibilities of action.

Surveillance is also associated with fragmentation. The more people are risk-profiled in terms of their population identities, the more they feel individualized, fragmented, fractured, and separated from those not so identified. The only integration that counts is based on common interests in the management of particular needs. Governance is privatized and dispersed across multiple institutions and spaces. It is based on an instrumentalism that extracts things from their wider social contexts and totalities and deals with them as fragmented interests.

Fragmentation signals inequality in risk society. There is inequality in knowledge of risk. The better-off are able to purchase risk technologies that meet their needs and provide security against the risks they have helped to produce. They also benefit from institutional support for risk taking and invite government regulation in this regard. The worse-off are demonized by the public media and subject to the institutionalized bias and selective discrimination of the risk technologies that regulate them. By definition, risk technologies create knowledge-structured inequality. They etch people into the institutional class structure of risk society. Class is constituted in terms of people who share a particular institutional classification, rather than in terms of communities that share overall communal interests.

The risk knowledge structure of inequality puts the onus on the classes it creates to look after their own governance. The perfection of biopower is self-governance, that is, having people accept the social identity of how they have been classified institutionally, to the point where such acceptance allows them to risk-manage their own lives. Acceptance of self-governance is underpinned by the interconnected discourses of morality, rights, responsibility, and accountability.

Risk discourse is deeply moral, but only in utilitarian terms. The norm or standard of acceptable risk is always both factual and moral. It signifies the typical or usual, but also the ethical, constraint. Risk classifications infuse moral certainty and legitimacy into the facts they automatically produce. People experience the facts of risk assessment as normative obligations and therefore as scripts for action.

The legitimacy of utilitarian morality in risk discourse is underpinned by the discourse of rights. Risk discourse has expanded with the decentralization of politics into risk institutions, which employ peculiar means of distributive justice. Rights discourse provides an ethics of the possible and probable, embedded in legal rules of right. It forms part of the politics of difference, which morally contests risk classifications regarding the security they do or do not provide.

In the condition of self-governance, one is to contribute to the whole by being accountable for one's part, including the risks one creates for oneself and others. One is to be self-sufficient, creating one's own political economy through available institutional risk classifications. One is to risk-manage one's biography competently in order to capitalize on the institutional meaning of life. The result is not individual autonomy but rather the institutional structuration of individual identities for practical purposes. While individual responsibility may be fostered at the individual level, it is governed at the institutional level.

At the systemic level of communication among risk institutions there are different forms of autonomy and self-governance. While the demands for responsibility and accountability are also great at this level, they are ever-elusive because of the juggernaut quality of risk communication systems. The more knowledge of risk that is produced, the greater the demand and the more it has to be managed and regulated. Risk communication systems exemplify the scandal of rationality. Solutions to problems concerning knowledge of risk are sought in technical terms that are themselves generators of the problems.

The greatest risk to risk society is not that it believes in itself totally and becomes a closed system. Rather, it risks leaving too much to dispersed institutional sites of governance connected only by the circuitry of risk communication. Within a given institution, individuals must either accept the institution's risk management system or not participate in what it has to offer. Within risk society, individuals must make risk choices among institutions in order to take care of themselves. The faith is that disparate institutions will somehow take care of each and all. The result is agnostic liberalism.

References

Abbott, A. 1988. *The System of Professions: An Essay on the Division of Expert Labor.* Chicago: University of Chicago Press

Adler, M., et al. 1991. 'The Sociology of Social Security,' in M. Adler et al., eds., *The Sociology of Social Security,* 1–14. Edinburgh: Edinburgh University Press

Altheide, D. 1985. *Media Power.* Beverly Hills: Sage

– 1993. 'Electronic Media and State Control: The Case of Azscam.' *Sociological Quarterly* 34: 53–69

– 1995. *An Ecology of Communication: Cultural Formats of Control.* New York: Aldine de Gruyter

Altheide, D., and R. Snow. 1991. *Media Worlds in the Postjournalism Era.* New York: Aldine de Gruyter

Andrew, D. 1989. *Philanthropy and Police: London Charity in the Eighteenth Century.* Princeton: Princeton University Press

Archer, M. 1988. *Culture and Agency: The Place of Culture in Social Theory.* Cambridge: Cambridge University Press

Baldwin, J. 1993. *Preparing the Record of Taped Interviews.* Research Study Number 2. Royal Commission on Criminal Justice. London: HMSO

Balkin, J. 1992. 'What Is Postmodern Constitutionalism?' *Michigan Law Review* 90: 1966–90

Barry, A., T. Osborne, and N. Rose, eds. 1996. *Foucault and Political Reason: Liberalism, Neo-Liberalism and Rationalities of Government.* London: University College London Press

Baudrillard, J. 1983. *Simulations.* New York: Semiotext[e]

Bauman, Z. 1992a. 'Life-World and Expertise: Social Production of Dependency,' in N. Stehr and R. Ericson, eds., *The Culture and Power of Knowledge: Inquiries into Contemporary Societies,* 81–106. Berlin and New York: Walter de Gruyter

– 1992b. 'Soil, Blood and Identity.' *Sociological Review* 40: 675–701

Bay, C. 1981. *Strategies of Political Emancipation*. Notre Dame: University of Notre Dame Press

Bayley, D. 1988. 'Community Policing: A Report from the Devil's Advocate,' in J. Greene and S. Mastrofski, eds., *Community Policing: Rhetoric or Reality*, 225–37. New York: Praeger

Beattie, J. 1986. *Crime and the Courts in England 1660–1800*. Princeton: Princeton University Press

Beck, U. 1992a. *Risk Society: Toward a New Modernity*. London: Sage

– 1992b. 'Modern Society as Risk Society,' in N. Stehr and R. Ericson, eds., *The Culture and Power of Knowledge: Inquiries into Contemporary Societies*, 199–214. Berlin and New York: Walter de Gruyter

Beck, U., A. Giddens, and S. Lash. 1994. *Reflexive Modernization: Politics, Tradition and Aesthetics in the Modern Social Order*. Cambridge: Polity Press

Becker, H. 1963. *Outsiders: Studies in the Sociology of Deviance*. New York: Free Press

Becker, T. 1974. 'The Place of Private Police in Society: An Area of Research for the Social Sciences.' *Social Problems* 21: 438–53

Bell, D. 1985. 'Gutenberg and the Computer.' *Encounter* (May): 15–20

Bennet, T. 1993. 'Community Policing in Britain,' in D. Dölling and T. Feltes, eds., *Community Policing: Comparative Aspects of Community-Oriented Police Work*, 127-43. Holzkirchen, Germany: Felix-Verlag

Benson, D. 1993. 'The Police and Information Technology,' in G. Button, ed., *Technology in Working Order: Studies in Work, Interaction and Technology*, 81–97. London: Routledge

Bercal, T. 1970. 'Calls for Police Assistance.' *American Behavioral Scientist* 13: 681–91

Best, J. 1990. *Threatened Children*. Chicago: University of Chicago Press

Bittner, E. 1967. 'Police Discretion in Emergency Apprehension of Mentally Ill Persons.' *Social Problems* 14: 278–92

– 1970. *The Functions of the Police in Modern Society*. Rockville, Md.: National Institute of Mental Health

Black, D. 1968. 'Police Encounters and Social Organization: An Observational Study.' PhD thesis, University of Michigan

– 1976. *The Behavior of Law*. New York: Academic Press

– 1980. *Manners and Customs of the Police*. New York: Academic Press

Boas, M., and S. Chain. 1976. *Big Mac: The Unauthorized Story of McDonald's*. New York: New American Library

Bohm, R. 1984. 'The Politics of Law and Order.' *Justice Quarterly* 3: 449–55

Böhme, G. 1984. 'The Knowledge-Structure of Society.' in E. Bergendal, ed.,

Knowledge Policies and the Traditions of Higher Education, 5–17. Stockholm: Almquist and Wiksell International

– 1992. 'The Techno-Structures of Society,' in N. Stehr and R. Ericson, eds., *The Culture and Power of Knowledge: Inquiries into Contemporary Societies*, 39–50. Berlin and New York: Walter de Gruyter

Bok, S. 1979. *Lying: Moral Choice in Public and Private Life*. New York: Vintage

Bourdieu, P. 1984. *Distinction: A Social Critique of the Judgement of Taste*. London: Routledge and Kegan Paul

Brodeur, J.-P. 1983. 'High Policing and Low Policing: Remarks about the Policing of Political Activities.' *Social Problems* 30: 507–20

Brogden, M., T. Jefferson, and S. Walklate. 1988. *Introducing Police Work*. London: Unwin Hyman

Brubaker, R. 1984. *The Limits of Rationality: An Essay on the Social and Moral Thought of Max Weber*. London: Allen and Unwin

Burchell, G. 1991. 'Popular Interests: Civil Society and Governing "the System of Natural Liberty,"' in G. Burchell, C. Gordon, and P. Miller, eds., *The Foucault Effect: Studies in Governmentality*, 119–50. Chicago: University of Chicago Press

Burchell, G., C. Gordon, and P. Miller, eds. 1991. *The Foucault Effect: Studies in Governmentality*. Chicago: University of Chicago Press

Cambrosio, A., C. Limoges, and E. Hoffman. 1992. 'Expertise as a Network: A Case Study of the Controversies over the Environmental Release of Genetically Engineered Organisms,' in N. Stehr and R. Ericson, eds., *The Culture and Power of Knowledge: Inquiries into Contemporary Societies*, 341–61. Berlin and New York: Walter de Gruyter

Carlen, P. 1976. *Magistrates' Justice*. London: Martin Robertson

Carriere, K., and R. Ericson. 1989. *Crime Stoppers: A Study in the Organization of Community Policing*. Toronto: Centre of Criminology, University of Toronto

Castel, R. 1991. 'From Dangerousness to Risk,' in G. Burchell, C. Gordon, and P. Miller, eds., *The Foucault Effect: Studies in Governmentality*, 281–96. Chicago: University of Chicago Press

Cavendar, G., and L. Bond-Maupin. 1993. 'Fear and Loathing on Reality Television: An Analysis of "America's Most Wanted" and "Unsolved Mysteries."' *Sociological Inquiry* 63: 305–17

Chan, J. 1997. *Changing Police Culture: Policing in a Multicultural Society*. Melbourne: Cambridge University Press

Chatterton, M. 1983. 'Police Work and Assault Charges,' in M. Punch, ed., *Control in the Police Organization*, 194–221. Cambridge: MIT Press

– 1989. 'Managing Paperwork,' in M. Weatheritt, ed., *Police Research: Some Future Prospects*, 107–36. Aldershot: Gower

– 1991. 'Organizational Constraints on the Uses of Information Technology in

Problem-Focused Area Policing.' Paper presented to the British Criminology Conference (July)

Chermak, S. 1995. *Victims in the News: Crime and the American News Media*. Boulder: Westview Press

Christie, N. 1986. 'Suitable Enemies,' in H. Bianchi and R. Van Swaaningen, eds., *Abolitionism: Towards a Non-Repressive Approach to Crime*, 42–54. Amsterdam: Free University Press

Clarke, R. 1988. 'Information Technology and Dataveillance.' *Communications of the ACM* 31: 498–512

Clarke, R., and M. Hough. 1984. *The Effectiveness of the Police*. Home Office Research Unit. London: HMSO

Cohen, S. 1985. *Visions of Social Control: Crime, Punishment and Classification*. Cambridge: Polity

Coleman, C. 1993. 'The Influence of Mass Media and Interpersonal Communication on Societal and Personal Risk Judgements.' *Communication Research* 20: 611–28

Comrie, M., and E. Kings. 1975. 'Study of Urban Workloads: Final Report.' London: Home Office Police Research Services Unit

Cooney, M. 1994. 'Evidence as Partisanship.' *Law and Society Review* 28: 833–58

Cooper, R. 1992. 'Formal Organization as Representation: Remote Control, Displacement and Abbreviation,' in M. Reed and M. Hughes, eds., *Rethinking Organizations*, 254–72. London: Sage

Couch, C. 1984. *Constructing Civilization*. Greenwich, Conn.: JAI Press

Cumming, E., I. Cumming, and L. Edell. 1965. 'Policeman as Philosopher, Guide and Friend.' *Social Problems* 12: 276–86

Dandeker, C. 1990. *Surveillance, Power and Modernity: Bureaucracy and Discipline from 1700 to the Present Day*. New York: St. Martin's Press

Davis, K. 1969. *Discretionary Justice*. Baton Rouge: Louisiana State University Press

Davis, M. 1990. *City of Quartz: Excavating the Future in Los Angeles*. London: Verso

Defert, D. 1991. '"Popular Life" and Insurance Technology,' in G. Burchell, C. Gordon, and P. Miller, eds., *The Foucault Effect: Studies in Governmentality*, 211–33. Chicago: University of Chicago Press

DiMaggio, P., and W. Powell. 1991. 'Introduction,' in W. Powell and P. DiMaggio, eds., *The New Institutionalism in Organizational Analysis*, 1–38. Chicago: University of Chicago Press

Ditton, J. 1979. *Controlology: Beyond the New Criminology*. London: Macmillan

Donzelot, J. 1979. *The Policing of Families*. New York: Pantheon

– 1991. 'The Mobilization of Society,' in G. Burchell, C. Gordon, and P. Miller, eds., *The Foucault Effect: Studies in Governmentality*, 169–79. Chicago: University of Chicago Press

Doob, A. 1991. *Workshop on Collecting Race and Ethnicity Statistics in the Criminal Justice System*. Toronto: Centre of Criminology, University of Toronto

Douglas, M. 1986. *How Institutions Think*. Syracuse: Syracuse University Press

– 1990. 'Risk as a Forensic Resource.' *Daedalus* 119: 1–16

– 1992. *Risk and Blame: Essays in Cultural Theory*. London: Routledge

Douglas, M., and A. Wildavsky. 1982. *Risk and Culture: An Essay on the Selection of Technical and Environmental Dangers*. Berkeley: University of California Press

Doyle, A. 1996. 'COPS: Reality Television as Policing Reality.' Paper presented to the annual meeting of the American Society of Criminology, Chicago

Doyle, A., and R. Ericson. 1995. 'Fixing the Public: The Police, the Media and Vancouver's Stanley Cup Riot Review.' Unpublished paper, Green College, University of British Columbia

Draper, H. 1978. *Private Police*. Harmondsworth: Penguin

Durkheim, E. 1973. *Moral Education*. New York: Free Press

Eck, J., and W. Spelman. 1987. 'Who Ya Gonna Call? The Police as Problem Busters.' *Crime and Delinquency* 33: 31–52

Edelman, M. 1988. *Constructing the Political Spectacle*. Chicago: University of Chicago Press

Edgerton, R. 1985. *Rules, Exceptions and Social Order*. Berkeley: University of California Press

Ellul, J. 1964. *The Technological Society*. New York: Vintage

Ericson, R. 1975. *Criminal Reactions: The Labelling Perspective*. Farnborough, England: Saxon House

– 1981. 'Rules *for* Police Deviance,' in C. Shearing, ed., *Organizational Police Deviance: Its Structure and Control*, 83–110. Toronto: Butterworths

– 1982. *Reproducing Order: A Study of Police Patrol Work*. Toronto: University of Toronto Press

– 1991. 'Mass Media, Crime, Law and Justice: An Institutional Approach.' *British Journal of Criminology* 31: 219–49

– 1993. *Making Crime: A Study of Detective Work*. 2nd ed. Toronto: University of Toronto Press

– 1994a. 'The Division of Expert Knowledge in Policing and Security.' *British Journal of Sociology*. 45: 149–75

– 1994b. 'The Royal Commission on Criminal Justice System Surveillance,' in M. McConville and L. Bridges, eds., *Criminal Justice in Crisis*, 113–40. Aldershot: Edward Elgar

– 1994c. 'The Decline of Innocence.' *University of British Columbia Law Review* 28: 367–83

– 1995a. 'The News Media and Account Ability in Criminal Justice,' in P. Stenning, ed., *Accountability for Criminal Justice*, 135–61. Toronto: University of Toronto Press
– ed. 1995b. *Crime and the Media*. Aldershot: Dartmouth
– 1995c. 'Promoting Security: The Division of Expert Knowledge in Policing,' in K. Miyazawa and S. Miyazawa, eds., *Crime Prevention in the Urban Community*, 11–60. Deventer and Boston: Kluwer
– 1996. 'Why Law Is Like News,' in D. Nelken, ed., *Law as Communication*, 195–230. Aldershot: Dartmouth
Ericson, R., and P. Baranek. 1982. *The Ordering of Justice: A Study of Accused Persons as Dependents in the Criminal Process*. Toronto: University of Toronto Press
Ericson, R., P. Baranek, and J. Chan. 1987. *Visualizing Deviance: A Study of News Organization*. Toronto: University of Toronto Press; Milton Keynes: Open University Press
– 1989. *Negotiating Control: A Study of News Sources*. Toronto: University of Toronto Press; Milton Keynes: Open University Press
– 1991. *Representing Order: Crime, Law and Justice in the News Media*. Toronto: University of Toronto Press; Milton Keynes: Open University Press
Ericson, R., and K. Carriere. 1994. 'The Fragmentation of Criminology,' in D. Nelken, ed., *The Futures of Criminology*, 89–109. London: Sage
Ericson, R., and C. Shearing. 1986. 'The Scientification of Police Work,' in G. Böhme and N. Stehr, eds., *The Knowledge Society: The Growing Impact of Scientific Knowledge on Social Relations*, 129–59. Dordrecht: Reidel
Ettema, J., and D.C. Whitney. 1994. 'The Money Arrow: An Introduction to Audiencemaking,' in J. Ettema and D.C. Whitney, eds., *Audiencemaking: How the Media Create the Audience*, 1–18. Thousand Oaks: Sage
Evans, R. 1993. *The Conduct of Police Interviews with Juveniles*. Research Study Number 8. Royal Commission on Criminal Justice. London: HMSO
Ewald, F. 1991a. 'Insurance and Risk,' in G. Burchell, C. Gordon, and P. Miller, eds., *The Foucault Effect: Studies in Governmentality*, 197–210. Chicago: University of Chicago Press
– 1991b. 'Norms, Discipline and the Law,' in R. Post, ed., *Law and the Order of Culture*, 138–61. Berkeley: University of California Press
Featherstone, M. 1991. *Consumer Culture and Postmodernism*. London: Sage
Feeley, M. 1979. *The Process Is the Punishment*. New York: Russell Sage Foundation
Feeley, M., and J. Simon. 1994. 'Actuarial Justice: The Emerging New Criminal Law,' in D. Nelken, ed., *The Futures of Criminology*, 173-201. London: Sage

Fleissner, D., et al. 1991. *Community Policing in Seattle: A Descriptive Study of the South Seattle Crime Reduction Project*. Seattle: South Seattle Crime Reduction Project

Foucault, M. 1973. *The Order of Things: An Archaeology of the Human Sciences*. New York: Vintage

– 1977. *Discipline and Punish: The Birth of the Prison*. New York: Pantheon

– 1978. *The History of Sexuality*, vol. 1: *An Introduction*. New York: Vintage

– 1980. *Power/Knowledge: Selected Interviews and Other Writings 1972–1977*. New York: Pantheon

– 1991a. 'Politics and the Study of Discourse,' in G. Burchell, C. Gordon, and P. Miller, eds., *The Foucault Effect: Studies in Governmentality*, 53–72. Chicago: University of Chicago Press

– 1991b. 'Questions of Method,' in G. Burchell, C. Gordon, and P. Miller, eds., *The Foucault Effect: Studies in Governmentality*, 73–86. Chicago: University of Chicago Press

– 1991c. 'Governmentality,' in G. Burchell, C. Gordon, and P. Miller, eds., *The Foucault Effect: Studies in Governmentality*, 87–104. Chicago: University of Chicago Press

Gandy, O. 1993. *The Panoptic Sort: A Political Economy of Personal Information*. Boulder: Westview

Garland, D. 1990. *Punishment and Modern Society*. Chicago: University of Chicago Press

– 1996. 'The Limits of the Sovereign State: Strategies of Crime Control in Contemporary Society.' Unpublished paper, Centre for Law and Society, University of Edinburgh. Forthcoming in *British Journal of Criminology*

Geertz, C. 1983. *Local Knowledge: Further Essays in Interpretive Anthropology*. New York: Basic Books

Geller, W., and N. Morris. 1992. 'Relations between Federal and Local Police,' in M. Tonry and N. Morris, eds., *Modern Policing*, 231–348. Chicago: University of Chicago Press

Gergen, K. 1991. *The Saturated Self: Dilemmas of Identity in Contemporary Life*. New York: Basic Books

Giddens, A. 1984. *The Constitution of Society: Outline of the Theory of Structuration*. Cambridge: Polity

– 1985. *A Contemporary Critique of Historical Materialism*, vol. 2: *The Nation-State and Violence*. Cambridge: Polity

– 1990. *The Consequences of Modernity*. Cambridge: Polity

– 1991. *Modernity and Self-Identity: Self and Society in the Late Modern Age*. Stanford: Stanford University Press

– 1994. *Beyond Left and Right: The Future of Radical Politics*. Cambridge: Polity

Gluzol, J. 1981. 'Police, Law and Security in France: Questions of Method and Political Strategy.' *International Journal of the Sociology of Law* 9: 361–82

Goldberg, D. 1995. 'Taking Stock: Counting by Race.' Paper presented to the Law and Society Association, Toronto (June)

Goldsmith, A., ed. 1990. *Complaints against the Police: The Trend to External Review.* Oxford: Oxford University Press

Goldstein, H. 1987. 'Toward Community-Oriented Policing: Potential, Basic Requirements and Threshold Questions.' *Crime and Delinquency* 33: 6–30

– 1990. *Problem-Oriented Policing*. New York: McGraw-Hill

Goldstein, J. 1960. 'Police Discretion Not to Invoke the Criminal Process: Low Visibility Decisions in the Administration of Justice.' *Yale Law Journal* 69: 543–94

Gordon, C. 1991. 'Governmental Rationality: An Introduction,' in G. Burchell, C. Gordon, and P. Miller, eds., *The Foucault Effect: Studies in Governmentality,* 1–51. Chicago: University of Chicago Press

Gouldner, A. 1954. *Patterns of Industrial Bureaucracy.* Glencoe: Free Press

Greene, J., and S. Mastrofski, eds. 1988. *Community Policing: Rhetoric or Reality.* New York: Praeger

Gusfield, J. 1981. *The Culture of Public Problems: Drinking-Driving and the Symbolic Order.* Chicago: University of Chicago Press

– 1989. 'Constructing the Ownership of Social Problems: Fun and Profit in the Welfare State.' *Social Problems* 36: 431–41

Habermas, J. 1975. *Legitimation Crisis*. Boston: Beacon

Hacking, I. 1982. 'Biopower and the Avalanche of Printed Numbers.' *Humanities in Society* 5: 279–95

– 1986. 'Making up People,' in T. Heller, et al., eds., *Reconstructing Individualism,* 222–36. Stanford: Stanford University Press

– 1990. *The Taming of Chance*. Cambridge: Cambridge University Press

– 1991. 'How Should We Do the History of Statistics?' in G. Burchell, C. Gordon, and P. Miller, eds., *The Foucault Effect: Studies in Governmentality,* 181–95. Chicago: University of Chicago Press

– 1992. 'Statistical Language, Statistical Truth and Statistical Reason: The Self-Authentification of a Style of Scientific Reasoning,' in E. McMullin, ed., *The Social Dimensions of Science,* 130–57. Notre Dame: University of Notre Dame Press

– 1995. *Rewriting the Soul*. Princeton: Princeton University Press

Hawkins, K. 1984. *Environment and Enforcement: Regulation and the Social Definition of Pollution*. Oxford: Oxford University Press

– 1990. 'Compliance Strategy, Prosecution Policy, and Aunt Sally: A Comment on Pearce and Toombs.' *British Journal of Criminology* 30: 444–66

– 1991. 'Enforcing Regulation: More of the Same from Pearce and Toombs.' *British Journal of Criminology* 31: 427–30

Heidegger, M. 1974. 'The Principle of Ground.' *Man and World* 7: 207–22

Hirst, P. 1994. *Associative Democracy: New Forms of Social and Economic Governance*. Cambridge, England: Polity

Holloran, J., P. Elliott, and G. Murdock. 1970. *Demonstrations and Communication: A Case Study*. Harmondsworth: Penguin

Hoogenboom, B. 1991. 'Grey Policing: A Theoretical Framework.' *Policing and Society* 2: 17-30

Hutchinson, A. 1995. *Waiting for CORAF: A Critique of Law and Rights*. Toronto: University of Toronto Press

Inbau, F., and J. Reid. 1967. *Criminal Interrogations and Confessions*. 2nd ed. Baltimore: Williams and Wilkins

Jepperson, R. 1991. 'Institutions, Institutional Effects, and Institutionalism,' in W. Powell and P. DiMaggio, eds., *The New Institutionalism in Organizational Analysis*, 143–63. Chicago: University of Chicago Press

Jorgensen, B. 1981. 'Transferring Trouble: The Initiation of Reactive Policing.' *Canadian Journal of Criminology* 23: 257–78

Kashmeri, Z. 1981. '"Battlestar" Fortress to Protect Peel Police.' Toronto *Globe and Mail*, 5 August

Katz, J. 1987. 'What Makes Crime "News"?' *Media, Culture and Society* 9: 47–75

Kelling, G., et al. 1974. *The Kansas City Preventive Patrol Experiment: A Summary Report*. Washington, D.C.: Police Foundation

Kinsey, R. 1985. *Merseyside Crime and Police Surveys: Final Report*. Liverpool: Merseyside County Council

Klockars, C. 1988. 'The Rhetoric of Community Policing,' in J. Greene and S. Mastrofski, eds., *Community Policing: Rhetoric or Reality*, 239–58. New York: Praeger

Landau, T. 1994a. 'Policing and Security in Four Remote Aboriginal Communities: A Challenge to Coercive Models of Police Work.' PhD diss., Centre of Criminology, University of Toronto

– 1994b. *Public Complaints against the Police: A View from Complainants*. Toronto: Centre of Criminology, University of Toronto

Lasch, C. 1980. *The Culture of Narcissism: American Life in the Age of Diminishing Expectations*. New York: Norton

Lash, S. 1993. 'Reflexive Modernization: The Aesthetic Dimension.' *Theory, Culture and Society* 10: 1–23

Lash, S., and J. Urry. 1987. *The End of Organized Capitalism*. Cambridge: Polity

Latour, B. 1987. *Science in Action*. Cambridge, Mass.: Harvard University Press

Law Reform Commission of Canada. 1975. *Studies on Diversion*. Ottawa: Information Canada

– 1983. *Police Powers: Search and Seizure in Criminal Law Enforcement*. Working Paper 30. Ottawa: Ministry of Supply and Services

Leighton, B. 1991. 'Visions of Community Policing: Rhetoric and Reality in Canada.' *Canadian Journal of Criminology* 33: 485–522

Lovekin, D. 1991. *Technique, Discourse and Consciousness: An Introduction to the Philosophy of Jacques Ellul*. Bethlehem, Pa.: Lehigh University Press

Lowi, T. 1979. *The End of Liberalism: The Second Republic of the United States*. 2nd ed. New York: Norton

– 1990. 'Risks and Rights in the History of American Governments.' *Daedalus* 119: 17–40

Macdonell, D. 1986. *Theories of Discourse*. Oxford: Blackwell

Maguire, M., and C. Norris. 1993. *The Conduct and Supervision of Criminal Investigations*. Research Study Number 5. Royal Commission on Criminal Justice. London: HMSO

Mann, E., and J. Lee. 1979. *RCMP vs The People*. Toronto: General Publishing

Manning, P. 1977. *Police Work: The Social Organization of Policing*. Cambridge: MIT Press

– 1980. *The Narc's Game: Organizational and Informational Limits on Drug Law Enforcement*. Cambridge: MIT Press

– 1982. 'Organizational Work: Structuration of Environments.' *British Journal of Sociology* 33: 118–34

– 1983. 'Organizational Control and Semiotics,' in M. Punch, ed., *Control in the Police Organization*, 169–93. Cambridge: MIT Press

– 1987. 'Ironies of Compliance,' in C. Shearing and P. Stenning, eds., *Private Policing*, 293–316. Beverly Hills: Sage

– 1988. *Symbolic Communication: Signifying Calls and the Police Response*. Cambridge: MIT Press

– 1992a. 'Information Technology and the Police,' in M. Tonry and N. Morris, eds., *Modern Policing*, 349–98. Chicago: University of Chicago Press

– 1992b. 'Technological Dramas and the Police: Statement and Counterstatement in Organizational Analysis.' *Criminology* 30: 327–46

– 1993. 'Discourses of Policing: Policing Discourses.' Unpublished paper, Department of Sociology, Michigan State University

Manning, P., and K. Hawkins. 1989. 'Police Decision-Making,' in M. Weatheritt, ed., *Police Research: Some Future Prospects*, 139–56. Aldershot: Gower

Marx, G. 1988. *Undercover: Police Surveillance in America*. Berkeley: University of California Press

Marx, K. 1967. *Writings of the Young Marx on Philosophy and Society.* Edited by L. Easton and K. Guddat. New York: Anchor

Massumi, B., ed. 1993. *The Politics of Everyday Fear.* Minneapolis: University of Minnesota Press

Mastrofski, S. 1988. 'Community Policing as Reform: A Cautionary Tale,' in J. Greene and S. Mastrofski, eds., *Community Policing: Rhetoric or Reality,* 47–67. New York: Praeger

McBarnet, D. 1979. 'Arrest: The Legal Context of Policing,' in S. Holdaway, ed., *The British Police,* 24–40. London: Edward Arnold

– 1981. *Conviction: Law, the State and the Construction of Justice.* London: Edward Arnold

McConville, M. 1993. 'An Error of Judgement.' *Legal Action* (September)

McConville, M., and C. Mirsky. 1993. 'The Skeleton of Plea Bargaining.' *New Law Journal* (9 October): 1373–4, 1381

– 1995. 'Guilty Plea Courts: A Social Disciplinary Model of Criminal Justice.' *Social Problems* 42: 216–34

McConville, M., A. Sanders, and R. Leng. 1991. *The Case for the Prosecution: Police Suspects and the Construction of Criminality.* London: Routledge

McGaw, D. 1991. 'Governing Metaphors: The "War" on Drugs.' Unpublished paper, Department of Political Science, Arizona State University

McMahon, M. 1992. *The Persistent Prison? Rethinking Decarceration and Penal Reform.* Toronto: University of Toronto Press

Meehan, A. 1993. 'Internal Police Records and the Control of Juveniles: Politics and Policing in a Suburban Town.' *British Journal of Criminology* 33: 504–24

Menzies, R. 1987. 'Psychiatrists in Blue: Police Apprehension of Mental Disorder and Dangerousness.' *Criminology* 25: 901–25

– 1989. *Survival of the Sanest: Order and Disorder in a Pre-trial Psychiatric Clinic.* Toronto: University of Toronto Press

Meyer, J., and R. Scott. 1983. *Organizational Environments: Ritual and Rationality.* Beverly Hills: Sage

Meyrowitz, J. 1985. *No Sense of Place: The Impact of Electronic Media on Social Behaviour.* Oxford: Oxford University Press

Miller, P., and N. Rose. 1990. 'Governing Economic Life.' *Economy and Society* 19: 1–31

Miyazawa, S. 1992. *Policing in Japan: A Study on Making Crime.* New York: State University of New York Press

Moore, M. 1992. 'Problem-Solving and Community Policing,' in M. Tonry and N. Morris, eds., *Modern Policing,* 99–158. Chicago: University of Chicago Press

Moroney, M. 1951. *Facts from Figures.* Harmondsworth: Penguin

Moynihan, D. 1993. 'Defining Deviance Down.' *The American Scholar* 62: 17–30.
Murphy, C. 1986. 'The Social and Formal Organization of Small Town Policing: A Comparative Analysis of RCMP and Municipal Policing.' PhD diss., Department of Sociology, University of Toronto
– 1988a. 'The Development, Impact and Implications of Community Policing in Canada,' in J. Greene and S. Mastrofski, eds., *Community Policing: Rhetoric or Reality*, 177–89. New York: Praeger
– 1988b. 'Community Problems, Problem Communities, and Community Policing in Toronto.' *Journal of Research in Crime and Delinquency* 25: 392–410
Nelken, D. 1990. *The Truth about Law's Truth*. Working Paper No. 7. Faculty of Laws, University College, London
Nelson, B. 1984. *Making an Issue of Child Abuse*. Chicago: University of Chicago Press
Newman, O. 1972. *Defensible Space: Crime Prevention through Urban Design*. New York: Macmillan
Nietzsche, F. 1914. *Beyond Good and Evil*. London: Foulis
Nock, S. 1993. *The Costs of Privacy: Surveillance and Reputation in America*. New York: Aldine de Gruyter
O'Malley, P. 1991. 'Legal Networks and Domestic Security.' *Studies in Law, Politics and Society* 11: 171–90
– 1992. 'Risk, Power and Crime Prevention.' *Economy and Society* 21: 252–75
Packer, H. 1968. *The Limits of the Criminal Sanction*. Stanford: Stanford University Press
Pasquino, P. 1991. 'Theatrum Politicum: The Genealogy of Capital – Police and the State of Prosperity,' in G. Burchell, C. Gordon, and P. Miller, eds., *The Foucault Effect: Studies in Governmentality*, 105–18. Chicago: University of Chicago Press
Pearce, F., and S. Tombs. 1990. 'Ideology, Hegemony and Empiricism: Compliance Theories of Regulation.' *British Journal of Criminology* 30: 423–43
– 1991. 'Policing Corporate "Skid Rows": A Reply to Keith Hawkins.' *British Journal of Criminology* 31: 415–26
Pearson, G. 1983. *Hooligan: A History of Respectable Fears*. London: Macmillan
Percy, S., and E. Scott. 1985. *Demand Processing and Performance in Public Service Agencies*. University, Ala.: University of Alabama Press
Perrow, C. 1984. *Normal Accidents: Living with High-Risk Technologies*. New York: Basic Books
Policy Studies Institute. 1983. *Police and People in London*, vol. 3: *A Survey of Police Officers*. London: Policy Studies Institute
Poster, M. 1990. *The Mode of Information: Poststructuralism and Social Context*. Cambridge: Polity

– 1995. *The Second Media Age*. Cambridge: Polity

Powell, W. 1991. 'Expanding the Scope of Institutional Analysis,' in W. Powell and P. DiMaggio, eds., *The New Institutionalism in Organizational Analysis*, 183–203. Chicago: University of Chicago Press

Priest, G. 1990. 'The New Legal Structure of Risk Control.' *Daedalus* 119: 207–27

Pudifin, M. 1991. 'A Study of Technical Means to Improve the Acquisition of Data on Motor Vehicle Events.' Unpublished paper, Transport Canada

Punch, M. 1979. *Policing the Inner City*. London: Macmillan

– ed. 1983. *Control in the Police Organization*. Cambridge: MIT Press

Putnam, H. 1981. *Reason, Truth and History*. Cambridge: Cambridge University Press

Reich, R. 1991. 'Secession of the Successful.' *New York Times Magazine*, 20 January, 16–17, 42–5

Reichman, N. 1986. 'Managing Crime Risks: Towards an Insurance Based Model of Social Control,' in S. Spitzer and A. Scull, eds., *Research in Law, Deviance and Social Control*, 151–72. Greenwich, Conn.: JAI Press

Reiner, R. 1992. *The Politics of the Police*. 2nd ed. Toronto: University of Toronto Press

Reiss, A. 1971. *The Police and the Public*. New Haven: Yale University Press

– 1982. 'Forecasting the Role of the Police and the Role of the Police in Social Forecasting,' in R. Donelan, ed., *The Maintenance of Order in Society*, 132–56. Ottawa: Supply and Services Canada

– 1983. 'The Policing of Organizational Life,' in M. Punch, ed., *Control in the Police Organization*, 78–97. Cambridge: MIT Press

– 1984a. 'Consequences of Compliance and Deterrence Models of Law Enforcement for the Exercise of Police Discretion.' *Law and Contemporary Problems* 47: 83–122

– 1984b. 'Selecting Strategies of Social Control over Organizational Life,' in K. Hawkins and T. Thomas, eds., *Enforcing Regulation*, 23–35. Boston: Kluwer-Nijhoff

– 1987. 'The Legitimacy of Intrusion into Private Spaces,' in C. Shearing and P. Stenning, eds., *Private Policing*, 19–44. Beverly Hills: Sage

– 1989. 'The Institutionalization of Risk.' *Law and Policy* 11: 392–402

Reiss, A., and D. Bordua. 1967. 'Environment and Organization: A Perspective on the Police,' in D. Bordua, ed., *The Police: Six Sociological Essays*, 25–55. New York: Wiley

Rock, P. 1986. *A View from the Shadows: The Ministry of the Solicitor General of Canada and the Making of the Justice for Victims of Crime Initiative*. Oxford: Oxford University Press

– 1990. *Helping Victims of Crime: The Home Office and the Rise of Victim Support in England and Wales*. Oxford: Oxford University Press
– 1993. *The Social World of an English Crown Court: Witnesses and Professionals in the Crown Court Centre at Wood Green*. Oxford: Oxford University Press
Rosenbaum, D. 1987. 'The Theory and Research behind Neighborhood Watch: Is It a Sound Fear- and Crime-Reduction Strategy?' *Crime and Delinquency* 33: 103–34
Royal Canadian Mounted Police. 1991. *Annual Report on Canada's Missing Children*. Ottawa: Royal Canadian Mounted Police
Royal Commission on Criminal Justice. 1993. *Report*. Cmnd. 2263. London: HMSO
Royal Commission on New Reproductive Technologies. 1993. *Proceed with Care: Final Report of the Royal Commission on New Reproductive Technologies*. Ottawa: Minister of Government Services, Canada
Sacks, H. 1972. 'Notes on Police Assessment of Moral Character,' in D. Sudnow, ed., *Studies in Social Interaction*, 280-93. New York: Free Press
Sartre, J.-P. 1966. *Being and Nothingness: An Essay on Phenomenological Ontology.* New York: Washington Square Press
Scheingold, S. 1990. 'The War on Drugs in Context: Crisis Politics and Social Control.' Paper presented to the Law and Society Association, Berkeley (June)
Schlesinger, P., and H. Tumber. 1994. *Reporting Crime: The Media Politics of Criminal Justice*. Oxford: Oxford University Press
Schur, E. 1971. *Labeling Deviant Behavior: Its Sociological Implications*. New York: Harper and Row
Scott, R. 1991. 'Unpacking Institutional Arguments,' in W. Powell and P. DiMaggio, eds., *The New Institutionalism in Organizational Analysis*, 164–82. Chicago: University of Chicago Press
Scott, R., and J. Meyer. 1991. 'The Organization of Societal Sectors: Propositions and Early Evidence,' in W. Powell and P. DiMaggio, eds., *The New Institutionalism in Organizational Analysis*, 108–40. Chicago: University of Chicago Press
Scull, A. 1984. *Decarceration: Community Treatment and the Deviant – A Radical View.* 2nd ed. Cambridge: Polity
Shadgett, P. 1990. 'An Observational Study of Police Patrol Work.' Master's thesis, Centre of Criminology, University of Toronto
Shearing, C., ed. 1981. *Organizational Police Deviance: Its Structure and Control.* Toronto: Butterworths
– 1984. *Dial-a-Cop: A Study of Police Mobilization*. Toronto: Centre of Criminology, University of Toronto
– 1992. 'The Relation between Public and Private Policing,' in M. Tonry and N. Morris, eds., *Modern Policing*, 399–434. Chicago: University of Chicago Press

Shearing, C., and R. Ericson. 1991. 'Culture as Figurative Action.' *British Journal of Sociology* 42: 481–506

Shearing, C., and P. Stenning. 1981. 'Modern Private Security: Its Growth and Implications,' in M. Tonry and N. Morris, eds., *Crime and Justice: An Annual Review of Research*, 3: 193–245. Chicago: University of Chicago Press

– 1982. 'Snowflakes or Good Pinches: Private Security's Contribution to Modern Policing,' in R. Donelan, ed., *The Maintenance of Order in Society*, 96–105. Ottawa: Supply and Services Canada

– 1983. 'Private Security: Implications for Social Control.' *Social Problems* 30: 493–506

– 1984. 'From the Panopticon to Disney World: The Development of Discipline,' in A. Doob and E. Greenspan, eds., *Perspectives in Criminal Law*, 335–48. Aurora, Ont.: Canada Law Book

Sherman, L. 1992. 'Attacking Crime: Police and Crime Control,' in M. Tonry and N. Morris, eds., *Modern Policing*, 159–230. Chicago: University of Chicago Press

Sherman, L., P. Gartin, and M. Buerger. 1989. 'Hot Spots of Predatory Crime: Routine Activities and the Criminology of Place.' *Criminology* 27: 27–55

Short, J. 1990. 'Hazards, Risks, and Enterprise Approaches to Science, Law and Social Policy.' *Law and Society Review* 24: 179–98

Simon, J. 1987. 'The Emergence of Risk Society: Insurance, Law and the State.' *Socialist Review* 95: 61–89

– 1988. 'The Ideological Effects of Actuarial Practice.' *Law and Society Review* 22: 772–800

– 1993. *Poor Discipline: Parole and the Social Control of the Underclass, 1890–1990*. Chicago: University of Chicago Press

Skogan, W. 1990a. *Disorder and Decline*. New York: Free Press

– 1990b. *The Police and the Public in England and Wales: A British Crime Survey Report*. Home Office Research Study No. 117. London: HMSO

Skolnick, J. 1966. *Justice without Trial: Law Enforcement in Democratic Society*. New York: Wiley

Skolnick, J., and D. Bayley. 1986. *The New Blue Line: Police Innovations in Six American Cities*. New York: Free Press

Skolnick, J., and J. Woodworth. 1967. 'Bureaucracy, Information and Social Control: A Study of a Morals Detail,' in D. Bordua, ed., *The Police: Six Sociological Essays*, 99–136. New York: Wiley

Smart, B. 1983. 'On Discipline and Social Regulation: A Review of Foucault's Genealogical Analysis,' in D. Garland and P. Young, eds., *The Power to Punish*, 62–83. London: Heinemann

Solicitor General of Ontario. 1991. *Community Policing: Shaping the Future*. Toronto: Queen's Printer for Ontario

South, N. 1988. *Policing for Profit: The Private Security Sector*. London: Sage
Southgate, P., and C. Mirless-Black. 1991. *Traffic Policing in Changing Times*. London: HMSO
Sparks, R. 1992. *Television and the Drama of Crime: Moral Tales and the Place of Crime in Public Life*. Milton Keynes: Open University Press
Sparrow, M. 1988. 'Implementing Community Policing.' Perspectives on Policing Paper No. 9. Washington, D.C.: National Institute of Justice
– 1991. 'Information Systems and the Development of Policing.' Working paper 91–05–11, John F. Kennedy School of Government, Harvard University
Spitzer, S. 1987. 'Security and Control in Capitalist Societies: The Fetishism of Security and the Secret Thereof,' in J. Lowman, R. Menzies, and T. Palys, eds., *Transcarceration: Essays in the Sociology of Social Control*, 43–58. Aldershot: Gower
Spitzer, S., and A. Scull. 1977. 'Privatization and Capitalist Development: The Case of the Private Police.' *Social Problems* 25: 18–29
Stallings, R. 1990. 'Media Discourse and the Social Construction of Risk.' *Social Problems* 37: 80–95
Stehr, N. 1992. *Practical Knowledge: Applying the Social Sciences*. London: Sage
– 1994. *Knowledge Societies*. London: Sage
Stehr, N., and R. Ericson, eds. 1992. *The Culture and Power of Knowledge: Inquiries into Contemporary Societies*. Berlin and New York: Walter de Gruyter
Stenning, P., ed. 1995. *Accountability for Criminal Justice*. Toronto: University of Toronto Press
Stenson, K. 1993. 'Community Policing as Governmental Technology.' *Economy and Society* 22: 373–99
Stinchcombe, A. 1963. 'Institutions of Privacy in the Determination of Police Administrative Practice.' *American Journal of Sociology* 69: 150–60
Sudnow, D. 1965. 'Normal Crimes: Sociological Features of the Penal Code in a Public Defender's Office.' *Social Problems* 12: 255–72
Swaan, A. de. 1990. *The Management of Normality*. London: Routledge
Task Force on Policing in Ontario. 1974. *The Police Are the Public and the Public Are the Police*. Toronto: Solicitor General of Ontario
Teubner, G. 1993. *Autopoietic Law*. Oxford: Basil Blackwell
Toch, J., and J. Grant. 1991. *Police as Problem Solvers*. New York: Plenam
Tocqueville, A. de. 1840. *Democracy in America*. London: Saunders and Otley
Trojanowicz, R., and B. Bucqueroux. 1990. *Community Policing: A Contemporary Perspective*. Cincinnati: Anderson Publishing
Trojanowicz, R., and D. Carter. 1988. 'The Philosophy and Role of Community Policing.' East Lansing: National Neighborhood Foot Patrol Center, Michigan State University

Trojanowicz, R., and M. Moore. 1988. 'The Meaning of Community in Community Policing.' East Lansing: National Neighborhood Foot Patrol Center, Michigan State University

Trojanowicz, R., et al. 1982. *An Evaluation of the Neighborhood Foot Patrol Program in Flint, Michigan*. East Lansing: Department of Criminal Justice, Michigan State University

Tuan, Y.-F. 1979. *Landscapes of Fear*. Oxford: Basil Blackwell

Tumber, H. 1982. *Television and the Riots*. London: Broadcasting Research Unit, British Film Institute

Valverde, M. 1990. 'The Rhetoric of Reform: Tropes and the Moral Subject.' *International Journal of the Sociology of Law* 18: 61–73

– 1991. *The Age of Light, Soap and Water: Moral Reform in English Canada*. Toronto: McClelland & Stewart

Van den Daele, W. 1992. 'Scientific Evidence and the Regulation of Technical Risks: Twenty Years of Demythologizing the Experts,' in N. Stehr and R. Ericson, eds., *The Culture and Power of Knowledge: Inquiries into Contemporary Societies*, 323–40. Berlin and New York: Walter de Gruyter

Van Maanen, J. 1983. 'The Boss: First-Line Supervision in an American Police Agency,' in M. Punch, ed., *Control in the Police Organization*, 275–317. Cambridge: MIT Press

Waegel, W. 1981. 'Case Routinization in Investigative Police Work.' *Social Problems* 28: 263–75

Waddington, P. 1984. 'Community Policing: A Sceptical Appraisal,' in P. Norton, ed., *Law and Order and British Politics*, 84–96. Aldershot: Gower

Walden, K. 1982. *Visions of Order: The Canadian Mounties in Symbol and Myth*. Toronto: Butterworths

Walsh, W. 1986. 'Patrol Officer Arrest Rates: A Study of the Social Organization of Police Work.' *Justice Quarterly* 2: 271–90

Webber, M. 1991. *Street Kids: The Tragedy of Canada's Runaways*. Toronto: University of Toronto Press

Weber, M. 1964. *From Max Weber: Essays in Sociology*. Edited by H. Gerth and C.W. Mills. London: Routledge and Kegan Paul

– 1978. *Economy and Society*. 2 vols. Berkeley: University of California Press

Webster, J. 1970. 'Police Task and Time Study.' *Journal of Criminal Law, Criminology and Police Science* 61: 94–100

Weick, K. 1979. *The Social Psychology of Organizing*. 2nd ed. Reading, Mass.: Addison-Wesley

White, J. 1984. *When Words Lose Their Meaning: Constitutions and Reconstitutions of Language, Character and Community*. Chicago: University of Chicago Press

Williams, R. 1976. *Communications*. Harmondsworth: Penguin

– 1983. *Keywords: A Vocabulary of Culture and Society.* London: Fontana

Wilson, J. 1968. *Varieties of Police Behavior.* Cambridge: Harvard University Press

Wilson, J., and G. Kelling. 1982. 'Broken Windows.' *Atlantic Monthly* (March): 29–38

Winkel, F. 1991. 'Police, Victims and Crime Prevention: Some Research-Based Recommendations on Victim-Oriented Interventions.' *British Journal of Criminology* 31: 250–65

Zimring, F., and G. Hawkins. 1991. *The Scale of Imprisonment.* Chicago: University of Chicago Press

– 1993. 'Crime, Justice and the Savings and Loan Crisis,' in M. Tonry and A. Reiss, eds., *Beyond the Law: Crime in Complex Organizations,* 247–92. Chicago: University of Chicago Press

Zuboff, S. 1988. *In the Age of the Smart Machine: The Future of Work and Power.* New York: Basic Books

Index